Press, Power, and Culture in Imperial Brazil

PRESS, POWER, AND CULTURE IN IMPERIAL BRAZIL

Edited by Hendrik Kraay,
Celso Thomas Castilho,
and Teresa Cribelli

UNIVERSITY OF NEW MEXICO PRESS · ALBUQUERQUE

© 2021 by the University of New Mexico Press
All rights reserved. Published 2021
Printed in the United States of America

First paperback printing 2023

ISBN 978-0-8263-6227-8 (cloth)
ISBN 978-0-8263-6500-2 (paper)
ISBN 978-0-8263-6228-5 (electronic)

Library of Congress Control Number: 2020949897

Designed by Mindy Basinger Hill
Composed in 11/14 pt Garamond Premier Pro

CONTENTS

vii List of Illustrations

ix Preface

xi Abbreviations

xiii Note on Currency and Orthography

1 INTRODUCTION   From Colonial Gazettes to the "Largest Circulation in South America"   *Hendrik Kraay, Celso Thomas Castilho, Teresa Cribelli*

33 ONE   The "Print Arena": Press, Politics, and the Public Sphere, 1822–1840   *Marcello Basile*

54 TWO   "Adapted to Our Customs and Dictated by Our Interests": The Press and the African Slave Trade, 1831–1840   *Alain El Youssef*

72 THREE   Printers, Typographers, and Readers: Slavery and Print Culture   *Rodrigo Camargo de Godoi*

90 FOUR   Outbreaks, Shares, and Contracts: The Press and the Migrant Trade   *José Juan Pérez Meléndez*

111 FIVE   Fictionalizing *Crônicas*: Transformations of an Article Genre   *Ludmila de Souza Maia*

132 SIX   "FOR RENT" and "FOR SALE": Newspapers, Advertising, Property, and Markets in Rio de Janeiro, 1820s–1890s   *Matthew Nestler and Zephyr Frank*

154 SEVEN   Much More Than Images: Visual Culture and the Public Sphere in Illustrated Satirical Magazines   *Arnaldo Lucas Pires Junior*

175 EIGHT   To "Judge the State of This Province": Correspondence to Rio de Janeiro Newspapers from Bahia, 1868   *Hendrik Kraay*

196 NINE   *Apedidos* and Public Discourse: Paid Letters and Articles in the *Jornal do Commercio*, 1870   *Teresa Cribelli*

220   TEN   The Sun Rises in the North: Brazilian Periodicals Published in the United States in the 1870s   *Roberto Saba*

242   ELEVEN   A "Gallery of Illustrious Men of Color": Recife's *O Homem*, the Black Press, and Transatlantic Literary Genres   *Celso Thomas Castilho*

261   Bibliography
295   List of Contributors
299   Index

ILLUSTRATIONS

Figures

56   FIGURE 2.1   Number of Newspapers and Political Associations in Rio de Janeiro, 1830–1840

57   FIGURE 2.2   Volume of the Slave Trade (Brazil and South-Central Region), 1822–1840

63   FIGURE 2.3   Brazilian Coffee Exports, 1823–1840

73   FIGURE 3.1   A Literate Slave Reading His Mistress's Correspondence, 1872

75   FIGURE 3.2   Two Dapperly Dressed Slave Men, ca. 1860

84   FIGURE 3.3   Slaves Reading the Abolitionist Newspaper, *O País*, 1887

139   FIGURE 6.1   Number of Pages in Newspapers with *Aluguéis* Mentioned, 1810–1899

140   FIGURE 6.2   Number of Advertisements for Sales (*Vendas*) and Rents (*Aluguéis*) in the *Jornal do Commercio*, 1828–1898

163   FIGURE 7.1   Number of Illustrated Satirical Periodicals in Circulation by Year and Province, 1860–1889

166   FIGURE 7.2   A Homeopathic Coachman, 1866

168   FIGURE 7.3   Retrospective Mirrors, 1863

168   FIGURE 7.4   His Majesty Is Traveling, 1875

171   FIGURE 7.5   The Little Marshals of Ouvidor Street, 1868

181   FIGURE 8.1   Number of Letters by Month and Newspaper, 1868

185   FIGURE 8.2   Number of Letters by Days from Writing to Publication, 1868

227   FIGURE 10.1   How Farming Is Done in the West of the United States, 1871

Tables

16   TABLE 1.1   Literacy Rates Among Free Adult Population by Province and Capital City (Select Provinces), 1872

17   TABLE 1.2   Literacy Rates Among Free Adult Population (Six Largest Provinces and Rio de Janeiro), 1872

36   TABLE 1.1   Newspapers Published Outside of Rio de Janeiro, Microfilmed and Cataloged by the Biblioteca Nacional

37   TABLE 1.2   Number of Periodicals Founded and Circulating in Rio de Janeiro, 1822–1831 (by Year)

39   TABLE 1.3   Number of Periodicals Founded and Circulating in Rio de Janeiro, 1831–1840 (by Year)

46   TABLE 1.4   Number of *Gazeta do Brasil* Subscribers, 1827

83   TABLE 3.1   Occupations of Literate Slaves, 1821–1831

141   TABLE 6.1   Advertisements Per Capita, 1828–1898

141   TABLE 6.2   Advertisements for Rents (*Aluguéi*s) Per Capita, 1828–1898

141   TABLE 6.3   Advertisements for Sales (*Vendas*) Per Capita, 1828–1898

210   TABLE 9.1   *Apedido* Signatories, January 1870

Hendrik Kraay, Celso Thomas Castilho, and Teresa Cribelli

PREFACE

This book began as two panels that we organized for the January 2017 annual meeting of the American Historical Association in Denver, Colorado. Our purpose, both for the panel and for this book, is to analyze newspapers' role in nineteenth-century Brazilian public life—the evolution of the public sphere—and to consider the implications for research in Brazilian history of the Hemeroteca Digital Brasileira (HDB), the country's open-access digital newspaper archive. Our panel title may not have been the most felicitous, for a blogger on History News Network suggested that it was "hard even for historians to get excited by the opportunity to sit through the reading of three or four papers on subjects such as 'Imperial Brazilian Newspapers, the Hemeroteca Digital Brasileira, and Historical Research, Part 1: Context, Content, and Research in a Digital Archive.'"[1] He had not attended the session, for if he had, he would have written about the large audience and the rapt attention to the papers that reflects the flourishing of scholarship on Brazilian newspapers since the HDB's July 2012 launch. Each of us has long worked with Brazilian newspapers and, by the time of the panel, had published books heavily based on newspaper sources, mostly or entirely researched in the predigital era.[2] We felt that it was time to devote some attention to newspapers themselves and to critically engage with the press itself, rather than just use periodicals as sources. And, given the burgeoning Brazilian scholarship on newspapers, we felt that it was time to introduce some of this work to English-language readers.

This book is the result. Five of the eight presenters at the January 2017 panels are included in this book; for different reasons, Ângela Alonso, Roderick J. Barman, and Ian Read were unable to contribute to this volume, but we thank them for their participation in the discussions that led to this book. We would also like to thank the University of Alabama Cartographic Research Lab for formatting the graphs, and George Thompson, University of Alabama Publisher in Residence, for his assistance and advice. Hendrik Kraay acknowledges support from the Social Sciences and Humanities Research Council (Canada) and the Calgary Institute for the Humanities during the editing process. Celso Castilho is grateful for a research scholar grant from Vanderbilt University that allowed protected time to work on this project. Teresa Cribelli would like to thank Dr. Márcia Motta of the Universidade Federal Fluminense for first introducing to her the richness of nineteenth-century public letters in the Brazilian press. We thank Vanderbilt University for supporting the indexing of this book.

Notes

1. Shenkman, "Here's What Historians Said."
2. Kraay, *Days of National Festivity*; Cribelli, *Industrial Forests*; Castilho, *Slave Emancipation*.

ABBREVIATIONS

ABN	*Anais da Biblioteca Nacional*
ACD	*Anais da Câmara dos Deputados*
AGCRJ	Arquivo Geral da Cidade do Rio de Janeiro
AHI	Arquivo Histórico do Itamarati
AN	Arquivo Nacional
APEBa	Arquivo Público do Estado da Bahia
APEPe	Arquivo Público do Estado de Pernambuco
BN	Biblioteca Nacional
CLB	*Coleção das Leis do Brasil*
CM	*Correio Mercantil* (Rio de Janeiro)
Corr.	Correspondência
CP	Carta Particular
DP	*Diário do Povo* (Rio de Janeiro)
DRJ	*Diário do Rio de Janeiro*
GN	*Gazeta de Notícias* (Rio de Janeiro)
HDB	Hemeroteca Digital Brasileira
JC	*Jornal do Commercio* (Rio de Janeiro)
ONM	*O Novo Mundo* (New York)

Unless otherwise indicated, all newspapers cited were published in Rio de Janeiro.

NOTE ON CURRENCY AND ORTHOGRAPHY

During the nineteenth century, the Brazilian currency was the *mil-réis*, 1,000 *réis* (singular, *real*), written 1$000; 1,000 mil-réis was known as a *conto*, and was written 1:000$000. The mil-réis fluctuated considerably in value from the 1820s to the 1890s, although for much of the period its value remained close to US$0.50.[1] To make rough comparisons possible, we provide US dollar equivalents for the mil-réis figures mentioned in the text. To avoid confusion with US dollars, we render currency amounts less than one mil-réis (1$000) as, for example, 800 réis, rather than $800.

Portuguese orthography has undergone several changes since the nineteenth century. Following convention, we have modernized the spelling of names and newspaper titles in the text, retaining the original spelling in the notes and bibliography except when, by convention, the archaic spelling is used. The most frequent instance of this is Rio de Janeiro's *Jornal do Commercio*, which maintained the nineteenth-century spelling of its name until it ceased publication in 2016.

Note

1. Duncan, *Public and Private Operations*, 183.

Hendrik Kraay, Celso Thomas Castilho, and Teresa Cribelli

INTRODUCTION FROM COLONIAL GAZETTES TO THE "LARGEST CIRCULATION IN SOUTH AMERICA"

The scarecrow [that drives away] terrible despots
Unrivaled queen of [public] opinion,
Who blinds and silences slanderers,
Before the majesty of reason;
Daughter of Gutenberg, you are the safeguard
That ensures that the pen triumphs over the sword
That saves peoples from harsh laws;
You are the glory of genius,
And, while not seeking to monopolize enlightenment
You refuse your spark to stubborn kings![1]

With this pedestrian verse, Bahian poet Rozendo Moniz Barreto began his 1868 ode "To the Press," celebrating the enlightened role that he envisaged for newspapers and magazines in the Brazilian empire (1822–1889). Much had changed in the Brazilian press in the six decades since the exiled Portuguese monarchy had launched the *Gazeta do Rio de Janeiro* on September 10, 1808. By the time that the poet was writing, major Brazilian cities supported several dailies and a shifting cast of often ephemeral, less frequently published periodicals, depreciatively known as the "petty press [*pequena imprensa*]" to distinguish it from the larger-format dailies that styled themselves the "great press [*grande imprensa*]." Three years earlier, the first historian of the Brazilian press, Manuel Duarte Moreira de Azevedo, proudly reported that "the periodical, political, and literary press's development among us is easy to recognize; our dailies are not inferior to those of Europe, neither in format, nor in variety of content, nor in accuracy [*nitidez*] of printing." He went on to describe the press as orderly and respectful.[2] While both men correctly signaled the press's importance in nineteenth-century Brazilian society and its rapid development since 1808, as well as its place in a larger Atlantic World history of printing and publishing, many contemporaries would have held that they exaggerated its higher calling and its orderly and respectful nature.

A very different view emerges from Joaquim Manuel de Macedo's brilliant satire of imperial politics, *Memórias do sobrinho do meu tio* (Memoirs of my uncle's nephew, 1867–1868). When the title character decides to enter politics, he must launch a newspaper to defend his candidacy. It cannot be a small weekly, he explains, for "nowadays, only the daily giant-format gazette is acceptable"; small periodicals were lamps that go out for want of oil and quickly become "wrapping paper." Chiquinha, another character, wonders whether he plans to found a permanent newspaper, but Sobrinho assures her that his will be a short-lived journal, just for the election. He then launches into a lengthy disquisition about the four kinds of newspapers in the country. The "exceptional gazette" was a serious publication that debated weighty issues and delved deeply into them, resorting neither to "calumny" nor to personal attacks. By contrast, the "radical [*exaltada*] gazette" defended its "clearly-defined principles" tooth and nail by constantly insulting its adversaries, in whom its editors could see no merit or honor. The editor of a "pillory periodical" amounted to "a base street-corner assassin" who shamelessly attacked and defamed his enemies. The *Espada da Justiça* (Sword of Justice), as Sobrinho proposes to name his newspaper, is of the fourth kind, a "civilized pillory: a gazette without ideas that [nevertheless] proclaims itself idealist, that has no honor [*consciência*] but always speaks of it, that affects gravity in its editorial articles and spreads poison in the anonymous articles of its own making, that uses these instruments to destroy the honor of others, when this serves its purposes, or the hatreds of those who buy" its services. Although also a "pillory," unlike the third kind of periodical, this type was "distinguished [*afidalgado*]."[3]

The cynical bare-knuckled politics espoused by Macedo's Sobrinho contrasts sharply with the Bahian poet's idealization of the press's noble role in the public sphere and Moreira de Azevedo's celebration of Brazilian journalistic achievement, yet each captures important aspects of the nineteenth-century Brazilian press. Besides highlighting its political and social importance, all three writers also underscore the press's cultural prominence, central themes in this volume, which offers new perspectives on questions of power and culture during the empire (1822–1889). The chapters range from discussions of the press and politics to analyses of the social and intellectual histories of the press to probing studies of the article genres that heavily influenced the norms and forms of public discourse. The contributors to *Press, Power, and Culture* take a contingent view of newspapers, imagining them as projects and as constitutive of social processes in their own right. We thus interrogate how the press constructed, challenged, and reinvented notions of time, place, markets, and order during the nineteenth century and so illuminate the press's broad resonance. Finally, we establish new points of departure for narrating the origins, trajectory, and social significance of the press. In this introduction, we present a brief overview of the nineteenth-century Brazilian press, setting it in an Atlantic World context, and highlight key themes in the burgeoning Brazilian historiography on nineteenth-century newspapers, much of it little known outside of Brazil.

A Latecomer to the World of Print?

Europe's first newspapers developed from manuscript news-sheets that were sold to and circulated among merchants, nobles, and officials in centers of late medieval and early modern commerce. The news contained in these *avvisi* or *gazetta*, as they were titled in Italy, was extremely valuable to merchants who had no other way to discern business conditions in faraway locations. It is no accident that Italy and Germany, two of the first European centers of the printing press and the book trade, both developed expansive newspaper cultures by the end of the seventeenth century. Primarily focused on commercial and political information, these first newspapers set the parameters for printed news for centuries to come.[4]

Although newspaper content subsequently evolved to meet changing tastes and broader readerships, as the scholarship in this volume demonstrates, at the heart of the genre remains the distribution of political and commercial information. Brazil's most important nineteenth-century paper, Rio de Janeiro's *Jornal do Commercio*, demonstrated this early modern lineage in its inaugural edition with the promise to provide the city's "Gentlemen Merchants" with "daily information on all matters relating to commerce."[5] Founded in 1827, the *Jornal do Commercio* followed a centuries-old format that had developed within an expanding European—and increasingly global—trading network. From the seventeenth to the nineteenth centuries, European commercial networks and newspapers grew in tandem.

The seventeenth-century expansion of the printing press coincided with— and was also a catalyst for—the Enlightenment practice of civic engagement through print. If early modern newspapers primarily focused on selling information, by the eighteenth century in Europe they joined political pamphlets, broadsides, and books as forums in which private individuals engaged in public debate. In contrast to books and pamphlets, newspapers were printed at regular intervals and sold at modest prices that made them accessible to a larger reading public.[6] On the eve of the age of revolutions, newspapers had evolved into a mature genre that outsold long-standing competitors: pamphlets, manuscript newsletters, and broadsides.[7] Across Europe, and particularly in France, Germany, and Great Britain and its American colonies, a vibrant—if still often financially precarious—newspaper culture was firmly in place.

Jürgen Habermas drew on this historical context in theorizing about the public sphere, which he conceptualized as a lettered space for debating political matters that he imagined as open, rational, and potentially free of state interference. Highly influential, the concept has also been much criticized for its failure to acknowledge the numerous exclusions from the public sphere that actually existed. Historians of Latin America have nevertheless productively used the framework of the public sphere to integrate research on the press, associations, and space with questions about hierarchies and inequalities.[8] They approach these processes as embedded in structures shaped by the state and social norms. This newer scholarship is attentive to how the world of newspapers itself constituted a space of power and contestation. It is less about documenting what was or was not *in* the public sphere, and more about analyzing how issues become part *of* public life. Without idealizing the press as an emancipatory space, a public-sphere approach can also help us better understand the perpetuation or remaking of power relations; this is exemplified in Alain El Youssef's chapter on the press's role in legitimizing the reopening of the illegal slave trade in the 1830s (chapter 2). Rozendo Moniz's comments about the majesty of reason and the press's preeminence in forging public opinion demonstrate that Brazilians of his social class recognized and acted in the name of a public sphere in the nineteenth century, even if the actual public sphere fell far short of Habermas's ideal.

Another highly influential thinker about the role of the press is Benedict Anderson. He saw the proliferation of newspapers as constitutive of the "imagined communities" of nations that were emerging as central to the Western experience in the nineteenth century. In a few off-the-cuff remarks about Latin America, he argued that the late-colonial gazettes helped to create the national communities that won independence in the 1810s and 1820s.⁹ Many have observed that his analysis of Latin American independence is empirically wrong, but the concept of imagined communities remains a powerful one and it is clear that, as the press expanded *after* independence, it both reflected and created national communities.

When the *Gazeta do Rio de Janeiro* first circulated in what had just become the de facto capital of the Portuguese empire, Brazil finally joined what already had a well-established history in Europe and elsewhere in the Americas. Such gazettes had long circulated in some Spanish American capitals and both the independent United States and the Anglo-American colonies were home to vibrant periodical presses. Brazil's second city, Salvador, got its gazette, the *Idade de Ouro do Brasil*, in 1810, and a handful of ephemeral literary and cultural periodicals were also launched in this decade.[10] Observations like these about the press in the decade after 1808 typically frame arguments about how Brazil was a latecomer to the world of print but, as Marco Morel has recently observed, they overlook the eighteenth-century Portuguese periodicals that had long circulated throughout the empire (he attributes this oversight to the misplaced nationalism of both Brazilian and Portuguese historians).[11] Moreover, as Rebecca Earle has noted, Mexico City's privileged position in the world of print (documented by François-Xavier Guerra) was exceptional in Latin America, and Brazil more resembled New Granada, Chile, Quito, or Upper Peru (Bolivia), none of which had significant colonial presses; in these areas—as in Brazil—the political conflicts that led to independence produced a flourishing press.[12]

Press Freedom and Independence

The liberal regime borne of the 1820 revolution in Porto instituted press freedom throughout the Portuguese empire and ultimately led to Brazil's independence as a constitutional monarchy under Emperor Pedro I (1822–1831).[13] With censorship lifted, Brazil went through its version of what Jorge Basadre called Peru's "periodical orgy [*orgia periodística*]"[14]; countless political pamphlets and periodicals appeared in major centers as Brazilians debated citizenship, the nation, and other concepts of the new era. Indeed, even before printing presses arrived in São Paulo and São Luís, manuscript periodicals briefly circulated in these provincial capitals; a faction blocked from accessing

Salvador's press also circulated a manuscript periodical in 1821.[15] The arrival of a printing press in São Luís meant that *O Conciliador* (The Conciliator) could be printed as of November 10, 1821. Its title suggests something of how its editors sought to adapt new constitutional ideas to the realities of Brazil's slave society.[16] The first periodical printed in Belém, *O Paraense*, devoted most of its inaugural issue to printing the Portuguese constitutional regime's law of press freedom.[17] Newspapers from Portugal also circulated widely at this time and, already in late 1820, reports from Salvador advised that liberal periodicals from Portugal were being read aloud to groups of people on the streets, to much applause.[18]

The press, along with the 1823 constituent assembly and, after 1826, the annual session of Parliament, dominated the new country's public sphere, although many historians have noted that there was also what James Sanders calls the "broader, more chaotic public sphere of the streets."[19] In the mid-1820s, Emperor Pedro I attempted to close down political debate. After disbanding the constituent assembly in November 1823, he turned against the press and, for a few years, there was little space for independent journalism. In the late 1820s, led by Evaristo Ferreira da Veiga's *Aurora Fluminense* (1827–1835), the liberal press recovered and, by the early 1830s, a raucous partisan political press debated the great political questions of the day in Rio de Janeiro and the major provincial capitals (see chapter 1, by Marcello Basile). In the capital alone, one historian has calculated that the political press produced 2,027 newspaper issues between 1827 and Pedro I's abdication on April 7, 1831; these periodicals published 4,640 articles and 2,014 letters to the editor commenting on political issues.[20] Editors like Evaristo, Cipriano José Barata de Almeida, Ezequiel Correa dos Santos, and Antônio Borges da Fonseca were leading political figures, whose influence extended deeply into urban society.[21] Women's and Black newspapers formed part of this wave of the political press. In Porto Alegre, a women's paper vigorously defended the monarchy against republican agitation in the region. Other women's political titles also emerged in São Paulo and São João del-Rei.[22] In the imperial capital, a handful of Black papers railed against military and political exclusions. Like the women's press, these periodicals represented a variety of partisan perspectives.[23]

Among the liberal reforms passed by Parliament was legislation to regulate the constitutional provision that "all may communicate their thoughts by word and text and publish them in the press, without prior censorship, as long as they bear responsibility for abuses of this right, in the cases and according to the procedures that the law specifies."²⁴ The 1830 press law enumerated a relatively narrow range of abuses subject to prosecution: advocating the destruction of the representative monarchy and rebellion against the emperor (as well as the regents and members of the imperial family), incitement to disobey the law and constituted authorities, denying the existence of God, and blasphemy. Libelous accusations against government officials or institutions could lead to short jail terms and substantial fines, but the law contemplated a defense of truth. In its third article, the law specifically allowed "reasoned analysis" of the constitution and religious principles and customs. Responsibility for publications lay first with the printer, then the editor, then the author, and finally the seller (if the publication did not include the publisher's name). There was no obligation for article authors to publish their names, something that enabled the flourishing culture of anonymous paid articles and unsigned provincial correspondence that Teresa Cribelli, in chapter 9, and Hendrik Kraay, in chapter 8, analyze. The law further specified a complex system of trials for abuse of press freedom, beginning with an indictment by a sort of grand jury, followed by a jury trial. The onus was on the offended party to bring his or her case to the district judge to launch a prosecution. The law's principal terms were subsequently incorporated into the criminal code.²⁵

We know of no systematic study of trials for abuse of press freedom, but there are scattered indications that authorities found it difficult to win convictions. While the radical liberal Cipriano Barata complained in 1831 that the new law squeezed him like "an iron bit sent by the Holy Alliance," a contemporary historian of Bahia judged that juries could do nothing to contain the "periodical war."²⁶ Even before the 1830 law's passage, Rio de Janeiro's *Astreia* won eleven acquittals.²⁷ The law thus laid the groundwork for what numerous foreign observers judged the "unlimited" press freedom that Emperor Pedro II (1840–1889) himself generally defended (he assiduously read newspapers and frequently inquired about what he had read).²⁸ Foreigners marveled at the publication of republican periodicals even in the empire's capital, as did Benjamin Vicuña Mackenna in 1855.²⁹ In Salvador, Domingos Guedes Cabral's *O Guaicuru* survived indictments for abuse of press freedom and remained a thorn in the side of provincial governments in the 1840s.³⁰ In Limoeiro, Pernambuco, the local police delegate, lamented the circulation of the "base and incendiary journals, the *Diário Novo* and the *G[uarda] N[acional] Destacado*," from the provincial capital that gave heart to the "handful of anarchists that lamentably" infested his district in early 1843.³¹ This was only a few months after the defeat of the 1842 liberal revolts of Minas Gerais and São Paulo, a time when a reactionary government was in power nationally, but radical periodicals continued to circulate.

Based on this evidence, some have argued that press freedom was greater in the Brazilian empire than in later republican regimes, but this may overstate the freedom that the imperial press enjoyed.[32] Governments closely watched Borges da Fonseca, editor of the republican periodical that Vicuña Mackenna noted; they sometimes managed to buy off radical journalists.[33] The eleven trials that *Astreia* faced amounted to costly harassment, while legal protections mattered little when authorities turned a blind eye to extra-legal repression, most famously in the 1883 murder of Apulco de Castro, editor of Rio de Janeiro's widely read, scandal-mongering *O Corsário*.[34] Aristides Ricardo de Santana, editor of Salvador's *O Alabama*, a similarly critical periodical, survived a brutal beating in 1872, and during the Conservative reaction in late 1868, Bahian Liberals lamented the impressment of typographers and other employees of their periodicals in the province's interior.[35] Another famous incident was the late 1830 murder of Libero Badaró, a radical liberal journalist who had criticized the *ouvidor* (district judge) of São Paulo.[36] In times of political tension, opposition periodicals might suffer what in Portuguese is known by the delicious metaphor of an *empastelamento*, a sack of their printing press, reduced to the chopped filling of a meat pie (*pastel*). In December 1833, the Moderado (moderate liberal) government silenced the conservative restorationist periodicals by encouraging a mob to sack their press; *O Corsário* suffered an empastelamento in 1881 (Apulco failed to heed this warning).[37]

Growth and Differentiation of the Press

Already in the 1820s there were signs of differentiation in the press, as other genres joined the predominant political periodicals. The *Diário do Rio de Janeiro* (1821–1878) and the *Jornal do Commercio* (1827–2016) published extensive commercial advertising and thus served the business community; the regular publication of food prices soon earned the former the title of "butter daily."[38] Both developed into major dailies that by the 1840s published a variety of articles: local, provincial, and foreign news; literary works; *crônicas* (chronicles); shipping news; announcements and advertising; *apedidos* (paid articles); provincial correspondence; provincial or national legislative debates and government decisions; and occasional lengthy editorials, the so-called *artigos de fundo*. By this time, major provincial capitals typically had one or two newspapers that fit this mold.

Alongside this "grande imprensa," an enormous variety of other periodicals circulated in Brazilian cities by midcentury. Together, they transformed urban sensibilities—altering perceptions of time, space, and order, and changing people's relationship with the printed word. Not only was there a greater variety of newspapers and periodicals, but they published a greater variety of articles; as one historian has put it for Spanish America, newspapers became "more complex artifacts."[39] More than simply offering newspapers from which to read about local changes, the expansion of the press is itself a register of growing cities and evolving urban cultures. One scholar argues in another context that nineteenth-century newspapers "engaged in a geographical process to reproduce the city, to render it" legible to readers.[40] Experimental columns in newspapers became fixtures of quotidian affairs. Crônicas and apedidos became some of newspapers' most interesting features. The former afforded (mostly) men ways of creating their reputation through commenting on everything from street processions, to the latest operas, to parliamentary matters, and much more, while the latter allowed anyone with a small amount of money to get his or her views into print (on these genres of articles see, respectively, the contributions by Ludmila de Souza Maia [chapter 5] and Cribelli [chapter 9] in this volume).

Moreover, these innovations on the inside pages of dailies and weeklies mirrored the increasing variety of newspapers and periodicals, which included literary, women's, scientific, and illustrated journals, not to mention the radical *pasquins* (small-format newspapers) and politicized newspapers that continued to echo the press of the 1820s and 1830s. A wave of short-lived radical pasquins from 1848 to the early 1850s kept alive the radical-liberal program defeated with the Praieira Rebellion in Pernambuco in 1849; these included the coordinated publication of *Argos* periodicals in northern provinces. Another wave of these ephemeral periodicals appeared in the early 1880s.[41] Whether they were pillories, and which kind of pillory they were, to use the terminology of Macedo's character, depended on one's point of view.

Fully thirty-four periodicals directed at women appeared throughout Brazil in the 1850s and 1860s. The *Jornal das Senhoras*, founded in 1852 by the Argentine schoolteacher and political exile Juana Manso, is probably the best known, and it ran in Rio de Janeiro for three years. Other shorter-lived women's newspapers also emerged in Recife, Salvador, Aracajú, São Luís, and Belém.

Female journalists, who also published in the mainstream press, often took on the issue of education. They made it a topic of their serialized stories and editorials, connecting it to debates over citizenship. In the 1870s and 1880s, the number of women's newspapers almost doubled again, and two Rio de Janeiro periodicals, *A Mai de Famílias* and *Éco das Damas*, achieved notable longevity, circulating from 1879 to 1888.[42]

As elsewhere in Latin America, the press expanded and diversified in the last decades of the empire and historians of the era have long turned to newspapers to probe its major moments, such as the Paraguayan War (1864–1870), the abolition of slavery (1888), modernization, popular politics, and the making of the republican regime proclaimed in 1889.[43] Some of the chapters in this book touch on these themes, such as those by Arnaldo Lucas Pires Junior (chapter 7), Rodrigo Camargo de Godoi (chapter 3), Roberto Saba (chapter 10), and Kraay (chapter 8), but by focusing on the press itself, they offer rich methodological insights for studying visuality, slaves' engagement with print culture, Brazilian periodicals published abroad, provincial life, and intellectual history more generally. This was also the time when the press became increasingly popular and accessible. The illustrated weekly magazines that proliferated after 1860 provided visual commentary on society and politics (see Pires Junior's chapter). José Ferreira de Souza Araújo's *Gazeta de Notícias*, founded in Rio de Janeiro in 1875, pioneered a new genre of daily with shorter articles, more news, and fewer lengthy editorials and other opinion pieces. It sold for only 40 réis per issue; that same year, Salvador's *Diário de Notícias* emulated this model of journalism in Brazil's second city.[44] These Brazilian exemplars of what is elsewhere known as the "new journalism" quickly established themselves with large print runs and were sold both by subscription and through street sales by newsboys, themselves fixtures of late nineteenth-century cities, louder than parrots as they peddled their wares, according to one traveler.[45] The new newspapers marked a major change in the press, which increasingly became a business, more or less neutral in party politics, seeking profit from delivering "news" to readers.[46]

Much less is known about the provincial press than about Rio de Janeiro–based newspapers; indeed, in classic and more recent overviews of the press, what appeared in the provinces is often treated as an afterthought.[47] Nevertheless, major provincial capitals had lively presses, lovingly cataloged by early twentieth-century historian-librarians.[48] The *Diário de Pernambuco*, in fact, has long held the title as Latin America's oldest continually published newspaper (and the oldest one in the Portuguese-speaking world), as it proudly proclaims on its masthead (and now on its website).[49] Those in the country's North got their foreign news directly from Europe and North America, and readers skipped the outdated foreign news summaries in the *Jornal do Commercio* and other Rio de Janeiro papers when they arrived weeks or months later. Even seemingly isolated Teresina, capital of Piauí since 1852, supported three newspapers by the 1860s, and they printed foreign news obtained from European newspapers imported through São Luís.[50] As Pires Junior notes, illustrated satirical magazines were also produced in many provincial centers, but little is known about them.[51] The relative lack of scholarship on provincial presses derives from the limited scope of the Biblioteca Nacional's national microfilming project in the 1970s, which did not reach the large collections of periodicals in state archives, libraries, and historical institutes in places like Salvador, Recife, and São Luís.[52] While some states have taken steps to preserve what survives of their nineteenth-century periodical holdings, many crumbling collections of nineteenth- and twentieth-century periodicals still await preservation by modern technologies, and we are today running serious risk of losing much of the surviving provincial press (in the meantime, these collections are now often inaccessible to researchers).[53]

Politics, Circulation, Readership, and Production

As several of the contributors to this volume demonstrate, the Brazilian press, like its counterparts in the North Atlantic world, was a precarious business, reliant on imported newsprint, presses, and ink. Even a well-connected and successful printer and periodical publisher like Francisco de Paula Brito faced regular bankruptcies before his death in 1861.[54] An old hand in the publishing business recalled that *O Despertador* (1838–1841), which for a time constituted serious competition to the *Jornal do Commercio*, folded leaving a debt of 200:000$ (US$122,000), despite shareholders' investment of about half of that amount.[55] In their chapters, Basile shows how periodicals rose and fell with the fortunes of the political group that sponsored them in the 1820s and 1830s, while Pires Junior describes the hand-to-mouth existence of most illustrated magazines.

Few major newspapers survived without subventions until the 1870s, an open secret, as both government and opposition sought to influence the press. Many short-lived periodicals resembled Sobrinho's *Espada da Justiça* as they championed candidacies or particular interests. Longer-lived party periodicals depended on patrons with deep pockets or governments' slush funds. The *Correio da Tarde* (1848–1852), the Conservative government's organ, cost 4:000$ per month to produce but barely brought in 900$ from subscribers and advertisers (the average value of the mil-réis in these years was US$0.55).[56] In the late 1840s, the British legation quietly subsidized *O Filantropo*'s campaign against the slave trade.[57] Opposition newspapers regularly criticized their rivals who, they alleged, lived from a minister's "secret funds." In 1855, Justiniano José da Rocha broke with the Conciliação cabinet and famously denounced the government monies that he had long received for his work as a hired pen for mostly conservative groups.[58] Fifteen years later, Minister of Justice José de Alencar complained that the *Diário do Rio de Janeiro*, receiving a subsidy to promote colonization, was nevertheless criticizing him, and proudly held up his *Dezesseis de Julho* (1869–1870) as a newspaper that had never taken government money.[59]

Much the same happened in the provinces; in April 1868, Salvador's *O Progressista* reportedly only survived on "money from the police," but neither government nor opposition had unlimited funds.[60] In May 1870, Bahia's chief of police complained that he had exhausted his secret budget of 4:000$, most of which had gone to a 300$ monthly subsidy to the "*Interesse Público* for the services that it does for this department" (that year, the mil-réis was worth US$0.45).[61] In October 1868, a "society or company composed of Conservatives" had bought this newspaper, which joined the *Jornal da Bahia* to defend the Conservative government against the "subversive doctrines" of the "Progressista opposition."[62] In addition to direct subsidies, the lucrative contracts to publish national or provincial legislative debates and government notices kept some major newspapers afloat and ensured that they supported the government. In these respects, the Brazilian press before the 1870s closely resembled that of the early republican United States, where low barriers to entry made for precarious newspapers that had to rely on party patronage, and therefore amounted to "boosters of a particular political organization."[63]

The mid-1870s marked an important change in the press's relationship to politics. The new dailies, like Rio de Janeiro's *Gazeta de Notícias*, espoused an ideal of political neutrality or impartiality; published more appealing content; deployed reporters (a word that entered Brazilian Portuguese at that time); sought out advertising; relied mostly on street sales; but still opened their pages to apedidos, an important source of revenue. Brazil's version of the new journalism was an effective business model and increasing numbers of writers earned a (precarious) living in newspapers, where they satisfied their literary aspirations.[64] While one man who had worked as a small-town publisher commented about his years in the business (1876–1880) that "backwoods journals resemble those of the Court [Rio de Janeiro] in [their capacity] to relieve their owners of their last pennies," his frustrations do not tell the whole story.[65] The press's late nineteenth-century expansion and investors' willingness to put money into new newspapers in the 1870s and 1880s reveals that there was profit to be made in Rio de Janeiro, even if newspapers were probably not "one of the most lucrative investments" available at the time, as one historian has recently claimed.[66] Of course, the absentee-owned *Jornal do Commercio* had long been a profitable business and, already in 1863, it had 3,000 subscribers throughout the country. Advocates of politically engaged journalism, however, criticized the generally conservative *Jornal* for seemingly being most interested in making money. In the 1870s and 1880s, it did not adopt the new journalism's innovations, but continued to turn a profit.[67] Very little is known about how smaller periodicals managed to stay afloat but, by the 1880s, Ângelo Agostini's *Revista Ilustrada* had also become a profitable business.[68]

Just as the press's business aspects remain obscure, there is little reliable data on circulation, for partisan periodicals had a strong incentive to exaggerate the number of subscribers; the data presented by Basile for two Rio de Janeiro periodicals in the early 1830s (print runs between 500 and 1,000 copies) is consistent with what Marcelo Cheche Galves has found for São Luís in the 1820s, when the major periodicals typically produced 500 copies for a city of 30,000 people.[69] Data for later in the empire are a bit more reliable, even if newspapers likely had an incentive to exaggerate their circulation to attract paid advertising and to justify the prices that they charged for printing apedidos. According to foreign observers, the *Jornal do Commercio* produced 15,000 copies per day in the 1860s and early 1870s; it usually published more than 360 days per year.[70] In 1881, four Rio de Janeiro dailies had a combined circulation of 46,000 in a city whose population grew from 229,000 in 1872 to 423,000 in 1890.[71] Eight years later, the city's eight morning and three afternoon dailies reportedly published 87,500 copies; later in 1889, *O País* claimed "the largest circulation in South America," with a press run of 32,500.[72] Provincial capitals' dailies had a similarly large presence in their cities. In 1886, São Paulo's five dailies boasted a combined circulation of 12,300 in a city whose population stood at just over 44,000.[73] Salvador's *Gazeta da Tarde* announced a print run of 6,600 in 1887, when the city's population stood at close to the 145,000 counted in the 1890 census.⁷⁴

The size of print runs does not alone tell the whole story, for circulation is also a matter of distribution over geographical space.⁷⁵ Already in 1830, a keen observer of Brazilian affairs remarked (albeit with a bit of exaggeration) that "the sensation" caused by reactions to news of the Bourbon monarchy's fall in France "was instantly communicated throughout the entire Empire, through the instrumentality of the public journals."⁷⁶ Evidence from the important Minas Gerais town of São João del-Rei suggests that readers there constituted part of a geographically broad public sphere. In 1829, the town's library had periodicals from Maranhão, Pernambuco, Bahia, and Rio de Janeiro, as well as local ones (it is not clear, however, how many issues of each it had, nor how regularly it received newspapers from distant provinces).⁷⁷ In the 1830s, reported Ferdinand Dénis, the Imperial Library received periodicals from Rio de Janeiro and the provinces.⁷⁸ Three decades later, there was an intense circulation of correspondence and newspapers between Rio de Janeiro and Bahia (see Kraay's chapter), and the lengthy summaries of provincial news in the capital's newspapers and the summaries of news from the North and the South in provincial capitals' newspapers further indicate how the press undergirded a national imagined community, knit together by steamship lines and mule trains and, later, railroads.

How far this print community extended into the countryside remains to be determined. Evidence from Bahia is mixed. In 1853, a Boston carpenter working on a plantation outside of Santo Amaro remarked that it was "odd to have no papers to read Sundays but the people dont [sic] seem to care about know [sic] anything beyond their plantation."⁷⁹ A German visitor complained in 1878 that mail service was very limited in this area and that the only way to get newspapers was to have someone bring them from Salvador; he and his hosts eagerly awaited news from outside.⁸⁰ Some years earlier, the proprietor of the *Jornal da Bahia*, which had recently become the new Conservative government's mouthpiece, complained of delays in shipping into the interior, where opposition newspapers were preferred.⁸¹ Likewise, the complaints of Limoeiro's delegate indicates that Recife's radical periodicals circulated beyond the provincial capital's limits in the early 1840s.

Circulation of course also implies readership, and this raises the issue of literacy. Unfortunately, very little is known about how census-takers arrived at the oft-cited 18.6 percent literacy rate recorded in the 1872 census. To conclude that these one-in-five Brazilians amounted to an "island of literates" bobbing in a "sea of illiterates," as one historian characterizes nineteenth-century Brazil, oversimplifies the story,[82] for it is clear that popular sectors engaged with the press (and with politics more generally). Indeed, a recent edited book on Rio de Janeiro questions the generally accepted view that the popular sectors were distant from literate culture.[83] Both the press's expansion and the heightened political ferment of the 1870s and 1880s raise the issue of how people with different levels of literacy engaged with the politicized print world, a question that needs further research.

Instead of taking the census's literacy rate as an accurate measure of who read and who did not, we use the census data to pose new questions about both the census itself and about the spread of information. Unfortunately, there is no earlier national census against which to compare the 1872 data, so it is impossible to trace change over time. This census, like all others, was a state project, and political considerations influenced its conclusions.[84] Students of slavery have shown that in some cases it misconstrued the nature of the "free" population and that it sometimes miscounted the enslaved. Census-takers counted conditionally freed slaves as "free" even though they were still subject to long-term obligations to their former owners.[85] In Pernambuco, the 1872 census undercounted the more rigorously enforced 1873 slave registration by almost 17 percent (89,028 instead of 106,236 slaves).[86] Whether underreporting on this scale happened with literacy is not knowable, but these examples underscore the arbitrary and politicized nature of census data.

Nonetheless, the census offers insights into literacy rates at the national, provincial, and municipal levels. While there is growing attention to the subject of slave literacy (see Godoi's chapter), we focus on the free population, for literacy among the enslaved was statistically very low (the census deemed less than 1 percent of the total enslaved population as literate).[87] Table I.1 presents the national literacy figures, along with data from select provinces and their capital cities. The gender breakdown is generally consistent across the country, with men registering about a 10-percentage point higher literacy rate than women. Equally unsurprisingly, literacy rates in provincial capitals and Rio de Janeiro city, the imperial capital, were markedly higher than the provincial or national rates; in most cases, they were around double the provincial rate (Salvador's was almost triple Bahia's), which is consistent with the print world's concentration in cities and towns.

The most urbanized parishes in capital cities boasted literacy rates several

TABLE 1.1 Literacy Rates Among the Free Adult Population by Province and Capital City (Select Provinces), 1872. Brazilian and provincial data exclude the capital city. In addition to the adult literacy data, the census recorded separately the number of students enrolled in schools. They are not included in this table. Calculated from Brazil, *Recenseamento*.

	NUMBER LITERATE	TOTAL POPULATION	PERCENT LITERATE
BRAZIL			
Rio de Janeiro (city)			
Male	65,164	133,880	48.7
Female	33,992	92,153	36.9
TOTAL	*99,156*	*226,033*	*43.9*
Rest of Brazil			
Male	1,012,097	4,318,699	23.4
Female	550,981	4,100,973	13.4
TOTAL	*1,563,078*	*8,419,672*	*18.6*
PERNAMBUCO			
Recife (city)			
Male	20,266	54,234	37.4
Female	15,942	47,211	33.8
TOTAL	*36,208*	*101,445*	*35.7*
Rest of Pernambuco			
Male	72,398	327,241	22.1
Female	38,717	323,735	12.0
TOTAL	*111,115*	*650,976*	*17.1*
BAHIA			
Salvador (city)			
Male	23,878	59,820	40.0
Female	15,125	53,821	28.1
TOTAL	*39,003*	*113,641*	*34.3*
Rest of Bahia			
Male	102,117	570,543	17.9
Female	33,314	527,608	6.3
TOTAL	*135,431*	*1,098,151*	*12.3*
SÃO PAULO			
São Paulo (city)			
Male	5,056	13,692	36.9
Female	2,673	13,865	19.3
TOTAL	*7,729*	*27,557*	*28.0*
Rest of São Paulo			
Male	87,921	334,612	26.3
Female	36,425	318,573	11.4
TOTAL	*124,346*	*653,185*	*19.0*

times higher than the national rates. Almost half of urban Rio de Janeiro's free population was literate (table I.1). Likewise, Recife's three most urbanized parishes had literacy rates of 43 percent: in Santo Antônio Parish, where Recife's presses and theater were located, census-takers judged fully 57 percent of the population literate.[88] While male literacy rates exceeded female literacy rates, around one-third of free women in Rio de Janeiro (36.9 percent), Salvador (28.1 percent), and Recife (33.8 percent) were counted as literate, which undergirded the pronounced growth of the women's press in the 1870s and 1880s. In short, in major cities, 30–40 percent of the population was, by census-takers' metrics, squarely part of this print sphere. While the total number of possible readers in Rio de Janeiro city was much larger than that of most provincial capitals, the national circulation of newspapers linked big and small publics alike; deeper research into the provincial press will certainly enrich the national perspective derived mostly from work on Rio de Janeiro.

Table I.2 lists the six most populous provinces and their literacy rates, providing further insight into the concentration of centers of information. None of these provinces—Bahia, Minas Gerais, Pernambuco, São Paulo, and Rio de Janeiro—are unexpected in a listing of this sort, but the absolute numbers of potential readers in provinces like Minas Gerais and Bahia should compel scholars of the press and print culture to take a closer look at them. These provinces also had the largest slave populations, revealing the coexistence of large concentrations of free literate people with the highest concentrations of

TABLE I.2 Literacy Rates Among the Free Adult Population (Six Largest Provinces and Rio de Janeiro), 1872. Calculated from Brazil, *Recenseamento*.

PROVINCE	LITERATE POPULATION			TOTAL POPULATION	PERCENT LITERATE
	Male	*Female*	*Total*		
Minas Gerais	145,207	78,271	223,478	1,669,276	13.4
Bahia	161,937	87,135	249,072	1,211,792	20.6
Pernambuco	92,664	54,659	147,323	752,511	19.6
Ceará	58,657	20,903	79,560	689,773	11.5
São Paulo	92,977	48,090	141,067	680,742	20.7
Rio de Janeiro	69,997	44,603	114,600	499,037	23.0
Rio de Janeiro (city)	65,164	33,992	99,156	226,033	43.9
Brazil	1,012,097	550,981	1,563,078	8,419,672	18.6

enslaved people; in other words, while vibrant antislavery movements flourished in these places, comparatively higher literacy rates were still compatible with proslavery orders.

This presentation of the literacy data, with all its caveats, provides a broader-than-usual view of this information. It shows variation at the urban, provincial, and even gender levels, and will hopefully encourage more work on literacy and the census. Nevertheless, it should not be forgotten that the census deemed more than 80 percent of the population illiterate. As we have suggested, this is not necessarily an objective or accurate statistic, but it is one of the reference points that historians must engage with when trying to understand the world of the press. It also suggests that more work is needed on the intersections and exchanges between print and oral forms of information. As elsewhere in the Atlantic World, Brazil's public sphere extended beyond those who could read and write. A German observer remarked in the late 1820s that Brazil's newspapers expanded the "inferior classes' ideas," even as he lamented their extreme partisanship.[89] The *Diário de Pernambuco* reported in 1881 that Conservatives in the town of Caruaru eagerly read news about the electoral reform, "showing it to each other, even in shops and stores," an indication of the linkage between literate and oral culture.[90] The newsboys who shouted about the latest news as they sold their copies in the 1870s and 1880s ensured that nobody could walk down major city streets without entering into newspapers' communication networks.[91]

How much newspapers cost to readers has yet to be the subject of systematic research. As Basile points out in his chapter, the forty or eighty réis per issue that periodicals typically cost in the 1820s and 1830s was a modest amount, equivalent to a pound of brown sugar or a pound of potatoes. Others suggest that newspapers then cost about as much as a loaf of bread.[92] At that time, one could subscribe to the *Jornal do Commercio* for 1$000 per month, a figure that went up to 16$000 per year by 1835, and 20$000 by 1850, and 30$000 by the 1880s (for most of this period, the mil-réis's value fluctuated around US$0.50).[93] When it was launched in 1884, *O País*, like the other new dailies, sold for 40 réis per issue and offered annual subscriptions for 20$000; for 1885, it lowered its subscription price to 12$000 for readers in Rio de Janeiro and Niterói, but kept the 20$000 price for subscribers in other provinces. Subscribers in Rio de Janeiro, in other words, would get 63 free issues (that year, *O País* published 363 issues). As Pires Junior points out in his chapter, illustrated periodicals were considerably more expensive, 500 to 1,000 réis, and a subscription to the weekly *Revista Ilustrada* could be had for 20$000. Both Basile and Pires Junior, like other scholars who have written about the press, suggest that these were relatively low prices and that people of modest means could have access to newspapers. It is more likely that they were casual purchasers rather than regular subscribers and, of course, yesterday's newspaper was probably available as a hand-me-down from a better-off neighbor who subscribed.[94] What seems clear is that newspapers were accessible in some way to large segments of urban Brazilian society, as is implied by the steadily growing circulation figures and the urban literacy rates recorded in 1872.

Scattered sources offer hints of reading practices among the literate. Dénis reported that, in the 1830s, the periodical collection in the Imperial Library attracted "a great concourse of readers belonging to all classes and all colors."[95] On the train from Rio de Janeiro to São Paulo in 1882, Ina von Binzer observed that most men buried their noses in the *Jornal do Commercio*'s large pages (which then measured approximately 19 by 31 inches).[96] The proliferation of streetcar lines after the 1860s and passive commuting meant that people had time for reading; not surprisingly, newsboys crowded around downtown streetcar stops to peddle their wares. Beyond the individual reader, other passengers were exposed to both the headlines on the front page and the advertisements on the final page, a strategic design that amplified the number of viewers for a given advertisement.[97] Historians have described how the serialized novels published in the *folhetim* (a section that published literature and social commentary) were read aloud in family gatherings, which gave illiterate members of the household access to these literary works. When a character in *Uma família baiana* (A Bahian family, 1888), wins the hand of her preferred suitor over several rivals, Bahian novelist Xavier Marques describes her gloating as even greater than that of the opposition gazette's folhetim when a government candidate is routed at the polls, an indication of how deeply newspaper culture had entered daily life.[98]

Other literary sources provide further indications of reading practices and how they were shaped by class and gender. The São Luís merchant, Manuel Pescada, in Aluísio Azevedo's *O mulato* (Mulatto, 1881), set in the early 1870s, "likes to read during his leisure hours, and respectfully subscribed to the better newspapers of the province and even some from Lisbon," but he does not "like his clerks always reading newspapers"; the senior clerk castigates a junior clerk for his reading habits. An elderly matron in this novel criticizes the newfangled sewing machines that gave young women the time "to read the newspapers, delve into novels, or even take to the indecency of the piano!"[99] In F. C. Duarte Badaró's 1881 abolitionist novel, *Fantina*, set in 1871 in rural Minas Gerais, the wealthy Luiza is more attuned to literary culture than her boorish planter suitor, Frederico, who can barely handle the *Jornal do Commercio*'s large sheets and does not know the difference between the editorial (*artigo de fundo*) and the folhetim. After he reads the right article to her, they agree that they both prefer the folhetim's light novel to news about "the man who wants to free that which is not his," in other words, the Viscount of Rio Branco, who had just secured the passage of the Free Womb Law.[100] Alessandra El Far's recent analysis of love notes published in the *Jornal do Commercio* in the 1870s suggests that male suitors expected the female objects of their affection to pore over this newspaper's densely printed advertising sections to find their missives.[101]

We know of no substantial scholarship on the laborers who produced Brazilian newspapers, but their experience reflected the big changes that took place in production processes, not just in Brazil but throughout the Atlantic World. At the beginning of the nineteenth century, print shops on both sides of the Atlantic were artisanal operations that depended on skilled manual and intellectual labor, often combined in the same person.[102] By the end of the century, newspaper presses developed into large-scale industrial manufacturing operations that collectively employed thousands of workers.[103] Whether artisanal or industrial, nineteenth-century printers were manufacturers in two senses: they produced a material object that required machinery, skilled labor, raw material, and a transportation network to bring their product to readers; at the same time newspapers were intellectual creations that depended on human knowledge, observation, and networks of information sharing that became ever more dependent on and shaped by nineteenth-century technology.

At the beginning of the 1800s, a skilled staff of typesetters, inkers, and machinists oversaw production runs of up to 200 impressions per hour using flat-bed presses.[104] By the 1870s, cylindrical and rotary presses transformed printing into steam-powered industrial operations that could produce from 12,000 to 15,000 impressions per hour.[105] The *Chicago Tribune*, for example, jumped from a circulation of 1,200 copies per day in 1850 to 24,000 in 1860 with the adoption of a Hoe cylinder press; such technological advances likewise enabled Brazilian newspapers' circulation growth.[106] In the 1880s, major Rio de Janeiro newspapers acquired French-made Marinoni rotary presses and publicly celebrated their new machinery's installation.[107]

Transportation and information technology also transformed newspaper production and content. The coastal steamers that linked Brazilian ports after the late 1830s, followed by regular transatlantic steam lines, some of them subsidized like the United States and Brazilian Steamship Company created in 1865, as well as the railroads that inched their way into some parts of Brazil's interior, all sped news—and newspapers—to readers.[108] The transatlantic cables that connected the United States and Europe in 1858, and Brazil and Europe in 1874, enabled virtually instantaneous transmission of news. However, early telegraph communication was costly, and in the late 1880s, Havas—which quickly dominated the South American market for cable news—supplied scarcely 350 words per month to its customers in the region. Most foreign news still came in the form of correspondents' letters or European and North American newspapers sent by steamer.[109]

Rising literacy and burgeoning populations in industrializing cities such as Rio de Janeiro, São Paulo, Chicago, Manchester, San Francisco, Buenos Aires, and New York increased demand for newspapers, in turn spurring the creation of new content that appealed to both a wider—and sometimes more specialized—audience. After its 1875 launch, Rio de Janeiro's *Gazeta de Notícias* developed new sections that captured the interest of a growing urban readership and outsold its more staid rival, the *Jornal do Commercio*, although the *Gazeta* was soon overtaken by *O País*. In short, Brazil's newspaper production was fully in synch with commercial, stylistic, and technological advancements unfolding in the North Atlantic, as Joaquim Maria Machado de Assis wryly observed about the speed with which news traveled to Brazil in Morse code via the transatlantic cable.[110] When Moreira de Azevedo celebrated the Brazilian press's achievements by claiming that Rio de Janeiro's newspapers compared favorably to those of Europe, he was expressing exactly those views. For the members of Brazil's intellectual elite, matching Europe's achievements and joining the Atlantic World's print culture were essential steps to creating the nation that they desired. In these ways, newspapers on both sides of the Atlantic were both a product of and an expression of modernity.[111]

Research and the Digital Revolution

One of this book's aims is to make Brazilian scholarship on newspapers more accessible to English-language readers. We seek to foster a dialogue between the English- and Portuguese-language scholarship; the press has been the focus of dozens of studies coming from the Brazilian academy, but the topic has received considerably less attention in Anglophone scholarship. The reasons for the striking difference in emphasis have to do with the notable expansion in Brazilian higher education and the interdisciplinary attention that the study of the press has received from scholars in Brazilian literature, communication, and history departments. Organized by a group of scholars at the Universidade Estadual do Rio de Janeiro, a series of conferences and workshops leading up to the 2008 bicentennial of the press's establishment in Brazil launched the contemporary genre of edited books on the Brazilian press.[112] Many more such volumes have appeared in the last decade, often drawing on the work of research groups organized around key questions.[113]

A quick overview of recent scholarship highlights several tendencies in research on the Brazilian press and suggests areas for future work. There are detailed analyses of the content of Brazil's first newspapers, the late colonial gazettes of Rio de Janeiro and Salvador.[114] Historians of independence and the imperial state's construction have long pored over crumbling yellowed paper copies and dimly lit microfilmed versions of the political press of the 1820s and 1830s to reconstruct the wide-ranging political debates in the new nation-state's emerging public sphere; countless chapters in edited books and journal articles continue to explore these themes, often providing an in-depth analysis of a single periodical.[115] Likewise, the influential illustrated press launched with Henrique Fleiuss's *Semana Ilustrada* (1861–1876) and further developed by Ângelo Agostini's *Revista Ilustrada* (1876–1898), has attracted considerable scholarly attention; far less is known about the provincial illustrated press (see Pires Junior's chapter).[116] Literary historians have studied some of the *crônicas* (sometimes also known as *folhetins*, after their usual location at the bottom of the front page, known in French as the *feuilleton*), the periodic (usually weekly) columns about culture, mores, politics, and society that appeared regularly in newspapers after mid-century; their focus, however, has been on those written by well-known literary figures like José de Alencar and Machado de Assis (on this scholarship, see Maia's chapter).[117] Many more anonymously written crônicas remain unexamined. Women's periodicals are a flourishing area of research, and historian Constância Lima Duarte has identified more than 140 titles published across Brazil.[118]

That the murdered Apulco and the roughed-up Aristides were Afro-Brazilians says much about both how the press served as an opportunity for social mobility and political engagement for men of color and about the limits of the spaces open to them, an issue that Celso Thomas Castilho examines further in chapter 11. Ana Flávia Magalhães Pinto has identified what she calls a "Black press" in nineteenth-century Brazil; journalists who raised racial questions in debates about citizenship and belonging constantly struggled against the dominant culture's denial of difference.[119] Biographies of notable journalists and publishers have recently appeared, joining the broader wave of biographical studies in Brazil. Journalists are ideal subjects for biographies as, even if they did not leave personal papers, their published record offers a wealth of information about their lives and their publicly expressed views.[120] Intellectual and cultural historians have long studied literary and cultural magazines like *Minerva Brasiliense* (1843–1845) and *Guanabara* (1849–1855).[121] Historians are of course most familiar with the *Revista do Instituto Histórico e Geográfico Brasileiro*, continuously published since 1838 and one of the oldest extant history journals in the world.

We have deliberately left to the end of this introduction what others might have chosen to start with—the digital revolution that came to scholarship on Brazilian newspapers with the July 2012 launch of the Biblioteca Nacional's Hemeroteca Digital Brasileira (HDB), reportedly the largest open-access online newspaper archive in the world. The millions of pages of nineteenth-century Brazilian newspapers now available anywhere to anyone with a computer and an Internet connection constitute a vast, mostly unexplored, terrain for historians. Much remains to be done before we can navigate confidently through the HDB's swelling sea of pixels (at the time of its launch, the HDB claimed five million pages; in November 2016, a pop-up window on the site boasted ten million pages and this number continues to grow).[122]

Despite the HDB's limited search function, scholars are eagerly mining it for useful nuggets of information and the tech-savvy among us are devising ways to extract more data from the HDB.[123] Nevertheless, many hits prove to be duds and (although we will never know for sure) it is likely that just as many search terms are missed thanks to the limitations of optical character recognition software, irregular nineteenth-century typefaces, and the faded quality of so many of these periodicals, which neither microfilming nor digitizing from microfilm masters can improve. No doubt, the search function will improve over time, but this will only increase the higher-level dangers of decontextualization that Lara Putnam has recently discussed. When we can almost instantaneously access all the occurrences of a keyword (or at least what the search function says are all of them), we lose sight of the larger context in which the concept was discussed and abandon the possibility of serendipitous discovery.[124] Of course, digitization enables certain new types of research, but such work is always dependent on the quality of the digitization.[125]

Impressionistically, it appears to us that the number of citations to nineteenth-century newspapers has soared in Brazilian and Brazilianist historical scholarship, just as the use of Toronto's *Globe and Mail* and the *Toronto Star* increased exponentially in Canadian history after these newspapers' digitization in the early 2000s. As Ian Milligan has cautioned, this methodological revolution in Canadian history took place without any reflection on the appropriate protocols for documenting research methods (the keywords and variations used, the scope of the material searched, the date of the search, among many other things that may affect results). Just as the online availability of the two Toronto newspapers may have pushed Canadian history toward a focus on that city and its southern Ontario hinterland, so the HDB may reinforce nineteenth-century Brazilian history's concentration on Rio de Janeiro because the collections of the imperial capital's newspapers in the Biblioteca Nacional are far more complete than those of provincial newspapers. At the same time, however, the HDB makes the provincial newspapers held in the library's collections more accessible to readers everywhere.[126]

Our embrace of all things digital must thus be tempered with a recognition of their limits, frank discussion of methodology, and renewed attention to context. By making newspapers much more widely available, the HDB, in fact, offers an opportunity to do badly needed basic research on the Brazilian press. What is striking about the chapters in this book is that, although they are based on research in the HDB, only Matthew Nestler and Zephyr Frank's chapter constitutes a digital history in the sense that its authors use data generated through the HDB's search function to analyze markets in Rio de Janeiro (chapter 6). Nevertheless, they are fully conscious of the HDB's limits. All the other authors rely not so much on counting or keyword searches but on the venerable methodology of closely reading texts and images.

Press, Power, and Political Culture begins with Marcello Basile's analysis of the "print arena" of the 1820s and 1830s, when the press first assumed its central place in politics and Brazil's public sphere. He closely connects the press's expansion and retraction to the political conflicts of these years and argues that the partisan press flourished during, and contributed to, periods of political division. Next, Alain El Youssef demonstrates that, contrary to historians' assumptions, the early press extensively debated slavery and the slave trade in the 1830s, after Parliament passed the November 1831 law that formally banned the import of slaves. He shows how the trade's opponents used the press to call for effective measures against it (and to criticize slavery), while the reactionaries of the late 1830s likewise used the press to legitimize their views about the need to continue the illegal trade; they effectively silenced the trade's critics. Slavery is also a theme in Rodrigo Camargo de Godoi's chapter as he examines the diverse ways in which slaves engaged in the print world. Some were literate workers in print shops while others knew about what was being discussed in the public sphere and acted politically on that knowledge. In chapter 4, José Juan Pérez Meléndez examines how newspapers debated one of the solutions proposed for slave labor—slaves' replacement by free immigrant workers. Not only were newspapers the vehicles through which colonization companies conducted much of their business, the press also served as a forum for debating colonization policy in the 1830s and 1840s.

The rest of the book focuses on the press after midcentury. Ludmila de Souza Maia examines the popular literary and journalistic genre of crônicas that increasingly combined fictionality with opinion and commentary on contemporary affairs. Leading literary lights contributed to these regular columns and, for this reason, they have attracted considerable attention from literary scholars. Matthew Nestler and Zephyr Frank study classified advertising, particularly those for rental and sale of slaves and real estate, to document the development of markets and property. They demonstrate how newspaper advertising aided in the expansion of an impersonal citywide market and demonstrate some of the possibilities of—as well as some of the limits to—digital history based on the HDB. Arnaldo Lucas Pires Junior examines the culture of visuality that both enabled and emerged from the illustrated satirical magazines that became a highly visible and influential genre after 1860. He argues that they constituted an interface between visual and literary culture; like crônicas, illustrated periodicals have long been the subject of scholarship, but he shows that there is much more to be learned about this genre. Hendrik Kraay analyzes a single year's worth of provincial correspondents' letters from Bahia published in Rio de Janeiro's major newspapers. Although it took up many columns from the 1850s through the 1870s, few have paid much attention to this genre of article, which formed part of a larger web of reporting that linked provinces and the national capital in the imagined community of the Brazilian nation. Teresa Cribelli similarly focuses on a little-studied but important genre of article—apedidos or articles published on request, in other words, by payment. She sets this genre in the context on scholarship on public letters in Atlantic World newspapers and then carefully analyzes the 923 apedidos that appeared in one month in the *Jornal do Commercio* to examine how the press and the public came together in nineteenth-century Brazil. Roberto Saba turns to the influential role of a small number of periodicals published in the United States for distribution in Brazil during the 1870s. These monthlies circulated widely in the expanding coffee plantation districts of São Paulo and presented favorable views of progress in the post–Civil War United States that, he argues, served as models for modernizing planters. Celso Thomas Castilho concludes this volume with a careful analysis of the "Gallery of Illustrious Men of Color," a regular column published in Recife's *O Homem*. An intellectual approach to the press, this chapter reappraises the literary genre of "illustrious men" from the perspective of a Black newspaper in the 1870s. While the chapters in this volume do not provide an exhaustive overview of the imperial Brazilian press, they provide a snapshot of the field and point the way for future research.

Notes

1. Moniz Barretto, "A imprensa," February 28, 1868, in *Cantos*, 477.
2. M. Azevedo, "Origem," 223–24.
3. Macedo, *Memórias*, 287–91. The views expressed by Moniz, M. Azevedo, and Macedo were shared by many others. See J. Araújo, *Bravos*, 85–87.
4. McIntyre, "Avvisi," 69–72; Weber, "Strassburg," 390–92.
5. *JC*, October 1, 1827.
6. Weber, "Strassburg," 387.
7. John and Silberstein-Loeb, "Making News," 1.
8. Habermas, *Structural Transformation*; Guerra and Lempérière, eds., *Espacios públicos*; Piccato, "Public Sphere"; Sábato, ed., *Ciudadanía*; Uribe-Uran, "Birth"; Trumper, *Ephemeral Histories*; Sabato, *Republics*, 132–68; Castilho, "Press."
9. Anderson, *Imagined Communities*, 61–63. For criticisms of Anderson, see Guerra, "Forms," 3–7; and, more generally, the other essays in Castro-Klarén and Chasteen, eds., *Beyond Imagined Communities*. For a pioneering analysis of the role of periodicals in creating a Latin American "nation," see Unzueta, "Periodicos."
10. M. B. N. Silva, *Gazeta* and *Primeira gazeta*; Meirelles, *Imprensa*; Kury, ed., *Iluminismo*.
11. Morel, "Da gazeta," 165.
12. Earle, "Role," 20–30; Unzueta, "Periodicos"; Posada-Carbó, "Newspapers"; Bedoya H., *Prensa*. On the high rates of late-colonial Mexico literacy and

the viceroyalty's precocious press, see Guerra, *Modernidad*, 276–88. On the nineteenth-century Mexican press more generally, see Torre, *Empresa*; Chávez Lomelí, *Público*; Piccato, *Tyranny*, 23–99; Piccato, "Notes," 35–43; Zeltsman, "Defining"; and the 2019 special section in *Historia Mexicana*, organized by Gantús, "Libertad."

13. On Brazilian independence, the most accessible overview remains Barman, *Brazil*.

14. Basadre as cited in Walker, "Orgia," 8. For similar developments in Buenos Aires and Montevideo, see Acree Jr., *Everyday Reading*, 24–27.

15. Schwarcz, *Retrato*, 56; Galves, *"Ao público,"* 108; Cadena, "Dois de Julho," 204.

16. Galves, *"Ao público,"* 135–37, 135n11.

17. *O Paraense* (Belém), May 22, 1822. On the early press in Pará, see Coelho, *Anarquistas*.

18. Cailhé de Geine to Intendente Geral da Policia, Rio, January 2, 1821, BN, Manuscritos, II, 22–33, 54.

19. Sanders, *Vanguard*, 15. See also Morel and Barros, *Palavra*, 44–50; Morel, *Transformações*, 205, 209, 224; Carvalho, Bastos, and Basile, "Introdução," 16, 22, 23, 30, 31; F. Cabral, *Conversas*.

20. Wisser, "Rhetoric," 14.

21. On Evaristo, see Basile's chapter; Morel, *Cipriano Barata*; Basile, *Ezequiel Corrêa dos Santos*; M. M. Santos, *Homem*; Ricci, *Atuação*.

22. Muzart, "Espiada," 229; Duarte, *Imprensa*, 70–71; Jinzenji, *Cultura*; W. Silva, "'Amáveis patrícias.'"

23. I. Lima, *Cores*, 51–67. Thomas Flory considers these periodicals a "mulatto press" in "Race," 207–15; Ana Flávia Magalhães Pinto in *Imprensa* (15–22) and, more recently, Petrônio Domingues, in "Imprensa negra" (253–59), see them as part of a longer lineage of the Black press that flourished in the early twentieth century.

24. §4, Art. 179, Lei, March 25, 1824, *CLB*.

25. Lei, September 20, 1830, *CLB*. On this law, see Nunes, "Liberdade," 72–95; Godoi, *Editor*, 105–12.

26. "Reflexões," *Sentinella da Liberdade* (Salvador), February 16, 1831; I. Silva, *Memorias*, 4:238.

27. Nunes, "Liberdade," 71. See also D. Araújo, "Política," 133–38.

28. For one observation from each decade, see Radiguet, *Souvenirs*, 279; Wetherell, *Brazil*, 108–9; Ribeyrolles, *Brasil*, 2:100–1; Aimard, *Mon dernier voyage*, 63; Hilliard, *Politics*, 382. On Pedro II and the press, see Barman, *Citizen Emperor*, 183–84; Façanha, *Política*, 37–38, 53–54; R. Araujo, "Caminhos," 239.

29. Vicuña Mackenna, *Paginas*, 2:329.

30. D. Araújo, "Política," 135–38.

31. Delegado Interino, Limoeira, to President of Pernambuco, Limoeira, January 7, 1843, APEPe, PC 6, fol. 6.

32. J. Carvalho, *D. Pedro II*, 84; *Construção / Teatro*, 46–47; Holanda, "Do Império," 72.
33. Pinho, *Cotegipe*, 472–75; Kraay, *Days of National Festivity*, 136.
34. Holloway, "Defiant Life."
35. "Provincia da Bahia," *A Republica*, April 2, 1872. On the 1868 impressment, see Kraay's chapter.
36. Barman, *Brazil*, 158.
37. Kraay, *Days of National Festivity*, 81; Holloway, "Defiant Life," 83; R. Araujo, "Caminhos," 110, 217–18, 255. For other periods of extralegal repression, see Godoi, *Editor*, 102. Rodrigo Camargo de Godoi has begun a research project on empastelamentos (https://bv.fapesp.br/pt/auxilios/101844).
38. Sodré, *História*, 123.
39. Sabato, *Republics*, 154.
40. Mackintosh, *Newspaper City*, 35–62 (quote, 51).
41. Sodré, *História*, 206–7, 265; Rosas, "Da 'Constituinte,'" 297; Kraay, *Bahia's Independence*, 90; R. Araujo, "Pasquins."
42. Duarte, *Imprensa*, 19.
43. For a few examples, see J. M. Silva, *Raizes*; Schwarcz, *Retrato*; H. Machado, *Palavras*; M. Silveira, *Batalha*; Alonso, *Flores*; Castilho, *Slave Emancipation*; Cribelli, *Industrial Forests*; Pires Junior, *Imprensa*; J. Carvalho, *"Clamar"*; E. Silva, *Prince*.
44. Sodré, *História*, 257; Kraay, *Bahia's Independence*, 130.
45. Binzer, *Alegrias*, 55. On newsboys, see R. Araujo, "Caminhos," 205–27. On "new journalism," see Nord, "Victorian City," 73–74; Schudson, *Discovering*, 88–89.
46. For an analysis of this process, see R. Araujo, "Caminhos," 28–65.
47. Sodré, *História*; Molina, *História*; Vianna, *Contribuição*.
48. See, for example, Ignotus, *Imprensa*; "Catalogo dos jornaes"; Bellido, *Catalogo*; Carvalho and Torres, *Anais*.
49. http://www.diariodepernambuco.com.br/.
50. J. Araújo, *Bravos*, 99, 102. On the press in Piauí more generally, see Rego, *Imprensa*.
51. See, however, A. E. M. Lopes, *Traços*; I. Araujo, "Flecha."
52. Brazil, *Catálogo*.
53. See, for examples, the Projeto Memória do Jornalismo Piauiense, memoriadojornalismopi.com.br (accessed September 2, 2020); the Coleção Jornais Século XIX-Recife, http://www.acervocepe.com.br/acervo/colecao-jornais-seculo-xix---recife (accessed September 1, 2020); the Recuperação e Memória da Imprensa no Rio Grande do Sul: Preservação da Memória da Imprensa de Porto Alegre, 1827–1836, https://www.ihgrgs.org.br/hemeroteca/cd_jornais_poa/CD/Abertura

.htm (accessed September 1, 2020); the Hemeroteca Digital Catarinense, http://hemeroteca.ciasc.sc.gov.br/ (accessed September 2, 2020); and the Arquivo Público do Estado de São Paulo's Repositório Digital, http://www.arquivoestado.sp.gov.br/site/acervo/repositorio_digital/jornais_revistas (accessed September 2, 2020). Other states have integrated digitized periodical collections into their state library holdings; see, for example, the Biblioteca Pública Estadual de Minas Gerais, http://www.bibliotecapublica.mg.gov.br/index.php/pt-br/digitalizacao-de-acervo-hemeroteca (accessed September 2, 2020).

54. Godoi, *Editor*.
55. Nabuco, *Estadista*, 342n*. On *O Despertador* as competition to the *JC*, see Sandroni, *180 anos*, 96–97.
56. Nabuco, *Estadista*, 342n*.
57. Mamigonian, *Africanos*, 278–79.
58. "Cá e lá mais fadas há," *CM*, November 4, 1848; Barman, "Justiniano José da Rocha," 12–21; Nabuco, *Estadista*, 183–85.
59. Façanha, *Política*, 44–48, 53.
60. CP 2, April 13, *JC*, April 20, 1868. The HDB holds no issues of *O Progressista*. On subventions, see Molina, *História*, 1:449–56; Nabuco, *Estadista*, 183–85.
61. Chief of Police to President of Bahia, Salvador, May 10, 1870, APEBa/SACP, m. 2970.
62. Corr., October 28, *DRJ*, November 6, 1868. The HDB contains only twenty issues of *O Interesse Público*, scattered over the years of 1860, 1861, 1864, and 1867.
63. Adelman and Gardner, "News," 48, 51; Schudson, "Was There Ever a Public Sphere?" 155.
64. R. Araujo, "Caminhos," 152–73; Needell, *Tropical Belle Époque*, 189.
65. Assumpção, *Narrativas*, 130.
66. R. Araujo, "Caminhos," 51–112 (quote 89).
67. On the *JC*'s subscribers, see M. Azevedo, "Origem," 191. On its business aspects, see Sandroni, *180 anos*, 123, 137, 147–49. For the critique, see Ribeyrolles, *Brasil*, 2:99–100.
68. Balaban, *Poeta*, 346, 348.
69. Galves, *"Ao público*,*"* 47–49, 48n103.
70. Canstatt, *Brasil*, 220n*; Mulhall, *Handbook*, 81.
71. H. Machado, "Imprensa," 249.
72. R. Araujo, "Caminhos," 32–34; *O Paiz*, September 1, 1889.
73. Schwarcz, *Retrato*, 83, 49
74. *Gazeta da Tarde* (Salvador), March 18, 1887.
75. For analysis of this point for Peru, see Jacobsen, "Public Opinions," 281–83.
76. Armitage, *History*, 2:80.
77. R. Silva, "Universo," 54.

78. Dénis, *Brésil*, 119.
79. "Journal of George Dunham, 1853," Woodson Research Center, Rice University, Americas Collection, ms. 518, p. 68.
80. Naeher, *Excursões*, 143–44.
81. Francisco José da Rocha to President of Bahia, Salvador, ca. October 1868, APEBa/SACP, m. 1545.
82. J. Carvalho, *Construção / Teatro*, 55.
83. Secreto and Venancio, "Apresentação," 11.
84. Loveman, "Race," 435–39; Bissigo, "Censo," 11–12.
85. Bissigo, "Censo."
86. Eisenberg, *Sugar Industry*, 149.
87. S. Graham, "Writing"; Ferreira, ed., *Com a palavra;* M. Barbosa, *Escravos*; Mac Cord, Araújo, and Gomes, eds., *Rascunhos*; Mota, "On the Imminence"; Wissenbach, "Letramento"; and the 2019 *dossiê* (special section) in *Estudos Avançados*. Machado, ed., "Tinta."
88. Castilho, *Slave Emancipation*, 19.
89. Bösche, "Quadros," 233.
90. Quoted in F. Souza, *Eleitorado*, 135.
91. R. Araujo, "Caminhos," 249–50.
92. Wisser, "Rhetoric," 16–17. Galves, in *"Ao Público,"* 188–89, notes the higher price of up to 200 réis per issue for *O Conciliador*, published in São Luís in the early 1820s.
93. Sandroni, *180 anos*, 47, 82. Unless otherwise indicated, the rest of the data in this paragraph is derived from the HDB.
94. For contemporary comments on such "readers who borrow [*leitores de empréstimo*]," see D. Silveira, "Trabalho," 691; R. Araujo, "Caminhos," 248.
95. Dénis, *Brésil*, 119.
96. Binzer, *Alegrias*, 75; Sandroni, *180 anos*, 173.
97. R. Araujo, "Caminhos," 35–36, 242, 245–46.
98. Sodré, *História*, 279; X. Marques, *Familia*, 98–99.
99. A. Azevedo, *Mulatto*, 33–34, 51, 82.
100. Badaró, *Fantina*, 92–93.
101. El Far, "Bilhetes."
102. Zeltsman, "Defining," 197–99; Godoi, *Editor*, especially 115–24. Small periodicals that sought to maintain their independence often retained some of this character until well into the twentieth century; see, for example, Buffington, *Sentimental Education*, 29–32.
103. R. Araujo, "Caminhos," 190–207.
104. Adelman, *Revolutionary Networks*, 32.
105. Hudson, *Journalism*, 775.
106. Nord, "Victorian City," 80; Schudson, *Discovering*, 32.

107. R. Araujo, "Caminhos," 44–51.
108. Saba, "American Mirror," 127–30.
109. Caimari, "News," 621, 631; R. Araujo, "Caminhos," 126–38.
110. Quadros, "Print Technologies," 199–202, 208–11.
111. Motte and Przyblyski, "Introduction," 4.
112. Neves, Morel, and Ferreira, eds., *História*; Lessa and Fonseca, eds., *Entre a monarquia*; Fonseca and Corrêa, eds., *200 anos*.
113. In addition to the edited books cited in this introduction, see the recent journal special sections in *Almanack* (Basile, ed. "Regência"), *Varia História* (Gomes, Kodama, and Fonseca, eds., "Imprensa"), and *Ágora* (Campos, Siqueira, and Mota, eds., "Imprensa").
114. M. B. N. Silva, *Primeira gazeta*; *A Gazeta do Rio de Janeiro*; Meirelles, *Imprensa*.
115. Contier, *Imprensa*; C.H.L.S Oliveira, *Astúcia*; Galves, *"Ao público"*; L. Neves, *Corcundas*; Morel, *Transformações*; Lustosa, *Insultos*; Wisser, "Rhetoric."
116. For examples of this work, see M. Silveira, *Batalha*; Balaban, *Poeta*; Margingoni, *Angelo Agostini*; A. E. M. Lopes, *Traços*; Knauss et al., ed., *Revistas*. For a reading of Agostini's antislavery images, see Wood, *Black Milk*, 132–88.
117. Chalhoub, Neves, and Pereira, eds., *História*; Ramos, *Máscaras*. Collections of crônicas by prominent literary figures have made their writing more familiar: Strzoda, ed., *Rio*; Paranhos, *Cartas*; Alencar, *Ao correr da pena*; França Júnior, *Política*; Laet, *Crônicas*.
118. Duarte, *Imprensa*.
119. A. F. M. Pinto, *Imprensa*.
120. In addition to the biographies cited above, see H. Machado, *Palavras*; Luz, *Incendiarias folhas*; and the much older precursor, Mascarenhas, *Jornalista*.
121. For examples, see Neves and Guimarães, eds., *Minerva Brasiliense*; D. Andrade, "Imprensa."
122. The HDB is available at http://memoria.bn.br/hdb/periodico.aspx. We know of no scholarship on the HDB, but for an overview of its creation, see Bettencourt and Pinto, "Hemeroteca Digital Brasileira."
123. Ian Read (Soka University of America) is developing a program called PyMeta to facilitate searching in the HDB (http://pymeta.org), email from Ian Read to Hendrik Kraay, August 28, 2020.
124. Putnam, "Transnational."
125. Mussell, "Digitization."
126. Milligan, "Illusionary Order."

Marcello Basile   Translated by Hendrik Kraay

ONE   THE "PRINT ARENA"
Press, Politics, and the Public Sphere, 1822–1840

Printing presses and periodicals came late to Brazil. While printing presses functioned in Mexico City, Lima, and the Anglo-American colonies in the sixteenth and seventeenth centuries, and periodicals were launched in these regions, as well as in Guatemala, Havana, Bogotá, and Quito, by the eighteenth century, Portuguese America's first press dates to 1808. After fleeing Lisbon for Rio de Janeiro, the Portuguese monarchy set up the Impressão Régia (Royal Printing Press), which produced Brazil's first newspaper, the *Gazeta do Rio de Janeiro*, from 1808 to 1822. After this late beginning, the Brazilian press shared in the main developments of the international printing business, combining Old-Regime survivals with modern innovations.[1]

Until the end of 1820, during the government of João (prince-regent until 1816 and King João VI thereafter), only one other periodical was published in Rio de Janeiro, while another two appeared in Bahia. By contrast, the press expanded dramatically in the next two years amid the political effervescence unleashed by the August 1820 Portuguese constitutionalist movement, which instituted press freedom and ultimately led to Brazil's independence. The establishment of new printing presses made possible the publication of at least twenty-one periodicals in Rio de Janeiro, ten in Bahia, eight in Pernambuco, three in Maranhão, and one in Pará by 1822, the year of independence. Nevertheless, the principal vehicle for political debate consisted of the approximately five hundred pamphlets that circulated at this time.[2] Although Brazil's independence movement was not as violent as those of the Spanish- and Anglo-American colonies, it was nevertheless marked by what a well-known pamphlet of the time referred to as an intense "literary war."[3]

This chapter analyzes the Brazilian press's development from independence (1822) to 1840; these years encompassed Emperor Pedro I's reign (1822–1831) and the Regency (1831–1840), when Emperor Pedro II was a minor. Its focus is on the newspapers published in Rio de Janeiro, the Corte (Court), as the country's capital city was known. The city was the center of Brazil's publishing trade. The first sections of this chapter present data on the number of periodicals and the press's uneven expansion throughout Brazil during these decades. Most, but not all, periodicals were devoted to politics, and most were published anonymously. Editors and publishers were, by definition, members of the country's intellectual and cultural elite, although there were important differences among them and their political engagement. They invoked public opinion and sought to shape it, as well as to educate their readers about new political concepts. Less is known about circulation and readership, as is common for newspapers of this time, but their printed texts did not displace manuscript and oral communication for political purposes. Newspaper writers deployed virulent rhetoric against their enemies, demonstrated their erudition by invoking ancient and contemporary writers, and, somewhat contradictorily, laced their prose with vernacular expressions and ordinary speech, which made their publications accessible to those who could only hear them when they were read aloud. In this chapter, the press is understood as an arena of political participation and cultural exchange in the public sphere, closely connected to other realms of political and cultural sociability like civic rituals, protest movements, associations, and Parliament.[4]

The Brazilian Periodical Press: An Overview

Printing and publishing were essentially artisanal trades in the early nineteenth century. Wooden manual presses were more common than their mechanized metal counterparts. A single editor, aided by occasional collaborators, typically launched a newspaper. Few devoted themselves full-time to journalism; most who dabbled in it did so alongside other occupations. In 1830, one of the era's principal journalists, Evaristo Ferreira da Veiga, estimated that about two hundred people earned their living from newspapers, including owners, editors, typesetters, printers, distributors, and sellers.[5] That year, at least twelve print shops existed in the city, and twenty-five periodicals circulated. When it came to production and technology, the Brazilian press of the 1820s and early 1830s was still firmly in what Roger Chartier calls "printing's Old Regime."[6]

The publications of this period demonstrated journalism's vigorous but still incipient nature; newspapers were created in the heat of the moment, closely connected to political questions. The most stable newspapers upheld the doctrines of the political group that they represented, criticizing the government or their rivals; the more ephemeral ones addressed a single issue or directly attacked a rival periodical or politician. Contemporaries characterized the latter as *pasquins*, short-lived irregularly published small-format newspapers with few sections, highly partisan content, and virulent language, which often resembled pamphlets in these respects.[7] In quarto or octavo format, they generally had four to eight pages and appeared one to three times per week. The majority of them never made it to their fiftieth issue (sometimes not even to their second or third), and they rarely lasted more than three months or a year. Their price depended on their format and the number of pages; eighty réis was the most common, but many cost half this. By way of comparison, eighty réis was the price of a pound of brown sugar or a bottle of vinegar in 1831; a pound of potatoes or one sheet of Dutch paper could be had for forty reís. That year, a slave cook working on his own account and a butcher both earned 400 réis per day, five or ten times newspapers' base prices.[8] Voters (those who cast ballots in the first round of elections) were required to have an annual income of only 100$000, which works out to only 274 réis per day, while electors (those who voted in the second round) had to have double this income.[9] Newspapers, therefore, were quite accessible for the literate middle-class public and even for people of lower incomes.

A survey of newspapers published in Rio de Janeiro during the Regency (1831–1840) reveals that they fit this profile: 77 percent did not reach their fiftieth issue (32 percent did not produce ten issues); 44 percent appeared one to three times per week (only 4 percent were dailies); 73 percent had four to eight pages; at least 44 percent cost forty or eighty réis; 76 percent dealt primarily with political questions, and almost all of them were linked to a political faction. Only 8 percent described themselves as literary or scientific, the same percentage that adopted a less polemical and more informative tone. They frequently changed printing presses and only three of the longest lived were printed in the same shop over their entire life.[10]

This same survey reveals the periodical press's development in early nineteenth-century Rio de Janeiro. While only 2 newspapers were produced between 1808 and 1820 and 21 from 1820 to 1822, these numbers soared to 68 in the First Empire (1822–1831) and reached 215 in the Regency. In the first decade of Pedro II's reign (1840–1850), this figure fell to 155. Given the lack of comparable counts for the empire's other provinces, one way to obtain a partial overview of the national press during this time is to count the titles listed in the Biblioteca Nacional's microfilm catalogue (table 1.1). While not a complete collection of Brazil's newspapers, it is the country's largest newspaper

TABLE 1.1 Newspapers Published Outside of Rio de Janeiro, Microfilmed and Cataloged by the Biblioteca Nacional. Compiled from *Catálogo de periódicos brasileiros*.

PROVINCE	1808–1820	1820–1822	1823–1831	1831–1840	TOTAL
Alagoas	0	0	0	2	2
Bahia	1	3	7	28	39
Ceará	0	0	3	6	9
Goiás	0	0	1	1	2
Maranhão	0	1	15	15	31
Mato Grosso	0	0	0	1	1
Minas Gerais	0	0	11	15	26
Pará	0	0	1	3	4
Paraíba	0	0	1	2	3
Pernambuco	0	0	8	20	28
Piauí	0	0	0	2	2
Rio Grande do Norte	0	0	0	2	2
Rio Grande do Sul	0	0	3	24	27
Santa Catarina	0	0	0	2	2
São Paulo	0	0	4	6	10
Sergipe	0	0	0	3	3
TOTAL	1	4	54	132	191

archive, and its holdings suggest that the provincial press's growth followed the capital's trajectory before 1840.

The Press in Pedro I's Reign (1822–1831)

In the years after independence, printing presses were set up in another six provinces: Minas Gerais (1823), Ceará (1824), Paraíba (1826), São Paulo, and Rio Grande do Sul (1827), and Goiás (1830); combined with the existing presses in Rio, Bahia, Pernambuco, Maranhão, and Pará, Brazil had printing presses in ten of its eighteen provinces by 1830. Expansion of the press, however, was neither linear nor uniform. In 1823, the press changed little from the previous two years as periodicals assiduously covered the Constituent Assembly's debates. In the next two years, however, the press contracted dramatically, thanks to the repressive measures adopted by the imperial government after it dissolved the assembly in November 1823 and the outbreak of the revolutionary Confederação do Equador (Confederation of the Equator) movement in Pernambuco (July 1824). The first session of the Brazilian Parliament in 1826 and the greater freedom of expression that followed allowed the press to grow, albeit slowly. The emergence of two political factions in opposition to the court faction that controlled the government contributed greatly to this development: the so-called moderate liberals, who came together in 1826; and the radical liberals, who gained prominence after 1829. The majority of the periodicals launched in the late 1820s were closely linked to one of these groups.[11] The data on the number of periodicals published in Rio de Janeiro during the Pedro I's reign demonstrates this irregular trajectory (table 1.2).

The founding of newspapers was unevenly distributed over this period.

TABLE 1.2 Number of Periodicals Founded and Circulating in Rio de Janeiro, 1822–1831 (by Year). Data drawn from research in progress by Marco Morel and Marcello Basile.

YEAR	FOUNDED		CIRCULATING
	Number	*Percent*	
Before 1822	9	11.7	–
1823	9	11.7	14
1824	2	2.6	7
1825	3	3.9	7
1826	6	7.8	12
1827	9	11.7	17
1828	7	9.1	19
1829	5	6.5	15
1830	15	19.4	25
1831	12	15.6	29
TOTAL	77	100.0	–

Fully 35 percent of the newspapers founded in the Brazilian capital during Pedro I's reign published their first issue in the sixteen months from January 1830 to his abdication. By contrast, only 6 percent of the new titles appeared in 1824–1825. On average, ten newspapers circulated in each year from 1823 to 1826, a figure that more than doubled to twenty-one between 1827 and 1831. The seventy-seven periodicals founded before the end of 1831 accounted for 17 percent of the total number of titles published between 1808 and 1850. Nine dated from the independence era and the remaining sixty-eight were launched from 1822 to 1831. Only two of these newspapers were published in provincial towns, one in Niterói and the other in Campos dos Goitacazes. Eighteen different presses were listed, but the Tipografia Nacional, the *Diário do Rio de Janeiro*'s press, and Pedro (Pierre) Plancher's press printed most of these periodicals. More than three-quarters of the newspapers focused on political questions, and almost all of them were linked to a faction.

As the main venue for political debate, alongside Parliament, the press was an important factor in both the legitimization and the later delegitimization of Pedro I's government.[12] Amid the controversies and political unrest that characterized this period, the emperor's supporters hailed him as the "FATHER OF THE COUNTRY [*PÁTRIA*], to whom the Brazilian nation owes the *proclamation of independence*"; the "August Founder of the Great Empire of Brazil"; the "Heroic Monarch"; or even "Brazil's Guardian Angel."[13] By contrast, Moderados' and Exaltados' increasingly bitter criticisms of the government contributed decisively to the crisis that led to the abdication as they lambasted the "nefarious absolutist government," the "government of assassins," the "government that has only plotted the Pátria's ruin," or the "government that makes common cause with our enemies."[14] This political crisis provided fertile ground for the press's growth.

The Press in the Regency (1831–1840)

The nine years during which four Regency governments succeeded each other, from Pedro I's abdication to the declaration of Pedro II's majority on July 23, 1840, constituted the period during which the press reached the peak of its development before midcentury. Printing presses reached six more provinces: Santa Catarina and Alagoas (1831); Rio Grande do Norte, Sergipe, and Piauí (1832); and Espírito Santo (1840). More important was the significant increase in the number of newspapers, especially in Rio de Janeiro. However, just like in the First Reign, this trajectory was not a linear one and, rather, resembled a bell curve.

The Regency's first years saw a rapid growth in the number of periodicals published. Among the factors that contributed to this were Pedro II's minority and the ensuing intensification of conflict within political and intellectual elites (now divided among a Moderado government, opposed on the left by Exaltados and on the right by the Caramurus), the expansion of the public political sphere, the debates about constitutional reform, and the proliferation of printing presses. With a few exceptions, this period was followed by years of decline in the number of newspapers, deriving from two simultaneous and linked processes. First, the political realignment of the post-1837 conservative Regresso reflected a decline in conflicts within the elite (now divided between Regressistas and Progressistas, nuclei of the future Conservative and Liberal Parties).[15] Second, the public sphere shrank as the number of newspapers, associations, and civic demonstrations declined (see table 1.3).[16]

Half of the periodicals published in Rio de Janeiro during the Regency appeared from 1831 to 1833, with the latter year accounting for almost 25 percent

TABLE 1.3 Number of Periodicals Founded and Circulating in Rio de Janeiro, 1831–1840 (by Year). Data drawn from research in progress by Marco Morel and Marcello Basile; and Basile, "Inventário," 43.

YEAR	FOUNDED		CIRCULATING
	Number	*Percent*	
Before 1831	16	6.9	–
1831	37	16.0	53
1832	26	11.3	51
1833	54	23.4	81
1834	5	2.2	21
1835	19	8.2	32
1836	22	9.5	34
1837	16	6.9	30
1838	14	6.1	30
1839	12	5.2	29
1840	10	4.3	26
TOTAL	231	100.0	–

of the total number of titles. The other half appeared over the course of the next seven years, and the number of periodicals launched per year gradually fell, to the point that the last three years of the period accounted for only 16 percent of the total. In the Regency's first three years, the average number of periodicals in circulation was 62, more than double the 30 titles that circulated each year in 1835–1840. This decade's 231 periodicals account for half of all of the titles published between 1808 and 1850. Before the start of the Regency only 16 of them had been founded, and they remained in circulation after the abdication, while the remaining 215 were launched during this period. Only 12 were published in Rio de Janeiro province's interior (in Niterói, Campos dos Goitacazes, Itaboraí, and Valença) and Rio de Janeiro accounted for the other 219 titles. Fully 52 presses produced at least 1 newspaper, but the leaders in printing periodicals were Fluminense de Brito e C. (on Francisco de Paula Brito, see chapter 3) and the *Diário do Rio de Janeiro*'s press, followed by R. Ogier and Thomaz B. Hunt and Company. More than 75 percent of these periodicals dealt with political questions, and almost all of them were linked to a political faction.

As one pamphleteer aptly put it, the press constituted a "print arena [*arena tipográfica*]," so closely was it linked to political conflicts.[17] More than in any other area, political identities and political projects were clearly defined, as the press spanned the political spectrum from republicans to restorationists, those who sought a return of Pedro I. In addition to bitter political disputes between individual periodicals, some newspapers were closely linked to the other centers of political activity like Parliament, associations, and street movements. A large proportion of newspaper editors were deputies or senators, members of the political associations or secret societies whose numbers soared during these years, or active participants in demonstrations and street protests.[18] All of the major issues debated in Parliament echoed in newspapers and pamphlets and, in many cases, their editors took partisan positions in these debates. They also promoted the associations' activities by publishing their statutes, the minutes of their meetings, membership lists, and notices of their political, social, and other activities. Many associations were represented by a newspaper or published their own periodical. In the same way, several newspapers, especially those of the Exaltados, contributed to the more than forty protests and revolts that took place throughout the country during these years, sometimes with vociferous calls to revolution or unabashed support for the rebels; some amounted to propaganda sheets for the rebels' causes.

Beyond Politics

Notwithstanding the numeric predominance of the political press, other types of periodicals had been produced since the 1810s. The newspapers that described themselves as *commercial* (a common designation at this time) published content similar to that of the contemporary press, with regular sections devoted to a variety of topics (government acts and parliamentary debates; registers of port traffic; mail and telegraph service schedules; lottery results; communiqués; letters to the editor; classified advertisements for the purchase, sale, and rental of goods; and, after 1838, serialized novels). In Rio de Janeiro, these newspapers accounted for less than 8 percent of the titles published in 1822–1831 and only 3 percent in 1831–1840; however, in comparison to the rest of the press, the commercial periodicals had larger formats and longer press runs, appeared more frequently (often daily), and lasted longer. The best known and longest-lived of these were the *Jornal do Commercio* (1827–2016) and the *Diário do Rio de Janeiro* (1821–1878).[19]

Periodicals with a cultural orientation, focusing on literary, scientific, or, more rarely, religious topics, accounted for less than 8 percent of the titles published in 1822–1831, a share that fell to below 6 percent in 1831–1840. The majority of these appeared monthly or bimonthly, and they generally had many more pages, higher prices, and fewer issues than the political press. The first of these was published in Bahia in 1811, followed by another in Rio de Janeiro in 1813–1814. In the 1820s and 1830s, Rio de Janeiro publishers issued some two dozen of these periodicals, including *O Beija-Flor* (1830), *Semanário de Saúde Pública* (1831–1890), *O Auxiliador da Indústria Nacional* (1833–1892), *Selecta Católica* (1836–1837), and Brazil's first illustrated periodical, *Museu Universal* (1837–1844).[20] They focused on a diverse array of topics, including literature, fine arts, history, geography, medicine, natural history, agriculture, technology, theology, morals, and even politics. Still in an embryonic state during this time, this genre of periodical would expand significantly after 1840, as would the magazines illustrated with lithographs that became highly influential in the 1860s and later.[21]

The 1820s and 1830s also saw the appearance of the first periodicals written for a female readership. Men wrote most of their articles, but they also published articles by women and accepted letters to the editor from women readers. The first of these was *O Espelho Diamantino*, which circulated in Rio de Janeiro from 1827 to 1828; it was followed by *O Mentor das Brasileiras*, published in São João d'El Rei from 1829 to 1832. Recife's *O Espelho das Brasileiras* (1831) published articles anonymously written by Nísia Floresta, an important early defender of women's rights in Brazil. Most of these periodicals, however, published articles on topics considered appropriate for the "fair sex" like fashion, literature, art, manners, education, morals, and virtues. Just like the political periodicals that sometimes published articles for female readers (some Exaltados went so far as to call for equal political rights for both sexes and women's involvement in politics), the women's periodicals also discussed politics. Usually they sought to foster women's patriotism, to encourage them in their role as mothers of citizens, and to make them aware of social problems like the love of luxury.[22]

Editors and Public Opinion

Most newspapers did not identify their editors, a custom of editorial anonymity that persisted throughout the imperial regime but was especially strong before 1850. The 1830 criminal code and the press law of September 20, 1830 upheld this right by not requiring the identification of authors in published, lithographed, or engraved materials; only the printer's name and the place and year of publication were required. In the case of abuse of press freedom, authorities would first hold the printer responsible, followed in order by the editor, the author, and finally the work's seller.[23] This meant that the vast majority of newspapers, pamphlets, and even articles and letters published in periodicals did not indicate the author or were signed with pseudonyms. This generalized anonymity facilitated the publication of banned ideas—for example, calls for revolution, a republican regime, or the restoration of Pedro I—as well as libel, calumny, and other personal attacks. It also made it easier for their authors to avoid reprisals such as the criminal charges, arrests, insults, and even physical attacks that many journalists faced during these years.[24] Under this cover of anonymity, the press became a weapon as it conveyed private conflicts into the public arena. Many editors did identify themselves while they were still publishing their newspapers, sometimes to respond to criminal charges or to public accusations or invective, or later. In other instances, editors can only be identified based on contemporary comments.

The available data for the 1820s and 1830s allows us to trace the profile of known editors, all members of the intellectual and cultural elite.[25] Most were relatively young men in their thirties, born in Portugal or in one of

Brazil's larger provinces like Rio de Janeiro, Bahia, São Paulo, Pernambuco, and Minas Gerais. If they were not clerics or military men, they usually had degrees in law or medicine from Coimbra University, from the medical-surgical academies of Rio de Janeiro and Bahia, or from the Sorbonne. Alongside their journalism and their involvement in political or civil associations, these men were civil servants or exercised liberal professions (above all, teachers in higher-education institutions or medical doctors). Many were also part of the imperial or provincial elites and served as deputies.[26] This meant both that the press lacked independence from the political world and also that it served as a gateway into political life, projecting some men of modest social origins, including Blacks and men of mixed race, to prominence despite their lack of family connections or patrons.[27]

The careers of José da Silva Lisboa, Evaristo Ferreira da Veiga, and Ezequiel Corrêa dos Santos reveal the different paths to prominence via the press. Born in Salvador, Lisboa (1756–1835) graduated from Coimbra with a law degree in 1779, after which he held administrative posts in Brazil and Portugal; he belonged to the so-called Generation of 1790, mentored by Portuguese statesman Rodrigo de Souza Coutinho. After the court's transfer to Rio de Janeiro, he was appointed director of the Impressão Régia and censor of the Mesa do Desembargo do Paço (Supreme Court). Elected deputy to the 1823 Constituent Assembly from his home province of Bahia, Lisboa was appointed to the Senate in 1826; Pedro I named him Baron of Cairu in 1825 and raised him to viscount the following year. He authored more than forty books, pamphlets, and periodicals that advocated economic liberalism and defended the centralized constitutional monarchies of João VI and Pedro I. The most prolific court publisher of Pedro I's reign, he edited *Atalaia* (1823), *O Grito da Razão na Corte do Rio de Janeiro* (1825), *Triunfo da Legitimidade contra Facção de Anarquistas* (1825–1826), and *Honra do Brasil Desafrontada de Insultos da Astréa Expadaxina* (1828). After the abdication, he aligned himself with the Caramurus in opposition to the Moderado government, continuing to defend conservative positions until his death.[28]

Born in Rio de Janeiro, Evaristo Ferreira da Veiga (1799–1837) completed preparatory studies, but he decided not to go to Coimbra and, instead, worked as a clerk in his father's bookstore. An autodidact, he opened his own bookstore in 1827. Amid the political effervescence of the years before independence, he wrote poetry that celebrated the homeland (*pátria*), liberty, and constitutional monarchy; one of these became Brazil's independence anthem. He continued to expound these ideas as the editor of the *Aurora Fluminense* (1827–1835), Rio de Janeiro's leading moderate liberal newspaper, which launched his political career. His vigorous journalism quickly carried him to the Moderados' leadership and gained him considerable popularity; he won election to the Chamber of Deputies from Minas Gerais for the Parliaments of 1830–1833, 1834–1837, and 1838–1841 (his premature death meant that he did not serve this latter term). As a novice deputy, he first opposed Pedro I and, after the abdication, he defended the Regency government against the attacks from Exaltados and Caramurus. He was one of the most influential founding members of Rio de Janeiro's Sociedade Defensora da Liberdade e Independência Nacional (Society for the Defense of Liberty and National Independence). In 1832, he was slightly injured in an assassination attempt, likely for political motives. His well-known disdain for high office and honors meant that, despite his prestige, he held no posts other than deputy. Disillusioned with the Regresso and the support for this conservative reaction from many erstwhile Moderados, he died of a fever at the young age of 37; his death marked the end of the party to which he had devoted his entire political career.[29]

A contemporary of Evaristo, Ezequiel Corrêa dos Santos (1801–1864) was born in Pilar parish in Rio de Janeiro province. He received a pharmacy degree from Rio de Janeiro's Medical-Surgical Academy in 1819 and quickly entered politics, first as a member of the Sociedade dos Amigos Livres (Society of Free Friends), sometimes also known as the Sociedade dos Amigos Unidos (Society of United Friends), a secret society opposed to Pedro I's government. He gained political prominence as the editor of *Nova Luz Brasileira* (1829–1831), Rio de Janeiro's main radical newspaper, campaigning bitterly against the emperor and then against the Regency, calling for revolution and a republic. Ezequiel participated in several protest movements and his pharmacy was a gathering place of radical liberals. In December 1831, he founded the Sociedade Federal Fluminense (Fluminense [Rio de Janeiro] Federal Society), linked to Exaltados, whose principal aim was the establishment of a federal system of government. At the same time, he served as procurator for Rio de Janeiro's municipal council. Disappointed with the collapse of the Exaltado faction, Ezequiel continued to participate quietly in politics, eventually joining the Liberal Party, under whose banner he was twice elected city councilor. Instead of politics, he devoted more time to his profession and became the capital's most respected midcentury pharmacist. He was a life member and first president of the pharmaceutical section of the Academia Imperial de Medicina

(Imperial Academy of Medicine), founder and president of the Sociedade Farmaceutica Brasileira (Brazilian Pharmaceutical Society), and editor of *Revista Farmaceutica*. He authored several scientific papers based on research conducted in his laboratory, and Pedro II named him the court pharmacist.[30]

These men of letters aligned their rhetoric with what contemporaries called public opinion, a new source of political legitimacy within modern political culture.[31] They directed themselves to this new abstract organism, still incipient but ever more active and politicized. In light of the importance that public opinion acquired as politics became more public, this was not merely a rhetorical device. The proliferation and increasing variety of periodicals thus indicated not just the increasingly bitter political disputes but also the "evident expression of public opinion."[32] Journalists presented themselves as the spokesmen for public opinion, which they celebrated as the queen of the world, holder of reason, or sovereign tribunal, whose judgment was infallible, but also determined to guide it and to use it to legitimize their positions rather than merely to subject themselves to it. They thus exercised a sort of civic pedagogy, which aimed to instruct, to persuade, and to mobilize public opinion (as well as authorities) to align with their political projects. Moreover, they needed public opinion's support to legitimize their newspapers and make them financially viable.

What constituted public opinion, whether real or imagined, remained unclear. Some adopted a radical view of it, drawing on Rousseauian and Jacobin ideals that linked it to the general will, defined as the "public and uniform expression of the opinion of more than half of a people [*povo*] on any questions: from this derives the influence, power, and direction that it gives to all affairs." This understanding was thus closely connected to the notion of *public spirit*, "the general opinion, formed by the understanding that a People has of its rights, and the general principles that establish and uphold these rights."[33] By contrast, the advocates of a juste-milieu, imbued with a moderate view that restricted politics to a qualified citizenry, held that such a general public opinion "did not exist, for only a very limited number of men are capable of forming the public opinion"; the common people "can never have an opinion."[34]

It is difficult to go beyond journalists' imaginings to identify newspapers' readers. First, there is a lack of data on circulation. The few references that exist were, in most cases, presented by newspapers themselves and, therefore, cannot be completely trusted. The *Aurora Fluminense*, for example, claimed to have about 1,100 subscribers in 1831; *O Caramuru* declared that it sold more than 1,000 copies per issue the following year, the same figure that *A Mulher do Simplício* mentioned in one of its issues three years later. According to one contemporary writer, the *Jornal do Commercio* and the *Diário do Rio de Janeiro* each had no fewer than 4,000 subscribers in 1837.[35]

Thanks to two financial statements from *O Homem e a América* to Rio de Janeiro's Sociedade Defensora da Liberdade e Independência Nacional, its publisher, we have reliable data on its press run, the number of subscribers, and sales of individual issues, as well as revenue and expenditures. According to the December 1831 report, this periodical printed 500 copies per issue; 116 of them went to subscribers, 102 were distributed to other societies or exchanged with other publishers, while 282 were sold to individuals. The 95 people who paid for their subscriptions and the sale of individual issues brought in 402$650;

TABLE 1.4 Number of *Gazeta do Brasil* Subscribers, 1827. *Gazeta do Brazil*, August 25-26, 1827, cited in Morel, *Transformações*, 213–14; Morel and Barros, *Palavra*, 35–37.

PROFESSIONAL CATEGORIES	NUMBER	PERCENTAGE
Merchants	246	35.5
(Brazilians)	*(187)*	*(27.0)*
(Foreigners)	*(59)*	*(8.5)*
Military Men	158	22.8
(Army Officers)	*(115)*	*(16.6)*
(Navy Officers)	*(43)*	*(6.2)*
Clergy	101	14.6
Parliamentarians	47	6.8
(Senators)	*(28)*	*(4.0)*
(Deputies)	*(19)*	*(2.8)*
Doctors and Surgeons	35	5.0
Diplomats	18	2.6
Employees of the Customs House	15	2.2
Employees of Other Government Departments	1	0.1
Miscellaneous	72	10.4
TOTAL	693	100.0

the seven issues published that month cost 122$000, leaving the periodical with a balance of 280$560 (that year, the mil-réis, 1$000, was worth US$0.51, and it appreciated to US$0.71 the following year). In May 1832, the press run remained unchanged; the number of subscribers had risen to 156 and the editors continued to exchange copies with other periodicals. However, only 41 of the subscribers had paid and there were no sales of individual issues (these had likely been suspended). The monthly revenue amounted to only 164$000 and expenses came to 263$400; carryover from the previous three months of 280$560 covered the shortfall but left only 181$160 for the next month.[36]

The *Gazeta do Brasil*, a newspaper closely connected to the palace, is another revealing case. In 1827, it claimed to have 693 subscribers, whom the editor listed by professional categories: merchants accounted for more than a third of the subscribers, while army and navy officers accounted for almost a fourth. Parliamentarians, clergy, and other government employees counted most of the other subscribers (table 1.4). It is likely that periodicals with other political orientations would have had different subscriber bases, but there is no doubt that merchants, liberal professionals, civil servants, clergy, and military officers formed a large proportion of newspapers' and pamphlets' primary readership.

Circulation of Ideas and Reading Practices

The appearance of printing presses in Brazil and the spread of a great variety of printed materials no doubt contributed to the increased circulation of ideas and the expansion of political debate in Brazil. But the printed word did not displace forms of communication and reading inherited from the colonial period. Manuscript texts and oral communication remained important ways of disseminating ideas, which demonstrates the interaction between literate and popular culture, between written and oral communication.

While there are no official or reliable statistics on the number of illiterates in early nineteenth-century Brazil, the literacy rate was certainly low at this time. The 1872 census counted 15.8 percent of the entire population—including minors, women, and slaves—as literate, but literacy rates were much higher in the Corte (36.2 percent and 44.8 percent in just the urban parishes). Fully 62.7 percent of the city's free men could read and write.[37] Four or five decades earlier, rates must have been lower. Those who could not read nonetheless had access to the printed word, for newspapers and pamphlets were commonly read, heard, and discussed in public squares, in commercial establishments (bookstores, print shops, and taverns), in reading rooms, and even in homes and private gatherings.[38] In this way, they reached an audience that extended far beyond the literate, spreading news, ideas, and customs among virtually all social groups.

Manuscript pamphlets particularly fulfilled this role. Facing neither the costs of printed materials nor the political constraints on what presses produced, the so-called flyers (*papelinhos*) were furtively affixed to walls and poles in public places—and sometimes distributed for free—to be read aloud by anonymous speakers to the varied audience that gathered around these incendiary papers. The backs of some of these documents still hold vestiges of the mortar or glue that held them to walls. Authorities tore down many of them to prevent rebellion or to disperse crowds, often considered illegal gatherings. Frequent spelling errors and the coarse and vulgar language reveal these pamphleteers' limited education and popular origins.[39]

A handful of manuscript newspapers were produced and, with the help of copyists, reproduced. The first thirty-four issues of Maranhão's first newspaper, *O Conciliador*, appeared in manuscript form over the course of seven months in 1821, until a printing press was established there that November. Likewise, *O Paulista*, circulated in São Paulo for a few months in 1823, four years before the establishment of a printing press in that province.[40]

The old custom of public proclamations (*bandos*) also persisted; through this custom, official decrees and orders, even those printed in the press, were announced aloud in streets and squares for the benefit of the public. Another indication of the close connection between print and oral culture was the propagation of rumors through newspapers and pamphlets; these often had a great capacity to mobilize people as they spread by word of mouth through the streets, especially when they reinforced political beliefs or social fears.[41]

Forms of Discourse: Political Rhetoric and Vocabulary

In their literary and rhetorical style, newspapers and pamphlets also betrayed oral culture's influence, even as they sought to instruct readers and reach a broader public. Consistent with most periodicals' mission of political indoctrination, writers used various argumentative strategies.[42] One of these was to promise civility and impartiality in debate, as well as to pledge to eschew personal attacks, all as a way to fulfill the press's role of instructing the populace. Such promises, however, were quickly forgotten amid the "wars of opinion," "wars of doctrine," or "wars of the pen," as journalists themselves readily confessed, recognizing the bitterly partisan nature of political debate.[43] Regardless of their political alignments, editors abandoned their enlightened ideals and resorted to invective, "carried along by the floodwaters' force," as Evaristo explained.[44]

Thus, a notable feature of these texts is the virulence of their discourse, attributed to the heat of the political moment and the obligation to tell the brutal truth. To those who were offended by this kind of language, a radical newspaper retorted: "Out with the wimps [*Fora delicados*]!"[45] Criticism descended into personal attacks against rival journalists and political adversaries and did not even spare the regents in the 1830s. Journalists' rhetorical style often amounted to ad hominem attacks on rivals' reputations rather than criticisms of their arguments.[46] Passions ran so high in these debates that violent language not rarely turned into real violence against journalists.[47]

Recourse to authority was another widely used rhetorical strategy. It was almost obligatory to cite a large number of authors, especially foreign ones, to demonstrate writers' erudition and to confer legitimacy on their ideas. Journalists invoked authorities from different periods, places, and traditions, from ancient Greek and Latin writers (Aristotle, Plato, Cicero, Horace, Virgil, Seneca, and Cato) to modern and contemporary writers (Machiavelli, Hobbes, Locke, Montesquieu, Voltaire, Diderot, Rousseau, Paine, Raynal, De Pradt, Mably, Burke, Guizot, and Constant), not to mention biblical writers and Scholastics. These were always cited instrumentally and selectively appropriated in support of journalists' arguments and factions' political projects. Nevertheless, they constituted part of the intellectual repertoire and, in important ways, served as external reference points for the Brazilian press.[48]

Certain didactic techniques and literary styles demonstrate oral culture's influence on the press. Slang, simple words, and vernacular expressions, typical of ordinary people's speech, caught readers' attention, made newspapers easier to understand, and facilitated reading them aloud. So did aphorisms, anecdotes, and the direct, fluent style, close to the spoken word, as well as the polemical and emotional tone that caught people's attention. Ellipses, interjections, exclamation and question marks, and vigorous calls to action frequently appeared, as did a variety of figures of speech (metonymy, metaphor, allegory, hyperbole, irony, and interruptions). Many articles were presented in the form of dialogues, in which two or more characters with different points of view discussed the country's political situation. Newspapers also published poems and anthems (to be recited or sung during political gatherings in theaters, homes, or streets), prayers and political catechisms (parodies of religious speech), and fictional letters written to friends and relatives.

The political dictionaries published in newspapers and pamphlets after independence best demonstrate the press's didactic function and provide important insights into contemporary political vocabulary. These usually listed political concepts and expressions whose precise and true meaning they pledged to elucidate; they thus demonstrate semantic shifts and distinct meanings attributed to certain terms. The largest of these consisted of the 108 terms defined over the course of 49 issues in 1830's *Nova Luz Brasileira*. In a world polarized between liberalism and despotism, the editor of *Nova Luz* defined absolutist government, mixed government, state, homeland [*pátria*], nation, representation, citizen, rights, virtue, people [*povo*], aristocracy, noble, friars, patriotic societies, public opinion, sovereignty, insurrection, and anarchy.[49] He justified this dictionary's publication on the grounds that he wanted "to present the light to those who [were] in the darkness of little knowledge." Others had the same goal: "Yes," explained one, "I write for the so-called ignorant ones of the povo, who do not know the meaning of constitution, rights, citizens' guarantees, and the pátria's liberty."[50] Using this style and language, they sought to reach an audience composed not just of the literate but also the less-educated sectors of society. In this way, the press proffered a citizens' political pedagogy.

The Brazilian press of the first half of the nineteenth century was not an autonomous journalistic field.[51] There was still no established market for the production, circulation, and use of publications outside of the political realm. Periods of criticism and crisis prompted the proliferation of publications, which in turn contributed to these crises.[52] More generally, the press's trajectory followed the evolution of the public sphere into which it was inserted, which for its part, was tightly connected to the level of cohesion among the political and intellectual elites. On the one hand, the expansion and invigoration of the public sphere was encouraged by the crisis deriving from the divisions and violent disputes among these elites at the end of Pedro I's reign and during the first Regency governments; this opened up space for the emergence of new political actors and political participation by subaltern groups. On the other hand, the contraction of this public space that took place after the middle of the 1830s derived from the collapse of the old political factions and the political realignments of the Regresso, whose leaders, alarmed at the Regency's anarchy, sought to reduce the level of intra-elite conflict. Not coincidentally, the press's partisan activities diminished, as did the number of associations, demonstrations, and protest movements. Over the course of Pedro II's reign, the press remained at the whim of political disputes, but it gradually professionalized and modernized and gained greater autonomy.

Notes

1. Rizzini, *Livro*, 309–64; Sodré, *História*, 11–40; Morel and Barros, *Palavra*, 11–21; Lustosa, *Nascimento*, 7–20; T. Cardoso, "*Gazeta*"; M. B. N. Silva, *Gazeta*; Meirelles, *Imprensa*.

2. L. Neves, *Corcundas*; Lustosa, *Insultos*; Nascimento, *História*, vol. 4; Coelho, *Anarquistas*; M. B. N. Silva, *Primeira gazeta*, *Semanário*, and *Diário*; Galves, "*Ao público*." On manuscript and printed pamphlets, see Carvalho, Bastos, and Basile, eds., *Às armas* and *Guerra*.

3. Carvalho, Bastos, and Basile, eds., *Guerra*, 1:742.

4. On the concept of the public sphere, see Habermas, *Mudança*; and Guerra and Lempérière, eds., *Espacios*. On the concept's application in different contexts, see Calhoun, ed., *Habermas*. For Brazil, see Morel, *Transformações*.

5. Morel and Barros, *Palavra*, 78–79.

6. Chartier, "Ancien Régime."

7. An 1832 dictionary noted that *pasquim* derived from *pasquinada*, "a written satire presented to the public affixed" in a public place. The definition of *Pasquino* followed: "A statue in Rome where satires were posted, which then gained the name of *pasquins*," L. M. S. Pinto, *Diccionario*, q.v. *pasquim*. The same definitions appear in the 1813 edition of A. M. Silva, *Diccionario*, 405.

8. *DRJ*, April 9, 16, and 25, April 1831.

9. "Constituição Politica do Imperio do Brasil," March 25, 1824, *CLB*.

10. Basile, "Inventário." This text is part of an ongoing research project with Marco Morel to compile an analytical catalog of the periodical press in the city and the province of Rio de Janeiro from 1808 to 1850.

11. On these factions' projects and political activities, see Morel, *Transformações*, 99–147; and Basile, "Império," "Ezequiel, and "Governo."

12. Marques Júnior, "Verdadeiros Constitucionais"; Basile, "Governo," "Anarquistas," 9–28; I. Souza, *Pátria*, 327–50.

13. *Honra do Brasil Desafrontada de Insultos da Astréa Expadaxina*, April 12, 1828 (italics in original) and *O Grito da Razão na Corte do Rio de Janeiro*, February 23, 1825. See also *O Novo Censor*, March 5, 1831.

14. *Nova Luz Brasileira*, December 9, 1829 (italics in original); *O Tribuno do Povo*, December 29, 1830; *Aurora Fluminense*, March 18, 1831.

15. On the Regresso, see Needell, *Party of Order*, 73–116.

16. Morel, *Transformações*, 261–300; Kraay, *Days of National Festivity*, 86–111.

17. *Refutação á Exposição*, 1.

18. On associations' growth, see M. Azevedo, "Sociedades"; Morel, *Transformações*, 261–300.

19. Sandroni, *180 anos*; Gouvêa, *Impressão*.

20. In addition, *Nitheroy*, the magazine that launched the Romantic movement in Brazil, was published in Paris in 1836.

21. C. Costa, *Revista*, 85–197.

22. Buitoni, *Imprensa*; Jinzenji, *Cultura*; W. Silva, "Amáveis patrícias"; Basile, "Império," 167–71, 362–64.

23. Tinoco, *Codigo*, part 4, chap. 8; Lei, September 20, 1830, *CLB*.

24. Basile, "Radicalismo," 35–38; Lustosa, *Insultos*.

25. On the concept of a cultural elite, see Sirinelli, "Elites," 261.

26. Morel, *Transformações*, 167–99; Basile, "Império," 38–41, 149–52. On the concept of a political elite, see J. Carvalho, *Construção / Teatro*, 43–54, 129–80.

27. The perceived use of the press for secret or opportunistic purposes was frequently criticized at the time of independence by those who condemned the "plague of petty periodicals [*praga periodiqueira*]" and during Pedro II's reign by Joaquim Manuel de Macedo's satires. Carvalho, Bastos, and Basile, eds., *Guerra*, 3:16–17; Macedo, *Memórias*.

28. Kirschner, *José da Silva Lisboa*; Marques Júnior, "Verdadeiros Constitutionais"; Basile, "Governo."

29. Sousa, *História*, vol. 6; M. Andrade, "Família."

30. Basile, *Ezequiel*.

31. Baker, "Politique," 55; *Inventing*, 167–99; Habermas, *Mudança*, 274–90. For this concept's use in the Brazilian context, see Morel, *Transformações*, 200–22; L. Neves, "Opinião."

32. *Caramuru*, January 23, 1833.

33. *Nova Luz Brasileira*, February 16 and 19, 1830.

34. Patroni, *Biblia*, 14.

35. *Aurora Fluminense*, September 30, 1831; *Caramuru*, April 14, 1832; *A Mulher do Simplicio*, December 12, 1835; *JC*, April 10, 1837.

36. *O Homem e a America*, January 5 and August 18, 1832.

37. Brazil, *Recenseamento*, 1:429–30. For a fuller discussion of literacy rates, see this book's introduction.

38. There are various allusions to these practices, especially in pamphlets. M. B. N. Silva, *Movimento*, 12–15; L. Neves, *Corcundas*, 103–4; Morel, *Transformações*, 223–39.

39. For examples of such pamphlets at the time of Independence, see Carvalho, Bastos, and Basile, eds., *Às armas*, 24–25, 40–41, 108, 130–31, 144, 180.

40. Galves, "*Ao público*," 108; C. E. F. Oliveira, *Poder*, 45.

41. Such rumors usually proliferated at times of political agitation, such as revolts or debates about controversial legislation. See Basile, "Império." For other contexts, see Ploux, *De bouche*; Farge, *Dire*; Girardet, *Mitos*; Delumeau, *História*; Lefebvre, *Grande Medo*.

42. J. Carvalho, "História"; Basile, "Anarquistas," 132–42; R. Souza, *Império*.

43. *Astréa*, February 7 and 9, 1832 (first two citations); *Honra do Brasil Desafrontada de Insultos da Astréa Expadaxina*, April 8, 1828.

44. *Aurora Fluminense*, March 2, 1832.

45. *Nova Luz Brasileira*, January 12, 1830 (italics in original).

46. Perelman and Olbrechts-Tyteca, *Tratado*, 333–47; Lustosa, *Insultos*.

47. Basile, "Radicalismo," 35–38.

48. J. Carvalho, "História," 142–45; Basile, *Anarquistas*, 143–71.

49. Basile, "Luzes." *O Exaltado* also filled two December 1831 issues with the definitions of twenty-three concepts related to the founding and types of government and sovereignty, Basile, "Anarquistas," 126–30. The Pernambucan press offered other examples, S. Fonseca, *Ideia*, 364–73. Several independence-era pamphlets took the form of dictionaries, Carvalho, Bastos, and Basile, eds., *Guerra*, 3:253–542.

50. *Nova Luz Brasileira*, January 15, 1830; *Luz Brasileira*, February 3, 1830.

51. On the concept of field, see Bourdieu, *Poder*, 59–73.

52. Koselleck, *Crítica*.

Alain El Youssef   Translated by Demetrius Murphy

TWO   "ADAPTED TO OUR CUSTOMS AND DICTATED BY OUR INTERESTS"

The Press and the African Slave Trade, 1831–1840

In studies of nineteenth-century slavery and the slave trade, scholars working from different approaches have held that slavery and the slave trade were not important subjects in the press or in the public sphere more generally. From the introduction of the printing press to Brazil in 1808 to the beginnings of slavery's crisis in the 1860s, they argue, the press rarely debated slavery. These mischaracterizations are readily found in scholarly literature. In writing about imperial politics, José Murilo de Carvalho states that, given the consensus between Liberals and Conservatives regarding slavery and the trade, "important texts [on these subjects] were not published until the 1860s." "The press," he writes, "debated these matters as they surfaced, such as around the abolition of the trade [1850]. Yet, newspapers would again go silent soon thereafter." Scholars of the press itself advance similar arguments. Marco Morel and Mariana Monteiro de Barros write that "between 1808 and the end of the 1870s, a defense of or silence in the face of slavery prevailed" in Brazilian newspapers. Classic works in the field of slave studies, like Mary Karasch's groundbreaking book on urban slavery in Rio de Janeiro, include observations that newspapers "generally accepted the institution of slavery and did not question it nor seek to reform it." Christiane Laidler de Souza echoes this view in her analysis of slavery through newspapers, in which she concludes that there was "no debate in the [Rio de Janeiro] press about the institution of slavery."[1]

As these quotations suggest, the view that discussions about slavery and the slave trade were absent from Brazilian newspapers for much of the nineteenth century has persisted. A consensus exists around both issues and, so the thinking goes, differing perspectives were not expressed in the public

---

The author thanks the São Paulo Research Foundation (FAPESP) for the doctoral scholarship (2015/04292-1).

sphere. However, the basis for these generalizations begins to unravel when we consider that the Brazilian empire was one of the main slave societies of the nineteenth century; that the slave trade generated much dispute in Parliament; that some slave revolts affected national politics; and that, for almost two decades, Great Britain threatened Brazilian sovereignty over its continuing participation in the illegal slave trade. Did the press effectively detach itself from these most pressing social issues of the time or was it part of them, and did it thus shape their outcome?

This chapter answers this question by analyzing the press debates about slavery and the slave trade in the 1830s. It illustrates the debates' public character and, therefore, takes a first step toward revising the standard historiography. By focusing on newspaper articles published in Rio de Janeiro during the Regency (1831–1840), in light of the changing political, economic, and social processes experienced in the Brazilian empire and the Atlantic World, it demonstrates how, early in the decade, liberals used the press to criticize slavery and the slave trade, and to advocate for the latter's effective abolition. Subsequently, the press became a central means through which the Regresso governments of the late 1830s legitimized their policy toward the illegal slave trade. In effect, I will show how the Regressistas, who represented the base of the future Conservative Party and who mostly hailed from the booming coffee regions of Rio de Janeiro and Minas Gerais, were able to silence the dominant antislavery discourse of the Regency's early years and stymie Moderados' anti–slave trade measures. This ensured the continued smuggling of African slaves and, for most of the 1830s and 1840s, effectively rendered meaningless the 1831 law that was to end the transatlantic slave trade.

The Moderados and the Campaigns against the Trade

Pedro I's abdication on April 7, 1831, ushered in a period of unprecedented political unrest and an expansion of public political debate in Brazil's main urban centers. In the capital city alone, the number of political associations and newspapers rose significantly. The number of the former doubled from 1830 to 1831, from two to four, and peaked at seven in 1834. The growth in newspapers inaugurated a "real blast of the public word." From twenty-one newspapers published in 1830, the number spiked to forty-three the following year, and rose to seventy-six in 1833; the total number of newspapers increased threefold in three years (figure 2.1). Associations and the press thus quickly

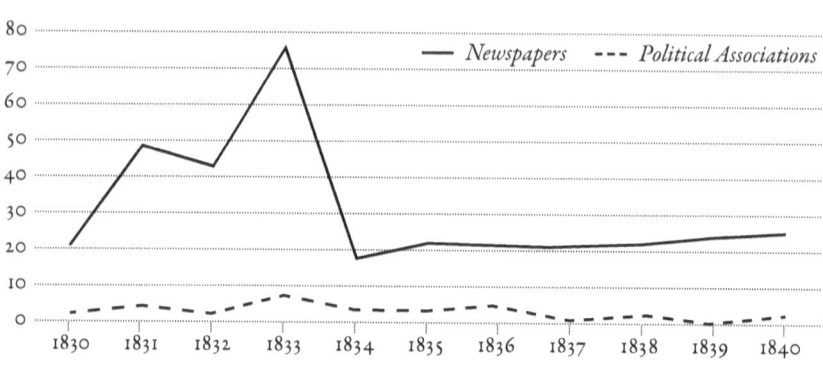

FIGURE 2.1 Number of Newspapers and Political Associations in Rio de Janeiro, 1830–1840. Morel, *Transformações*, 204, 261, 298.

became the privileged means for structuring partisan networks and debating state projects (on these themes, see also Marcelo Basile's and José Juan Pérez Meléndez's chapters).

This new space transformed imperial politics, shaping the strategies of the three main political groups that emerged after the abdication. The first group, known as the Moderados (Moderate Liberals), was organized around the Sociedade Defensora da Liberdade e Independência Nacional (Society for the Defense of Liberty and National Independence) and the newspaper *Aurora Fluminense* (1827–1836). They supported revisions to the 1824 constitution that would strengthen Parliament and grant greater autonomy to the judiciary. The second group, the Exaltados (Exalted or Radical Liberals), banded around the Sociedade Federal Fluminense (Fluminense [Rio de Janeiro] Federal Society) and newspapers such as the *Nova Luz Brasileira* (1829–1831). They defended a more radical political program that called for popular sovereignty and an end to what they characterized as despotism. Restauradores (Restorationists), nicknamed Caramurus, the third group, had their bases in the Sociedade Conservadora da Constituição (Society for the Conservation of the Constitution), the Sociedade Militar (Military Society), and the newspaper *O Caramuru* (1832). They defended a more literal interpretation of the 1824 constitution and Pedro I's return to the throne.[2]

These rival groups, although largely built around competing ideas about the framework of the state, did not differ all that much when it came to the slave trade. In the early 1830s, the prevailing view held that the trade's days

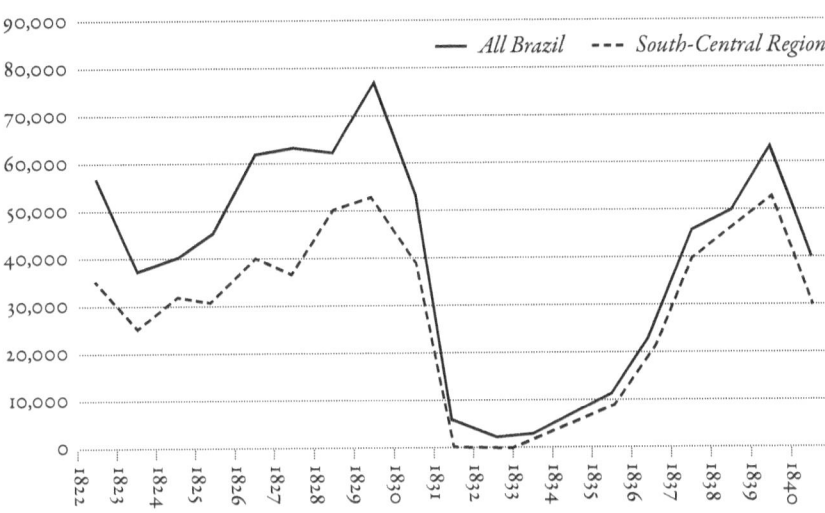

FIGURE 2.2 Volume of the Slave Trade (Brazil and South-Central Region), 1822–1840. Number of Slaves Imported by Year. Compiled from www.slavevoyages.org (December 5, 2019).

were numbered. In addition to the fact that the empire had signed a treaty with Great Britain in 1826–1827 that mandated the end of the slave trade as of September 1830, European powers and other American countries had already followed this path, ending the infamous trade through national laws and international treaties. Certain that they were living in the end of an era, slaveholders acquired large numbers of enslaved Africans in the late 1820s to prevent the labor shortages that they feared (figure 2.2). Meanwhile, merchants working in the trade also sought to transfer their businesses into other sectors. If, at that point, one were to bet on the prospects of the traffic, it would have been hard to find takers who believed in the future of this commerce.[3]

Consistent with these expectations, in May 1831, Senator Felisberto Caldeira Brant Pontes, the Marquis of Barbacena, introduced a bill to prohibit the transatlantic slave trade. Approved without much opposition on November 7, 1831, the new law significantly strengthened the existing Anglo-Brazilian treaty, which had branded the trade an act of piracy, set up joint commissions for trials of vessels seized on the high seas, and established that Africans who arrived illegally were to be freed. The new law imposed harsher consequences on the "traffickers"—broadly defined to include those funding the trade, crew members, those buying the enslaved, and anyone else otherwise tied to this commerce. It also established that smuggled Africans were to be declared "free," and not "freed," upon reaching Brazil. Thus, far from having been created "to please the English [*para inglês ver*]," a Brazilian expression that reportedly derived from its ultimate failure, the 1831 law initially represented a wholesale effort to effectively end this heinous traffic, to close ranks against all those involved, and to grant full freedom to those victimized by the trade.[4]

Proof that this was the government's intention can be seen in two executive decisions that complemented the 1831 law. First, even before Parliament began to debate the bill, the regents issued notices to all municipal councils and provincial presidents instructing the local judges of the peace to ensure "full police vigilance regarding this issue [the traffic of Africans]." Shortly afterward, the regents ordered the navy to patrol the coast to enforce the law and to apprehend illegal traders.[5]

As the Regency became more securely established, its administrations worked hard to restrict the slave trade. Under the moderate liberal from São Paulo, Diogo Antonio Feijó, the Ministry of Justice ordered that notices be posted throughout the country to announce the fines, penalties, and rewards instituted by the 1831 law. He also went after traffickers on the high seas. The combined effects of these actions produced results. According to official reports, the imperial navy captured fully half of the slavers seized in 1834. In 1835, Brazilian cruisers seized five of the seven slavers that were sent to Rio de Janeiro's mixed commission.[6]

These relative successes, however, paled in comparison to the actual numbers of Africans still being brought into Brazil. This residual smuggling—that which was done against the government's expressed desire to end the trade and which rejected the anti-slave trade discourse in the public sphere (as opposed to the later illegal trade that would come to depend on the state's and the public sphere's complicity)—dropped initially, but soon showed signs of recovery. If in 1832 and 1833, the import of Africans fell to negligible levels—respectively, 2,514 and 3,129 people illegally landed—in the following two years the increase was exponential, to 6,680 and 11,352, respectively, thanks to demand from the south-central region, responsible for acquiring about 80 percent of these captives (figure 2.2). This growth demonstrated that the state could not carry out its policy effectively. For the Moderados, who controlled the legislature and executive, the situation was alarming. They openly wondered how they could reassert control over a trade that had seemed on the verge of extinction.

They tried to reverse the situation by a campaign in the public sphere. Led by Evaristo Ferreira da Veiga, deputy director of the Sociedade Defensora and editor of the *Aurora Fluminense*, Moderados asserted that "the primary means to obtain the effective abolition of the traffic is via persuasion." In a coordinated effort through the press and other partisan associations, Evaristo and his followers also appealed to "the planters and ... capitalists," who would serve as examples "to the rest of the population." This approach, moreover, did not preclude "the use of administrative measures, and the enforcement of criminal laws which until now have unfortunately been a dead letter." Thus, Moderados believed that a two-pronged approach was necessary to end the traffic: a rigorous application of existing legislation and effective persuasion in the public sphere.[7]

The Sociedade Defensora took an initial step in this direction in 1834, when it sponsored a public competition with a reward of 400 mil-réis for "the best study of the odious traffic of African slaves." It published the requirements for the competition, written by Evaristo after extensive discussions in the Sociedade. According to the minutes of one such meeting, printed in *A Verdade*, the Sociedade declared that "our honor, as a civilized nation, [and] our fortune and development as a free state demand measures of His Majesty's Government" to prevent the slave trade. For this purpose, the Sociedade advocated harsher penalties against vessels caught trafficking Africans into the country and called for the creation of a sort of "fire brigade" to monitor the regions where this most happened. This way, they thought, it would be possible "to fully implement the sensible Law of November 7, 1831," whose practical implementation was considered paramount to achieving their aim.[8]

The group drew direct inspiration from the English abolitionist movement. Echoing William Wilberforce, the British parliamentary abolitionist, Evaristo began to argue that slavery hindered the Brazilian nation and impeded the development of its "industry," by which he actually meant agriculture. He continued that slavery corrupted the country because it "Africanized even the creoles" and introduced "the germ of corruption into the heart of the families." Additionally, he claimed that the slave trade had been "a plague that infiltrated our land and delayed the true prosperity of a blessed country, thereby degrading the industry that vivifies everything, without which there is no wealth." It was, in short, a social problem that produced serious economic consequences.[9]

For these reasons, the moderate liberal leader warned the traffickers to stop placing "powder kegs in this threatening mine that is African slavery!"

The metaphor alluded to something specific, as Evaristo explained that the enslavement of Africans imported after 1831 was illegal and that the law guaranteed their freedom. His fear was that, in the end, "by becoming ladinos, and knowing the law, [these slaves] can and will demand a better future or, to obtain their freedom, will even resort to means that threaten the tranquility of the country [and] property and even compromise the obedience of the remaining slaves." Fearing an eventual uprising, the *Aurora*'s editor did not stop warning landholders that their continued buying of recently arrived Africans was tantamount to gathering "the firewood that could at some point burn them all."[10]

Despite these notable public efforts, the Moderados' arguments did little to persuade planters and merchants. The number of slaves brought in illegally more than doubled from 1834 to 1835, rising from 11,352 to just over 23,000 (figure 2.2). An increase of this magnitude in the number of slaves imported raises the question of how to explain Feijó and Evaristo's failure. A closer examination of the broader political, economic, and social transformations taking place in Brazil and in the Atlantic World shows how they rendered ineffective the Moderados' efforts in the political arena and in the public sphere to end the slave trade.

Political and Economic Shifts

Moderados' internal cohesion eroded rapidly during the early 1830s. While the group was united after Pedro I's abdication, tensions emerged over changes in the coffee economy, constitutional reforms, and the Regency's internal workings. In addition to the consequent political realignments, the divisions among Moderados facilitated the emergence of dissident views regarding the slave trade and slavery, bringing these issues to the forefront of political debate.

The first fissures opened in mid-1832, amid wider debates about the state's nature. A bill proposed by Deputy José Cesário Miranda Ribeiro sparked discussions over the terms of the 1824 constitution as it called for a federative monarchy and proposed abolishing the unelected council of state, the emperor's moderating power, and senators' life terms. The bill also proposed the creation of provincial assemblies and the establishment of a single regent, instead of the three-man Regency that had governed Brazil since the abdication, as the constitution mandated. Exaltados strongly backed the bill, but divisions appeared among the Moderados, who splintered into three camps. On one end of the spectrum, a group led by Diogo Feijó and Antônio Paulino Limpo de

Abreu, fully supported the bill; in the middle, men like Evaristo and Bernardo Pereira de Vasconcelos supported some measures but not others; and, finally, at the other end of the spectrum, Cândido José de Araújo Vianna and Cândido Batista de Oliveira opposed changing any aspect of the 1824 Constitution.[11]

Ultimately, a majority of deputies endorsed the bill, and it easily won approval in the Chamber of Deputies. Its fate, however, changed in the Senate. Despite a supporting petition from the Sociedade Defensora, senators significantly altered the proposal, accepting the creation of the provincial assemblies but rejecting the other reforms. The rejection of term limits for senators led some Moderados to discuss the possibility of a coup. Led by Feijó, they devised a plan to bring down the Regency and to install him as regent. Feijó would then approve the so-called Pouso Alegre constitution, a draft charter that incorporated the main elements of Miranda Ribeiro's bill.[12]

However, things did not unfold according to plan. At first, the cabinet and the regents resigned, but Deputy Honório Hermeto Carneiro Leão altered the course of events with two speeches in the Chamber of Deputies in which he urged his colleagues to abide by "the path of legality" and called on the regents to return to their posts. He reiterated the constitution's legitimacy and thus convinced the majority of the deputies to abandon the coup, leaving Feijó and the other leaders of the movement without a political base. He thus ensured that any constitutional changes would follow legal procedures, but this came at the cost of Moderados' cohesion. Although the group remained the majority in the lower house, these events deeply divided Moderados.[13]

Demonstrating the new divisions among the group, Vasconcelos began publishing *O Sete d'Abril* (1833–1839) in an attempt to challenge the *Aurora*'s dominant position in Rio de Janeiro's press. Its first article immediately illuminated the growing schisms between those aligned with Vasconcelos's newspaper and those who supported Feijó and Evaristo: "In our view, Moderados and Exaltados are more or less impatient patriots. Only anarchists and Caramurus actually want our ruin; so them, and only them, will we treat like slaves who lack the ability to contain themselves; we will not altogether dispense with censuring Exaltados and Moderados if they act unreasonably." While demonstrating a splintering of Moderado opinion, Vasconcelos also revealed that, because of the opposing factions (Caramurus and Exaltados), Moderados preserved some unity.[14]

This stance, however, continued to evolve, especially after the passage of the Additional Act in 1834, which enshrined key reforms of the Miranda Ribeiro project: provincial legislative assemblies, the single regent, and the council of state's abolition. The Exaltados, for their part, satisfied with the incorporation of their proposals and facing harsh repression for their leadership of urban protests, withdrew from institutional and noninstitutional politics. In different ways, the Caramurus also retreated from the public sphere. Besides suffering a major political defeat with the Additional Act's passage, those who supported the former emperor's restoration lost their principal raison d'être when the news of his death reached Rio de Janeiro in late 1834. After losing this key symbol, they found it difficult to maintain their partisan identity.[15]

The disappearance of the two groups enabled the dissident Moderados to systematically counter those who followed Feijó and Evaristo. The first opportunity arose during the 1835 elections for the single regent. At the end of 1834, different groups launched candidates for the chief executive office, but the race came down to two men: Feijó, supported by Evaristo and the Sociedade Defensora, and Antônio Francisco de Paula Holanda Cavalcanti de Albuquerque, a politician from Pernambuco whose candidacy had been backed by Honório to unite the former Caramuru Pedro de Araújo Lima with the dissident Moderados Vasconcelos and Joaquim José Rodrigues Torres, whose political power was based in Rio de Janeiro's hinterland and in Minas Gerais.[16]

Equally important, this election, whose campaign played out largely in the press, occurred amid a broader set of shifts in Atlantic slavery that influenced, and was influenced by, growing Brazilian coffee production. In 1833, the British Parliament abolished slavery, ending captivity throughout their empire after a six-year apprenticeship for the newly freed people. At that point, the production of sugar and other commodities began decreasing in the British colonies, seemingly confirming the fears of those who expected that abolition would lead to economic ruin.[17]

In addition to the impact of the "mighty experiment," as Seymour Drescher dubbed British abolition, another political decision in the North Atlantic also influenced the Brazilian economy more directly. Beginning in 1831, the US Congress gradually reduced import taxes on coffee. Under heavy pressure from Southern representatives in what became known as the Nullification Crisis, the US Congress, which had set the coffee tariff at five cents per pound in 1831, lowered it to nothing in 1833, which boosted coffee consumption in the United States. Well supplied with labor thanks to the massive disembarkation of Africans before 1831, coffee planters, especially those in the Paraíba River Valley, significantly expanded their output. Coffee exports more than

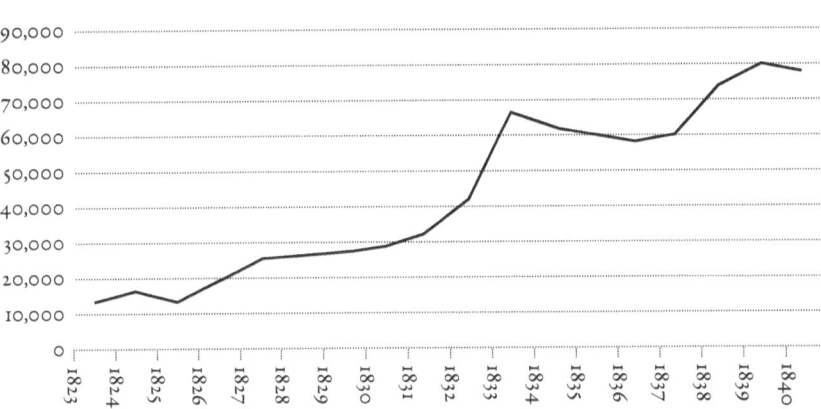

FIGURE 2.3   Brazilian Coffee Exports, 1823–1840 (Metric Tons). Clarence-Smith and Topik, eds., *Global Coffee Economy*, 432.

doubled between 1831 and 1833, rising from 32,940 to 67,230 metric tons (figure 2.3). But to sustain such a marked expansion of production, it was essential to reestablish pre-1831 levels of labor supply for the coffee plantations. In the producers' view, the only way to achieve this was to resume the transatlantic slave trade.[18]

These economic transformations in the Atlantic World coincided with the divisions among the Moderados and with the emergence of public calls in defense of the transatlantic slave trade and slavery. One of the first instances of this latter phenomenon happened in May 1834, during a municipal council meeting in Bananal, located in the Paraíba Valley. Local planters signed a petition asking for the repeal of the 1831 prohibition against the slave trade.[19] Months later, Feijó followed suit in *O Justiceiro* (1834–1835), a periodical that he established in São Paulo to support his campaign for regent. On December 25, 1834, in an attempt to win votes from slave owners, especially in São Paulo, Rio de Janeiro, and Minas Gerais, the Moderado leader gave them the ultimate Christmas gift when his newspaper published "Do tráfico dos pretos Africanos" (On the African slave trade), a call for the trade's restoration.

In the beginning of this article, the candidate drew on several historical examples to construct what amounted to a narrative about universal law: sometimes "habits," even when contrary to humanitarian values, were capable of imposing "a new nature on men." Feijó then introduced the article's main points, arguing that customs linked to captivity bred "very sad consequences" for the country, such as the naturalization of a slave order and the spread of violence against captives. These points coincided with criticisms that Evaristo had raised in his writings. Unlike his ally, however, Feijó left behind these antislavery thoughts and, based on the premises about universal law that he had enunciated at the outset, he explained that it was the planters' "habits" that guided their disregard for the November 7, 1831, law:

> In Brazil, plantation agriculture is in its infancy: a scythe, a hoe, and an ax are all the tools a farmer needs. If the land is fertile and nature lavishes her gifts, the slave's brute work provides the landowner's wealth. But if the land needs to be worked, the slave, who is obliged to labor excessively, almost without eating and sleeping, and surely subject to a premature death—this will spell financial troubles for the owner. This latter scenario is quite common among us. Now in this fledgling state of our agricultural economy, to press for an end to the slave trade is to want the impossible. At first it seemed that at least the moral position would prevail, even if at the expense of economic interests, but to the contrary, everything has worsened.[20]

In this exercise of historical analysis, Feijó held that, although "humanitarianism" had dictated "the treaty that the former Emperor had signed with England" and the November 7, 1831, law's passage, "all had been deceived." The lack of "prudence" on both occasions, coupled with the growth of smuggling, made it "inevitable . . . that the authorities would give in" to the "people's" demands.

Giving in, in this case, meant something very specific. For Feijó, this law should, "as soon as possible[,] be repealed to stop its current and future negative consequences." Instead of strengthening enforcement, as the government had been doing, Feijó preferred making the policing of the slave trade Britain's sole responsibility. This would allow, he argued, the government to create agricultural schools and to focus on importing free colonists to work the land. He envisioned that these measures would together change the population's habits and, consequently, would create the conditions for the prudent abolition of slavery in the not-so-distant future (on colonization, see José Juan Pérez Meléndez's chapter).

While seeking to reconcile antislavery and proslavery interests, Feijo's article in *O Justiceiro* set an important precedent in imperial politics. By openly defending measures that would increase the slave trade and provide legal cover for the already illegally imported Africans, Feijó was elected regent. While his cultivation of links to slave interests helped to secure his victory, these interests soon turned against him. This is because the article's implications did not pass unnoticed by those in Holanda Cavalcanti's camp, who took note of the electoral gains that Feijó's pro-trade shift had brought.

The Regresso and the Press in Reopening the Slave Traffic

As Brazilians are well aware, campaign promises rarely become public policy after candidates win elections. Caught in the sway of politics, Feijó did not buck this trend. Joining an antislavery wave that followed the January 1835 Malê revolt in Salvador, he effectively buried the slave traders' hopes and pursued an approach that contradicted the position that he had staked out in *O Justiceiro*. This shift became evident in his inaugural address. On this occasion, he presented the guiding "principles" of his administration as wedded to the "execution of all laws," an oblique reference to the November 1831 law. Feijó also defended the importation of more colonists "to render slavery unnecessary." It was such a persuasive speech that *O Fluminense* (1835–1836) had no doubt that "the proclamation of the new regent promises to reduce landholders' support for the traffic."[21]

Indeed, Feijó meant what he said. He ordered the Ministry of Justice to bolster inspections of suspected slave ships, which would prevent local justices of the peace from conspiring with smugglers. He also instructed Foreign Minister Manuel Alves Branco to add three articles to the 1826–1827 treaty with Britain that would make it easier to identify slave ships on the high seas. He then negotiated a bilateral agreement with the Portuguese government to end smuggling on both sides of the Atlantic. Finally, he sent Barbacena to England with special instructions to sign a new Anglo-Brazilian convention for "effectively suppressing the trafficking of Africans at sea."[22]

The Regent's efforts, however, conflicted with the interests of Brazilian planters and merchants, prompting greater opposition after the election. Lines were more firmly drawn between the wing of the Moderados that followed Feijó and Evaristo and the one led by Vasconcelos and Honório. By the end of 1835, the coalition that would make the Regresso was taking shape. This group brought together dissident Moderados, former restorationists, and new leaders mostly from the province of Rio de Janeiro, such as Rodrigues Torres, Paulino José Soares de Sousa, and Eusébio de Queirós Coutinho Matoso da Câmara;

they linked themselves to planters and merchants, among whom their defense of the slave trade and slavery won them political capital.[23]

In general, the Regressistas supported revoking key policies instituted after the abdication. These included undoing the 1832 reforms to the criminal code, the 1834 Additional Act, and the November 7, 1831, law. The core of the group, however, mostly advanced a pro–slave trade political agenda. In Parliament, Vasconcelos and his followers started arguing against a harsher anti–slave trade law. This group also protected planters' illegal slave property, thus indirectly encouraging increased importation of Africans. The Regressistas made these points through the press, just as Feijó had done during the election, but they did so more successfully.[24]

These developments occurred in 1835, amid the worries prompted by Salvador's slave uprising. In June, a representative from the Bahian provincial assembly petitioned Parliament to close the slave trade at once. The proposal stirred the capital's press and the *Jornal do Commercio* proclaimed that the "general vote of the Brazilians" was in favor of the measure.[25] Nevertheless, while this petition was under discussion in the chambers of deputies, Vasconcelos came forward with a chilling proposal: to repeal the November 7, 1831, law altogether. In the parliamentary debates printed in the *Jornal do Commercio*, the deputy's speech was mentioned but not transcribed.[26] *O Sete d'Abril*, closely connected to Vasconcelos, conveyed his position more explicitly:

> Mr. [Vasconcelos] said that the enslavement of Africans was not as odious as others have claimed; that it had been adapted to our customs and dictated by our interests. It was also doubtlessly beneficial to the Africans since it improved their condition. He based these claims on the ancient philosophers and, with the examples of all civilized and uncivilized nations, he concluded that the abolition of the traffic should not be decided by law, but rather that it should be left to the prerogatives of the country [*país*]. That once the traffic no longer suited public and private interests, they would be its most pronounced enemies.[27]

To be sure, Vasconcelos did not again defend the trade for another year, but from that point onward, *O Sete d'Abril* campaigned for reopening the trade. It did so in terms that went beyond the points established in the article in *O Justiceiro*. In this campaign, it criticized Feijó and the "saintly Evaristo," who allegedly fancied himself a Brazilian Wilberforce. Furthermore, Vasconcelos's paper plainly stated that "the extinction of slavery will not happen in our day" and "that its continuation is indispensable and will continue to be so in Brazil for years, and perhaps for centuries." *O Sete d'Abril* also spread the notion, based on the British example, that "an immediate path to abolition could cause much damage to the rural economy." More generally, the paper fanned anti-British sentiment, rejecting any inspiration from Britain's laws, its history, and its way of life. Its central point, meanwhile, was to press for the repeal of the 1831 law. It was thus in the press that the Regressistas most fully developed and articulated their proslavery position. This turned Vasconcelos's newspaper into the main link between the politicians of the Regresso and their constituents, the coffee planters.[28]

By late 1835 and 1836, intense debates over slavery occupied the Rio de Janeiro press, pitting *O Sete d'Abril* against the *Aurora Fluminense* and other moderate newspapers. Of these, *O Fluminense* impugned the "Legislator Journalists"—a reference to Vasconcelos—who "seem, with their doctrines, to endorse the infamous commerce, and the disobedience of [our country's] Laws ... thinking that they will be favored in the next elections." The editor of *O Fluminense* went as far as to regard these defenders of slavery as "men of elastic interest." They seemingly seek to move "from the detestable system of slavery to a generous one of freedom," yet their actions could not be trusted: "At first one wants to believe them, but once you catch on to their agenda, it is clear that they will laugh at you."[29]

The problem that the trade's critics faced, meanwhile, was that beyond being unable to articulate as coherent a platform as the Regressistas, they were also hampered by the closure of many newspapers and associations in the second half of the 1830s, among them the *Aurora Fluminense*. Taking advantage of this shrinking public sphere (figure 2.1), the result, to a great extent, of the political changes mentioned above, Vasconcelos's group increasingly placed the slave trade's critics on the defensive, eventually silencing them. The outcome was evident in a letter printed in the *Jornal do Commercio* in 1837. "The Enemy of Traffic in Human Flesh," as its anonymous author identified himself, declared that, despite the "noble and philanthropic feelings ... [that] still exist in certain hearts," "fear ... and the wretched political climate maintain them in a damaging silence."[30]

The absence of significant anti-slavery support in the public sphere undercut any chance that Feijó's anti–slave trade policies would garner broader backing. They were seen as failures, and along with the pressures of an escalating regional conflict in the far south (the Farroupilha Rebellion broke out in September 1835 and lasted until 1845), as well as the growing opposition within Parliament, they prompted the regent's resignation in September 1837. This revealed the political capital that the Regressistas had accrued on the basis of their pro-slavery platform. Before Feijó resigned, he designated Araújo Lima as his substitute. In his first act, the new regent appointed a cabinet composed of prominent Regressistas: Vasconcelos (justice and empire), Miguel Calmon du Pin e Almeida (treasury), and Rodrigues Torres (navy). As *O Sete d'Abril* had predicted a few days before Feijó's resignation, the change would result in "a scaling back of the detrimental efforts currently deployed to prevent the importation of Africans, who are so necessary to Brazil's livelihood."[31]

This is precisely what transpired. However, despite having won power, the Regressistas could no longer openly advocate for the repeal of anti–slave trade legislation, since this could be considered a violation of their obligation to abide by the law. As a result, they were forced to deploy other tactics to bolster the smuggling of Africans into Brazil. On the one hand, now that they controlled the government, they loosened the oversight that the navy had exercised over illegal trading. On the other, they also turned to a strategy of what could be considered vertical integration: they established ties with prominent editors in the capital who would help normalize their activities in the public sphere. Both of these complementary strategies sought to give a free hand to smugglers and planters, broadcasting that the slave trade was justified and that the government was turning a blind eye to offenders.[32]

At that point, three newspapers fell in line with Regressista politics: *O Sete d'Abril*, which was closest to Vasconcelos; *O Cronista*, which broke ranks with the Moderados and lent unconditional support to the new government; and the *Correio Oficial* (1833–1841), which Justiniano José da Rocha, the group's "hired pen [*pena de aluguel*]," took over at the end of 1837. Of these, Justiniano's departure from *O Cronista* to the *Correio Oficial* was the most surprising. Despite having been Evaristo's protégé and a longtime critic of the slave trade, he attributed his political shift to the influence of the "current government," which was relying "on the powers of the press to, in alignment with other social forces, reorganize the bases of Brazilian society." If still somewhat ambiguous, Justiniano was able to, better than others, convey the Regressistas' approach: to use the press as a forum to advance their and the planters' interests, even if they amounted to creating an even more African Brazil.[33]

In concert, then, with the government's strategies, the Regressista press avoided printing articles that called for the outright repeal of the 1831 law. Instead, these papers publicized memoirs, pamphlets, and other texts that defended slavery and the slave trade, reprinting favorable reviews of these works. They ran articles about the illegal continuation of the slave trade in Africa, and the contraband networks that carried slaves to the French colonies. They also discussed the financial ruin that followed the British and Spanish abolitions of the slave trade. Thus, without touching on the 1831 law, these editors promoted smuggling, disseminating a narrative in which the slave trade's continuation, despite laws and treaties that had banned it, was in lockstep with similar developments elsewhere.[34]

This collusion among politicians, planters, and the press was directly responsible for one of the greatest crimes in Brazilian history. Between 1835 and 1840, more than 230,000 Africans were illegally brought into Brazil, a significantly higher number than the 18,000 who were imported between 1831 and 1834, when critiques of the slave trade were hegemonic in the public sphere and Parliament. Some 80 percent of these Africans—approximately 200,000 men, women, and children—disembarked in south-central Brazil, the region where coffee boomed and where the Regressistas were strongest (figures 2.2 and 2.3). These numbers highlight just how much success Vasconcelos and his group had with their project of social reorganization. They overturned the anti–slave trade ideas that had prevailed at the dawn of the 1830s. As a result, the Brazilian politics, economy, and society that emerged from the Regency was all the more rooted in the exploitation of smuggled Africans. Without the press, moreover, this project would not have consolidated in the ways that it did.

By way of conclusion, it is useful to ponder why the relationship between the press and slavery and the slave trade has been so misunderstood in scholarship on nineteenth-century Brazil. Without having done systematic research on the nineteenth-century press, the historians who have written about this issue likely interpreted it in light of the public silence that Regressistas imposed on antislavery voices. It is true that antislavery articles could still be found in the late 1830s in the remaining Moderado newspapers. But they grew increasingly rarer, and this likely left the impression among overhasty twentieth-century scholars that neither slavery nor the trade were important issues of debate. In this light, it would not be an exaggeration to say that this historiographical error derived, even if indirectly, from the actions of the proslavery factions that came to power in the mid-1830s. It is thus crucial to reveal the complexities behind these historical narratives to free such interpretations from the frameworks initially constructed to support slavery and the slave trade.

Notes

1. J. Carvalho, "Escravidão," 35–64; J. Carvalho, *Construção / Teatro*, 123–24; Morel and Barros, *Palavra*, 98–99; Karasch, *Slave Life*, xvi; C. Souza, "Mentalidade," 111.

2. Morel, *Transformações*, 61–147; Basile, "Império," 29–109, 130–250, 338–87.

3. For a comparative view of abolition in the Atlantic World, see Blackburn, *Overthrow*, 265–418. On the withdrawal of traffickers from this commercial branch and the intensification of direct purchases by owners, see Florentino, *Em costas*, 43–44, 203–4.

4. The text of the 1826–1827 Convention can be found in A. P. Pinto, *Apontamentos*, 1:389–93; Lei, November 7, 1831, *CLB*. On this law's passage, see Parron, *Política da escravidão no Império*, 84–90. That this law was not "for English to see" has been discussed by several other authors, including Florentino, *Em costas*, 37–60; Florentino and Góes, *Paz*, 61–71; Youssef, *Imprensa*, 111–20; and Mamigonian, *Africanos livres*, 58–89.

5. *Diario do Governo*, June 20, 1831; Bethell, *Abolição*, 92.

6. Conrad, *Tumbeiros*, 95, 102–3.

7. *Aurora Fluminense*, October 3, 1834.

8. *Aurora Fluminense*, March 10, 1834; *A Verdade*, February 27, 1834. Frederico Leopoldo César Burlamaqui won this essay contest with his memoir about the trade and the "evils of domestic slavery." See *Memoria*.

9. *Aurora Fluminense*, May 14, 1834. References to Wilberforce can be found in *A Verdade*, February 27, 1834; and in *JC*, January 17, 1834.

10. *Aurora Fluminense*, April 7, 1834.

11. Basile, "Laboratório," 55–119.

12. Basile, "Laboratório," 55–119; Sousa, "Tentativa," 82–106. For the Sociedade Defensora's petitions, see *Aurora Fluminense*, July 27, 1832. For *Aurora Fluminense*'s views on the reforms, see the issues of August 7, 1833; June 4, and August 4 and 28, 1834.

13. Sousa, "Tentativa," 82–106; Needell, *Party of Order*, 47–50.

14. *O Sete d'Abril*, January 1, 1833.

15. Needell, *Party of Order*, 51–59; Basile, "Império," 440–41, 450–51.

16. Needell, *Party of Order*, 55–57.

17. On the role of the press in the electoral race, see, among others, *Aurora Flu-*

minense, March 9, 20, 21, 27, and 30, 1835; May 4, 1835; *O Sete d'Abril*, March 7 and 17 1835; May 2, 1835; June 16, 1835; and *O Pão d'Assucar*, March 21, 1835. On the impact of British abolition, see Drescher, *Mighty Experiment*, 121–201.

18. Parron, "Política da escravidão na era," 224–66. On the development of coffee cultivation in the Paraíba Valley, see Marquese and Tomich, "Vale."

19. Bethell, *Abolição*, 104.

20. *O Justiceiro* (São Paulo), December 25, 1834.

21. The speech is published in Caldeira, ed., *Diogo Antônio Feijó*, 172–74. *O Fluminense* published its review on November 3, 1835. On the Malê Revolt's repercussions, see Reis, *Rebelião*, 509–43.

22. On inspections, see Parron, *Política da escravidão no Império*, 133–34. Additional acts may be consulted in A. P. Pinto, *Apontamentos*, 1:394–98. J. Marques discusses the initiative to broach an agreement with the Portuguese government in *Sons do silêncio*, 242–43. On sending Barbacena to London, see Bethell, *Abolição*, 140–45; and Ellis Jr., *Feijó*, 224–29.

23. Needell, "Party Formation," 259–308.

24. On slave smuggling policy, see Parron, *Política da escravidão no Império*, 123–78.

25. *JC*, July 14, 1835.

26. *JC*, July 24 and 27, 1835.

27. *O Sete d'Abril*, August 1, 1835.

28. *O Sete d'Abril*, October 31, 1835; November 7 and 18, 1835; January 27, 1836; February 13, 1836; July 27, 1836.

29. *O Fluminense*, November 3, 1835. On the debates between the moderate press and the Regressistas, see Youssef, *Imprensa*, 182–203.

30. *JC*, February 17, 1837.

31. *O Sete d'Abril*, September 2, 1837.

32. On the Regressistas' performance in the executive, see Parron, *Política da escravidão no Império*, 114–15. The notion of vertical expansion is developed in I. Mattos, *Tempo*, 180–81.

33. *O Chronista*, October 11, 1837.

34. The books and pamphlets published under Regressista patronage include Muniz Barreto, *Memória sobre a abolição*; [J. C. Silva], *Memória sobre o comércio*; and Taunay, *Manual do agricultor brasileiro*. Reviews of the last work can be found in *O Chronista*, February 7 and 9, 1839; *Correio Oficial*, February 14, 1839; *O Sete d'Abril*, February 9 and 11, 1839. The other texts were referred to in *O Sete d'Abril*, January 10, 1838; January 2 and 5, 1839; and *O Chronista*, May 15, 1838.

Rodrigo Camargo de Godoi   Translated by Henry Pratt

THREE   PRINTERS, TYPOGRAPHERS, AND READERS   *Slavery and Print Culture*

One of the cartoons published in *Semana Ilustrada* on February 18, 1872, shows a slave who can read (figure 3.1). He appears standing behind his mistress, craning his neck over her shoulder as she sits and reads a letter, unaware of his presence. The slave's intrigued smile suggests that there is something interesting in the text. Notwithstanding the humor in this illustration, its message was serious and clear. Titled "Um bom criado malcriado" (A badly behaved good servant)—the Portuguese pun is untranslatable—the cartoon warned members of the Brazilian slave-owning class about the dangers of literate slaves. As the rest of the caption explains, "These are the consequences when one teaches slave boys [*moleques*] to read and write: they get to know all of our secrets and become our confidants."[1]

Slave literacy and slaves' roles in the production and consumption of printed material in nineteenth-century Brazil are the subjects of this chapter. It focuses on slaves who gained knowledge of the Latin alphabet and written Portuguese. The slave trade from West Africa brought a significant number of Muslim slaves to Brazil, and in the nineteenth century, there are indications that Arabic manuscripts and printed texts circulated in Brazil, along with writings in African languages written in Arabic characters. Arabic writing played a prominent role among the African Muslim slaves and freed people involved in the 1835 Malê Rebellion in Salvador.[2] In the aftermath of this movement, the largest slave rebellion during Brazil's imperial regime, "Malê papers," the product of centuries-old Muslim literary and religious traditions, represented danger to masters.[3] From time to time, the police discovered and destroyed what were evidently *madrasas* (schools for Koranic education) throughout Brazil, from Recife to Porto Alegre.[4] French booksellers in Rio de Janeiro even specialized in supplying slaves and freed people with Korans imported from Europe.[5] This, however, remains a little-studied area in the history of Brazilian print culture.

Cultural historians have probed deeply into the relationship between print culture and subaltern groups, like the literate slave. The questions raised and the methods developed by scholars of reading practices like Natalie Zemon Davis, Roger Chartier, and Robert Darnton can help us rethink the relationship between enslaved Africans and their descendants and the nineteenth-century world of print.[6] To be sure, well before this wave of cultural history broke on the shores of Brazilian historiography, researchers had noted the regularity with which slaves were part of the nineteenth-century newspaper world.[7] Slaves appeared in editorials, advertisements, news stories, public solicitations, and even serialized fiction. In a short book first published in the early 1960s, anthropologist Gilberto Freyre studied approximately 10,000 runaway-slave advertisements from different Brazilian newspapers to analyze the fugitives' physical and cultural traits.[8] Other historians and anthropologists followed Freyre's path, among them Lilia Moritz Schwarcz, who studied the representations of slaves and freed people in late nineteenth-century newspapers from the state of São Paulo.[9]

New paradigms that emerged in the 1980s enabled historians to move beyond questions about Afro-Brazilians' visibility in the press and the study of slavery more broadly. Scholars turned to the perspectives of the free and enslaved people themselves; these approaches offered new ways of connecting the study of literate culture and unfree labor.[10] In Portuguese America, an early example of these connections can be found in the late eighteenth-century slave uprising on Santana plantation in Ilhéus (Bahia). There, the slaves killed their master, fled to the woods, and resisted the advances of colonial authorities.

FIGURE 3.1 A Literate Slave Reading His Mistress's Correspondence, 1872. *Semana Illustrada*, February 18, 1872.

What made this uprising exceptional was the proposed peace treaty written by the escaped slaves.[11]

Since then, and in part inspired by US historiography, Brazilian researchers have maintained an abiding interest in slave literacy rates and practices, as well as in schooling policies for the enslaved and their descendants.[12] As Marialva Barbosa has recently demonstrated, "slaves' spheres of communication" thrived in diverse forms, including reading, writing, and orality.[13] Barbosa underscores that it would have been impossible for slaves to remain immune from the increasingly complex systems of communication that took shape in nineteenth-century Brazil, especially the unprecedented circulation of books, magazines, and newspapers. "As historical agents," writes Marco Morel, slaves "left their mark on the world of print."[14]

This chapter provides fresh views on these discussions through its focus on nineteenth-century slaves' engagement in the production and consumption of print materials. It was common for free laborers and enslaved people to work in various capacities in the world of print.[15] Yet, scholars who have dealt with workers in the publishing industry focus on typographers and the ways in which they represented themselves as an intellectual elite and heirs to Gutenberg's legacy.[16] Slave printers certainly shared in these values. In light of, then, this appreciation of the relationship between slavery and print culture, conventional approaches to analytical problems, such as public opinion, need to be rethought.[17] Criminal court cases, police records, newspaper advertisements, travelers' accounts, private correspondence, autobiographies, among other sources, bring to light an unexpected universe of slave readers. Public opinion during the Brazilian empire was thus not restricted to white elites and, beyond merely producing newspapers, slaves also acted politically based on what they read.

Slavery and Print Production in the Brazilian Empire

We begin with a story that brings together many of this chapter's themes. Like the Rio de Janeiro enslaved people whom Christiano Júnior photographed in 1860s (figure 3.2), Theodoro probably dressed up on Sundays and saints' days. This was certainly the case on the afternoon of Sunday, June 22, 1862, when, at about 3:00 p.m., the eighteen-year-old left his residence at 85 Ouvidor Street wearing a blazer, white pants, and shoes. A wintry mist had prevented the sun from coming out that afternoon and the hills surrounding Guanabara Bay

FIGURE 3.2 Two Dapperly Dressed Slave Men, ca. 1860. Photograph by Christiano Junior. Courtesy of Museu Histórico Nacional (Rio de Janeiro), 874V (036.646).

were "cloudy and very foggy."[18] At about 8:00 p.m., Theodoro was seen on his way to a religious procession, perhaps the one in honor of Saint Joseph that was taking place that weekend.[19] It was an otherwise normal night until he reached Cadeia Street, where he was insulted by José Sapateiro, a policeman who lived in Cidade Nova. A confrontation ensued and Theodoro stumbled, falling to the ground. The reasons for this were unclear: he may have tripped because of the shoes that he was wearing or Sapateiro may have pushed him.

On some levels, this was a typical street incident. Free and enslaved Blacks routinely experienced coercion and humiliation on Rio de Janeiro's streets. They could be arrested on mere suspicion of vagrancy or escape. That same day, for example, the slave Josefa was detained "for being out during off-hours" and the slaves Matheus, Mathias, Justino, and Raphael were taken in on suspicion of flight.[20] Despite having his owner's permission to be out, and even when wearing his Sunday best, Theodoro's forays through the city were always subject to being cut short on the basis of someone's misgivings about his presence and status. As for Sapateiro, he left the scene while Theodoro was still on the ground. Theodoro, then, perhaps unwilling to continue following the procession in his now disheveled state, also left the scene and headed home for a change of clothes. On reaching Quitanda Street, he encountered a friend, whose name he would later forget, and he walked with him to Sé Square. From there, Theodoro continued alone toward Ouvidor Street.

Lined with cafés, tailor shops, and bookstores, Ouvidor was the capital's most elegant street. Theodoro apparently stopped in front of one of these famed storefronts and, from afar, he saw a wounded Black man fall to the ground. He asked a passing boy what was happening, but did not hear the response. At that moment, a Portuguese man grabbed Theodoro and shouted at the top of his lungs that the slave had stabbed the injured man.

This was Theodoro's version of the story, as told to the police during questioning the next day.[21] Taken into custody at the Casa de Detenção (House of Detention), Theodoro waited out a long trial in which he was found guilty of murder. The evidence that convicted him appeared compelling: a bloodstained pocketknife; testimony from the policeman Sapateiro; and, above all, the fact that the police knew him as a capoeira fighter. Theodoro initially received a life sentence, but his punishment was "reduced" to four hundred lashes on appeal. As his legal representative argued, "If the right to punish is a necessity of every well-ordered society, the right of property is nevertheless no smaller." In other words, he explained that it made no sense to "disable a slave" by keeping him imprisoned until the end of his days at his master's expense.[22] Theodoro was thus severely flogged.

Theodoro's master, who did not intervene at any point in the proceedings, was in fact no ordinary citizen at all, but rather Junius Villeneuve and Company, the firm that owned the largest daily newspaper in Brazil at the time, the *Jornal do Commercio*. Theodoro was born a slave of the Frenchman François Antoine Picot, editor of the *Jornal*, and, in addition to practicing capoeira, he operated the printing machine.[23] It is difficult to determine when Theodoro was sold or transferred to Junius Villeneuve and Company. Founded in 1827, by the Frenchmen Pierre Plancher, his son Émile Seignot-Planchet, and Dr. Joseph François Xavier Sigaud, this business included the newspaper and a print and book shop. Junius Villeneuve and his partner, R. A. Mougenot, acquired it for more than 50:000$000 (US$35,500) in 1832 and, within two years, Villeneuve consolidated it under his sole ownership.[24] Picot had come to Rio de Janeiro at a young age with his father, who founded a grade school in the city. After working as a French teacher, he joined the *Jornal do Commercio* as a printer. Picot eventually married Villeneuve's stepdaughter, a match that cemented the connection between the two immigrants. This trust was reaffirmed when Picot became director and later editor-in-chief of the *Jornal* after Villeneuve returned to Paris in 1845.[25]

We can assume that Theodoro learned about printing while still quite young. Child apprenticeship and child labor were vital to nineteenth-century print shops, and it is possible that enslaved children were apprentices and workers in the print shops.[26] Theodoro's job required mostly physical strength, for he had to handle the machine that pressed over the paper. The nature of his job may explain why he had not learned to read, a fact that he revealed during his trial. In response to a separate line of questioning, however, he revealed that he had been punished "because of his work."[27]

The history of the Brazilian press and printing dates to 1808, when the Portuguese court brought printing presses to Brazil as it fled Napoleon's invasion. The court's establishment in Brazil required setting up the official Impressão Régia (Royal Press) and laws that overturned previous censorship. The new legislation also sanctioned the establishment of privately owned presses, such as Silva Porto's in Rio de Janeiro and Silva Serva's in Salvador.[28] Because these were entirely new businesses, skilled labor was at a premium. This demand became more pronounced in the early 1820s with the exponential increase in the publication of newspapers and pamphlets during Brazil's independence movement (see Marcelo Basile's chapter). In November 1822, the Imperial Library opened a printing shop and Gaspar José Monteiro, the library's "official typesetter," offered his services to the new press, explaining that, since 1812, he had been teaching the trade in Rio de Janeiro. He also took credit for "having trained several typesetters who worked at Silva Porto's shop."[29]

As early as the 1830s, slave labor can be documented in print shops. In November 1831, the *Jornal do Commercio* ran an advertisement for the escaped "Antonio, a Black man who worked at the print shop." This fugitive slave was described as having a "good appearance and wearing striped pants and a blue shirt."[30] His specific skills or job, however, were not mentioned. Antonio may have been a typesetter, such as "the good slave typesetter" who was for sale in October 1867.[31] Nevertheless, slave typesetters appear to have been rare. Only two slaves with this profession appeared among the 239 literate slave runaways that Atilio Bergamini located in the *Jornal do Commercio* between

1830 and 1888.³² Other slaves worked as beaters, spreading ink on the presses. Francisco, a runway who presented himself as a freedman, had been in charge of ink barrels at Paula Brito's shop when he fled in 1858.³³

Most of the equipment and supplies for Rio de Janeiro's printing presses, including ink and typesetting machines, were European imports. Despite favorable conditions, including an abundance of natural resources and abundant waterpower, all attempts to establish a high-grade paper mill in Rio de Janeiro failed. Thus, the cost of importing supplies raised the price of publications.³⁴ The deliberate waste of valuable items, such as ink and paper, would no doubt have led to severe punishments for these slave workers, like the punishment that Theodoro had received at the *Jornal do Commercio*.

In the mid-1840s, African slaves were also employed as printers in Heaton and Rensburg's lithograph shop, described by the US visitor Thomas Ewbank as the "the largest lithographic establishment in Brazil."³⁵ The traveler noted George Heaton's astonishment at learning that, in the United States, lithographic printers received between ten and fifteen dollars weekly. Heaton explained that here, "a mil-réis (fifty cents) a day is a good wage, and slaves do not cost us a quarter of that."³⁶ Heaton was English and his partner, Eduardo Rensburg, was Dutch; they opened their lithograph shop in late 1839.³⁷ It is telling how both owners of this Anglo-Dutch firm, as well as the French owners of the *Jornal do Commercio*, quickly adapted to and came to participate in the Brazilian slave economy. Furthermore, the mix of people in the print and lithograph shops forces us to consider them as truly Atlantic World Towers of Babel. Although they produced mostly works in Portuguese, numerous languages must have been heard during the production process, not only English, Dutch, and French but also Bantu languages like Kimbundu and Kikongo spoken by West-Central African slaves.³⁸

A similar dynamic also took shape in the 1850s in the Casa de Correção (House of Correction), where liberated Africans worked in the bookbindery.³⁹ Far from being there because of criminal activity, these liberated Africans were hired out after being rescued from ships participating in the illegal slave trade. They spent considerable time at what became Rio de Janeiro's first prison to employ laborers. After completing the building, work continued with the establishment of bookbinding, shoemaking, carpentry, and tailoring workshops.⁴⁰ Workers learned to make book covers and document folders for government records, earning the Casa a favorable reputation for bookbinding. It is not coincidental, then, that liberated Africans Agostinho and Claro, both from Quelimane, were rented to Francisco de Paula Brito's printing business in the 1850s. At that time, the Afro-Brazilian Brito owned the largest printing operation in the empire.[41]

An 1844 tax decree on print shops further illustrates the importance of compulsory labor to this sector.[42] An annual tax, the rate differed in towns, coastal cities, interior cities, and the capital, but everywhere it was based on the number of free and enslaved people employed by the business. For example, in interior towns, printing companies that hired up to fifteen free workers would pay 40$000 (US$20) annually. In the case of "slave workers, alone or in conjunction with free workers," there was a surcharge of 10 percent. The law also specified that the term "workers" encompassed letter pressers, typesetters, machine operators, and apprentices. It also mandated that, at the end of each fiscal year, owners of printing companies submit a complete report of all workers, both free and enslaved, employed in their workshops. Keeping in mind that Brazilians often evaded taxes, we should not interpret the surcharge on enslaved laborers as an attempt to rid the printing industry of slavery. In fact, as Heaton told Ewbank, "printing slaves" were still an excellent investment.[43]

"Having Learned to Read and Count Some": Slave Literacy in Nineteenth-Century Brazil

Janet Duitsman Cornelius's research shows how slaves' own written accounts are extraordinary sources for learning how men and women became literate during slavery.[44] Unlike in the United States, slave autobiographies for nineteenth-century Brazil are exceedingly rare. There are only two: Mahommah Gardo Baquaqua's autobiography published in Detroit in 1854 and the letter that Luiz Gama wrote to Lúcio de Mendonça in July 1880.[45] Baquaqua, who was a slave in Brazil in the 1840s, offers scant evidence on slave literacy. He learned rudimentary Portuguese from slave interpreters on the ship that brought him to Pernambuco, where he worked for a baker. In Olinda, he learned to count to one hundred, which was crucial for someone who sold bread on the streets.[46]

Luiz Gama's story was different. He was born in Bahia in June 1830, the son of a free African woman from the Mina coast named Luiza Mahin. Although born free, at the age of ten, his father sold him into slavery. He was sent south, where coffee bushes, the basis of Brazil's wealth, sprawled for leagues and leagues across the provinces of Rio de Janeiro, Minas Gerais, and São Paulo.

There, Gama escaped slavery and became a formidable public figure. He gained a reputation as a writer and poet in São Paulo city, and served as a public defender in which capacity he fought for the freedom of hundreds of illegally imported slaves through the courts. In so doing, he became a linchpin of the abolitionist movement in the 1860s. In his autobiographical letter, he explains how he learned to read and write at the home of his owner, the respected lieutenant and slave dealer Antonio Pereira Cardoso:

> In 1847, I was 17 years old when a young Antônio Rodrigues do Prado Júnior—today a renowned ex-magistrate and coffee planter in Mogi-Guassu—came to live in Mr. Cardoso's house. He had come from Campinas to take a degree in the humanities. We developed a deep bond, of the brotherly sort. It was he who first taught me the letters. In 1848, having learned to read and count some, and having secretly obtained irrefutable proof of my freedom, I fled. I left Antônio Pereira Cardoso's house, although he had held me in high esteem, and went to enlist [in the state police].[47]

Gama's account makes clear the connections between becoming literate and challenging the slave system. Upon "having learned to read and count some," Gama gathered the necessary evidence to show the illegal basis of his captivity. From there, the ex-slave's embrace of print culture took off. After a stint as a police soldier, in 1859, Gama published a book of verses, *As primeiras trovas burlescas de Getulino* (Getulino's first burlesque ballads), and his public writings soon became more regular.[48]

It is also worth remembering the student who taught Gama to read and write. In light of the legal restrictions on slaves obtaining an education, people like the young Prado played a key part in this history of one slave's achievement of literacy. The 1827 law that created elementary schools for girls and boys in cities and townships across the empire did not contemplate opening these institutions to slave children; its silence on the matter suggests that the Viscount of São Leopoldo, author of the law, did not even consider it.[49] In the 1850s, a follow-up decree that reformed elementary and secondary education in the capital explicitly prohibited the admission of slave children to public schools.[50] This prohibition was reaffirmed in 1878, when the city launched its evening-school program.[51]

No laws, however, kept free children of African descent out of public schools. Rio de Janeiro had private schools geared toward free Blacks and *pardos* (people of mixed race), such as the school founded by the Black teacher Pretextato dos Passos Silva in 1853.[52] Schools like this one also may have enrolled children from Africa sent to Rio de Janeiro to be educated. Sons and daughters of slave traders from Benguela (Angola) had been studying in the Brazilian capital since the late eighteenth century.[53] Coincidentally, the same year that Pretextato opened his school, José Gonçalves de Carvalho Júnior, a local merchant, requested police authorization to receive one Guilherme da Costa Teixeira, the legitimate son of Guilherme Teixeira of Benguela, who had been sent to Brazil to study; authorities permitted the young Guilherme to come to Brazil.[54]

While Brazil's laws barred the admission of slaves into the city's public schools, I have yet to find evidence that they explicitly prohibited slaves from learning to read and write. Even in places where such laws existed, such as the antebellum United States, they were not entirely successful. Recent archaeological excavations in the US South, for instance, have uncovered evidence of writing tools and boards used by slaves despite the strict laws against slave literacy.[55] There is also evidence from Brazil that some slaves taught others to read. One Raimundo "[knew] how to read and write, and [enjoyed] talking, [and had] an affinity for teaching how to read, wherever he [was]."[56] Thus, it is possible to imagine circumstances under which slaves' workplaces could be transformed into miniclassrooms.[57]

The issue of teaching slaves came to the fore as the movement to abolish slavery took shape in the late 1860s. Liberal publicists insisted that emancipation would not be complete without measures to educate those who were freed. The 1871 Free Womb Law, for example, included some provisions for educating children born of slave mothers. This was a turning point in the history of educating Black children in Brazil. Later, in the 1880s, a number of abolitionist societies, such as the Club Gutemburg (Gutenberg Club) and Club dos Libertos contra a Escravidão de Niterói (Niterói Club of Freedmen against Slavery), created evening schools for slaves and free Blacks as part of their activism.[58]

The 1872 imperial census offers quantitative data on slave literacy.[59] One of the main reasons for conducting this census was to map out the contours of the slave population in light of the intensifying abolition debate. Altogether, the country's population stood at 9,930,489 people, of whom 84.7 percent—or 8,419,672—were free, and 1,510,806, or 15.2 percent, were captive. According to historian Sidney Chalhoub, the slave population had represented somewhere between 30 and 40 percent of the total in the first half of the century. Two notable reasons behind the decrease in the enslaved population were the end the transatlantic slave trade in 1850 and, a few years later, the cholera epidemics.[60] Only 1,403 of the more than 1.5 million slaves, or less than 1 percent, knew how to read and write, 958 were men and 445 women.[61] This marked gender difference was also evident among the free population of color, which comprised 42.7 percent of the total population. Overall, among the free, there were 1,012,078 literate men (12 percent of the population) and 550,973 literate women (6 percent of the population). More than 81 percent of the free, or almost 7 million people, could not read or write.

The census data's release in 1876 forced Brazilians to face uncomfortable truths about illiteracy rates. The *Gazeta Jurídica* opined that "the latest census ordered by the government upsets even the coldest of Brazilian hearts, by revealing a striking number of illiterates."[62] The satirical newspaper *O Mosquito*, by contrast, made light of the low literacy rate among women: At least "fathers will not have much to worry about in terms of their daughters writing their boyfriends!"[63] While the 1872 census revealed literacy rates at that moment, other sources must be consulted to ascertain literacy rates from earlier eras.

Using advertisements published in the *Diário do Rio de Janeiro* in the 1820s, it is possible to estimate free and enslaved workers' literacy rates.[64] This crucial period in Brazilian history, bookended by the process of independence and the abdication of the first emperor in 1831, also saw the rapid rise of the printed word and the development of a dynamic public sphere.[65] The *Diário do Rio de Janeiro* was then known as a cheap and accessible paper, primarily publishing advertisements. Because of its affordability, it was called the *Diário do Vintem*, which might be loosely translated as the Two-Penny Daily, and the *Diário da Manteiga* (Butter Daily), for its publication of commodity prices.[66] I analyzed 492 advertisements published between 1821 and 1831 in the following sections: Rentals, Clerks, Domestic, Runaway Slaves, Private Notices, and Sales. These categories overlapped significantly: while 445 or 90.4 percent of the slaves were found in the Private Notices section, the Rentals section included advertisements in which free and freed workers touted their services, like the "freed cook" who claimed to be a "good buyer, capable of every house service, loyal, and also knows how to read, write, and count."[67]

These advertisements provide rich insights into slaves' literacy. Just over 9 percent of the advertisements which mentioned reading and writing abilities dealt with slaves and freed people. Of these forty-three slaves and two freed people, only four were women. The latter included the skilled seamstress and cook, Alexandrina, who fled carrying her young son Sabino in April 1827; the advertisement indicated that she also knew how to read and write.[68] That same year, a group of newly arrived slaves from Bahia included a coachman or valet who also knew how to read and write.[69] The advertisements even revealed literate African slaves, like the "very ladino Black man, who is no different in his speech or otherwise from being creole"; he was described as a good cook and as one who knew how to read.[70]

The numbers also point to the specialized skills that correlated with slave literacy. Excluding entries that did not specify trades, or those which listed multiple trades—such as that of "the dark pardo, still a young man, who is good for every service, [who] knows how to read and write"[71]—thirty-one of the literate slaves were described as having specialized skills, or almost three-fourths of the forty-three described as literate; the largest number of them were tailors and shoemakers (table 3.1). These notices suggest that some runaway slaves could well have read the advertisements about their escapes, even while many leagues away. Pedro, "a young dark pardo born in Angola, who speaks good Portuguese and knows how to read and write a bit, between 16 and 18 years old more or less," might well have discovered through the *Diário do Rio de Janeiro* that his master was willing to give a "nice reward" for information on his whereabouts.[72]

Print Culture and Slave Revolt

Incidents of rebellion also highlight slaves' use of print culture. In October 1887, the popular *Revista Ilustrada* published a cartoon of a slave reading to his fellow captives (figure 3.3).

TABLE 3.1 Occupations of Literate Slaves, 1821–1831. Compiled from 492 *DRJ* advertisements, 1821–1831.

OCCUPATION	NUMBER
Tailor	7
Shoemaker	3
Barber (Bloodletting)	2
Caulker	2
Carpenter	2
Blacksmith	2
Driver	2
Mason	2
Barber (Hairdresser)	1
Butler	1
Seamstress	1
Cook	1
Domestic Servant	1
Foreman	1
Laundress	1
Sailor	1
Sawyer	1
Multiple Occupations	3
Unspecified	9
TOTAL	43

FIGURE 3.3 Slaves Reading the Abolitionist Newspaper, *O País*, 1887. *Revista Illustrada*, October 15, 1887.

The picture conveyed the planter's surprise when he discovered them holding the abolitionist *O País* in their hands. The caption reads: "A planter made a startling discovery that floored him: a field slave reading an abolitionist speech of Conselheiro [Manuel Pinto de Sousa] Dantas to his companions!"

Run by Quintino Bocaiuva, *O País* was, according to Angela Alonso, the "most reformist newspaper of the moment, abolitionist and republican."[73] The slaves represented in the cartoon were thus discerning in their reading material, for they had chosen a newspaper that defended their greatest interest: their freedom. It could also have been the case, however, that this reference to *O País* in *Revista Ilustrada* was but a courtesy between editors jointly engaged in abolitionism. The cartoonist could also have been inspired by articles published in the press that month about slaves in the coffee counties of São Paulo who had been caught by their overseer reading Dantas's speech. In this instance, they were reading the local *Imprensa Ituana* (from Itú) and not *O País*.[74] The cartoon in *Revista Ilustrada* thus commented on a recent event.

Although mass flight from the coffee plantations intensified in 1887, there is no direct evidence that these well-read slaves from Itú were among those who rose up and fled. This differed, however, from what happened exactly a decade earlier in Campos, in the province of Rio de Janeiro. There, the Brazilian-born Manuel do Sacramento read "inflammatory pages" to the other slaves of the Queimado plantation. Aware of the abolition debates in the press, these slaves planned an uprising.[75]

In the mid-1860s, news of the US Civil War echoed throughout Brazilian slave communities. In Belém, the capital of Pará, two hundred slaves on a plantation owned by the Carmelite Convent rose up, claiming that they would all be free as a result of the conflict between Yankees and Confederates.[76] From Diamantina, a worried deputy wrote to the provincial president about another imminent revolt. He could barely conceal the panic spreading among landowners who learned about "purchases of firearms by some of the most audacious, a certain state of agitation among them, gatherings and groups of four or more individuals, [and] cryptic and enigmatic conversations." The deputy blamed this agitation on "some slaves learning about the Civil War in the United States and passing information to those who did not know how to read." He concluded in no uncertain terms: "We have little-to-no means of containing them."[77]

First recorded by Xangô da Mangueira and Jorge Zagaia in 1972, "Moro na Roça" (I live on the farm) was a classic of partido-alto music.[78] Originating in neighborhood bars and Candomblé grounds in early twentieth-century Rio de Janeiro, partido-alto or Bahia samba was a musical style in which one improvised verses to the sound of rhythmic clapping, tambourines, the guitar, and the *cavaquinho* (a small guitar about the size of a ukulele).[79] At the time of its recording, "Moro na Roça" was already a popular song, widely known, whose composition date had been lost to time. Enduring, its verses are a powerful register of the deep relationship that connected the "Black sons of Angola" with some form of schooling and print culture:

I live on the farm, missy.
I have never lived in the city.
I buy the morning newspaper
To know what's going on.
. . .
Xique-xique macambira,[80]
Son of the Angolan Black man,
Good thing you can't read,
Since you want to be a schoolmaster.

These timeless Bahia samba verses encapsulate this chapter's argument. During the empire, most slaves lived and worked in the fields, but they also read the daily newspapers, knew the latest news, and used this information to fight the slave system. Slaves and liberated Africans were also crucial to the production of newspapers, pamphlets, books, and magazines in nineteenth-century Brazil; the men and women among them who were literate belonged to a modest, to judge by the 1872 census, group of consumers of print culture. The vibrant Black press that emerged after abolition represents the next part of this story.[81]

Notes

1. "Um bom criado malcriado," *Semana Illustrada*, February 18, 1872.
2. Reis, *Rebelião*, 158–282.
3. Dobranravin, "Não só mandingas."
4. Reis, Gomes, and Carvalho, *Alufá*, 54–59, 311–19.
5. A. C. Silva, "Buying and Selling"; Diouf, *Servants*, 113–14.
6. Davis, *Culturas*; Chartier, *Leituras*; Darnton, *Grande Massacre*.
7. Thérenty, *Littérature*, 78.
8. Freyre, *Escravo*.
9. Schwarcz, *Retrato*.
10. Chalhoub and Silva, "Sujeitos"; Wissenbach, "Cartas," 103–22; Mamigonian, "Bilhete," 379–85; Mamigonian, "Do que 'o preto mina' é capaz," 89–90; J. Rodrigues, "Ferro," 38–39; K. Oliveira, "E agora, com a escrita" and "Textos."
11. Schwartz, "Resistance," 69–81. On the culture of slave literacy in Portuguese America starting in the eighteenth century, see, Morais, "Ler"; Paiva, "Leituras." On British America, see the letter denouncing the evils of slavery drafted by slaves from Virginia received by the Bishop of London in 1723, Ingersoll, "Releese us Out of This Cruell Bondegg," 777–82.
12. M. Fonseca, *Educação dos negros*; Bergamini, "Escravos," 115–36. Regarding the US South, see Cornelius, *"When I can read my title clear."*
13. M. Barbosa, *Escravos*.
14. Morel, "Escravidão," 75.
15. Karasch, *Slave Life*; L. Soares, *"Povo."*
16. Vitorino, "Sonhos."
17. Darnton, *Poesia*, 20.
18. "Meteorologia," *CM*, June 22, 1862.
19. "Colchas: alugam-se ricas colchas de damasco lisas e bordadas para a procissão de São José," *CM*, June 21 and 22, 1862.
20. "Estatísticas da corte: Prisões," *DRJ*, June 24, 1862; Chalhoub, "Precariedade estrutural."

21. "Apelação criminal. A Justiça, autor. Theodoro, crioulo escravo de Junius Villeneuve e Cia, réu," AN, Corte de Apelação, n. 1184, caixa 160, Gal-C, 1863, fols. 9r–9v. I first analyzed the case of Theodoro in Godoi, "Trabalho."

22. "Apelação... Theodoro," fol. 62v.

23. According to baptismal records attached to the trial transcript, Theodoro was the son of Henriqueta, who remained the slave of Monsieur Picot for many years. In October 1863, Picot freed Amélia, her daughter, at her baptism. "Estatisticas," *CM*, October 30, 1863.

24. The total value of the transaction was 52:664$ (US$2,633.20). Macedo, *Anno*, 2:147–62; Morel, *Transformações*.

25. Biographical sketches of Picot were published in the Rio press upon his passing in Paris in 1902: "Falecimentos: Francisco Antonio Picot," *Cidade do Rio*, January 7, 1902; "Francisco Antonio Picot," *JC*, January 11, 1902; "Francisco Antonio Picot," *Jornal do Brasil*, January 11, 1902.

26. Godoi, *Editor*, 147.

27. "Apelação... Theodoro," fol. 10v.

28. Hallewell, *Livro*, 122–36.

29. "Gaspar José Monteiro, oficial compositor, oferece seus serviços à nova tipografia a ser instalada na Biblioteca Nacional e Pública do Rio de Janeiro, 1822," BN, Manuscritos, C-1062-40, docs. 4–5.

30. "Escravos fugidos," *JC*, November 11, 1831.

31. "Anuncios," *CM*, October 6, 1867.

32. Bergamini, "Escravos," 123.

33. "Atenção," *CM*, August 25, 1858.

34. Godoi, *Editor*, 310–17; Godoi, "Cartas."

35. Ewbank, *Life*, 193.

36. Ewbank, *Life*, 193.

37. Hallewell, *Livro*, 159. "Manifesto," *JC*, December 10, 1839.

38. On African languages spoken in the slave southeast, see Slenes, "'Malungu, ngoma vem!'"

39. On the illegal slave trade and liberated Africans, see Youssef's chapter in this volume and Chalhoub, *Força*, 30; Mamigonian, *Africanos*, 33–34, 100.

40. C. Araújo, "Cárceres," 182, 186, 265–66.

41. Godoi, *Editor*, 157.

42. Decreto 384, October 16, 1844, *CLB*.

43. Godoi, *Editor*, 145–48.

44. Cornelius, *"When I can read my title clear,"* 61.

45. Baquaqua, *Biography*. On Luiz Gama, see Schwarz, "Autobiografia," 136–41. Given that excerpts of Frederick Douglass's life began appearing in the Brazilian press in the early 1880s, I suspect that Gama disappointed Lúcio de Mendonça

when he merely summarized his life story in a letter instead of writing a full autobiography. "Frederico Douglass," *Gazeta da Tarde*, April 25, 1883; Gomes and Machado, "Abolição," 25.

46. Lara, "Biografia," 245; Lovejoy, "Identidade," 39.
47. Schwarz, "Autobiografia," 140.
48. E. Azevedo, *Orfeu*.
49. Lei, October 15, 1827, *CLB*.
50. Decreto 1,331-A, February 17, 1854, *CLB*.
51. Decreto 7,031-A, September 6, 1878, *CLB*.
52. A. M. P. Silva, "Escola."
53. R. Ferreira, "Biografia," 35–36.
54. A. M. P. Silva, "Escola," 154.
55. Rasmussen, "Attended with Great Inconveniences," 201–3; Bly, "Pretends he can read," 280.
56. Bergamini, "Escravos," 119.
57. Bergamini, "Escravos," 121–25.
58. M. Fonseca, *Educação*; Souza and Torres, "Liberdade."
59. The data in this paragraph are drawn from the 1872 census available from the UFMG Research Center in Economic and Demographic History (http://www.nphed.cedeplar.ufmg.br/). See also the discussion of literacy in the introduction.
60. Chalhoub, "População," 41–42.
61. Chalhoub, "População," 42.
62. *Gazeta Juridica*, 10 (January–March 1876).
63. *O Mosquito*, August 12, 1876.
64. Other authors have used newspaper ads in their research about slave literacy rates. For eighteenth-century United States, see Bly, "Pretends he can read." For nineteenth-century Brazil, see M. Barbosa, *Escravos*, 151–54; Bergamini, "Escravos."
65. Morel, *Transformações*.
66. Sodré, *História*, 123.
67. "Aluguéis," *DRJ*, September 20, 1822.
68. "Escravos," *DRJ*, April 20, 1827.
69. "Vendas," *DRJ*, January 11, 1827.
70. "Aluguéis," *DRJ*, April 20, 1827.
71. "Vendas," *DRJ*, October 14, 1825. My emphasis.
72. "Escravos," *DRJ*, November 30, 1825.
73. Alonso, *Flores*, 290.
74. M. Barbosa, *Escravos*, 133–34.
75. Soares and Gomes, "Sedições," 139–40. Signs of literacy appeared in other slave revolts. Diogo Rebolo, leader of a major plot in 1832 in Campinas, São Paulo, used a book that, according to reports from other slaves involved in the plot, could make predictions. Pirola, *Senzala*, 39–40.

76. Mota, "Vulcão," 192.
77. Mota, "Vulcão," 181.
78. Mangueira, *Rei*.
79. M. Cunha, *"Não tá sopa."*
80. These allusions to, respectively, a cactus and a bromeliad, may be references to the arid northeast of Brazil where they are common plants, and thus this line may be related to the postabolition migration from this region to Rio de Janeiro.
81. A. F. M. Pinto, *Imprensa*.

José Juan Pérez Meléndez

FOUR
OUTBREAKS, SHARES, AND CONTRACTS
The Press and the Migrant Trade

The Ship Entries section of the *Diário do Rio de Janeiro* reported the arrival of 3,408 *colonos* (immigrant settlers) from early 1836 to mid-1839. Of course, the numbers paled in comparison to the estimated 329,837 Africans brought to Brazil throughout the decade as part of the illegal slave trade then fully underway despite its ban in 1831.[1] Yet this smaller influx, consisting in large part of Azoreans who left their homeland without passports and thus without the Portuguese government's consent, not only represented a new trade in migrants but also unfolded in the public eye thanks precisely to newspapers such as the *Diário*. Opinion pieces, translations, advertisements, and logistical information pertinent to colonization made the press the primary platform for the articulation of this early migrant trade. While ship-entry listings allowed captains to announce the landing of colonos and the offices where interested parties could procure their services, Variedades sections advertised company shares, called shareholder meetings, and tendered requests for contractors to service the depots maintained by new companies specializing in selling out colonos services. In their back pages, several dailies emphasized the availability of especially skilled colonos and alerted the populace about the frequent escape of young ones.

Occurring decades before the mass migrations of the late nineteenth century, the orchestrated migrations of the 1830s were not spontaneous slave-substitution schemes concocted by forward-thinking planters interested in colonization.[2] Indeed, as newspapers in Brazil's main port cities show, a small set of profit-driven private companies were primarily responsible for organizing the transport and distribution of colonos from overseas. While certainly extolling the value of free labor, these companies' organizers exploited the new business environment afforded by the opening of provincial legislatures in 1835 and the resurgence of the press after the fall of Pedro I. As the main conduits for business information, newspapers abetted these firms' emergence by putting their symbolic arsenal in full view, publicizing the details of opening ceremonies or placing a relevant promotional pamphlet on a front page. As a business interface for these companies' operations, the press also lent them credence in the eyes of a reading and shareholding public. In 1838, barely two years after the launch of the Sociedade Promotora de Colonização (Society for the Promotion of Colonization), the most prominent of these enterprises, even Minister of Empire (Interior) Bernardo Pereira de Vasconcelos, a rabid stalwart of the slave trade (see Alain El Youssef's chapter), lauded the company for performing "its self-imposed duties efficaciously" and hoped "that Brazilians [would] try to imitate it in the most important maritime provinces."[3]

Historians have mentioned these companies only in passing due to the paucity of documentation on how they worked.[4] Adding to this lack of information is the fact that these migrant-trading firms did not last long after their establishment in Rio de Janeiro, Salvador, and Santos in 1835–1836. Thus, studies on the Regency, one of the most central political moments in Brazilian history, tend to ignore these firms despite the fact that the initial trickle of colonos they fostered increased significantly after company operations came to an end. According to one historian, throughout the 1840s free foreigners made up the fastest-growing segment of Rio de Janeiro's population, with Portuguese newcomers representing the largest foreign-born group in the city, even ahead of men and women imported illegally from Africa.[5]

More generally, contemporaries' caution regarding directed migration, or colonization, tends to offer but a partial view of these companies' performance and political interventions. The official record—parliamentary debates, ministerial reports, and executive decrees—only soberly addressed colonization schemes, in part out of pure noblesse oblige. Patronage tied the hands of critics. Vasconcelos, for instance, owed his ministerial post to Regent Pedro de Araújo Lima, the Sociedade Promotora's first president. In addition, parliamentary protocol barred lawmakers from directly attacking the colonization company figureheads in their midst. For other statesmen, the relative novelty of colonizing endeavors made their ultimate value hard to judge. This also appeared in the platitudes of politicians' reports that addressed the challenges and conflicting expectations around colonization without revealing the internal mechanisms of what was effectively a trade in migrants, whose services were increasingly advertised on notable newspapers' back pages.

It was in the press, not in the national Parliament, nor in the provincial assemblies, nor in cabinet meetings, that the full dimensions of a burgeoning colono trade came to view. This chapter uses newspapers as windows into a relatively sophisticated system that developed to identify, transport, and receive foreign migrants in Brazilian ports from 1834 to about 1841. Opinion pieces, translations, advertisements, and logistical information pertinent to colonization made the press the primary platform for the articulation of this early migrant trade. Newspapers' ship-entry listings gave captains and the Sociedade Promotora the opportunity to announce the landing of colonos and the offices where interested parties could procure them. Variedades sections in turn advertised company shares, called shareholder meetings, and tendered requests for contractors to service the Sociedade's depot. The back pages of several dailies also announced the availability of especially skilled colonos and alerted the populace about the frequent escape of young ones.

Simultaneously, the press served as a bastion of opposition, publishing blistering critiques of colonization dealings. Abandoning the decorum characteristic of government circles, many newspapers plunged into pasquinade wars around private colonization.[6] Hence, as the press delineated the colono trade's dynamics and profited from the advertisements placed by company administrators, it also chipped away at the ability of colonization advocates to convince potential shareholders and government officials of the feasibility of their efforts. Approaching company-run colonization dynamics through the press thus highlights both the migrant trade's business nature and the political contentions that it incited. Though newspaper reports, advertisements, and opinion pieces paved the way for future colonization advocates to perfect these early migrant importation schemes, dissenting perspectives and politically charged invectives against colonization's masterminds also populated the press for years to come.

The following pages first touch on newspapers' contribution to a framework of ideas and models that informed colonization, and then examine how colonization companies faced fierce criticism for their clumsy response to a number of crises. While the attacks leveled in the press forestalled new colonization projects, they did not entirely eliminate them. These early—and conflictive—initiatives, in fact, became precedents for similar efforts in the 1840s, 1850s, and 1860s, which signals the need to recast directed migrations as a central topic in the empire's periodicals and, by extension, as an integral part of imperial elites' political imaginary.

Incorporating Models: Foreign Blueprints and the Press

The press contributed decisively to the rise of colonization ventures in Brazil by reporting on similar efforts throughout the world. Coverage of colonization efforts looked beyond contexts such as the United States and Cuba, which as slave societies had pride of place in Brazilian print and political culture. *Astreia*, for instance, published future US secretary of state Edward Livingston's penal codes for the state of Louisiana, which became a reference for Brazil's first criminal and criminal procedure codes. Other journals discussed improvements in the Cuban sugar industry, republished foreign news on Cuban railroads, followed Governor Tacón's measures against slave unrest, and kept track of Havana's 1833 cholera outbreak.[7] Journalistic interest in Cuba and the United States increasingly faced competition from an eclectic array of allusions to political economy studies on population promotion. In 1830, for example, the *Diário Fluminense* and *Astreia* debated the means to attain population growth, respectively citing William Godwin's anti-Malthus tract, *Of Population* (1820), and Jeremy Bentham's *Théorie des peines et des récompenses* (1811, *The Rationale of Reward* [1825]), which advocated population management to prevent crime. It was no wonder that these ideas found resonance in lawmakers' efforts to revive the tradition of *degredo*, or banishment, as a model for hinterland colonization.[8]

Foreign examples invoked by the press spoke directly to Brazilian political concerns, providing a panoply of scenarios relevant to ongoing debates. For instance, shortly after the start of the first Brazilian parliamentary session (1826), the progovernment *Diário Fluminense* translated a review from the *Journal de Paris* of Scottish doctor Robert Lyall's report on Russian military colonies.[9] Arguing that state-run colonization efforts in the Caucasus had transformed soldiers into farmers, the piece coincided with the outbreak of the Cisplatine War (1826–1828) and was thus meant as a plan for the postwar settlement of the German mercenaries whom Pedro I had hired to fight for him. While some newspapers such as Vasconcelos's *O Universal* politicized the reference, hailing the Russian model as a potential counterweight to British interests, most newspapers focused on its practical implications. *O Farol Paulistano* extolled how Russian military colonies created "a class that will have rights as well as the means to protect them," thus calling for bestowing citizenship on the veteran mercenaries settling in southern Brazil. A naturalization law issued four years later, while the erstwhile editor of *O Farol*, José da Costa Carvalho, served as one of the regents, did exactly that.[10]

Newspapers also moved beyond politics by searching far and wide for relevant counterpoints to Brazilian colonization efforts. Any good finds in leading journals quickly rippled through other publications. Months after publishing the Sociedade Promotora's charter, the new government newspaper, the *Correio Oficial*, translated part of the report on slavery and free labor in Puerto Rico by Colonel George Flinter, an Irishman in the service of Queen Isabel II.[11] A little later, the first issue of the scientific and literary journal *Nitheroy* referred to Flinter to explain why, in contrast to Cuba, Puerto Rico offered "a rotund denial of slave owners' opinion that free colonos cannot endure the tropical sun."[12] From more temperate climates came Huerne de Pommeuse's descriptions of Dutch agrarian asylums and Belgian *colonies de bienfaisance* (charity colonies), which aroused considerable interest in the Brazilian press. The Swiss agricultural school of Hofwil also received ample attention in the *Correio Oficial* and, years later, in enthusiastic reports by one of Brazil's first illustrated magazines.[13]

No reference, however, sparked as much interest as Britain's colonies, Upper and Lower Canada, especially given their spectacular demographic growth. Already in 1833, an "English manufacturer" claimed in the *Correio Oficial* that Brazil could profit immensely from redirecting Canada-bound British emigration to its own shores, where "an Englishman ... even if he gets three times less tired than in Canada or in Van-Diemen's Land, will produce three times more in convertible value [and] consume a greater proportion of European products."[14] In 1835, the *Correio Oficial* highlighted Canadian success with a commissioned translation of Isidore Lebrun's *Tableau statistique et politique des deux Canadas* (1833, Statistical and political view of the two Canadas), by João Cândido de Deus e Silva, an independence veteran from Piauí.[15] Through running commentary in the footnotes, Silva directed readers' attention to Canada's schooling system, its construction boom, its many agricultural fairs, and, notably, its breathtaking migration statistics. More than 16,000 settlers had arrived in Canada from Great Britain in 1831 alone, not to mention the many Bavarians who came via Le Havre, a port with which the Brazilian empire had established regular packet service in 1834.[16] Notoriously poor, these German emigrants faced serious difficulties upon arrival in Canada, but the *Correio* highlighted how they quickly overcame these obstacles as they acquired land, cattle, and income. Silva attributed such fortunate outcomes to the preponderance of religious and mutual aid associations, not to mention land companies, as he lamented their dearth in Brazil. Did the Brazilian Constitution prohibit such associations, he wondered in the footnotes.[17]

Heeding the concern about the precariousness of associational life and the need to spur population growth through immigration, Miguel Calmon du Pin e Almeida's *Memória sobre o estabelecimento d'uma Companhia de colonisação* (1835, Memoir on the establishment of a colonization company), was a clarion call that placed companies at the forefront of orchestrated immigration and settlement initiatives. Published originally as a pamphlet and quickly reprinted by the *Jornal do Commercio*, Calmon's *Memória* also served as a corporate prospectus that highlighted his political experience, business savvy, and reputation as one of the Brazilian empire's leading improvers. In 1831, after leaving the Ministry of Finance, Calmon traveled to Europe, where he became acquainted with the many colonization companies operating in British domains. A local newspaper in Bahia revealed that, on his return from Le Havre, he brought with him three families of Swiss *colonos*. During the Atlantic passage, he may have sealed a pact to promote colonization with his fellow travelers, Raimundo da Cunha Mattos and the son of Domingos Borges de Barros, since all three became prominent colonization advocates in the following years.[18]

Calmon's *Memória* reached a considerable audience thanks to its re-publication in the press, through which it acquainted a greater number of Brazilians with colonization initiatives elsewhere.[19] The *Memória* reflected Calmon's work as the founding president of the Sociedade de Agricultura, Comércio e Indústria da Provincia da Bahia (SACIPB or Agricultural, Commercial, and Industrial Society of Bahia), in whose journal he had sought to educate Bahian planters with know-how culled from international publications such as the *Révue Britannique*, the *One Penny Magazine*, and the *Southern Agriculturist*.[20] Like Calmon's earlier publications, the *Memória* had immediate, practical import. As Calmon informed his readers, a *colono* trade was already underway in Rio de Janeiro, where "private enterprises" had begun "to promote colonization with free people ... [b]ecause the Imperial Government will protect such laudable projects." The arrivals of a ship with Chinese workers and of a schooner with a load of *colonos* from the Azores were, to Calmon, worthy of imitation. Such early trips in the migrant trade were carried out by independent captains who profitably returned from Portugal laden with *colonos* rather than ballast. Calmon's intention was to regularize this process while redirecting profits to the company's shareholders. To this end, despite his defense of companies against a public administration not yet consolidated, Calmon relied on support from the Brazilian government via diplomatic backchannels and the publicity afforded by the official press.[21]

Even a conservative, proslavery outlet such as Vasconcelos's *O Sete d'Abril* accompanied the *Correio Oficial* in reporting on a lavish company-launch ceremony attended by Bahia's elites at Salvador's Santa Teresa Convent in late 1835.[22] As a follow-up, a month later the *Correio* also excerpted Frances Wright's *Views of Society and Manners in America* (1821) to describe Pennsylvania's redemptioner system, following earlier suggestions from a Brazilian "patrician" living in Europe that US-style "emigrant protection societies" take charge of organizing migrations to Brazil. Wright's detailed exposé on the *redencionistas*—redemptioners, or the German-indentured emigrants bound first to ship captains, then to individual contractors—not only demonstrated that a market in migrant labor could function with a modicum of government oversight, but also that Calmon's proposed protocols for conveying and hiring out colonos had long-standing precedents.[23]

Apart from Calmon's company drive, the *Correio* publicized many other of the prominent Bahian's interventions. Calmon earned accolades for his speech at the SACIPB on how to increase sugar production and for his leadership in the Chamber of Deputies. The government's daily portrayed him as a born innovator, applauding his proposal for employing Protestant missionaries such as the Moravians to educate Brazil's unpacified Indians, and for establishing a practical school (*horto botânico*) centered on agricultural improvement methods.[24] As part of these modernizing efforts, Calmon's company aroused the interest of editors as well as of readers, planters, and politicians who expressed their support by purchasing 449 shares of 100$000 (US$80) each within a month of the company's founding.[25]

Enthusiasm for Calmon's venture bolstered a similar, almost parallel, initiative in Rio de Janeiro, where a larger and fully incorporated colonization company was established by early 1836. The new company derived from the Sociedade Auxiliadora da Indústria Nacional (SAIN, or Society for the Aid of National Industry), whose members discussed establishing an "Association to Aid the Immigration of Free Colonos" that would be in charge of recruiting colonos from ship captains, housing "them in a warehouse," and recouping the costs of transport and daily maintenance from the planters and manufacturers who would hire them.[26] In January 1836, a group of interested parties drafted the statutes of the Sociedade Promotora de Colonização. In what amounted to a tacit acknowledgment of its incorporation, Justice Minister Antonio Paulino Limpo de Abreu divulged the statutes as a complement to a new mandate for the public works inspector to hire free workers rather than slaves. Having secured formal government recognition, the Sociedade Promotora's official charter made its rounds through the newspapers.[27]

The new company then set to work with prodigious speed. Its board voted the future regent Pedro de Araújo Lima for president and for secretary chose Diogo Soares da Silva Bivar, a small-time Portuguese lawyer who had originally arrived in Bahia en route to an exile sentence in Mozambique, only to become coeditor in 1811 of the *Idade de Ouro do Brazil*, one of Brazil's first gazettes.[28] More than anyone else, Bivar saw to the efficient functioning of everyday operations, using newspapers as channels for business transactions. While the treasurer collected payments from the 355 initial shareholders, Bivar relied on his publishing experience and worked actively with newspapers by placing periodic announcements to improve company operations. In one, he called for those interested in importing colonos to submit proposals for transport by third parties. In others, he asked for someone to offer a warehouse to serve as migrant hostel (*depósito*) and for landowners to lease or sell lands to the Sociedade for its colonos to cultivate. Not by chance, these calls appeared in the *Diário do Rio de Janeiro*, the classic *Diário do Vintém* or inexpensive newspaper that had sided with conservative factions tied to Portuguese merchants since 1831.[29] With such access to the business community, and thanks to Bivar's effective work, the Sociedade received plaudits from a growing rank of supporters.[30]

At the same time that the Sociedade Promotora began to earn praise, it also faced a public backlash over migrant transportation. To be sure, migrants, especially Portuguese ones, were already arriving in Rio de Janeiro in considerable numbers before the Sociedade launched its operations. The same issue of the *Diário do Rio de Janeiro* that published the Sociedade's charter featured numerous rental ads requesting or offering Portuguese men of different ages to work in a broad array of occupations, from domestic service or managing rural properties to accompanying hay carts into the city or serving as shop clerks. Fully 23,548 migrants entered Rio de Janeiro from 1835 to 1842 according to police entry records. Of these, at least 3,819 were Azorean islanders, the same people whom the Sociedade Promotora targeted as the most suitable colonos for Brazil.[31] Colonization companies did not summon this market for migrant workers into existence; rather, they latched onto it and sought ways to amplify it by using the press as a loudspeaker. Nonetheless, in public discussions, the denunciations of poor treatment that dogged the colono trade increasingly targeted the Sociedade, which colonization opponents blamed for any mishaps in acrid columns published in various newspapers. While this did not stall colonization endeavors, it did force both the Brazilian government and the Sociedade to resolve crises directly, incurring high administrative expenses and paying an even greater price in the form of a tarnished public image.

Disease, Fugitives, and the Troubles of the Migrant Trade

Problems began in earnest with the arrival of the *Libertad*, a Spanish vessel calling at Rio de Janeiro from the Canary Islands, via Salvador, in June 1836. Originally bound for Montevideo and overcrowded with 570 colonos, the *Libertad* allegedly brought with it a strain of cholera morbus that had recently ravaged the ports of the Balearic Islands and Genoa. As soon as the ship anchored in Guanabara Bay, the Spanish consulate asked the Sociedade Promotora for help, protesting that colonos had arrived under conditions akin to those of slave transports. The *Libertad*'s captain fled.[32]

Without assuming any liability for this particular group of colonists, the Sociedade promptly sent two members to investigate: doctors Joseph François Xavier Sigaud, who had cofounded the *Jornal do Commercio* and *O Propagador das Ciências Médicas* in 1827, and Manuel do Valadão Pimentel, the future Baron of Petrópolis.[33] Years later, in an influential medical treatise, Sigaud explained that, rather than cholera, this had been a slow-incubating but highly contagious strain of typhoid that infected one hundred individuals, including colonos, some of the ship's crew, and the stevedores handling the vessel's cargo.[34] While the Sociedade Promotora helped determine the gravity of the situation, it lacked the capacity to contain the epidemic. Its assessment, however, prompted the government to quarantine the ship, transfer the infected colonos to the Santa Casa da Misericórdia hospital, and, later, when the Casa reached full capacity, to military installations on the Campo da Honra.[35]

The crisis stained the Sociedade Promotora despite its diligence. Although the epidemic was not ultimately a high mortality event (according to Sigaud, only nine of those infected died), and even though the government, not the Sociedade, was behind containment efforts, critics in the press blamed the company. *O Cronista* (1836–1839), a rabidly conservative newspaper published by Justiniano José da Rocha, did not miss a beat, forecasting that the "colonization society will only give us . . . a plague of ragged mendicants for our streets, as already happened with the Spanish colonos." A month later, the same newspaper lambasted the *colonos canarinos* affair by calling attention to the considerable government expenses incurred: "We ended up paying 2:355$742 [US$1,837.48] for those colonos . . . quite cheap did this market turn out for us," added Justiniano sarcastically. Indeed, when the Spanish chargé d'affaires in Rio de Janeiro asked Limpo de Abreu a few months later about the total costs incurred in caring for the colonos, the minister reported an amount of 3:689$936 (US$2,878.15), about 56 percent more than what Justiniano had considered excessive.[36]

Writing to the *Diário do Rio de Janeiro* to restore public confidence in colonizing endeavors, "an associate who purchased more shares" defended the Sociedade Promotora's decision to care for the ailing colonos. But the Sociedade did not need such defenses. As the government endeavored to avoid a health crisis, the Sociedade's board went about its business by contracting out the healthy colonos canarinos. The Spanish chargé d'affaires quickly demanded their return to his care. The Sociedade consented, while announcing publicly that it had never inscribed these colonos in its books—it simply did not make sense to fight over these particular migrants, which would only hurt the company's public image. After all, the colono trade from the Canary Islands was, like that of the Azores, picking up speed. Some weeks after the *Libertad* events, the Portuguese brigantine *Dois Amigos* arrived in Rio de Janeiro with 321 Canary Islanders, followed shortly by Uruguayan brig *Restaurador da Paz* with another 36.[37]

The Sociedade Promotora preferred to refrain from public opinion wars as demonstrated in the colonos canarinos affair. Newspaper articles could be double-edged swords even when amicable to the Sociedade. This was precisely the case with a contributor to the *Diário do Rio de Janeiro* calling himself "Cincinato." In a series of articles beginning in mid-1836, "Cincinato" defended colonization against the pernicious effects of slavery. In the long term, he claimed, the importation of Europeans would bring endless benefits, including the expansion of agriculture, industry, and commerce; the growth of a national, more homogeneous population; and an increase in government revenue. But there was a caveat. The law of November 7, 1831, that had officially abolished the slave trade had adversely affected the government's capacity to tax continuing slave imports. Ships that had to complete return voyages to Brazil in ballast rather than packed with slaves continued to sustain losses.[38] Cincinato argued that the trade should have been abolished only *after* the government had duly promoted colonization societies through subsidies and tax exemptions. In subsequent front-page opinion pieces, he insisted that colonization would have solved the problem of slavery, but "bad luck," rather than any inherent fault with the model, had "foiled such attempts." And so, while he supported colonization, Cincinato bluntly exposed its shortcomings.[39]

Bivar and others made sure that the Sociedade stood up for itself when necessary, especially in the international arena. In late 1836, for instance, Bivar responded to what he described as the "inexact apprehensions against the guiding principles of colonization in Brazil" that had appeared in London's *Evening Mail*. Countering accusations against the company's work, Bivar declared that, as per its statutes, the Sociedade Promotora would never accept colonos without a proper "testament to their morality" in the form of the certificate of good conduct that its overseas agents had instructions to obtain.[40] Yet Bivar's pronouncements demonstrate how newspapers could serve multiple, sometimes contradictory, ends. While Bivar defended the Sociedade's integrity in the Rio de Janeiro newspapers, Brazil's vice-consul on Terceira announced in the local press that he would offer expedited certificates of good conduct and other travel documents to "all the farmers who out of necessity wish to go live in the Brazilian empire."[41]

Meanwhile, local newspapers in the Azores caught on, and a few months after this announcement, a concerted campaign against colono recruitment took shape. Denouncing how "ships continue to pull into these islands to pick up mounting numbers of wretched men," *O Angrense* offered a series of horror stories. It accused the captain and the crew of one of the colono-recruiting vessels, the *Comêta*, of "abusing their authority" with Azorean women on board after locking their family members in the hold. It told of how a "colonizing society" put Azoreans in a "warehouse like those used for Blacks, so that they can be sold." It offered the story of one miserable Azorean, referred to as a slave, who, falling ill at the Baroness of São Francisco's plantation in Rio de Janeiro province, was taken back to the city and abandoned to die in a public square. This coverage contributed to a narrative on "white slavery [*escravatura branca*]" that began to emerge in the Azorean and Portuguese mainland press.[42] Calling attention to abusive and predatory recruitment practices, newspapers such as *O Nacional* called for more government regulation as they made every effort to reach a wide reading public. In São Miguel, a doctor who opposed emigration personally distributed copies of an issue of the *Diário do Povo* containing critiques of Brazilian recruiting before allegedly boarding a ship and sailing to Brazil himself.[43]

Even in Brazil, colonization companies faced opposition from Portuguese consuls. When the *Comêta* arrived in Bahia with a colono shipment in late April 1836, the Portuguese consul in Salvador, Francisco de Souza, protested that the ship's captain and his cosignatory had imposed "harmful [contractual] conditions" on the Azoreans, beginning with an "exorbitant passage" of 65$000 (US$50.70) per person. In the contracts that they had signed prior to departure, the colonos had agreed that, lacking the means to cover travel costs, upon arrival in Brazil they would have to remain on board until contracted out by the captain. The consul rightly argued that this was a direct violation of the Portuguese commercial code, under whose stipulations the captains were not fit to draw up contracts and could only to charge travel fares. The consul demanded that new contracts be drawn up at his desk in the Azoreans' presence, in his view the only way to guarantee fair contractual conditions in light of the fact that the colonos were "ignorant of the prices, uses and customs of the country" and were thus "easy to fool through contracts." In response, the captain and his partner invoked the imperial law of September 13, 1830, which regulated service-leasing (*prestação de serviços*) agreements drawn up in Brazil or abroad. Any disputes, they claimed, could be settled in Brazilian courts, whose protection both the captains and colonos could invoke.[44]

In truth, the 1830 statute was vague at best. Its approval came at Pedro I's behest in the context of mounting British investments in Brazilian mining and continued mercenary recruitment in the late 1820s. At the time, newspapers like the *Aurora Fluminense* had celebrated it as a law that would "help the poor find subsistence through their work and the rich to usefully employ their capital toward production and population."[45] However, in practice, the 1830 law barely gave a legal footing to Brazilians drafting commercial or service contracts overseas by giving local justices of peace jurisdiction over breach-of-contract cases. In situations in which foreign precedents or jurisdictions played a role, and a foreign representative could duly invoke them, the law provided few indications on how to proceed. In the *Comêta* case, authorities deliberately avoided going to court, with Bahia's president pleading with the Portuguese consul to cooperate with the colonization company director—Calmon—so that the colonos could be advantageously employed.[46]

Frequent colono escapes reinvigorated calls for a law that effectively adjudicated contractual frauds and breaches, and even prosecuted those who aided fugitives. The challenge posed by fugitive colonos was already evident in August 1836, when Secretary Bivar called on anyone who had hired workers from the Sociedade to report any escape so that the company's management could report it to the police. A few months later, the Sociedade responded much more aggressively to reports of escaped colonos. In one instance, it issued a warning that four Spaniards aged twenty to twenty-eight were missing from the hostel and that anyone housing them would be legally liable for having "seduced or hired them." More leniently, the Sociedade later offered a reward to whoever found a couple from the island of Pico who had, for the second time, fled from their employer's house.[47]

In light of these alleged contractual violations, the Sociedade presented a bill of its own making to the Chamber of Deputies. Quickly approved by a special commission, the bill breezed through Parliament without significant discussion and became law within a year. The new *lei de locação dos serviços* was not, as its literal translation would suggest, a "work-lease law," but rather a contract law that for the first time explicitly threatened criminal penalties for workers, as well as any person aiding them; it mandated prison sentences and fines for the evasion of contractual obligations.[48] The new law empowered the Sociedade Promotora to hold colonos accountable despite protests from their diplomatic representatives. It even took care of the concern expressed by some that the colonos hired from the hostel at the Largo da Lapa were often minors. To prevent Portuguese consuls from intervening as legal guardians, the law charged Brazilian *juízes de órfãos* (orphans' judges) with this role. Thus empowering the Brazilian judiciary, the law won conservative support, as evidenced by the fact that Vasconcelos' newspaper was still advertising it months after its approval.[49]

If the press served to police colonos' movement and to publicize a law that criminalized it, it also aided the Sociedade Promotora in holding its shareholders accountable for timely payments. Indeed, winning their participation in society operations constituted one of its top challenges. No-shows at meetings, sometimes due to bad weather, hobbled the Sociedade's communications with its shareholders. To fix this, the Sociedade's secretary repeatedly announced shareholder meetings in the *Diário do Rio de Janeiro* and other outlets well in advance. In addition, Bivar and other personnel published repeated notices in the press chiding shareholders for delays in paying their installments or patrons for failing to pay for colonos whom they had hired "on credit [*em confiança*]." Sometimes, the Sociedade threatened debtors that they "would be compelled by judicial means" if they failed to pay within a deadline. The Sociedade also warned that missed payments would accumulate under colonos' own debts, with an interest rate of 9 percent annually, which made colonos responsible for their employers' liabilities.[50]

Newspaper announcements regarding the Sociedade Promotora's financial activities provide a window into some of the reasons for the demise of this early trade in migrant workers. As Bivar announced in the press, by 1837 the Sociedade could boast of the arrival of its "neatly printed" *apólices*, or share certificates, from London. By then, however, the Sociedade's shares had depreciated considerably. With no restrictions on their sale to third parties, the Sociedade's shares remained transferable, and so unidentified subscribers began to resell or purchase company shares via third parties in locations throughout the city. Newspapers served as conduits for such transactions, connecting potential buyers and sellers (on newspapers' role in developing a commercial culture in Rio de Janeiro, see Matthew Nestler and Zephyr Frank's chapter). In August 1836, a business on Direita Street announced the sale of two of the Sociedade's shares. Around the corner on Ouvidor Street, Manoel José Cardoso's stationary store put out a call to buy two or three shares on the same day. Months later, another locale on São Pedro Street announced the sale of a public debt bond and one share in the Sociedade Promotora, which, the ad promised, would yield dividends. This was certainly not the case. By 1839, the Sociedade's shares were for sale at 25$000 (US$16) each, that is, at a fourth of their original value.[51] In part at least, this was a reflection of the larger financial crisis of 1837, which had begun with English credit contractions in late 1836 and expanded into a financial panic across the Atlantic.[52] In Rio de Janeiro and other Brazilian port cities where credit practices such as consignation and parceled payments had only recently solidified thanks to resident English firms, the use of apólices and other forms of paper money remained a work in progress.

Ad Hominem Attacks and Public Audits: Unwinding the First Migrant Trade

The financial situation of the Sociedade Promotora after 1838 was grist for the mill of those who opposed colonization as a private business. Leading the charge was the conservative *O Cronista*, with Justiniano at the helm. In its characteristically acrid style, the journal extolled colonization as a means to replace slavery with the "fertilizing sweat of the free, industrious man," but rejected colonization through companies.⁵³ Taking aim at the lucrative "colonization commerce" and its supporters, it urged the government to come up with a sensible colonization policy using the migrant conveyance process employed by the companies as a "new means of making a profit."⁵⁴ There may have been personal vendettas behind *O Cronista*'s diatribe against the companies: months earlier, in the Chamber of Deputies, fellow conservative Calmon had delivered a stern rebuke to Justiniano's request for a "modest indemnity" over damages incurred during his exile in 1823, following the Constituent Assembly's dissolution.⁵⁵ Likely thus targeting Calmon for reasons unrelated to colonization, the bilious language in *O Cronista* corroded the debate over government's role in colonization. Previously, newspapers had advocated for some degree of government involvement in the migrant trade. "As powerful and rich as colonization associations may be," declared the *Diário da Bahia* (approvingly quoted by *O Paquete do Rio*), "they cannot successfully meet their well-intended objectives by themselves if government does not aid them." In the *Diário da Bahia*'s view, as a "direct promoter of industry," the government had simply to support rather than implement migrant transport schemes lest it do "more harm than good." If anything, it should "act negatively" and remain a step removed from the migrant trade. When signaling that "this task belongs to individual citizens, all the more so if they come together into companies," the *Diário da Bahia* placed itself squarely within the camp that defended freedom of association and investments as the engines of colonization.⁵⁶ By contrast, *O Cronista* held that the government should rein in such ventures, warning that it should "meditate on the future, irremediable consequences of speculators' dealings and decide whether it should remain apathetic and inactive as vice and crime inoculate themselves among us."⁵⁷

Heating up due to external political circumstances, the debate over the most appropriate forms of colonization took a turn toward ad hominem attacks. Epithets became more callous after Brazil signed a treaty of commerce with Portugal in 1836, reportedly with the support of Calmon, who among other things was called a "a gigantic lowlife!! a Portuguese cashier!" by the radical *O Repúblico*.⁵⁸ Lusophobic (anti-Portuguese) invectives specifically against Calmon reached their peak in late 1837 when he took the finance portfolio offered by the newly elected regent Araújo Lima while Salvador was engulfed by the Sabinada revolt. "That traitor Calmon sends letters to the Portuguese in Bahia," proclaimed the rebels, "and has told them that he accepted a ministerial post to save them!"⁵⁹ Yet such radical rhetoric missed the mark when, a year later, Calmon proposed a burdensome tax on the contracting of foreign clerks (*caixeiros*), the majority of whom were Portuguese, and thus became the target of attacks by more conservative newspapers.⁶⁰ Calmon's appointment to his ministerial post by Araújo Lima not only galvanized him against these aspersions but also earned him praise in some quarters. "In Bahia," reported one newspaper, "no one ignores the enthusiasm with which Mr. Calmon, together with the majority of our landowners, threw themselves at that sea of misguided hope." But the fault fell on migrants' incapacity to "bear the sun's intensity and the other hardships of our fields," which Salvador's *Correio Mercantil* illustrated by referring to failed efforts to better colonos' working conditions on the plantation owned by Domingos Borges de Barros, whose son had traveled back from Europe with Calmon years earlier. Borges de Barros, by then the Viscount of Pedra Branca, had segregated colonos from slaves to improve the formers' productivity, but colonos did not boost their performance nor did segregation of laborers by status attract greater numbers of colonos to his plantation.⁶¹

The Sociedade Promotora confronted its own challenges after 1838. In a matter of years, the company had brought together some of the empire's most illustrious planters and politicians; a list of top shareholders in the *Diário do Rio de Janeiro* featured the Marquises of Barbacena and Baependi, planters from the Gonçalves de Moraes and Souza Breves clans, and political heavyweights like Francisco Gê de Acaiaba de Montezuma and Antônio Francisco de Paula de Holanda Cavalcanti. This stellar lineup notwithstanding, by 1839 the Sociedade was bankrupt.⁶² Conservative newspapers like *O Universal* half-heartedly lamented the fate of such a "promising establishment" while lancing it for laying waste "to the fortunes of its associates" without "its managers even informing the public of what led to such disastrous consequences."⁶³

Newspapers contain the only available evidence of the Sociedade Promotora's unwinding: the report of a commission appointed to study the Sociedade's accounts and make recommendations on whether it should continue operations.⁶⁴ Headed by Montezuma, the commission complained of the "lack of method" with which the Sociedade had kept track of its transactions as well as of missing treasury records and shareholder rosters, some of which was fortunately reported by the press. The fifty-two account books that the Sociedade did have at least contradicted the "calumnious assertions that the enemies of free colonization . . . had disseminated throughout Europe."

According to the auditors' findings, the Sociedade Promotora had fed colonos well, purveyed them with other necessities, and invested in improving the hostel's sleeping quarters. Its active debt was equivalent to its start-up capital of 75:000$ (US$ 60,000), but only about 70 percent of that debt was recoverable, according to the commission's estimate. Nonetheless, according to a summary published in *O Universal*, the commission recommended that the Sociedade not dissolve: "If on this day its books show no profits, its accounts lead us to expect them soon . . . [B]esides promising no small profit, this enterprise is eminently patriotic."[65]

In spite of the commission's positive outlook, the Sociedade Promotora did not operate much longer. Nevertheless, its work and that of Calmon's company set a significant precedent. By the time that Vasconcelos delivered the report to the Chamber of Deputies mentioned at the beginning of this chapter, the Sociedade Promotora had received 2,112 colonos in its hostel on the Largo da Lapa. Monthly arrivals of Portuguese migrants to Rio de Janeiro alone averaged 199 throughout much of the Sociedade's first year of existence, 1836. By 1850, according to historian Rosana Barbosa's estimates, they had increased to 358.[66]

As new land and colonization bills made their way to the Chamber of Deputies in 1840 and 1843, the idea of fomenting migration by providing subsidies to individuals or companies interested in the conveyance of overseas workers resurfaced.[67] By 1845, the imperial government set up its own model colony, which became Petrópolis, the emperor's retreat in the mountains above Rio de Janeiro. Two years later, liberal firebrand Teófilo Ottoni launched his trail-blazing Companhia do Mucury (Mucuri [River] Company), a colonization venture heavily reliant on government subsidies, and by 1855, the government inaugurated its own Associação Central de Colonização (Central Colonization Association), which not only established its own version of the Sociedade Promotora's hostel but was also directly overseen by Araújo Lima (now the Marquis of Olinda), the Sociedade's first president.[68]

Historians have long overlooked the extent to which these colonization efforts and the advent, more generally, of larger migration flows after 1850s harkened back to the colono trade of the 1830s. These early orchestrated efforts to convey free workers to the Brazilian empire have in part remained obscure due to the dearth of manuscript sources and the paucity of imperial government records in documenting colonization efforts before the 1860s, when national colonies became commonplace. Newspapers not only correct this problem, showing how migrant recruitment, conveyance, and hiring took place in the midst of the most fractious period of the Brazilian empire's history, but also shed light on their role in stoking, and questioning, consecutive colono trades.

The relationship between the press and colonization in fact survived the initial moment of crisis epitomized in Justiniano's offensive. Brazilian newspapers continued to facilitate orchestrated migrations and settlement initiatives of all kinds, even as they switched editors or ownership. The *Diário do Rio de Janeiro*, for instance, hosted debates about Confederate immigration and Chinese coolies after its acquisition by Joaquim Saldanha Marinho, a figurehead of emergent republican cadres best represented by his chosen editor, future immigration promoter Quintino Bocaiuva.[69] Meanwhile, Brazil's first English newspaper, *The Anglo-Brazilian Times*, advertised the empire as a desirable destination. The highlights echoed topics past: contract issues, this time between government and companies, periodic pandemics, invectives against perceived speculators. As the Brazilian empire re-embarked on the question of abolition, newspapers lay bare what an earlier press had suggested. Publishing news of Macao's coolie trade or of the freedmen's colony of Liberia, newspapers continued to show that orchestrated mobilities opened a world of troubles for many and opportunities for the few.[70]

Notes

1. Browne, "Government Immigration Policy"; Klein, *Atlantic Slave Trade*, 216–17 (the estimate of 338,182 slave entries).
2. The literature on the substitution of slaves by free migrants is vast: E. Costa, *Brazilian Empire*, 125–71; Holloway, *Immigrants*; Hall and Stolcke, "Introduction"; Seyferth, "Slave Plantation"; Gonçalves, "Procuram-se braços." On clandestine Azorean migration, see S. Silva, "Emigração."
3. Vasconcelos, *Relatório*, 30. On Vasconcelos's stances, see Needell, *Party of Order*, 138–42; Parron, *Política da escravidão no Império*, 133–56.
4. Alencastro, "Prolétaires," 126–28; and Ribeiro, *Liberdade*, 163, briefly mention at least one of the companies.
5. R. Barbosa, "Portuguese Migration," 43.
6. Sodré, *História*, 179–200.
7. Dantas, "Da Luisiana"; Youssef, *Imprensa*, 111–20; *JC*, March 13, 1834; *Diario de Pernambuco*, January 20, 1837, January 31, 1838.
8. *Diario Fluminense*, February 13, 1830; *Astréa*, March 23, 1830. See also Carneiro Leão's intervention on May 14, *ACD* (1833), 1:155–56.

9. *Diario Fluminense*, February 8 and 13, 1826; Lyall, *Notice*; Bitis and Hartley, "Russian Military Colonies."

10. *O Universal* (Ouro Preto), March 6, 1826, March 19, 1830; *O Farol Paulistano* (São Paulo), May 24, and August 2, 1828, April 27, 1830; Lei, October 23, 1832, *CLB*.

11. "Factos e informações que provão as vantagens do trabalho livre sobre o trabalho forçado," *Correio Official*, June 17–18, 20–23, 1836 (extracted from Flinter, *Account*, chap. 9).

12. Francisco Salles Torres Homem, "Considerações econômicas sobre a escravatura," *Nitheroy* 1 (1836): 35–82.

13. Huerne de Pommeuse, *Colonies*; *Correio Official*, November 15, 1837; January 17, February 1 and 20, June 8, 9, 11, 16, and 18, 1838; "Escola de Agricultura de M. de Fallemberg, em Hofwyl, na Suissa," *Correio Official*, November 11–12, 1835; *Museo Universal*, September 12, 1840.

14. *Correio Official*, August 31, 1833.

15. Isidore Lebrun, "Do quadro estatístico e político dos dous Canadás," *Correio Official*, April 14, 21, May 6, June 23, 25, 27, 30, July 24, August 1, 3, 4, September 7, 1835.

16. "Estabelecimento de comunicações regulares entre o Havre, e o Rio de Janeiro," *Correio Official*, November 25, 1834.

17. *Correio Official*, July 24, 1835.

18. *Gazeta da Bahia* (Salvador), December 2, 1831. See R. Mattos, "Memória." Borges de Barros held shares in Calmon's company.

19. *Jornal da Sociedade de Agricultura, Commercio e Industria da Provincia da Bahia* (Salvador) 38 (October 1835); *JC*, November 9, 1835. The *Correio Official* reprinted the company's prospectus and followed up on its provincial and central government concessions, November 14, 1835.

20. Miguel Calmon du Pin e Almeida, "Communicado sobre a importancia da boa redacção deste Jornal, e meios de conseguil-a," *Jornal da Sociedade de Agricultura, Commercio e Industria da Provincia da Bahia* (Salvador) 34 (June 1835): 691–99.

21. Almeida, *Memória*, 5.

22. *O Sete d'Abril*, December 5, 1835.

23. *Correio Official*, July 31, 1833; "Colonisação no Norte de América," *Correio Official*, December 18, 1835; F. Wright, *Views*, 342–46.

24. *Correio Official*, June 4, 1836.

25. *Aurora Fluminense*, November 30, 1835.

26. "Extracto da sessão da sua Assembléa Geral, reunida no dia 15 de Novembro," *O Auxiliador da Industria Nacional* 3, no. 12 (1835), 361–63; *DRJ*, November 9, 1835.

27. "Estatutos da Sociedade Promotora de Colonisação do Rio de Janeiro," January 15, 1836, *CLB*; *DRJ*, March 12, 1836.

28. Vianna, *Contribuição*, 18–21; M. B. N. Silva, *Primeira gazeta*, 233.

29. *DRJ*, April 20, 21, and 26, 1836.

30. *DRJ*, September 27, 1836.

31. *DRJ*, March 11, 1836; R. Barbosa, *Immigration*, 35. I have calculated Azorean entries based on a data set elaborated from the AN's *Movimentação dos portugueses* database, www.an.gov.br/baseluso.

32. Consul Mariano Carlos de Sousa Corrêa to Foreign Affairs Minister Manuel Alves Branco, Lisbon, October 30, 1835, AHI, e. 251, pr. 2, maço 14; *DRJ*, June 16, 1836.

33. *JC*, June 16, 1836. Sigaud, a Bonapartist émigré and Montpellier alumnus, arrived in Brazil in 1825, promoted medical journalism, and cofounded the Sociedade de Medicina do Rio de Janeiro (1829). Valladão Pimentel was one of young Pedro II's doctors and later headed the Military Hospital. On medical elites, see Coratini, "Grandes famílias."

34. Sigaud, *Du climat*, 98–102.

35. Empire Minister Antonio Paulino Limpo de Abreu to War Minister Manuel Fonseca Lima e Silva, Rio de Janeiro, June 16 and 22 1836, AN, IG[1] 339.

36. *O Chronista*, October 15, 1836, November 26, 1836; Spain's chargé d'affaires José Delavat y Rincón to Limpo de Abreu, Rio de Janeiro, February 27, 1837; Limpo de Abreu to Fonseca Lima, Rio de Janeiro, February 28, 1837, AN, IA[6] 155.

37. *DRJ*, July 8, 16, and 29; August 16, 1836.

38. *DRJ*, September 22, 1836. On these issues, see also Alain El Youssef's chapter in this volume.

39. *DRJ*, October 10, and November 11, 1836, January 7, 1837.

40. *JC*, November 7, 1836. The *Evening Mail*'s accusations originally appeared in Hamburg's *Schwäbischer Merkur*.

41. *O Observador* (Terceira), June 9, 1836.

42. *O Angrense* (Angra), October 15, 1836. On white slavery, see M. Carvalho, "O 'tráfico'"; and Ferraria and Sousa, "Emigração."

43. Sousa Corrêa to Alves Branco, Lisbon, April 20 1836, AHI, e. 251, pr. 2, maço 14.

44. *Paquete do Rio*, May 16 and 17, 1836.

45. *Aurora Fluminense*, August 23, 1830; Lei, September 13, 1830, *CLB*.

46. *Paquete do Rio*, May 16 and 17, 1836.

47. *DRJ*, August 31, 1836; February 12 and 20, 1837.

48. See the debates of September 1, *ACD* (1836), 2:237–39; and May 9 and 30, *ACD* (1837), 2:26–27, 153; Lei 108, October 11, 1837, *CLB*.

49. *O Sete d'Abril*, January 10, 1838.

50. *DRJ*, May 2 and 31, June 7, July 21, 1837; January 22, 1839.

51. *JC*, August 30, and October 10, 1836; December 7, 1837; *DRJ*, October 20, 1836, May 5, 1837; *O Universal* (Ouro Preto), January 18, 1839.

52. Lepler, *Many Panics*.

53. *O Chronista*, January 13, 1838.

54. *O Chronista*, November 20, 1838.

55. *Aurora Fuminense*, August 22, October 8, 1838; *O Chronista*, May 29, July 14, October 18, November 3, 1838.

56. *Paquete do Rio*, May 18 and July 16, 1836 (extracted from *Diario da Bahia*).

57. *O Chronista*, November 20, 1838.

58. *Collecção*, 132–33; *O Républico*, January 21, 1837.

59. *Jornal dos Debates*, November 18, 1837.

60. *O Parlamentar*, October 17, 1838; *O Universal* (Ouro Preto), October 29, 1838.

61. *Correio Mercantil* (Salvador), August 20, 1839.

62. *DRJ*, April 26, 1839.

63. *O Universal* (Ouro Preto), January 18, 1839.

64. "Relatório apresentado à Assembléa Geral dos Accionistas da Sociedade Promotora de Colonisação . . . pela commissão encarregada do exame das contas da mesma sociedade até o dia 31 de março de 1838," *O Parlamentar*, January 30, 1839.

65. *O Universal* (Ouro Preto), February 13, 1839.

66. R. Barbosa, *Immigration*, 36; Vasconcelos, *Relatório*, appendix 7.

67. J. Carvalho, "Modernização"; L. Silva, *Terras*, 95–110.

68. Chrysostomo and Vidal, "De depósito."

69. *DRJ*, January 17 and February 8, 1866.

70. *The Anglo-Brazilian Times*, August 22 and November 7, 1868, May 23, 1878.

Ludmila de Souza Maia

FIVE FICTIONALIZING *CRÔNICAS*
Transformations of an Article Genre

A lowly doctor,
One-eyed, one-armed, and lame
Is the man behind
These gazette pages.
...
He lays out a well-defined program,
To face the battle:
Neither flat, nor sharp,
Neither Cain nor Marcus Aurelius
He comes with no modern ideas,
Nor antiquated ones: he comes with nothing.
He comes on both his legs,
One healthy, the other broken.
...
Here I am, in perfect unity,
I approve or I contest,
Without the need
Of hearing protest and protest.[1]

On November 1, 1886, the *cronista* "Malvolio" signed the first *crônica* of a series titled "Gazeta de Holanda" (Dutch gazette) in Rio de Janeiro's *Gazeta de Notícias*. Joaquim Maria Machado de Assis, already a notable author of Brazilian literature and newspaper crônicas, was behind the pseudonym Malvolio. Through Malvolio's voice, Machado de Assis pushed the boundaries of the crônica genre by composing the entire series in verse. Malvolio described himself as a one-eyed, lame doctor, indicating to the reader a clearly delineated otherness that distinguished the author Machado de Assis from the fictional narrator Malvolio.[2] Published weekly or bi-weekly, crônicas comprised a popular section in the nineteenth-century Brazilian press. Cronistas—as their authors were known—wrote in a literary style that combined fictional narrative with news reporting. Since the genre's inception in Brazil in the 1830s, crônicas had undergone important transformations.

In the first crônica of the new series, the narrator Malvolio declared a clear agenda for his "Gazeta de Holanda." It consisted of a single work of literature that included discussions of political, social, and economic issues in the form of a free-style poem, spiced with doses of fiction. Malvolio commented on local news as well as international affairs, sometimes in the same strophe, as in the following passage: "I present to you:—The famous case / Of the schoolyard brawl / The case that eclipsed everything else / Everything, even the epidemic's outbreak."[3] Using poetic language syncopated by rhymes, Malvolio referred to the aggression against a student by a teacher in the Colégio Abílio (Abílio School) in Rio de Janeiro. The case was denounced widely by the student's father in local press,[4] an event that overshadowed, in Malvolio's opinion, the major cholera outbreak in Buenos Aires that same year.[5] Making literature out of news, crônicas were a hybrid genre mixing and re-creating poetry, fiction, and journalism.[6]

By the end of the nineteenth century, most notable Brazilian writers composed and published at least one series of crônicas. Indeed, crônicas became one of the most important sections of Brazilian newspapers at the time for they attracted readers and boosted sales. By the end of the century, the crônica genre had acquired such importance in the Brazilian press that it was unthinkable to run a newspaper without it.

During the nineteenth century, literature and the newspaper press were closely associated. Most Brazilian writers first published literary works in newspapers and only later issued the same texts as separately published volumes. Newspapers were filled with passages from novels, short stories, poems, and other literary genres. In both literary pieces and ordinary news, fiction was a useful means for journalists to discuss a variety of subjects such as the latest balls, breaking crime stories, urban reforms, political events such as the opening of Parliament, or even epidemics. Fictional and referential texts filled the pages of newspapers and, in the case of crônicas, both served as fodder for the narrative.[7]

This chapter surveys crônicas in the Brazilian press during the empire (1822–1889), focusing on the genre's origins and the diverse roles that crônicas played in the country. The wealth of material in crônicas demonstrates how they functioned as a specific newspaper section in which literature and reporting converged, resulting in the forging of a new literary and journalistic genre by the end of the century. From its beginning in the 1830s until the 1880s, crônicas were written with increasing levels of fictionality that included more complex literary narratives about daily life, political events, and recent events. Crônicas presented news in an innovative way that joined opinion with literary experimentation.[8] In this chapter, I argue that a long-term view of the genre across the century enables a deeper understanding of its transformation in form and function. Over time, the genre acquired increasing doses of recognizably literary quality that made newspapers even more important to prospective writers. If, by the time of their first appearance, crônicas had a more referential core that discussed fresh news more or less objectively, with time, fictionality took over the genre, and it became the preferred venue for many authors to launch their literary careers. Due to their fictional and referential elements, chronicles are rich sources for historians interested in uncovering nineteenth-century Brazilian daily life.

The Making of a Genre

The Portuguese word *crônica* originates from the French *chronique*. Crônicas or chroniques comprise a narrative form that dates to antiquity in which historical facts are related in chronological sequence. In the nineteenth century, the crônica emerged as a new literary form in European newspapers, developing into a narrative form in which authors distanced themselves from reality to explore a variety of daily themes drawn from their own inspiration.[9]

In the beginning of the nineteenth century, French newspapers reserved the footer of the first page for an entertainment section called the *Feuilleton*. At this time, French newspaper chroniques were merely descriptive texts narrating the most relevant events of the week, including political, theatrical, or anecdotal facts, in straightforward prose. By the 1830s, French chronique authors started a new writing trend by extending their text beyond simple description of daily events to embrace fictional digressions, dialogical language, and first-person narration, an entirely new style. In general, they avoided referential or chronological prose, using fictional touches to entertain readers based on the most recent events in society. Chroniques were part of a larger process of producing newspapers in a more attractive and literary fashion to reach wider audiences and raise sales. In short, chroniques were the epitome of the style of textual works that came to define the new mass-produced commercial product that appealed to a large audience.[10]

Just as scholars today recognize the Brazilian genre's French origin, Brazilian writers were themselves mindful of this foreign influence on their work. They were well aware that the genre originated in France, and they admitted finding their inspiration in French authors and newspapers. In Brazil and other parts of Latin America, French newspapers abounded in local markets. They were shipped across the Atlantic or republished overseas by local branches of French publishing houses in important editorial hubs like Recife and Rio de Janeiro. French novels were likewise quickly translated and eagerly read by Brazilians. Local newspapers often copied the trends that they observed in French newspapers, and upper-class Brazilians looked to France as a symbol of civilization and progress. The press served as the principal channel through which such inspiration traveled.[11]

As early as the 1820s, France became an important publishing and editorial market for Portuguese and Brazilian volumes, and some publishers specialized in distributing Portuguese-language volumes in local and international markets. In this way, the movement of French literary genres was no one-way flow but rather a constant circulation of ideas and publications between the two continents. Brazilian periodicals incorporated ideas from abroad at the same time that they spread innovative styles of writing back to Europe. Additionally, although the nineteenth-century French press was a major influence on its Brazilian counterpart, the evolution of literary genres assumed a path of its own in Brazil. *Acclimatization* was the term that Machado de Assis used to describe this process, emphasizing the development of something much more complex than the mere reproduction of French forms and styles in Brazil.[12]

In the early nineteenth century, following the French model of the feuilleton, Brazilian newspapers reserved the lower part of the front page for the editors' discretion. At first unnamed, this new section soon acquired the title of Variedades (Varieties). Over time, it evolved from a section that was heavily news oriented to one that was exclusively dedicated to entertainment.[13] This was not a straightforward process but one that had twists and turns along the way. Initially, Variedades included not only fictional prose such as serialized novels published chapter by chapter, but also nonfiction texts like crônicas. The section slowly migrated from the lower front page and acquired more space in other parts of the newspaper. From the beginning, this section proved to be very popular and therefore profitable to newspaper owners, who in turn grew increasingly conscious of the importance of entertaining readers. If we look at some of the major newspapers of the time, we can further grasp the subtle complexities of this transition.[14] The mainstream *Jornal do Commercio* adopted this innovation in the late 1830s, demarcating the lower front page and naming the new section Folhetim, a free translation of *feuilleton*. Over time, it became a section dedicated to the publication of serialized novels, sometimes sharing space with weekly or bi-weekly crônicas. Whether titled Variedades or Folhetim, these new sections revolutionized news reporting in Brazil.[15] Both are key primary sources for studying nineteenth-century Brazil, due to the genre's concern with quotidian aspects of Brazilian society.

Scholarship on Crônicas

Most of the analysis of crônicas focuses on notable cronistas, such as Machado de Assis and José de Alencar, who are most famous for their fictional works. As a result, studies that emphasize marginal and forgotten authors remain relatively scarce. However, scholars' interest in the work of canonical authors as cronistas has been much smaller than the interest in their novels, poems, or short stories. It was not until the late twentieth century that literary critics started to pay careful attention to these authors' newspaper productions, especially crônicas. Lúcia Granja argues that one of the reasons for this lack of interest in crônicas was that the authors themselves did not make any effort to publish their newspaper texts in edited volumes, judging crônicas a minor genre not meant to be published outside the periodical press. The lack of quality editions also helps in understanding why scholars ignored the subject for so long.[16] Recently, a massive number of new sources has become available online through the Hemeroteca Digital Brasileira. This new research tool, easily accessed all over the world, has dramatically changed research topics, methodological approaches, and, more broadly, the traditional forms of historiographical production. It has enabled scholars in diverse fields to discover crônicas as valuable primary sources.

John Gledson's 1986 work on Machado de Assis was one of the first efforts to recover crônicas' importance. This text opened the eyes of scholars of Brazilian literature who could perceive the richness of these texts as well as the silences around them. The fact that Gledson himself had to justify to his readers the importance of this newspaper literary production demonstrates that the value of studying these forgotten articles was far from obvious. Gledson's work on Machado was part of an awakening of interest for the subject.[17]

Literary critics such as Marlyse Meyer, Antonio Cândido, and Flora Sussekind participated in a joint effort to recover and discuss what they considered an important portion of Brazilian literature, hidden in old periodicals and forgotten in the past. After analyzing novels, poems, and short stories by canonical Brazilian authors, they turned to their crônicas, searching for links between these texts and their masterpieces.[18] In the 1992 edited volume *A crônica: o gênero, sua fixação e suas transformações no Brasil* (Crônicas: The genre, its establishment, and its transformation in Brazil), the notable Brazilian critic Antonio Cândido defines "crônicas" as a "step toward literature." He argues that they were unpretentious texts aiming to fit into daily life. In his opinion, these texts were not intended for posterity and were therefore a short-lived genre. Cândido and most of the authors in his edited volume were especially concerned with twentieth-century crônicas, as they shared the view that crônicas had only become consolidated as a national genre in the 1930s. Other authors in the book focused on crônicas in the late nineteenth century and the beginning of the twentieth century. Few scholars in the volume went so far as to consider the genre's arrival in Brazil and its nineteenth-century development.[19]

Antonio Cândido judges crônicas a "minor genre," texts made for ephemeral consumption in the daily press. They were not quite literature, in his view, but they were on the way. He also considers crônicas a uniquely Brazilian genre due to their originality and adaptability. Crônicas discussed serious topics through apparently trivial dialogue. For Meyer as well, crônicas were not a genre per se. In her opinion, crônicas were part of newspaper texts. The fact that they emerged from ordinary dialogues and street conversations meant that they cannot be considered a literary genre. Telê Lopez, also a contributor to Cândido's volume, regards crônicas as the middle ground between fiction and journalism, a definition frequently repeated since then.[20]

The search for crônicas by great authors guided the first efforts of scholars interested in the genre. In *Machado de Assis: ficção e história* (Machado de Assis: fiction and history), John Gledson introduces the important place that the genre held in uncovering and understanding Machado de Assis's ideas about his time; Gledson argues that crônicas are particularly relevant for interpreting Machado's other literary works and emphasizes Machado's dialogical narrative with his readers as one of his crônicas' most relevant features, a style that also appears in his fiction.²¹

Nevertheless, Gledson denies the literary features of crônicas and argues that the ambiguities of Machado's narratives should be interpreted as the author's irony. Gledson refuses to see crônicas as literature in which fictional creation plays an important role. He argues against the idea that crônicas possessed a fictional narrator, but acknowledges the possibility of the creation of a crônica persona. He believes that a single crônica possessed a specific fictional narrator, but he denies that an entire series was united under one narrative voice. Gledson interprets crônicas as a collection of independent texts. He acknowledges a literary intention in the crônicas, but his interpretation centers on the political debates that "Machado" depicted in his texts.²²

In addition to literary critics, historians also became interested in studying crônicas. Margarida de Souza Neves, for example, calls attention to the historical value of crônicas, arguing that they not only played a significant role in notable authors' literary production, but they also are important primary sources for studying nineteenth- and twentieth-century Brazilian daily life. In her view, crônicas reoriented contemporary readers to the relationship between fiction and history. She argues that crônicas were multilayered texts that expressed "the spirit of an era" and therefore shed light on daily life in Brazil.²³

Leonardo Pereira followed Neves's suggestions and employed nineteenth-century newspaper crônicas as primary sources for examining carnival in Rio de Janeiro. Pereira's interpretation of Machado de Assis's series "Bons dias!" (1888–1889) diverges substantially from John Gledson's analysis. Pereira considers Policarpo, the "Bons dias!" narrator's pseudonym, to be a fictional figure and not Machado de Assis himself. Instead, Pereira views Policarpo as a character in the series who intervenes coherently in discussions of then controversial issues. While Pereira's interpretation of "Bons dias!" did not convince John Gledson (who kept to his opinion that Machado's series lacks a fictional narrator and coherence throughout the texts), Pereira's interpretation opened up a new tradition in the analysis of crônicas, at least among social historians of literature and the press.²⁴

Historians Sidney Chalhoub, Margarida Neves, and Leonardo Pereira offer new insights into the genre's interpretation and definition from a social history perspective.²⁵ They criticize Cândido's definition as well as other literary critics like Gledson for considering crônicas the "bastard daughter" of literary art, because their authors did not write for posterity or seek transcendence. Gledson and Cândido claim that crônicas do not have the narrative elaboration of novels, poems, or short stories but are a mix of journalism and literature that resulted in unpretentious and dated texts. According to this view, cronistas faced the unpredictability and short deadlines of newspaper publication and so their crônicas lacked the refinement and creativity that true literary texts possess.[26]

According to Chalhoub, Neves, and Pereira, Cândido's and Gledson's ideas on crônicas ignore most of the ways that authors produced literature in nineteenth-century Brazil. Many of Brazil's greatest authors wrote their masterpieces and published them first in serialized newspaper versions, and only later issued them as a single volume. Thus, writers also had deadlines to publish novels, short stories, and poems, just as they did for crônicas. Crônicas were produced under conditions that were similar to those of other literary works and should be interpreted accordingly, argue Chalhoub and his colleagues, undermining arguments that depict crônicas as a minor genre.[27]

From the 1850s, crônicas were among the most important forms of literary production in the Brazilian press. Despite the different formulas developed by cronistas, texts in the genre share similar features. One of the most important characteristics is that cronistas created profiles for their series. Therefore, instead of analyzing them as individual texts, interpreters should pay attention to the development of crônicas as a whole. Besides engaging in the discussions of their times, authors sharpened their rhetoric and style, looking to meet the literary demands of their craft.[28] Cronistas carefully constructed series profiles that defined a theme for their crônicas and created a specific point of view for the narrative, delimiting their writing style. In general, these features were presented as a program or project in the first crônica of the series, even when the narrator claimed to have no plan at all. Thus, the first crônica in a series served as a guide for readers, orienting them to the sequence of texts to come.[29]

Social historians of literature such as Chalhoub, Pereira, Neves, and more recently Ana Flávia Ramos believe that, as they planned their crônicas, writers created pseudonyms not to hide their identity but rather to create character narrators or fictional narrators. Pseudonyms were a fundamental part of making crônicas as literary pieces. The choice of the pseudonym itself was usually a clear reference to the narrator's opinion and to the series' themes. Accordingly, to interpret crônicas, scholars must necessarily go back to newspapers and understand the context of production as well as dialogue with other newspapers or literary or art pieces. The indeterminate circumstances under which these texts were written is another important aspect. The unpredictability of daily life and the unexpected responses of readers played a major role in these texts' construction. The genre developed in the press itself, and crônicas were responsible for transforming nineteenth-century newspapers into a more attractive form of media that was responsive to the growing role and taste of the public reader. Newspaper audiences participated in the making of crônicas with their feedback through letters that were sometimes published in response to the crônicas.[30]

Certainly, Machado de Assis has received the lion's share of attention from scholars concerned with nineteenth-century crônicas. Scholars from the fields of history and literature dedicate much of their effort to canonical authors such as Alencar and Machado de Assis, giving special attention to their works during the final decades of the empire when the genre solidified its format. Nevertheless, there is still much to be explored in the Brazilian press, ranging from unknown authors—including female and Black writers—to smaller newspapers and magazines, as well as the use of crônicas as primary sources for the study of contemporary topics.

The First Crônicas

In 1836, editor and cronista Justiniano José da Rocha founded *O Cronista* in Rio de Janeiro, directly referencing the meaning that chronique had acquired in France in the early nineteenth century. Justiniano explained his new invention to readers:

> If by chance, my friend and reader, you know French, and when you have in your hands a French newspaper, when you anxiously unfold the long pages of the newspaper, you must be ingenuous, you shall confess, what are your eyes looking for? ... Usually in the lower part of the page, a thick and long black line stands out to your inquiring look, below this line, upper-case letters announce FEUILLETON, it emerges in a radiant, fascinating, charming way. Thus, you heave a sigh of satisfaction—your preferred FEUILLETON is placed apart, is carefully reserved to be read slowly, to be savored with pleasure, like a dessert in your reading feast.[31]

At that time, Justiniano perceived the crônica to be a distinct section dedicated to particular subjects like administration (Crônica Administrativa) or parliamentary debates (Crônica Parlamentar), to quote typical headings from his newspaper. Justiniano dubbed his delectable feuilleton as the "Folhazinha," a name that did not last long and later assumed its free French translation as folhetim. Nonetheless, the idea of the newborn crônica genre was already there, although temporarily under another name: "We need to provide for our population the primary need of modern civilization—the desire for reading... that takes one's mind off the tasks of life, the annoyances of work, the tedium of leisure, this is what we aim for, this is what we hope to deliver."[32] This was probably one of the first articles in the Brazilian press that both announced the new newspaper section (folhazinha or feuilleton) and defended a new type of journalism concerned with leisure and entertainment as well as with journalists' civilizational mission. The lower front page developed into a place for the free expression of ideas only permitted in this part of the newspaper, a fundamental space for the making of Brazilian press freedom.[33]

In *O Cronista*, the folhazinha became a place in which Justiniano spread the conservative ideas that also appeared in the newspaper's other articles, criticizing liberal values and institutions such as liberty, equality, the National Guard, and the jury. In addition to this major political focus, Justiniano included discussions about aesthetic options at a time when Romanticism was beginning to thrive in Brazil. Their criticism of romantic plays, for instance, related to their wider political view of the country.[34]

As the example of *O Cronista* demonstrates, in the late 1830s, the term *crônica* did not yet specifically refer to the crônica genre. Instead, crônicas described articles dedicated to a particular subject that were linked to what Justiniano termed "our material life." The folhazinha was a place for information, imagination, and entertainment, representing an early example of what later became the genre.[35]

In 1839, the *Jornal do Commercio* inaugurated its Feuilleton section with the publication of a French novel. The following year, the *Diário do Rio de Janeiro* adopted the new section as well, first under the title of Apêndice (Appendix) and later Folhetim. Similar innovations appeared in other major newspapers that started to devote separate sections to entertainment, thereby reaching a larger spectrum of readers. In the folhetim, novels shared the lower front page with weekly or biweekly theater and opera reviews. Once a week or twice per month, pieces on the latest theatrical performances or novelties in the theater or opera were printed. By the 1840s, crônicas continued to refer to a particular theme, but they were slowly shifting their focus to entertainment.[36]

The genre gained strength with Luiz Carlos Martins Pena's 1846–1847 "A Semana Lírica" (The Opera Weekly) in the *Jornal do Commercio*. Martins Pena commented on operas and musical spectacles, as he explained in early 1847: "When we write our folhetim, we have the single purpose of communicating to the audience which operas went on stage and how they were performed. Naturally, a critique must occupy the majority of our writings."[37] Martins Pena proclaimed his objectivity as an author and suggested that subjective critiques would only be a minor part of the weekly section.[38] Despite this disclaimer, Martins Pena's objectivity gradually assumed a more critical tone on performances, the administrative feuds within opera companies, the habits and mores of opera audiences, and the social life of the performing arts scene. He filled his prose with humor and transitioned from a straightforward and objective observer to an agent of and participant in the city's cultural life. As the case of Martins Pena's crônicas suggests, in the late 1840s, folhetim authors focused on one particular subject at a time. This dialogue-based, opinion-heavy narration was full of subjectivity and humor, with the purpose of entertaining readers while also catering to the tastes of an elite opera-going audience.[39]

Already in the 1840s, folhetins started to cover different topics. They moved away from articles dedicated to a single subject like "A Semana Lírica" and incorporated a variety of themes. By the 1850s, the genre was fully developed in Brazil, as articles in the section addressed daily events and recent news in a style that combined opinion, subjectivity, critique, and humor in a single narrative.[40]

Some scholars consider José de Alencar to be one of the most important names in the development of the crônica genre in the 1850s.[41] He is the author of "Ao correr da pena" (At the whim of the pen), a series published in Rio de Janeiro's *Correio Mercantil* between September 1854 and July 1855. While he was neither the first nor the only one to write crônicas at the time, he was among the set of authors who started writing about different subjects in one text. He described his role as a "folhetinista" (or cronista) in the following passage:

> To compel a man to follow all of the events, to move from pleasantries to a serious matter . . . to transform the writer into a hummingbird zigzagging back and forth, and to sop up the nectar, the grace, the salt, and the spirit that must necessarily accompany the essence of any fact![42]

The image of a hummingbird, flying from one theme to another in a single narrative, represents the cronista's work, a metaphor originally invoked by

French authors. The title reinforces the image of a free-flowing writer who, like a hummingbird, moves from flower to flower, going wherever his pen leads him.[43]

One of the subjects that Alencar's hummingbird chose was the art of crônica writing itself. Elucidating the construction and composition of a text was one of his habits and common to other cronistas of the 1850s. The strategic use of such metanarratives could also help authors meet the exact number of lines that they were expected to deliver to the editor: sometimes the article was shortened due to lack of space in the newspaper, or the font size was expanded as a space filler. In both cases, such digressions added to the fictional dimensions of crônica writing and are important sources for the study of the genre.[44]

In addition to digressions, cronistas such as Alencar progressively explored a form of dialogue within their narratives. Not only did they describe their own work as authors, but they also engaged in conversation with a fictional reader—often a female—which became a stylistic fashion for folhetins. Employing an epistolary style, Alencar's crônicas created an intimacy with readers that was based on actual dialogue. It was very common for readers to write to the newspaper with comments or complaints about the crônicas. The editors even published some of these letters and the cronistas sometimes made it a point to address them in their texts. This dialogical style became a defining characteristic of crônica writing in midcentury Brazil and it may be explored by scholars who want to deepen their knowledge of readerships.[45] This dialogical aspect also contributed to the genre's increasing fictionalization.

The folhetim and its crônicas appeared not only in mainstream newspapers such as *Diário do Rio de Janeiro* but also in smaller weekly, biweekly, or monthly periodicals. In general, these newspapers were not restricted to politics; rather, they explored other subjects such as social life, literature, and the lives of women, only occasionally addressing current events. These smaller periodicals played a considerable role in the genre's popularization. Through those publications, the term *crônica* started to be used more frequently to describe this new genre, although it was still used interchangeably with *folhetim*.[46]

The weekly *Jornal das Senhoras* (Ladies' Journal, 1852–1855) is an example of a smaller newspaper that published crônicas. Most of its articles discussed themes like women's emancipation, the duties of mothers and wives, and the social life of balls and concerts. Upper-class female readers from Brazilian families interested in entertainment and instruction made up the newspaper's primary audience. In 1852, a female cronista named "Belona," likely a pseudonym, brought her supposed reader into her "Crônica dos Salões" (Parlor chronicle) every other week:

> This, we shall reconcile now, my dear female reader, in this very moment, do you agree? (...) Very well, then, I will tell you the reason for my absence last Sunday, and you shall see in your soul and consciousness if I did not deserve your excuses.[47]

In addition to thus dialoguing with readers, Belona also divulged her writing process. For example, she explained how she made use of her doorman, turning him into an assistant who collected stories in the streets of Rio de Janeiro.[48] Social norms of the time dictated that upper-class women in Brazil avoid fraternizing in the streets and involving themselves in public conversations, so Belona gave the doorman another task:

> From now on, you must wander through the streets of the city whenever and how you want: stop, talk, listen, pay attention to everything, but nobody shall suspect you, pay attention, Santos! Later, you shall come back at your whim and tell me everything you saw and heard during the day.[49]

Belona's subjectivity and conversational style indicates that this aspect of the crônica genre had had gained ground and was becoming consolidated.[50] In another newspaper's crônica, the narrator, Varela, states:

> I must clear my conscience to you, the reader. The author behind these entries, the sharp-witted Alfredo Cramer, to whom you owe [this column], is absent, and only for this reason did I dare to take his place and attempt to test your patience with my unsalted and unflavored sentences, because I took on the purpose of opposing your civilized habits through the exposition of my retrograde ideas.[51]

In this case, the pseudonym suggests the development of a style of narration that helped to distinguish between the ideas of the narrator Smarra and those of the author Varela. The usage of pseudonyms came to characterize crônicas, especially in the later decades of the empire, adding an extra literary layer to the genre.[52]

Between 1861 and 1864, *Semana Ilustrada* published a collectively authored series titled "Crônicas do Dr. Semana" (Dr. Weekly's chronicles) (on *Semana Ilustrada*, see Arnaldo Lucas Pires Junior's chapter). The pseudonym spoke to the character's main function of commenting on the week's major events. In this series, different authors had to write in the same style to create the voice of the fictional narrator. One of the series' authors was Machado de Assis, who at that time had already authored crônicas in a variety of newspapers. Nevertheless, it seems that it was through his work in "Crônicas do Dr. Semana" that he started seeing the value of using pseudonyms in the fictional elaboration of character-narrations.[53]

Before "Crônicas do Dr. Semana," Machado de Assis had already written three crônica series, making his debut as a folhetinista in 1859. He enjoyed a forty-year career writing crônicas and is considered by many scholars to be the most significant cronista in Brazil. Building on previous crônicas, Machado discussed his crônica writing in his first series:

> The folhetinista (cronista) is the fusion of the pleasant and the useful, the curious and unique birth of the serious in partnership with the frivolous.... The entire world belongs to the folhetinista, even politics.[54]

This excerpt is part of a short series titled "Aquarelas" (Watercolors) published in *O Espelho* in 1859. In it, Machado de Assis revealed his new-found objective of writing frivolous prose about any topic in society, including the more serious realm of politics. In addition to "Aquarelas," during the 1860s, Machado wrote two different series in the mainstream liberal newspaper, the *Diário do Rio de Janeiro*, along with a collaboration in the smaller periodical, *O Futuro*. However, it seems that it was with Dr. Semana that he became more conscious of the fictional and literary possibilities of the genre. As a cronista, Machado de Assis incorporated several innovations into the genre, such as the creation of complex character-narrators and the development of a crônica series as a coherent literary narrative, just to name a few novelties. His career continued and expanded in the following decades and scholars agree that his contributions to and transformation of the genre in the 1860s were vital to the establishment of crônicas as both a literary and a journalistic form.[55]

Much more could be said about the period between the arrival of crônicas in Brazil in the 1830s and the genre's early development. As the analysis of these few crônicas and their authors demonstrates, crônicas moved from the political discussions found in Justiniano's writings—from a single topic like theater or opera to acquire a hummingbird-like style that combined diverse subjects into a single narrative. In smaller newspapers, the genre often depended on the topic of the periodical, but their diversity demonstrated that crônica-style texts were very effective at holding readers' attention. Crônicas developed a fictional tone over time, especially with the rise of dialogical and metanarrative styles, along with the creation of pseudonyms of character-narrators. As these examples show, by the end of the empire, crônicas had consolidated into a distinct genre and became a key feature of Brazilian newspapers. The genre acquired increasing doses of fictional elements, but it remains an important source for scholars interested in nineteenth-century Brazilian history, literature, and culture.

Late Nineteenth-Century Crônicas

The Brazilian press went through significant changes after the mid-1870s. Newspapers increasingly became commercially profitable enterprises that, unlike their predecessors, amassed a sufficient subscriber base to stay afloat, a process of massification in the press. The expansion of railroads and the installation of telegraph networks in 1874 were factors that helped the consolidation of newspapers as representative of the modernizing process. Readers were looking for impartial information and explanations about the nation's movement toward modernity.[56] In this context, crônicas remained an important section in the major newspapers and in turn helped to further their popularization. Readers consumed crônicas, along with other newspaper sections, with the hope of achieving a better understanding of the changes to modern society. At the same time, the creative possibilities for cronistas expanded and the genre became increasingly more literary and fictional.[57]

As an example of these changes, the collectively authored "Balas de Estalo" crônica (the title may be loosely translated as Blank Cartridges), published between 1883 and 1886 in Rio de Janeiro's *Gazeta de Notícias*, enjoyed great success. Different authors took turns discussing a variety of news, offering different and, most important, clashing perspectives. Nevertheless, politics and humor were vital features that held the series' crônicas together. "Balas" authors used several pseudonyms and one author may have been responsible for more than one fictional narrator. Authorship and the character-narrator were again subject to experimental writing: the series started with five different narrators and, after the confirmation of its success, the editor raised the number to ten. The political agenda of the group centered on the decline of imperial institutions such as slavery, the Catholic Church, and the monarchy.

By discussing political events in a broad context, they aimed to encourage debate about politics. Each narrator engaged a particular perspective that re-created relevant social issues of the day.[58]

"Balas de Estalo" reveals the importance that the genre assumed in the late empire. Crônicas not only brought together important authors, intellectuals, and journalists, but also became an indispensable section of newspapers and thus editors' priority. For writers, crônicas offered a way to make a living through a regular paid activity, and the means to form an audience and to experiment with fiction on a daily (or at least weekly) basis. The creation of individual and collective fictional narrators who embodied particular features and styles of prose testifies to this creative exploration.[59]

In the 1870s and 1880s, Machado de Assis published several crônica series in mainstream newspapers and in weekly and monthly periodicals. As one of the most important and restless authors of the period, he developed fictional narrators for each series that underscore the genre's literary possibilities. In general, the first crônica of a new series announced what to expect from the upcoming crônicas and from its narrator, demarcating themes and shaping points of view. The choice of pseudonym and title foreshadowed what would come in each text. Even though the themes covered in crônicas were always at the mercy of daily events and news, Machado de Assis directed the narrative, maintaining a set of themes in the style and voice of the fictional narrator. The creative process that Machado de Assis and other authors employed in developing their fictional narrators differed little from that of novelists.[60]

In the 1880s, Machado de Assis took a further step as cronista by abandoning prose and creating an entire series in rhymed verses. The "Gazeta de Holanda," the series that opened this chapter, was composed of forty-eight crônicas published between 1886 and 1888 in the *Gazeta de Notícias*. He wrote under the pseudonym Malvolio, a character from Shakespeare's *The Twelfth Night*.[61] The series title was inspired by "Les Gazettes de Hollande," described in Pierre Larousse's *Grand dictionnaire universel du XIXe siècle* (1872) as newspapers or pamphlets published in Amsterdam and Leiden by French refugees in the seventeenth and eighteenth centuries. Readers sought out these gazettes to read scandalmongering and calumnious texts.[62] Machado's "Gazeta de Holanda" had another historical reference in its epigraph: "There you have what is said about me in the *Gazette de Hollande*," the opening refrain of all crônicas in the series. The phrase originated in an operetta by Jacques Offenbach, Henri Meilhac, and

Ludovic Halévy, *La Grande Duchesse de Gérolstein*, first presented in Paris in 1867. The operetta later met with great success in Rio de Janeiro. It tells the story of a charmless prince engaged to a lascivious duchess; preferring the company of uniformed military men, she postpones the wedding day as long as she can. The prince then complains to his fiancée about being a victim of general mockery by using the phrase that Machado de Assis quoted.[63] His sources of inspiration demonstrate that crônicas had great literary elaboration, despite the fact they were meant for daily consumption and were not meant to endure.

Born from diverse literary influences, Malvolio was also always looking for the best way to make money and to gain the upper hand, a drive founded in the nineteenth-century belief that, in life, the strongest and smartest were winners. Malvolio, who appears to be a follower of Social Darwinism, believed in and followed the law of survival of the fittest, a frequent topic of Machado de Assis's literature that was one of the most important ideologies of Brazilian society in the second half of the nineteenth century. He played with Malvolio by constructing verses about bizarre situations in which Malvolio often defended an absurd point of view.[64] For instance, in the first crônica of the series, Malvolio discusses the case of two young enslaved women who were severely beaten by their female master. The case caused a scandal in Rio de Janeiro and mobilized abolitionists; Joaquim Nabuco organized a procession with the two girls to publicly demonstrate their wounds. The case went to court and so many people followed the trial that it demonstrated the need for a new building capable of accommodating the eager spectators. Malvolio speculated that if a new building were indeed constructed, the two enslaved women would have to be celebrated for their contribution to architecture.[65] He shares his illogical hypothesis:

> Example: To read that the solution is
> To construct a new building
> For the jury;—colonnades,
> A vast, Greek frontispiece.
> And that this bizarre idea
> Was born right now, now,
> When it went to trial
> Like a distinguished lady;
> When the swell of people

Was such, that the judge
Unrestrained, had to
Ask to borrow soap;
I told myself:—how good it was
That Joaninha died
From a chest disease,
That Eduarda went blind.
Only in this way could we have a building
For the trial without anything else;
It was not death, it was a remedy;
It was life, it was not a tragedy.
...
Therefore, if one or the other female slaves
Fought without feeling,
The reason for such great brave action
Was to build a monument.
At this point, I lay ink on the final period
And say good-bye in the point
Each new drop of ink,
Is not a period, it is a post period.[66]

The verses of the "Gazeta de Holanda" reveal Machado de Assis's craft as a cronista. The careful choice of names for the narrator and for the series reveals the inextricable process of literary creation that marked crônicas as a genre. The making of Malvolio, for example, is similar to the construction of the fictional characters in Machado's novels or short stories. However, the "Gazeta de Holanda" also reveals the differences between crônicas and other literary genres. Crônicas need to be placed in their context and in relation to the format in which they appeared (edition, number, and page), because they belonged to a literary style that more than any other cannot be understood or interpreted apart from its own time, place, and process of production. Simply put, without the press, there are no crônicas. The mutual dependency between crônicas and newspapers is fundamental for a better understanding of the genre. For more than a year, Machado de Assis gave life to the clumsy narrator Malvolio, commenting on the most important or bizarre events from the news with a particularly humorous and cynical eye. During this process, he challenged the boundaries between literature and news, fiction and nonfiction.

As the "Gazeta de Holanda" demonstrates, the genre attained a new status in the fictional elaboration of characters, narrators, and narratives that distinguished it from earlier iterations of the genre. In the late 1880s, crônicas became a genre in which the fictionalization of daily life provided a way for writers to intervene in society with humor and irony, a trend that helped editors to sell more copies of their newspapers. Crônicas allowed authors to build their audiences and keep them entertained. Several scholars describe crônicas as a genre responsible for helping readers to better perceive the world and its transformations, a task Malvolio seems to perform in a backward fashion. Flora Sussekind rightly points out that crônicas followed the professionalization of journalism, the construction of a large audience, and the incorporation of literary production into the press.[67]

Despite the diverging opinions among scholars who study crônicas, all agree that they are a rich, important source of research material for the study of Brazilian literature, history, and society. The birth of crônicas in Brazil was related to the development of the press during the empire, not only because famous nineteenth-century Brazilian authors found these newspapers to be useful outlets for their literary creations, but also because, rather than a minor genre, crônicas were a form of literature in their own right. The genre was the result of literary experimentation, subjectivity, and referential information that introduced a new way of creating journalism. Crônicas provide indispensable source material for scholars interested in gauging the social, political, and literary transformations of imperial Brazil and, indeed, the nineteenth-century Atlantic World.

Although crônicas were originally a genre imported from France, they were transformed upon their arrival in Brazil. The increasing importance of crônicas for Brazilian newspapers was accompanied by the growing demand of authors and readers for the genre's fictionalization. From the 1830s to the late century, cronistas gained space and importance in Brazilian newspapers, seducing audiences with their mix of news and fiction, referential arguments, and literary prose. By pleasing readers, writers built their literary careers and developed crônicas into a literary genre in which fiction played an essential role. As a result, crônicas became one of the most important newspaper genres, today serving as a gateway to exploring and understanding nineteenth-century Brazilian society and culture.

Notes

1. "Gazeta de Holanda," *GN*, November 1, 1886.
2. "Gazeta de Holanda," *GN*, November 1, 1886.
3. "Gazeta de Holanda," *GN*, December 6, 1886.
4. "Gazeta de Holanda," *GN*, November 1, 1886.
5. "Gazeta de Holanda," *GN*, November 20, 1886.
6. Chalhoub, "Crônica"; Paixão, "Elementos," 23; "Gazeta de Holanda," *GN*, December 6, 1886.
7. Chalhoub and Pereira, eds., *História*.
8. Gallagher, "Rise."
9. Vaillant, "Crônica."
10. Meyer, "Voláteis," 96; Thérenty, "Pour une histoire," 625–33; Thérenty, "Vies"; Thérenty, "Crónica."
11. M. Soares, *Crônica*, 11–13.
12. Cooper-Richet, "Paris"; Paixão, "Elementos," 25–30; M. Soares, *Crônica*, 12–13.
13. Meyer, *Folhetim*, 57.
14. Paixão, "Elementos," 23–24; M. Soares, *Crônica*, 97.
15. Cano, "Justiniano José da Rocha," 24.
16. Granja, "Das páginas," 387.
17. Gledson, *Machado de Assis*; Granja, "Das páginas."
18. Cândido, *Crônica*.
19. Cândido, "Vida."
20. Lopez, "Crônica," 167.
21. Gledson, "Introdução," in *Semana*, 12; Granja, "Das páginas."
22. Gledson, "Introdução," in *Semana*; Gledson, "Introdução," in *Bons dias!*
23. M. Neves, "Escrita do tempo," 76.
24. Chalhoub, "John Gledson"; Pereira, *Carnaval*.
25. Chalhoub, Neves, and Pereira, *História*.
26. Chalhoub, Neves, and Pereira, "Apresentação."
27. Chalhoub, Neves, and Pereira, "Apresentação."
28. Chalhoub, Neves, and Pereira, "Apresentação."
29. Chalhoub, Neves, and Pereira, "Apresentação."
30. Chalhoub, Neves, and Pereira, "Apresentação," 14, 16; Chalhoub, "Crônica"; Ramos, *Máscaras*.
31. Quoted in Cano, "Justiniano José da Rocha," 23.
32. Quoted in Cano, "Justiniano José da Rocha," 23.
33. Cano, "Justiniano José da Rocha," 24–25.
34. Cano, "Justiniano José da Rocha."

35. Cano, "Justiniano José da Rocha"; M. Soares, *Crônica*, 139–41.
36. M. Soares, *Crônica*, 143–45.
37. "Folhetim," *JC*, January 14, 1847.
38. M. Soares, *Crônica*, 145.
39. M. Soares, *Crônica*, 147–48.
40. M. Soares, *Crônica*, 147–48
41. M. Soares, *Crônica*, 148.
42. Quoted in M. Soares, *Crônica*, 148.
43. M. Soares, *Crônica*, 148; Paixão, "Elementos," 172; Granja, "Crônica"; M. Soares, *Crônica*, 206, 211.
44. M. Soares, *Crônica*, 148.
45. M. Soares, *Crônica*.
46. M. Soares, *Crônica*, 164–65.
47. Quoted in M. Soares, *Crônica*, 173.
48. Quoted in M. Soares, *Crônica*, 173.
49. Quoted in M. Soares, *Crônica*, 173.
50. M. Soares, *Crônica*, 174.
51. Quoted in Paixão, "Elementos," 211.
52. Paixão, "Elementos," 211.
53. Granja, *Machado de Assis*, 15; Cavallini, "Monumento," 300.
54. Quoted in M. Soares, *Crônica*, 32.
55. Pereira, "Introdução"; Granja, *Machado de Assis*; Cavallini, "Monumento," 326.
56. Pereira, *Carnaval*, 39; Ramos, "'Balas de Estalo,'" 152.
57. Ramos, "'Balas de Estalo,'" 151–70.
58. Ramos, "Política."
59. Ramos, "Política"; Ramos, "'Balas de Estalo.'"
60. Pereira, "Introdução," 9–57; Chalhoub, "Crônica"; Ramos, *Máscaras*, 54–55.
61. Chalhoub, "Crônica," 240–41.
62. Quoted in Chalhoub, "Crônica," 240–41.
63. On this operetta, see http://imslp.org/wiki/La_Grande-Duchesse_de _G%C3%A9rolstein_(Offenbach,_Jacques). The performance occurred between 1867 and 1877, because the Alcazar Lyrique Theater, opened in 1859, changed its name in 1877, http://www.ctac.gov.br/centrohistorico/teatroXperiodo.asp ?cod=75&cdP=19&tipo=Identificacao (accessed December 23, 2017). See also Chalhoub, "Crônica," 240–41.
64. "Gazeta de Holanda," *GN*, December 6, 1886; Chalhoub, "Crônica," 240–41.
65. Chalhoub, "Crônica," 240–41; Chalhoub, "John Gledson," 110–15.
66. "Gazeta de Holanda," *GN*, November 1, 1886.
67. M. Neves, "Escrita do tempo," 76.

Matthew Nestler and Zephyr Frank

SIX   "FOR RENT" AND "FOR SALE"
Newspapers, Advertising, Property, and Markets in Rio de Janeiro, 1820s–1890s

In nineteenth-century Rio de Janeiro, newspapers helped to convey information and to expand the market for the rent or sale of real estate and enslaved persons. By the 1830s, rental and sales notices appear naturalized and ubiquitous, covering whole pages with the words *alugar* and *vender, aluga-se* and *vende-se, aluguéis* and *vendas* (all variations of, respectively, *for rent* and *for sale*). Research in the Hemeroteca Digital Brasileira (HDB) database shows that this predominance emerged over time and was not strongly present at the birth of the newsprint revolution in Brazil's capital. Thus, something that was "there"—in the sense that people paid other people for the temporary or permanent use of property or other people held as slaves—became something else. The act of renting, buying, and selling was transformed into a mediated practice that grew in scope and intensity and thereby helped to change the size of markets, the understanding of the uses of property, and the sense of the city itself as a space filled with "rentable" and "sellable" things and people. Moreover, individuals increasingly began to see themselves as property owners, advertisers, and people with attributes that could be expressed in the language of advertising. As a first step in our analysis, we explore the underlying logic behind the practice of newspaper advertisements with an emphasis on those ads that involved rents and sales in what we will call the classified section of the newspaper.[1]

Advertising, Rents, Sales, and Property: Theoretical Considerations

What are the specific features of newspapers as media in the context of a nineteenth-century city, and what is the relationship between newspapers and the creating and shaping of markets?[2] As sociologist Sarah Quinn puts it, media "influence[s] general perceptions, in part by developing and disseminating the frames with which people make sense of social practices."[3] In the nineteenth century, newspapers were a key medium through which these processes occurred.[4] The newspapers thus did more than merely make information available to a wider public—they also helped to create new frames for social and economic behavior. Of course, they did more than this, for instance in the political and cultural spheres, as other chapters in this volume show, but our focus is on the frames relating to market activity.

Before newspapers, the frames for property rentals and sales were constructed through social interactions, which formed the foundation of economic behavior. As Karl Polanyi argues, "the economic system is, in effect, a mere function of social organization," which means that economic relationships (e.g., markets) originate in society.[5] In other words, the market for rent or sale of property is a reflection of social processes and as such contains normative features. The point of these observations with regards to newspapers in nineteenth-century Rio de Janeiro is (1) to underscore that a preexisting set of practices and norms relating to rent and sales existed before the rise of the newspaper and that these likely left their imprint on the newly mediated market conjured up by print advertising; and (2) to suggest that the newspapers themselves should be seen as both adapting to existing frames of reference and also helping to create new ones.

For advertising to work, the markets for rent and sales must be governed by a set of normative assumptions, which, by extension, may enter into the wording of ad copy (which we will show later). Over time, and in the aggregate sense, it appears that these ideas coalesced into routine scripts that were legible and credible for the consuming audience. Ads with unfair prices or flawed descriptions certainly existed, but the quantity and proximity of ads generated a normative equilibrium by producing a constrained set of possible words and categories. If property owners wished to fudge the facts, they would have to do this within a narrow range of possible vocabulary. Description itself bore the imprint of wider social forces. Most striking, we see the social construction of slavery in market terms, from the perspective of slaveholders, manifest in the injection of qualitative claims referring to the character and attributes of enslaved people.[6]

Having outlined these considerations with respect to the social and normative features of markets and newspaper advertisements, we now turn to the core issue at hand. According to one established theory, the point of newspaper advertising is to convey information to consumers. Newspaper classified advertising fits well in this theoretical frame: it offers information to a wide set of media consumers at a very low marginal cost.[7]

We argue that classified advertisements in newspapers are best understood in this framework of information. According to Bagwell and Ramey's 1993 study of advertising, a simple three-stage game model can capture the underlying process involved in classified ads in newspapers. The first move in the game is made by the owner of property (P), who must decide whether to enter the game and place an advertisement. The second move is taken when the prospective renter or purchaser (R) scans the newspaper looking at the advertisements and decides to follow up on a particular placement. Here, by definition, it is only possible for R to visit one P at a time. P has paid to enter the game and to reach R. The third and final move in the game happens when P and R meet in person and decide whether to conclude the transaction.[8]

The utility of this advertising arises from at least two theoretical directions. First, because houses and enslaved people are heterogeneous by nature, a match-products-to-buyers effect is likely to be found.[9] For example, a given consumer may wish to purchase a particular kind of house, of a specific size and general location, and information conveyed in newspaper ads can help match these preferences to the seller with the best-fitting house on the market. Second, and especially in advertisements relating to enslaved persons, *qualitative* information was also often conveyed as a preliminary warrant of quality and as an aid in further matching preferences. This qualitative effect may also involve yet another dimension of advertising—the persuasive. It is possible that claims of quality will increase levels of demand and willingness to pay.

It is important to remember that such an economic explanation of advertising, based on the concept of utility, depends upon the existence of alternative modes of economic transactions. In this case, the two alternative options were the predominant means of carrying out economic transactions before newspapers appeared en masse—by word of mouth or at organized city fairs. Though these two options induced economic activity for centuries, they were limited by at least two important constraints, which can be translated into costs to weigh against the alternative. First, the geographic area covered would be limited, thereby restricting the total number of potential renters or buyers. Word-of-mouth suffered from the limitations in the reach of one's social network, and the city fairs, being in one specific location, restricted the number of people who could attend. Second, it took time to spread the word and make the journey to city fairs. In effect, newspapers improved upon both of these limitations and allowed people to reach more renters and buyers with a wider range of consumer preferences than was previously possible.

We believe that it is nearly certain that individuals pursued all three strategies simultaneously. The cost of placing an ad was low.[10] Because advertising is usually subject to diminishing returns, the threshold for most advertisers would be reached after the first placement of a classified.[11] Repeats were relatively infrequent, appear to be associated with brokers, and often involved clarifications or expansions of qualitative information, which we show later. Finally, we hypothesize that owners of property obtained some degree of leverage over prospective purchasers or renters through the very act of advertising. Having signaled information to a large number of prospective consumers with heterogeneous preferences, the owner holds a potential trump card in cases where buyers or renters are strongly motivated to conclude transactions. There is the threat that the desired house or enslaved person could be "stolen" by another consumer attracted by the ad with even greater willingness to pay.

As Rio de Janeiro grew, the transaction costs associated with searching—to find the most efficient matches between P and R—increased. Conversely, and driven by the same logic, the increasing scale of the urban scene and penetration of media into everyday practices meant that the leverage offered by mediation through ads was multiplied along with the size of the population and the number of readers of advertisements. Demographic and spatial changes associated with Rio de Janeiro's increased commercial and political role within the nascent Brazilian empire helped provide the preconditions in which newspaper media spread and helped to shape markets.

In concluding this section, we insert an important caveat regarding the relationship between newspaper advertising and real markets. Although newspapers helped to shape and expand the marketplace, especially with regard to the rent or sale of property through the conveyance of information to a growing number of consumers, these effects were limited in important ways. The clearest example underscoring this caveat is the relationship between the advertising of enslaved people and the actual market for rent or sale of these individuals. As we will show in the empirical sections of our paper, there were tens of thousands of advertisements for enslaved persons for sale or rent each year in the 1860s and 1870s. But there is no evidence whatsoever that tens of thousands of transactions actually took place in those same years. The HDB system makes quantification deceptively easy. More does not always mean more meaningful.

Alternative Sources and Context for Advertising

From a methodological standpoint it is useful to seek out alternative sources that contextualize and help confirm patterns found in the documentation under review. With respect to rent, we propose estate inventories as an independent check on the prevalence of rental income in wealth. While this source has its limitations, it is useful as an indicator of economic activity and markets in some sense. These sources suggest that the arrival of newspapers after the 1820s may have had an effect on the scale of the rental market. In the 1810s and early 1820s, before the newspapers were significant, only 11 of 176 estates listed "rents" as part of the total value, and those that did tended to list high values of rents. Only a few rich decedents appear to have lived in part on rents, which averaged more than four contos in value at the time of the accounting of their estates.[12] Virtually all of these individuals owned many urban properties as well as enslaved people. By the 1850s, when the newspapers were quite significant, 74 out of 363 estates listed rents in the total accounts, and the average value declined to 1.86 contos. In other words, many more people were living in part from rents at the time of death (20 percent compared to just 6 percent a few decades earlier). Renting enslaved people was a primary form of economic activity by this period and we will argue that the newspapers helped to expand and frame this market. In the 1870s, 18 out of 87 estates listed rents (~21 percent), which is a similar percentage to the 1850s.[13]

In sum, we can say that the salience of rent as part of property-owners' activities probably increased between the 1820s and 1850s–1870s. It is likely that much of this increase came from renting out enslaved people and, to a lesser degree, residential and commercial properties. At the very least, it is suggestive that the curve over time of assets in the form of rents owed to decedents shares a similar growth story reported in our next section on newspaper advertising and rent.

With respect to sales, we examined the transaction tax records for 1869 to generate an estimate of the frequency of completed transactions.[14] These records are not complete as they only cover roughly four months, and some sales likely took place without payment of transfer taxes. They do, though, provide a lower bound for property sales in the Rio de Janeiro marketplace. In addition, the ratio of types of property transacted can be compared to ratios in advertising to illuminate connections between market activity and newspaper ads.

Between January 2 and May 15, 1869, there were 1,746 transactions for which taxes were paid in the city. There are 134 days in this interval, yielding 13 transactions per day. Again, this is the bare lower bound for this activity. Average days in the 1860s featured 50 to 80 "for sale" advertisements. Even if the official tax records undercounted sales by a factor of two, there would have been at least twice as many ads as sales over time.

The ratio between advertisements offering enslaved people for sale to those offering real estate also offers instructive context. In the newspapers, ads for the sale of people outnumbered ads for the sale of real property by a factor of at least 15 to 1. By contrast, the tax records in this interval list only 66.5 percent of transactions as having to do with the sale of enslaved persons. Some variation between sources is always to be expected. This discrepancy, however, is large enough to raise questions about the underlying logic of newspaper classifieds and the social and economic world they reflected and shaped. To wit: if advertising works, why focus on selling enslaved people to such a degree and neglect real estate? Along these lines, why advertise so many more enslaved people in the newspaper than could possibly be sold?

Ads for Rent and Sale in Newspapers: A Quantitative Overview

To begin to answer the questions posed in this chapter, we turn to the newspapers themselves and provide initial evidence about the expansion of advertisements and newspapers in nineteenth-century Rio de Janeiro. The two principal newspapers containing advertisements for the renting and selling of different forms of property in the 1820s were the *Diário do Rio de Janeiro* and the *Jornal do Commercio*. Zeferino Vito de Meireles founded the *Diário* in 1821 and printed its initial issue on Friday, June 1, 1821. In this first issue, no rentals were offered, but under the "sale" category there were two ads for houses and two ads for enslaved people.[15] The first rental ad appears in the *Diário* in its sixth issue on Thursday, June 6, 1821, for houses, and the first rental ad for an enslaved person appears in its ninth issue on Saturday, June 9, 1821.[16] The *Jornal do Commercio*, directed chiefly toward Rio de Janeiro's merchant and business class, first appeared on Monday, October 1, 1827.[17] Its eighth issue, Monday,

October 8, 1827, was the first to contain a rental ad—two ads for houses and one for an enslaved person.[18]

A typical rental ad was simple as the following example illustrates: "RENT, at 49 Rua do Ouvidor, a Black (slave) who is strong and intelligent for all types of services."[19] Rental ads were generally placed alongside other advertisements for selling, seeking (*precisa-se*), auctions, and runaway slave announcements, which often were much more detailed.[20] Ads for sale looked similar in print and displayed analogous details as those for rent except that "ALUGA-SE" was replaced with "VENDE-SE." The nineteenth century saw a large increase in the number of newspapers in Rio de Janeiro, which suggests that these two newspapers faced competition from upstart rivals drawn to the newspaper business. In the HDB search function, the 1830s include 315,301 pages queried, whereas the 1890s include 1,254,830 pages. It is unclear the degree to which advertisements singularly contributed to this growth, but we believe that they remained a key feature of the newspapers throughout this period.

As a first step using the HDB's technological capabilities, we conducted simple searches for key words associated with rent over time. We compiled graphs like that seen in figure 6.1 for "aluga," "aluguel," "aluguéis," and "alugar." There are caveats to the data used in this analysis. The search function shows the number of pages in which there is at least one mention of a given term. In some years, specific newspaper pages mention a word twenty times whereas in other pages only once, but both of these examples would be counted as one occurrence. This shortcoming probably understates the pattern seen over time in figure 6.1, because by the latter half of the nineteenth century, some newspaper pages contain scores, even hundreds, of rental ads, whereas in the 1820s certain pages only contain one ad. The HDB's search function is also, frankly, unreliable. Often a search for "aluga" will yield no results, but when we view the queried newspaper there are several ads containing the word.

Despite these shortcomings, we see in figure 6.1 a clear upward trend in the number of rental ads in newspapers in Rio de Janeiro during the nineteenth century.[21] The total pages in which "alugeis" is mentioned doubles from the 1820s (1,502 pages) to the 1840s (3,044 pages), increases by about 40 percent from the 1840s through the 1870s, and then explodes in the 1880s (7,957 pages) and 1890s (14,208 pages).

To get a more reliable estimate of the changing number of advertisements in Rio de Janeiro, we looked at other quantitative measures in the *Jornal do Commercio*.[22] We again encountered difficulties in the HDB's word-searching

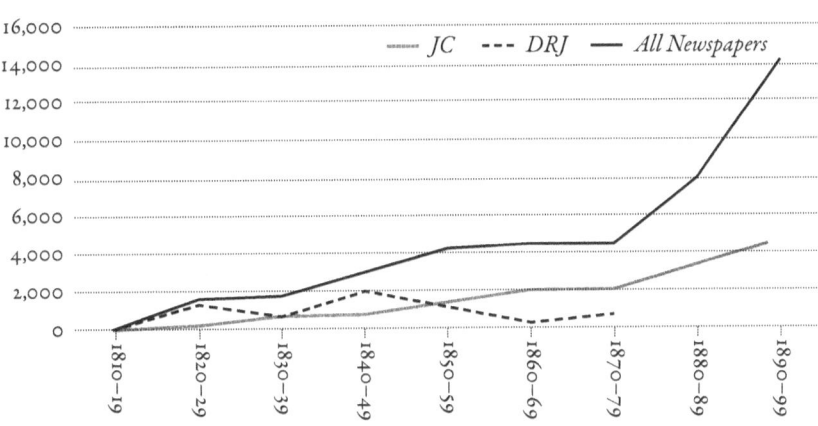

FIGURE 6.1 Number of Pages in Newspapers with *Aluguéis* Mentioned, 1810–1899. The *DRJ* ceased publication in 1878. HDB.

capabilities. Put simply, the system does not allow for a simple count of the appearance of the words "venda" or "aluguel" or any of their derivatives. The HDB does allow one to find these words in an incomplete and unsystematic manner, but there is no possibility of moving directly to a quantitative analysis. The system does not recognize the most frequent marker of an advertisement regarding rent—ALUGA-SE—which is typographically distinctive and simply ignored. Rather than rely entirely on the HDB search results, we used the system to identify and access relevant dates from the newspaper. We then hand counted the advertisements the old-fashioned way. As historians, we would argue that such hand counting should remain obligatory in any and all cases where the total number of observations can be identified by the human eye and counted adequately in a reasonable period of time.

Using the HDB database we randomly selected the newspaper issue from the *Jornal do Commercio* from the second Wednesday of May in five-year intervals between 1828 and 1898. Figure 6.2 plots the total number of advertisements for sales ("vendas") and rents ("aluguéis") over time. We see a strong growth trend from a very low base before the 1840s to a high but variable level in the period from the 1860s onward for rents. Sales advertisements appear to peak in the late 1850s and plateau throughout the rest of the period. These data corroborate what we found in the database of inventories as well as in the rough word frequencies estimates (such as in figure 6.1).

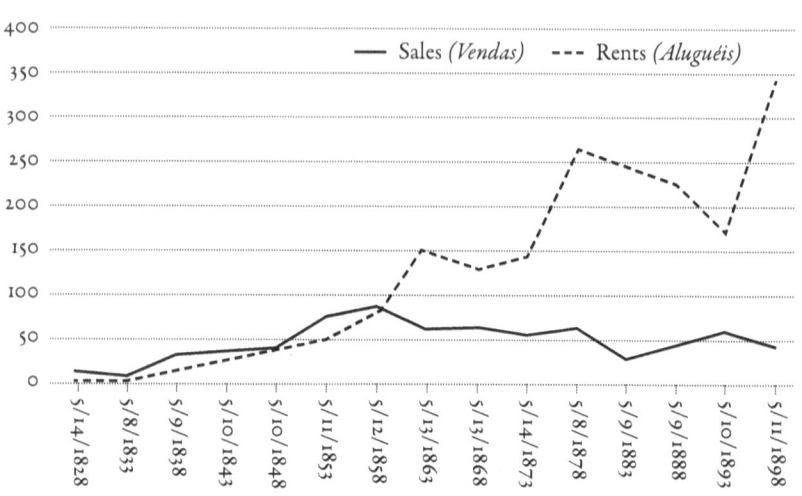

FIGURE 6.2 Number of Advertisements for Sales (*Vendas*) and Rents (*Aluguéis*) in the *Jornal do Commercio*, 1828–1898. JC.

Using these data from our hand-counting method, we can estimate rough figures for per capita advertising. We divided the sum of the ads for sales and rents in 1828, 1848, 1873, and 1888 by the population figures for the city of Rio de Janeiro from, respectively, 1822, 1849, 1872, and 1890. As seen in table 6.1, the results indicate that, per capita, advertisements more than doubled from the 1820s to the 1840s, doubled again from the 1840s to the 1870s, and then either remained about constant or declined from the 1870s through the end of the century.

We carried out the same analysis for rents only to compare to our previous findings. We can see in table 6.2 that, per capita, advertisements for rents jump massively from the 1820s to the 1840s, nearly triple from the 1840s to the 1870s, and then, depending on the year chosen, decreased or increased throughout the rest of the century. Significantly, we see a slightly lower rate of per capita advertisement for rents in the 1890s (taking the average of the figures from 1888, 1893, and 1898) compared to the 1870s. In sum, these findings corroborate the evidence presented from the inventories, as well as in figures 6.1 and 6.2.

Seeking to discover any differences between the markets for rents and sales, we also calculated per capita figures for advertisements for sale over this same period. Table 6.3 shows that sales advertisements per capita saw a similar pat-

TABLE 6.1   Advertisements Per Capita, 1828–1898. To correct for sample bias in the advertisement figures from 1888, 1893, and 1898, we included the figures for each of these years divided by the 1890 population figures, which gives a range of possible per capita figures. Population figures from 1822 and 1849 from Karasch, *Slave Life*, 62 and 66; population figures for 1872 and 1890 from IBGE: https://censo2010.ibge.gov.br/sinopse.

DATE	ADS/POPULATION	POPULATION/ADS
May 14, 1828	0.000151	6,615
May 10, 1848	0.000374	2,674
May 14, 1873	0.000702	1,425
May 9, 1888	0.000507	1,972
May 10, 1893	0.000423	2,365
May 11, 1898	0.000729	1,372

TABLE 6.2   Advertisements for Rents (*Aluguéis*) Per Capita, 1828–1898. For sources, see table 6.1.

DATE	RENTS/POPULATION	POPULATION/RENTS
May 14, 1828	1.16E-05	86,000
May 10, 1848	1.85E-04	5,419
May 14, 1873	5.02E-04	1,993
May 9, 1888	4.29E-04	2,333
May 10, 1893	3.14E-04	3,187
May 11, 1898	6.51E-04	1,537

TABLE 6.3   Advertisements for Sales (*Vendas*) Per Capita, 1828–1898. For sources, see table 6.1.

DATE	SALES/POPULATION	POPULATION/SALES
May 14, 1828	1.40E-04	7,167
May 10, 1848	1.89E-04	5,280
May 14, 1873	2.00E-04	4,999
May 9, 1888	7.84E-05	12,748
May 10, 1893	1.09E-04	9,169
May 11, 1898	7.84E-05	12,748

tern from the 1820s to the 1840s as seen for rental advertisements in table 6.2. However, sales advertisements diverged substantially from rental advertisements in the following decades. Whereas ads for rent per capita nearly triple between the 1840s and 1870s, ads for sale remain nearly identical per capita during this same period. What is more, the ads for sale fall by more than 60 percent from the 1870s to the 1890s. The average of 1888, 1893, and 1898[23] is not only much less than the rate in 1873 but is also nearly half the rate in 1828! These data suggest that the markets for real estate and enslaved people diverged during the nineteenth century.

Population figures for Rio de Janeiro provide context for the different fates of these markets. Recall that in the 1820s and 1830s, sales outnumbered rental ads in the *Jornal do Commercio*. There was a rental market, for both real estate and enslaved people, but it does not appear to have been particularly large or active in this early period, at least in the pages of the newspapers. The city in the 1820s was home to under 100,000 inhabitants, roughly half of whom were slaves.[24] It is likely that in the 1820s more families in the city owned homes and slaves as a proportion of all families than would be the case at any point in future decades. By the end of the 1840s, the population of the city had more than doubled.[25] There were two free residents for every one enslaved. Many new arrivals would rent rather than own their homes and servants. Consequently, the demand for rental properties and servants increased from this point forward, as the absolute and per capita figures above show.

Recall, also, that evidence from estate inventories further supports this conclusion: few estates in the 1810s and 1820s contained reference to rents; many did by the 1850s. Owners became more likely to offer property for rent and it stands to reason that this was largely due to the corresponding increase in prospective renters and thereby demand and prices. The increase in rentals means that the economic meaning of property ownership became more imbued with mediated values. For example, a house is a house, but it is also a word that can appear in an advertisement as something to rent. Moreover, there was more explicit concern with opportunity costs (underutilized property) and citywide markets. The newspaper stood at the center of this transformation in social and economic relations. It was a key mediating institution that brought property owners and slaveholders together with prospective renters or buyers, and in turn served to enlarge and entrench markets in a growing urban environment.

Efficacy of Advertising: Repeats, Rephrasings, Consummated Transactions

An important consideration for advertisers is how long they expect to run notices and whether to place the same version in a subsequent issue. To assess these questions, we randomly selected three weeks from the 1830s and 1840s and, by hand, looked at the ads placed to see whether a seller repeated them.[26] Due to the large volume of ads even by the late 1830s, it is difficult to conduct this type of analysis, yet we were able to identify advertisers by the street addresses included in the ads. The major discovery is that it appears that the vast majority of ads *did not repeat themselves*.

There are a few examples where the advertiser registered an additional ad a few days later but with different text. This suggests the first ad went unfulfilled and the advertiser decided to change the "selling text" to make it more appealing to potential renters. For example, an ad was placed on Thursday, January 14, 1830: "Whoever would like a *ladino* boy for all door service, inside and outside, as a servant for everything he knows how to do, he is loyal, whoever wants him, go to Rua dos Inválidos, number 74." Four days later on Monday, January 18, 1830, it appears the same person placed another ad: "Whoever would like a slave boy for door service, inside and outside, a great expert at purchasing, he is a good servant, he is very loyal, and he doesn't have vices; whoever wants him, go to Rua dos Inválidos, number 74, to make a deal."

The placer sharpened the language in the second ad by using the term *moleque* instead of *rapaz*, thus more clearly denoting an enslaved boy. Also, instead of saying the boy "is loyal," the second ad states that he "is very loyal" and adds the extra clause, "and he doesn't have vices." These subtle uses of language reveal an advertiser who is acutely aware of the specific meanings that words have for a potential renter and how a newspaper ad can be used to convey these meanings within a growing marketplace. Such modifications can be explained through the theoretical lens developed at the outset of this chapter—the ad in question offers information intended to facilitate consumer choice and to best match consumer preferences.

There are several interpretations for why most ads were one offs. For one, at least during these three weeks, we could assume that some of the ads were successful in drawing consumers and the rentals were completed after one ad placement. Second, lack of repetition could suggest that the advertiser used other methods (e.g., word of mouth) or gave up entirely. In addition, the advertisement could be seen by potential renters several days after the initial placement, so there would be no need to repeat the same ad.

At this point, the reader probably wants to know whether we have supporting documentation regarding the actual efficacy of advertising. On its face, advertising must have been at least somewhat effective because the number of ads grew dramatically over time and remained a major feature of the commercial papers from the 1830s onward. Still, one wants to see examples of when and how it worked. One such example, among many, involved the sale of a house at 90A Senado Street. Here, we have a very specific address listed for sale in the *Jornal do Commercio* on April 20, 1869. There can be no doubt that this is the same address as listed in the records of tax collection for the transfer of property on May 5, 1869: "To wit, Antonio Francisco Loureiro dos Santos was levied the 6% transfer tax on a purchase price of nine contos, paid as it were to José Lopes de Lima and his wife, former owners of said address."[27]

Having found this example of advertising probably leading to a real estate transaction, we also conducted a preliminary search for examples relating to the sale of enslaved people. Using the same tax rolls, we searched for fifteen addresses connected to sales of enslaved people. Although thirteen out of fifteen addresses appeared in the advertising section of the *Jornal do Commercio* in 1869, none of the addresses of sellers of enslaved people appeared in the newspaper (or better said, were identified by the HDB search system) in the weeks immediately preceding the transaction captured in the tax records.[28] This result was surprising. It suggests that in the case of sales of enslaved people there may be additional layers of mediation—the use of brokers as described in the next section—with transactions being consummated in locations other than the primary address of sellers. In addition, the tax records are incomplete and some records fail to include addresses. Thus, the failure to find evidence of advertisements tied to addresses in tax records should be taken as suggestive rather than definitive when it comes to sales of enslaved people.

Some ads must have resulted in sales, otherwise why pay for ads or take the time to write them? Even so, the lack of implicit matches between these two sources is surprising and raises a cautionary flag against assuming that all or even most ads were successful in generating transactions. With sales of enslaved people, we may be looking at a situation of very high quantity and relatively low yield. This might also help explain the relative lack of repeat ads. Many ads could be seen as essentially "fishing expeditions" where sellers sought to broaden the possible pool of buyers under the assumption that the next-best option, selling to a known individual, would suffice at some later date.

Undaunted by our initial failure to find examples of advertisements for enslaved people that matched a sample of transactions in the tax records, we looked until we found examples of ads that did correspond to sales. Although we cannot offer a quantitative measure of the success of such advertising, we can show that ads sometimes resulted in sales. For instance, on April 14, 1869, the broker Antonio Gonçalves Pereira Guimarães, located at 6 Lavradio Street, advertised an enslaved woman listed as Black, aged twenty-four. On May 5, a transaction tax was paid for Thomazia, a Black enslaved woman aged twenty-four, listed at the same address with the same individual as the seller. In keeping with the idea that newspaper advertising may have expanded the scale of market activity, note that the buyer in this case was listed at an address more than one kilometer from the broker.[29]

These results suggest an additional question about the balance between prospective renters and those wishing to rent out some property. If R is much greater than P, then P can find R more easily and there is less likelihood that missing out on one particular R would mean missing out on the ability to rent out the property. If there are more Ps chasing fewer Rs, then we might expect much more aggressive advertising. Yet it could also mean that in a world in which newspapers increasingly mediate the renting and selling of things, people believed that they had to place an ad—regardless of whether it got answered. Everyone could think of him- or herself as an advertiser in spite of the evidence that there probably were many fewer actual renters or buyers for each item of property. Placing an ad would therefore be considered normative behavior among property owners, thereby bringing them into this expanding mediated marketplace.

Brokers

An important group of participants present in the market for rental ads and property mediated by newspapers were the city's property brokers. The economic motivation behind the rise of the broker in this context would stress their role in collecting and transmitting information and possibly lowering risk and transaction costs. Even with cheap and numerous advertisements, there were still costs for property owners and prospective renters that could be lowered by using brokers. Most important, the broker could save P and

R on the risk inherent in any one-to-one transaction where time could be wasted (e.g., P and R do not agree on price or quality of property and no substitute is available) and act as a mediating buffer to resolve monitoring and collection-payment issues.[30] A broker could thus solve this informational problem and also help to reduce the risks that both the seller and renter faced. A sociological motivation for the broker would stress the personal relationships with prospective buyers and sellers of property. The buyer and seller might not know each other—and thus the transaction would be inherently risky and uncertain—but the buyer might know, and trust, a broker, and likewise the seller might also know, and trust, the same broker. The broker would then leverage his social relationships to connect people who otherwise would not be put in touch. What is more, as we will see, the repetitive nature of advertising would tend to encrust the location of a given broker's activities in a spatially legible frame for a much larger number of prospective owners and renters.

Although we cannot be certain that all brokers and commission agents operated in the space of newspaper advertising, we do know that some placed ads of their own and it is likely that these individuals kept a close eye on the classified section of the leading newspapers. Many brokers and agents were also listed in the *Almanak Laemmert*. In 1870, the *Almanak* listed thirteen men in the category of *escritórios e casas de consignação de comprar e vender escravos* (offices and consignment houses to buy and sell slaves).[31] Several of these people placed ads in the newspaper. For instance, João Joaquim Barbosa is listed as a slave broker in 1870. His address in the *Almanak* is given as 110 Prainha Street—a central location near the port zone of the city. Several ads were placed by an individual at this address in 1870. For example: "RENT: a young Black 18 years of age, for every kind of work; in the Rua da Prainha, n. 110." In the decade of the 1870s, this address appears 105 times in the *Jornal do Commercio* in the context of both rentals and sales of enslaved people. In 1872, the same address on Prainha Street is listed along with two advertisements for enslaved people for rent: "RENT: a good mess servant; in the Rua da Prainha, n. 110" and "RENT: a Black, for every kind of work; in the Rua da Prainha, n. 110."[32]

Although this evidence is not definitive, it appears that brokers were the most likely group to place repeat advertisements. For example, Manoel José Pinto Guimarães, with his business located at 95 Alfândega Street, placed different versions of the same advertisement for a "pretty and strong parda" along with her fifteen-month-old child on four out of five days in March 1869.³³ Economically, brokers were the most motivated of sellers in the market. They made money from concluded transactions and delays were lost income.

Landlords and Real Estate

If brokers helped match buyers to sellers, and renters to owners, the long and growing list of capitalists and landlords would also have made for interesting reading in the *Almanak Laemmert* for anyone in the market to buy or sell property. The *Almanak* provided names and addresses of men (and a few women) of property. Presumably this was not merely a sop to their vanity. It was a signal that they might be worth contacting in relation to property—whether buying or selling or seeking a property to buy or rent. By definition, an owner of dozens of properties would be the landlord for dozens of renters. Preliminary research, based on a small sample of major property owners, helps to clarify the amount of rental activity at this level of analysis—in today's terms, the "rate of churn" in the renting (and selling) of property in the case of owners of multiple properties. The results suggest that owners of multiple properties did place ads for rent or sale but that they did so rather infrequently. Unlike the case of enslaved people, there is less evidence here of "fishing" for prospects. For instance, Antonio Francisco Chaves is listed in the 1870 property tax rolls as the owner of thirteen properties clustered around the city center on Alfândega Street, Sabão Street, and São Pedro Street. Of these, nine addresses appear for certain in the HDB database within two years of the tax roll itself. Yet only one, at 237 São Pedro Street, appears connected to an advertisement for property rent—in this case a single room.³⁴

An alternative approach to this question is to begin with properties listed for sale or rent in the newspaper. These addresses can then be cross-checked with addresses in the tax rolls sorted by the name of property owners. At the very least, we can begin to form an impression of the profile of property owners likely to place advertisements. Unsurprisingly, preliminary research indicates that these owners tended to control multiple properties. For example, José Luis Alves Bastos owned seven properties in the city when he placed a rental ad for his property at 220 Hospício Street. This property was assessed at an annual rental value of 600 mil-réis. Given this value, we can assume that he stood to lose 50 mil-réis per month if the house failed to rent. Placing the ad indicates an apparently strong desire to find a renter and an equally strong desire to avoid leaving money on the table for this particular address. Women were also major property owners, holding roughly a third of real property in the city. They too were avid participants in the advertising market. Leocádia Joaquina Magalhães Garces, for example, owned three properties according to the 1870 tax roll. Of these, she offered the two-story structure at 17 Conde d'Eu Street for rent that same year.

The Addresses in Rental Advertisements

Despite its shortcomings, the HDB provides unparalleled access to newspapers and the ability to search by address. Both brokers and property owners can be approached in the HDB in this manner. Indeed, as advertising almost never included the names of individuals, the addresses are the most precious piece of information tying ads to specific places and, with more research, perhaps to specific people, as when these records are combined with other resources in the same database, such as the *Almanak Laemmert*. Further, it is possible to reconstruct a better picture of how information about rent and property diffused through the mediation of newspapers writ large.

Two critical facts bear elaboration with regard to the scope and intensity of this mediated marketplace. First, a process that began in the 1830s with the expanded number of advertisements had, by the 1870s, consolidated into a citywide mesh of information and connections. One of our initial questions in conducting this study focused on the scale of information and market activity. We sought to answer the question of scale through the unique affordances of the HDB, which allows us for the first time to assess what we term the *saturation* of property transactions, with a focus on rentals and sales. In other work, written by us and by others, the notion that renting and selling was a fundamental part of everyday life has been sustained through a variety of case studies and quantitative arguments.[35] What our new research shows is just how saturated everyday economic life became with information about enslaved people and properties for rent and for sale. Methodologically, the HDB system offers a clear path to measuring the scope of this phenomenon, not through the names of individuals involved but rather through their addresses. For any of these transactions to take place, in a world without electronic communication (telephones would appear only very late in the empire), face-to-face meetings were inevitable. These could only occur if the information in the newspaper included an address. The place of the market could not remain anonymous. As we have seen with 110 Prainha Street, some addresses were associated with slave brokers and thus appeared with frequency in the advertisements. It would be one thing if a few addresses accounted for most of the activity, but this was patently not the case.

To measure saturation, we developed a random sampling method for drawing lists of addresses from the universe of possible locations in the city. Property tax rolls provide the addresses and names of owners along with the implicit property values of every structure in the city. Using a random number generator, we pulled a sample of addresses from the 1849 and 1870 tax rolls and then checked whether those same addresses appeared in connection with rental or sale activity advertised in the newspapers in a five-year window (i.e., from 1847 to 1851 and from 1868 to 1872). Because the *Jornal do Commercio* had, by the 1840s, become the dominant venue, we restricted our search to its pages. At the outset, we had no idea whether these random addresses would result in hits in the HDB database. We expected that some would—perhaps a quarter or half, as we were only searching in the years surrounding the date of the tax rolls.

In 1849, fourteen of the thirty addresses queried yielded at least one match. One address, 14 Sabão Street, contained thirty-two matches between 1847 and 1851 whereas several other addresses saw only a handful of matches during these years. A 47 percent success rate from a random sample of addresses in 1849 was higher than we anticipated. It appears that market activity mediated by newspapers was already fairly widespread in Rio de Janeiro even by 1849. Given this relatively high rate, we were not sure what to expect with the addresses in 1870.

Astonishingly, in 1870, nearly all of the sampled addresses yielded matches. Saturation in the mediated marketplace was 83 percent according to a random sample of thirty addresses. What is more, the addresses turned up not one or two but dozens or more hits in nearly every case. The address at 256 Alfândega Street appeared at least 381 times in the decade of the 1870s, not only offering slaves for sale and rent but also offering to purchase slaves. The matched address with the fewest hits was 141 Saco do Alferes Street, where a book was offered for sale on four different occasions. Additional tests of saturation were conducted in a more ad hoc fashion in the course of researching other questions. The results confirm our finding of near total saturation in spatial terms during the 1860s and 1870s.[36]

Saturation, then. A world filled with information about people and things for sale. A city imbued with the language of commerce and increasingly impersonal and commodified interactions. This world of newspaper advertising did not go unnoticed in the cultural sphere. A terrific example that helps draw together the threads of our argument can be found in a play by Joaquim Manuel de Macedo. *O Primo da Califórnia* (The California cousin) was first performed at the opening of the season in the Ginásio Dramático Theater, on April 12, 1855. The play was explicitly crafted "in the French mode," copying the style of the comedy of manners popular in Paris at midcentury. The play's protagonist, Adriano, gets drunk on champagne that he can ill afford and confides to his friends that he has a cousin in California—"Paulo... Claudio... Genipapo," who he claims struck it rich in the Gold Rush. Being drunk, Adriano cannot help but give away the game and his friends decide to avenge themselves on their poor counterpart by placing a false notice in the newspaper attesting to the death of one Paulo Claudio Genipapo in California and calling upon Adriano Genipapo to collect a legacy as the sole heir of his defunct cousin.[37]

Adriano's lie turns into a golden opportunity when the news of his imaginary millionaire cousin's death spreads through the city, changing his social position instantly in the minds of his domestic servant, his tailor, his landlord, as well as in the minds of the theater impresarios and music publishers who have hitherto scorned Adriano's talent as a nobody with no connections. The idea that a bold lie such as this could change a young man's prospects overnight, while farfetched, is nonetheless much more understandable and plausible given what we have learned about the way newspapers and their advertisements and announcements permeated everyday life across the city. As such, the plot in this play passes the forensic test of comedy and uses certain truths of the social context as a foundation. To wit: we are dealing with a society in which the written word, particularly when printed in the newspaper, carried a great deal of weight.

Beyond this, the play also points to the way that the language of advertising could penetrate into everyday thought and lead, in certain cases, to comic bewilderment. In one scene, the landlord Pantaleão addresses the newly "rich" Adriano offering both his house and his daughter: "I am, as it were, obliged to sell some of my properties; now, as your lordship must know, I am the owner of a very well-built daughter and the father of a perfectly well-mannered house ... well... what I mean to say."[38] Mixing up people and possessions, Pantaleão refers to his daughter in terms of bricks and mortar and his house in terms of personal qualities. This mixing up is ridiculous, but it is also perfectly of a piece with the kind of language inserted in classified advertising every day in the commercial newspapers of the city. Such language, we argue, not only served to convey information, as theories of advertising indicate—but it also knit together a discourse of marketplace transactions and an evolving understanding of the words and concepts attached to property, people, and forms of labor.

Focusing on the case of Rio de Janeiro, we show in this chapter how newspaper advertising grew in scope and importance throughout the nineteenth century in connection with shifting notions of markets and property. The advertisements aided in the expansion of a citywide marketplace—thereby mediating the transition of Rio de Janeiro from small city to metropolis, from small markets and interpersonal networks to larger marketplaces and more impersonal transactions. The digital repository of nineteenth-century Brazilian newspapers, the HDB, provided the main sources for our analysis. Even though the HDB's shortcomings are many, we were able to discover aspects about the relationship among newspapers, property, and markets that would have been impossible in the past.

Notes

1. *Classified advertising* is the nearest cognate term we can think of to describe the section of the newspaper devoted to rental, sale, and want ads. Unlike contemporary classified advertising, the nineteenth-century Brazilian newspapers tended to organize ads in the classified section by the kind of transaction contemplated rather than the type of item for sale or rent.

2. For a general overview from the perspective of media studies, see Briggs and Burke, *Social History*, esp. chap. 6.

3. Quinn, "Transformation," 750–51.

4. Schwarcz, *Retrato*; Freyre, *Escravo*; Renault, *Rio antigo*. For a more general overview of this position, see Briggs and Burke, *Social History*. Freyre provides a classic statement on the importance of newspapers for historical purposes in *Escravo* as does Renault in *Rio*.

5. Polanyi, *Great Transformation*, 52.

6. For an example of this in advertisements for runaway slaves, see Read and Zimmerman, "Freedom," 405–11.

7. In the context of Rio de Janeiro, the most commonly advertised "products" for sale or rent in classified ads were human beings and houses or land. We are conscious of the problem inherent in discussing these practices in the flat language of economic theory. Changes in terminology will not resolve these ethical

challenges, but as a first step in this direction we will refer throughout this chapter to enslaved persons rather than slaves except in cases where we cite directly from nineteenth-century sources.

8. Bagwell and Ramey, "Advertising," summarized in Bagwell, "Economic Analysis," 1,785–86.

9. Bagwell, "Economic Analysis," 1,719.

10. Rates per line in the 1840s were around 80 réis. See, for example, *O Despertador*, January 1, 1841. Lower rates were often provided to subscribers. Put in context, the sale of a house in 1849 might fetch 5:000$000, so a five-line advertisement would run the seller 400 réis, or 0.00008 percent of the sale price. For data on the market prices fetched for properties in 1849, see Frank, "Urban Property," 565n11. The average value was 5:716$.

11. Bagwell, "Economic Analysis," 1,731.

12. The value of four contos in 1820 was significant. It represented more money than unskilled workers could hope to earn in a decade of labor. Thus, these assets in the form of collected rent stem not from small and episodic transactions, for example, the rent owed on a single enslaved person, but rather sums that correspond to rents from several houses over a year or more.

13. Estate inventory database derived from AN, Inventários. Discussion of collection and interpretation of inventory data can be found in Frank, *Dutra's World*, 171–85.

14. For a spatial analysis of the data discussed in this section, see Frank and Berry, "Slave Market."

15. *DRJ*, June 1, 1821.

16. *DRJ*, June 6 and 9, 1821.

17. *JC*, October 1, 1827.

18. *JC*, October 8, 1827.

19. *JC*, January 11, 1848.

20. Read and Zimmerman, "Freedom," 405–11.

21. The figures for the other three terms—*aluga*, *aluguel*, and *alugar*—show similar results.

22. By the 1860s, the *DRJ* had ceased to be a major competitor to the *JC*.

23. 8.87E-05 or 11,555 people per advertisement.

24. Frank, *Dutra's World*, 15. See also Karasch, *Slave Life*, 62; M. R. N. Silva, *Negro*, 53.

25. Karasch, *Slave Life*, 166. Karasch reports a jump from a population of ~86,000 in 1822 to ~206,000 in 1849.

26. *JC*, January 14–21, 1830; September 1–6, 1838; August 24–30, 1846.

27. Sizas, 1869. The coincidence in time is merely suggestive. There is no definitive proof that the sale of this house came about because of the placement of the advertisement.

28. Recebedoria, AGCRJ, 1869; *JC*, 1869.

29. Advertisement found in *JC*, April 14, 1869; tax record located in Recebedoria, AGCRJ, 1869.

30. The concept of consignment (*consignação*) inherent in these brokering agents' activities is predicated on the trade-off between the time and effort (thus costs) saved by the property owner by employing the intermediary broker and the lower return on property owing to the broker's commission.

31. *Almanak Laemmert* (1870): 606

32. *JC*, January 16, 1872.

33. *JC*, March 15, 16, 18, and 19, 1869.

34. Tax records found in Decima Urbana, 1870, AN. Addresses matched to HDB database for 1870–1872.

35. Frank, *Dutra's World*; Frank and Berry, "Slave Market."

36. For example, twelve of thirteen of Antonio Francisco Chaves's properties appeared within +/- five years of the listing of his properties in the 1870 tax rolls. The missing property appeared earlier, in 1863. Over any reasonable stretch of time, nearly every address will appear attached to a classified advertisement, at least from the 1860s onward.

37. Macedo, "Primo," 1:119–22.

38. Macedo, "Primo," 1:133.

Arnaldo Lucas Pires Junior   Translated by Hendrik Kraay

SEVEN   MUCH MORE THAN IMAGES
Visual Culture and the Public Sphere in Illustrated Satirical Magazines

Illustrated satirical magazines proliferated in Brazil in the 1860s and maintained their prominence until well after the end of the empire in 1889. This genre of publications shaped Brazilian visual culture; illustrated magazines defined political positions and debates, created new social networks and cultural practices, and, along with the development of an advertising market, contributed to new patterns of consumption. They adopted a standard form in the 1860s and were inseparable from the changes that took place in the larger Brazilian society. When examining the amusing cartoons in these periodicals, modern historians must take great care to understand their messages and the way in which they were designed to appeal to the reading public, which was their principal raison d'être. The images and texts in these periodicals were a fundamental part of public culture, and studying them gives access to social and political debates in the public sphere. And, no less important to historians, these publications offer clues about contemporary taste and how images were consumed.

The illustrated satirical magazines so closely associated with the last three decades of the imperial regime descended from illustrated variety magazines, Brazil's first periodicals to publish images, which first appeared in the late 1830s. Only rarely did cartoons appear on the latter's pages; most of their illustrations showed scenes of European landscapes, art, architecture, and customs as part of their project to educate and enlighten Brazilians. Critical cartoons only flourished in the later illustrated satirical magazines, whose earliest (but short-lived) examples appeared in the 1840s and 1850s. The genre came into its own in the 1860s, the subject of this chapter's first section. In the second, I argue that illustrated satirical magazines constituted an interface between visual and literary culture; they formed an integral part of the expanding public sphere, merging visuality and social criticism. These images help us to understand how satire and laughter became fundamental elements of the imperial press. While sometimes seen as merely light reading or frivolous amusement, illustrated magazines were central to the development of the public sphere, the construction of taste, and imperial social and political criticism. In addition to the content of the images analyzed in this chapter, it is important to recognize that these magazines were hybrid spaces that combined social criticism and political statements, as well as elite and popular culture. This is the approach that I take in the chapter's final section, in which I examine four cartoons from key illustrated satirical magazines to analyze the images' function within imperial society. While I focus on Rio de Janeiro, where the illustrated press flourished, it is important to note that similar illustrated satirical magazines regularly appeared in major provincial centers as well, although only a few of them have been systematically studied.[1]

The historical development of the illustrated magazine genre that led toward satire was directly connected to the social demand for visuality and the creation of a public sphere in which cartoons were accepted as legitimate instruments of criticism, demonstrating a transformation in readers' taste. The rise of caricatures as the dominant visual element in illustrated magazines is an example of the complex historical process of the "construction of taste"—the creation of a relationship between society and cultural goods via the imposition of a specific lifestyle or dominant discourses—that prompts changes in social life. It establishes hierarchies among cultural products that make it possible for marginalized cultural elements to gain acceptance within the dominant esthetic and ethic instruments of a given society.[2] The construction of taste is mediated by culture, class, and geography. In Brazil, the turning of illustrations into caricatures of social criticism did not change the intended audience, the literate minority. The 1872 census revealed that only 1.6 million Brazilians claimed to be literate out of a population of more than 10 million; in Rio de Janeiro, however, 43.9 percent of the 226,033 inhabitants were literate.[3] Despite writers' and caricaturists' intent—that their images be read along with the accompanying texts (much as I do in this chapter's last section)—the images might be interpreted quite differently by those who could not read. Some no doubt were as opaque to nineteenth-century illiterates as they are to twenty-first-century readers who lack the political and cultural knowledge that writers and artists assumed among the literate audience that they targeted. Others, however, were accessible to anyone with a minimal knowledge of society or politics.

From Varieties to Satire: The Birth of Illustrated Satirical Magazines

Illustrated satirical magazines descended directly from a little-known form of periodical that was fundamental in creating the demand for illustrated material in Brazil, the illustrated variety magazines (*revistas ilustradas de variedades*). Rather than deploying images for the purposes of humor and satire, these magazines published illustrations for pedagogical purposes and were designed to be collected. The pioneering *Museu Universal: Jornal das Famílias Brasileiras* (Universal Museum: Journal of Brazilian Families, 1837–1844), the first Brazilian periodical to publish illustrations, explained in its inaugural issue that it would "draw freely" from the best examples in Europe and publish illustrations of "the marvels of architecture," "beautiful landscapes" from around the world, examples of "popular dress" and "notable animals," and explanatory articles to promote Brazil's "enlightenment and progress."[4] Other examples of this genre included *Minerva Brasiliense* (Brazilian Minerva, 1843–1845), *O Ostensor Brasileiro* (The Brazilian Exhibitor, 1845–1846), *Brasil Ilustrado* (Illustrated Brazil, 1855–1856), *Museu Pitoresco Histórico e Literário* (Picturesque Historical and Literary Museum, 1848), as well as magazines directed at a female readership like *Jornal das Senhoras* (Ladies' Journal, 1852–1855) and *Correio das Modas* (Fashion Courier, 1839–1840).

Brasil Ilustrado lamented that, unlike their European counterparts, Brazil's illustrated variety magazines struggled to survive: they "practically die in the cradle, or eke out a meager existence for a few days, unless they take on the great commercial issues, embrace the partisan line of a political party, or turn their columns into support for those in power."[5] Presenting themselves as an Old World genre was one way for illustrated variety magazines' editors to promote their periodicals. The Argentine-born political exile Juana Paula Manso de Noronha, editor of the *Jornal das Senhoras*, explained that, although she was unusual in Rio de Janeiro, it was already quite common for women to edit newspapers in European countries.[6] As if anticipating criticism, she asked: "Should, by chance, South America, and only South America, remain stagnant in its ideas, while the entire world marches toward progress and tends toward the moral and material perfection of society?"[7] Her declaration was apparently well received, for this weekly appeared without interruption for three years, publishing serialized novels, articles about the latest trends in European fashions, and a series of essays on "the moral emancipation of women."

The *Jornal das Senhoras* published relatively few illustrations and did not see them as educational tools or instruments of critique. Its existence, however, demonstrates the press's tendency toward specialization and periodicals' efforts to reach narrowly defined reading publics. There is no evidence that female caricaturists produced images for the illustrated press during the empire—if they did exist, they hid their identities under pseudonyms.[8]

While originally publishing illustrations for educational purposes, illustrated variety magazines gradually became a privileged space for cultural discussion; they published novels, debates about plays performed in the capital's theaters, and even riddles and puzzles (*charadas*) that served the dual purpose of entertaining readers and encouraging them to buy the next issue where they could find the answers. Already in 1838, *Museu Universal* published a riddle that was particularly significant in a slavocrat empire: "It is the most terrible fate that a mortal can suffer. Always obeys [and] never freely finds happiness." The answer, published a week later, was "slave."[9] Visual satires also occasionally appeared among these magazines' illustrations of customs.[10]

Lanterna Mágica (Magic Lantern, 1844–1845), sometimes wrongly identified as the first Brazilian illustrated magazine, was in fact the first Brazilian illustrated *satirical* magazine.[11] Its failure, like the short-lived *Charivari Nacional* (National Charivari, 1859), reveals the difficult process of constructing the taste for caricatures. The justifications for these periodicals, as expressed in their first issues' editorials, differed strikingly from purposes of illustrated variety magazines. *Lanterna Mágica* claimed no pedagogical purpose and, rather, declared that it would represent "the principal scenes of our times . . . , without personal rancor and without the intention of mocking this or that individual." In other words, instead of a visual and educational almanac, *Lanterna Mágica* proposed "an epic for our time," a narrative about contemporary society, marked by humor and visuality.

The inclusion of fictional characters (*personagens-símbolo*), whose function is to accompany the reader, created an even closer relationship between the critiques presented in the magazine and its readers. These characters were essential to the construction of the narrative about society in *Lanterna Mágica*. It announced that its "protagonist" would be "the immortal Laverno, this extraordinary man, a sort of Mephistopheles," and that he would be accompanied by "his inseparable companion [and] close personal friend, Belchior dos Passos," as well as "a retinue of other characters who will lend luster to this great work."[12] Laverno was the first of these characters in Brazil, but the most famous of them was Dr. Semana (Doctor Weekly) in *Semana Ilustrada* (Illustrated Week, 1860–1875). Through ongoing contact with the character, whose personality and relationships with sidekicks like Laverno's Belchior dos Passos and Dr. Semana's Moleque (Boy) were developed over the course of many issues, readers felt as if they were discussing politics and current affairs with a friend. The characters served to create a space of discussion on the magazines' pages.

The short existences of *Lanterna Mágica* and *Charivari Nacional* are not surprising in light of the difficulties that most newspapers had in maintaining themselves. Despite constantly beseeching its subscribers to pay up, *Charivari Nacional* was forced to suspend publication for July and August 1859; when it reappeared, the editor, who used the pseudonym Capão Maior (Head Capon), blamed the printer, the Tipografia do *Diário* (the printing press that belonged to the *Diário do Rio de Janeiro*), which had tried to censor some of *Charivari*'s language.

> They squeezed me, although they couldn't separate me from my printing press, [but] they made it clear that they wanted to see me behind them.... And because I don't want anyone to be able to question me, I had to spend [my money] to buy a press where *Charivari* can be as sovereign as any of the world's rulers, so today I can assure my subscribers that there will be no more interruptions to this publication, and that I will remain among the press because I am indispensable for the well-being of the people of this land.[13]

The justifications for the editor's failures offer some indications of these periodicals' business model. They were typically run by a single individual or by a small group of editors and artists, who printed their periodical in a third party's press, and relied on sales of individual issues and annual or biannual subscriptions. It is impossible to know whether this censorship was the real reason for the failure of *Charivari Nacional* to publish (and for its ultimate demise), or whether this was merely the editor's excuse for his inability to live up to his commitments. Nevertheless, by revealing the difficult relationship between printing presses and editors, *Charivari Nacional* demonstrates some of the commercial considerations that shaped periodical production and publication in imperial Rio de Janeiro. None of this was unique to illustrated magazines, for the press under the empire was a risky business, especially for publishers who did not have large numbers of subscribers for their periodicals or who could not count on government favor. This precariousness, however, did not prevent the press's expansion and diversification, especially after 1860. In contrast to the years of Pedro I's reign, the freedom of the press encouraged the production of more visual content in periodicals, even if financial constraints often meant that illustrated magazines were ephemeral publications. Not surprisingly, the longest-lived illustrated magazine, Henrique Fleiuss's *Semana Ilustrada*, was often accused of receiving subsidies from the imperial household's coffers, to which rival caricaturists attributed the respectful way that Fleiuss portrayed the emperor.

Bankruptcies notwithstanding, the editorial innovations of *Lanterna Mágica* and *Charivari Nacional* caught on in the early 1860s, and caricatures emerged as the predominant instrument of criticism in the illustrated press. In that decade, illustrated satirical magazines proliferated and became a favored way of pointing out through caricature all that was funny in Brazilian society. The founding of Fleiuss's *Semana Ilustrada* in late 1860 signaled this transition to a new era in Rio de Janeiro. Because many have already written about this periodical and its German-Brazilian cartoonist, it is not necessary to dwell on its history here. The longest-lived and most successful illustrated magazine of the empire, the *Semana Ilustrada* solidified the genre of illustrated satirical magazines.[14] Its format of eight pages, two sheets of paper lithographed and typeset on opposite sides, folded in quarto, became the standard for the empire's illustrated periodicals.

Semana Ilustrada introduced itself to readers by invoking the Latin expression, "*Ridendo castigat mores* [Laughter corrects customs]":

> *Semana Ilustrada* appears today under this simple but meaningful motto, seeking the public's approval as it begins its many tasks. It will not tell readers about the latest developments in politics, which business deals were recently struck, how many petty thieves fell into the police's hands, so for what reason are we taking our first hesitant steps in the shadows, in spite of living in the century of light? No. The mission of the humble athlete who today enters the vast sandy plain of the press is more demanding, but also more transcendental. We will speak for him. Ignoring petty personal political conflicts and discussions of pointless matters [*niilidades*], hopefully supported by public favor, we principally propose to fulfill the epigraph that precedes these lines: *Ridendo castigat mores*.[15]

Embracing the idea of transforming the magazine's pages into a space for criticizing customs through humor, *Semana Ilustrada* embodied the ideal already seen in *Lanterna Mágica* and *Charivari Nacional*, and this would remain the principal raison d'être for the subsequent periodicals of this type. "Let's laugh! There is a ridiculous side of life that merits special attention, and this is what we will focus on, this is what we will occupy ourselves with.... We will critique laughingly and the reader will laugh with us," declared Fleiuss, as he invited readers into his magazine's discussions about the most important issues in politics, science, the arts, theater, and fashion, "an inexhaustible supply of material for the pencil and the pen."[16] This passage, part of the magazine's introduction to its readers, underscores that its editor envisioned the magazine as a space for interaction among readers, writers, and illustrators.

Three years later, following *Semana Ilustrada*'s model, the Dutchman Eduardo Rensburg launched *Bazar Volante* (Wandering Bazaar, 1863–1866) in the Brazilian capital. Produced by former contributors to *Semana Ilustrada* Joseph Mill, João Pinheiro Guimarães, and Flumen Junius (the pseudonym attributed to Ernesto Augusto de Souza e Silva), this magazine was a deliberate attempt to compete with Fleiuss's established weekly. Rensberg referred directly to his rival in his first issue, in which he also recognized the new taste for this genre of periodical:

> Here I am established! A model bazaar, a market containing more than 10,000 stores! A giant establishment open to the Brazilian public, which will find here all things in existence, [all things] possible and imaginable, and a few other little things as well.... It is a formidable task to write for a population that every week [*semana*] becomes more enlightened [*ilustrada*].[17]

The pun on the name of Rio de Janeiro's most important illustrated magazine made clear the new magazine's target. Humorous jibes at its rival filled the first issue of *Bazar Volante*, including the following dialogue between a mother and her daughter:

> "Mommy, are there now two *Semanas Ilustradas* every Sunday?"
> "No, daughter! One of these sheets is the *Semana*, the other the *Bazar*."
> "Oh! Right! But *Bazar*'s owner is more handsome than Dr. Semana."
> "Silence! Don't say this out loud, girl!"[18]

The joke, of course, demonstrates that *Semana Ilustrada* already had an established reputation in the capital and that the taste for caricatures and satirical periodicals was already well developed. That the girl called the new magazine "another illustrated week [*semana ilustrada*]" is an indication of these periodicals' and their caricatures' consolidation as key elements of visual culture in the empire's public sphere.

Illustrated periodicals proliferated in the next decades. They struggled to stay solvent, but as soon as one closed, others emerged under new owners or from new partnerships involving lithographers and caricaturists. There was continuity of staff among those different newspapers, and very often cartoonists offered their services to two or more periodicals. After a periodical's bankruptcy, its editors and journalists often launched a new periodical under another name. *Bazar Volante*, for example, shut down in 1866, but the following year, *O Arlequim* (The Harlequin, 1867) appeared, run by many of the same writers and artists who had worked on *Bazar Volante*; they soon replaced it with *Vida Fluminense* (Fluminense [Rio de Janeiro] Life, 1868–1874), the greatest competitor to *Semana Ilustrada*. *Vida Fluminense* in turn gave rise to *Revista Ilustrada* (Illustrated Review, 1876–1898), owned by the renowned Italian-born cartoonist Ângelo Agostini.

Scholarship on this period's illustrated periodicals has traditionally focused on the contrast between Fleiuss's *Semana Ilustrada* and Agostini's *Revista Ilustrada*.[19] The difference between the two men is not just historians' construct, for Agostini repeatedly provoked Fleiuss in his cartoons and challenged some of what the German advocated in his magazine. Fleiuss's favorable view of the imperial government was, in fact, unique among the illustrated press, and contrasted sharply with other illustrated periodicals' frequently virulent critiques of the regime and its politicians and policies. Agostini participated actively in the abolitionist movement and republican cause; Joaquim Nabuco, one of the antislavery campaign's leaders, called *Revista Ilustrada* "the abolitionist bible of the people who cannot read," an indication of how visual culture blurred the boundary between literate and nonliterate.[20] The contrast between Fleiuss and Agostini is well documented and forms part of the established history of Brazilian caricature, but this focus has led scholars to overlook the contributions of other artists and other periodicals.

From 1864 to 1870, a flurry of illustrated satirical periodicals appeared in Brazil. *Semana Ilustrada* and *Bazar Volante* were joined by no less than fifteen additional longer- or shorter-lived titles in Rio de Janeiro alone, while similar periodicals are known to have been published in São Paulo, Porto Alegre, Salvador, and Fortaleza. Indeed, from 1860 to 1889, no less than seventy-four illustrated satirical magazines appeared throughout Brazil, thirty-five in Rio de Janeiro and the rest in five other provinces (Ceará, Pernambuco, Bahia, São Paulo, and Rio Grande do Sul) (figure 7.1). Many were ephemeral publications—twenty-seven journals survived one year or less—and only a few lasted a decade or longer (*Semana Ilustrada*, *Revista Ilustrada*, and *O Mequetrefe* [1875–1892] in the capital, and Porto Alegre's *O Século* [1880–1889]). In only two years (1881 and 1888) did the number of provincial illustrated satirical magazines exceed that of the capital. These data demonstrate that, while the imperial capital remained the center of the illustrated press, by the 1880s significant numbers of illustrated magazines were appearing in the provinces. The expansion of the provincial illustrated press derived from the difficulty of distributing periodicals nationally in a continental-size country; the provincial magazines also engaged with local events and local political debates. The expansion of the illustrated press in other provinces not only demonstrates how these magazines catered to the national demand for this type of periodical, but it also reveals that they became a central venue for political disputes and social critique even in the far corners of the empire.

Nevertheless, to reduce the history of illustrated periodicals to the rivalry between Agostini and Fleiuss is to overlook the work of notable caricaturists like Cândido Aragonês Faria, Joseph Mill, Luigi Borgomainerio, and Vitor Mola, not to mention the cartoonists working in provincial capitals. The frequency with which these men reappeared as contributors to successive periodicals reveals their social network; they came together in varying combinations to found new periodicals and distanced themselves from the central figure of Agostini in the late 1870s. Faria and Mill, for example, created *O Mequetrefe*, which competed directly with Agostini's *Revista Ilustrada*, at a time when the Italian was increasingly distinguishing himself from his fellow caricaturists.[21] The break between Agostini and the other more radically republican caricaturists came after the arrival of Rafael Bordalo Pinheiro from Portugal in 1875; he engaged in a bitter rivalry with Agostini through cartoons published in his magazine, *O Besouro* (The Beetle, 1878).[22]

With a few notable exceptions, like the color cartoons that appeared in a few issues of *Bazar Volante*, illustrated magazines followed the same layout. They usually consisted of eight or twelve quarto-sized pages (8.5 by 11 inches) that had typeset text and lithographed illustrations on opposite sides. Al-

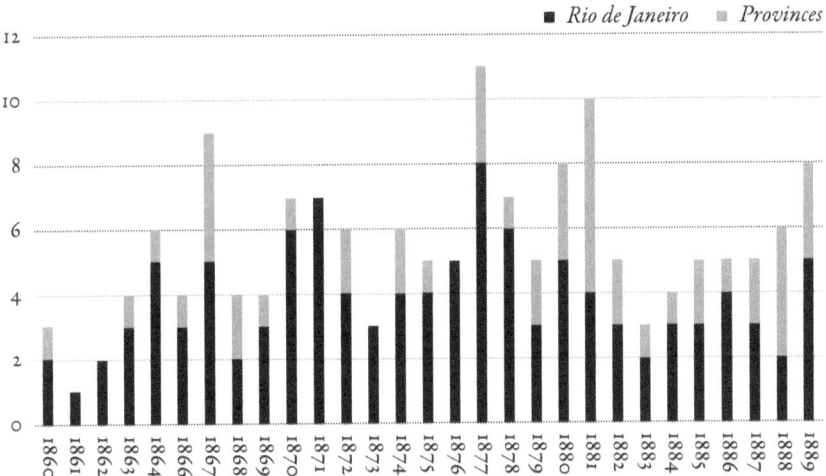

FIGURE 7.1 Number of Illustrated Satirical Periodicals in Circulation by Year and Province, 1860–1889. HDB, Arquivo do Instituto Histórico e Geográfico Brasileiro, and Museu da Comunicação Hipólito José da Costa (Porto Alegre).

though it was possible to print illustrations and text on the same page, the simple technology of rotary printing presses used by the lithographic printers prevented more innovative page layouts. Moreover, because these magazines were run by small groups of cartoonists, editors, and typesetters, a simple business model was essential for preserving their editorial independence and keeping prices reasonable.

There are indications that single-issue prices rose significantly from the 1860s to the end of the 1880s. When it was first launched in 1868, *Vida Fluminense*, for example, cost 500 réis per issue, but doubled its price to one mil-réis (1$000) in 1874; this was still the price in 1889. Prices for individual issues generally fell within this range, while subscriptions for six months usually cost around 11$000 and annual subscriptions cost from 18$000 to 20$000 réis (or considerably less than 400 réis per issue if the magazine published fifty-two times per year, a regularity of publication that not all achieved). While they were not expensive, illustrated magazines were beyond the reach of most. By way of comparison, at this time, a healthy adult slave cost around 1:200$000 (or sixty times the maximum price of an annual subscription); a three-square-meter (32.3 square feet) room in a tenement, with access to a shared kitchen and bathroom, rented for 14$060 per month, while the monthly salaries of the staff at a charity hospital ranged from 400$0000 for the bookkeeper to 100$000 for a clerk (from the 1860s to the 1880s, the mil-réis was usually worth around US$0.50).[23]

Like other newspapers, the illustrated magazines were sold on the street by newsboys, but they could also be purchased at their editorial offices, where subscriptions had to be paid. The US consul in Rio de Janeiro from 1882 to 1885, Christopher Columbus Andrews, remarked that the imperial capital was "a paradise for newspaper-boys." Barefoot, dressed in tattered clothing and smoking a cigarette, "they hover[ed] at the regular starting and stopping places of the street-cars, and [went] on a keen run from the newspaper-offices with the latest edition." Shouting the title of their newspaper, they made "a great deal of clamor, especially when it has a list of lottery-prizes."[24] No doubt, too, they touted the latest issues of illustrated magazines.

Toward New Visual Sensibilities

The history of illustrated satirical magazines is bound up with the histories of caricature and of visuality in Brazilian journalism. This form of journalism should be understood as part of the interplay between visual culture, political criticism, and public debate. Illustrated magazines were not separate from the broader space of public debate that shaped the country's literate culture. In their linkage of literate and visual culture, they offer historians particularly revealing insights into the great debates of Emperor Pedro II's reign, simultaneously discussed in texts and in illustrations on these magazines' pages. While these magazines were enabled by the technical innovations in printing and lithography of the second half of the nineteenth century, they were also the product of larger changes, such as the consolidation of professions linked to the press—cartoonists, journalists, publishers, booksellers—and the broadening range of subjects addressed in the illustrated press.

In the same way, these magazines shaped an emerging visual culture. In a society accustomed to religious imagery and civic mythology, the diverse images distributed by the thousands in the illustrated press amounted to a revolution in Brazilian visual culture. Nevertheless, this revolution built on existing visual culture, as the illustrated magazines brought civic and religious images into readers' hands and homes, as well as satires and curiosities. The changes in the loci for the appreciation of images did not eliminate the social reception of these visual elements; rather, they created a new visual culture that joined the existing social spaces for debate, always with the justification that Brazilians were thereby emulating "civilized" European habits. The parallel expansion of graphic advertising and a consumer culture shaped by the press, which began in the 1870s and accelerated in the first decades of the twentieth century, is another element that supports this hypothesis. Benedita Sant'anna emphasizes, for example, that the first poster advertisement in the streets of Rio de Janeiro promoted the launch of *Semana Ilustrada*.[25]

In short, to focus, as many have done, on defining illustrated magazines by their formal elements—format, number of pages, existence of illustrations, frequency of publication—is misleading, for defining a specific model for the illustrated press is inherently limiting by its exclusion of periodicals that, while they may not meet all the requisites for an illustrated magazine, can be considered part of the genre. Instead, illustrated magazines should be understood as an interface between visual and literary culture. They were the product of an expanding demand for visuality, a symbol of modernity that allowed readers (and those who produced these magazines) to feel close to what they perceived as the European vanguard so deeply desired as symbols of civility by the Brazilian empire's subjects. These magazines produced a dialogue between the visual culture of the society in which they circulated and their role as the creators of meaning and of a new visual sensibility.

A fundamental element of the illustrated press, humor, also constituted an interface, in this case between the existing culture of jocosity and its transformation into the visual *crônica* (chronicle) through the cartoonists' pens and crayons. Although humor became a fundamental feature of this press genre, it was not part of the first illustrated periodicals and only gradually became established over time. When illustrated periodicals assumed for themselves the role of critic and moderator of customs, humor and satire took pride of place. In this light, illustrated satirical magazines were, above all, unique vehicles of intertextuality and the construction of new meanings. Their pages exemplified a new visual culture.[26] Amid the myriad genres and styles of periodicals that flooded nineteenth-century Brazil, perhaps the most distinctive feature of the illustrated press, along with the systematic use of humor as criticism—the product of variety magazines' transformation into satirical magazines—was its capacity to create a new visual sensibility that endured until well into the twentieth century.

Um cocheiro homeopatha.
(Com o seu tilbury passando e repassando sobre as pernas de um homem).

VICTIMA: — Ai! minhas pernas miseras! Como heide agora andar?

COCHEIRO: — *Similia cum similibus*.... Pois vou-lh'as concertar.

FIGURE 7.2 A Homeopathic Coachman, 1866. *Semana Illustrada*, February 25, 1866.

Illustrated Magazines Speaking for Themselves

Up to this point, we have focused on defining the nature of illustrated magazines based on their editorial practices and discursive instruments; however, the best way to engage with these historical relics is to immerse ourselves in a few illustrations and use them to assess these caricatures' role in imperial society. Figure 7.2 is a jest with a specific target, a joke that made fun of homeopathic medicine, a popular practice in nineteenth-century Rio de Janeiro. Since its 1843 founding, the Instituto Homeopático Brasileiro (Brazilian Homeopathic Institute) offered clinical services to paying patients and even opened its doors "to the poor who bring a certificate of poverty signed by their parish priest."[27] Fleiuss plays with contemporary homeopaths' principal slogan, "*similia cum similibus* [like cures like]." Taking this to its logical but absurd conclusion, the cartoonist sketches in the first frame a traffic accident in which a coach's wheels run over a man's legs. In the second frame, the homeopathic coachman treats the victim by running back over him. The joke is made clear by a short verse that accompanies the illustration, an indication of these magazines' intertextual nature:

> VICTIM: "Oh, my hurting legs! / How will I walk now?"
> COACHMAN: "*Similia cum similibus* . . . / I'll treat them for you."[28]

This cartoon highlights that the illustrated press's caricaturists also commented on customs and social trends. There was much debate about the effectiveness of homeopathic treatments, and Fleiuss carried this to a ridiculous extreme. Exaggerating the logic of homeopathic treatment—curing like with like—the cartoon and its little rhyme expressed latent social tensions and worries. The cartoonist's exaggeration provoked laughter, but he spoke directly to a real social issue. The quality of street paving and drivers' failure to respect pedestrians were also constant subjects in these magazines' articles and illustrations, which thus portrayed the daily tensions of city life.

Figure 7.3 has a more traditional subject, imperial politicians, and it is one of the few cartoons that allows us to consider the intersection between criticism of customs and criticism of politics. Published in *Bazar Volante* by the French caricaturist and drawing teacher Joseph Mill, the illustration shows a "new invention for sale at the *Bazar*," a "retrospective mirror" that reveals the past of people who stand before it. Three middle-aged women pose before these mirrors eager to see their youthful selves and seem happy with what their reflections show. By contrast, two men speak privately in a corner of the cartoon:

> CLERK: "These are retrospective mirrors; they show everyone's past."
> THE BAZAAR'S OWNER: "This product is going to sell well to old women, to politicians not so much."[29]

Mill's great achievement lies in this illustration's linkage of two elements of critique in one satire. The critique of customs focuses on well-off women's efforts to regain, even if only in reflection, their youth. Twenty-seven years before the publication of Oscar Wilde's classic *Picture of Dorian Gray*, the cartoonist played with the idea of youth as an object of desire regained through a fantastical physical object. The bazaar owner's comment about how such a mirror would not please imperial politicians calls attention to their desire to distance themselves from their political pasts. In this way, Mill comments on party loyalty and the chaotic imperial party system. It is perhaps not coinci-

FIGURE 7.3 Retrospective Mirrors, 1863. *Bazar Volante*, October 4, 1863.

FIGURE 7.4 His Majesty Is Traveling, 1875. *O Mequetrefe*, October 7, 1875.

dental that, a few months later, the political order would go through one of its major changes with the establishment of the Liga Progressista (Progressive League), composed of dissident Conservatives and dissatisfied Liberals.[30] What Mill's mirror shows is that the distinctions between the two parties were more and more uncertain at this time. Combining criticism of customs and political criticism, this illustration underscores this chapter's argument that illustrated magazines were a great cauldron in which social and political tensions found expression and interacted with each other.

A more conventional imperial political cartoon appears in figure 7.4. Published on the eve of the 1875 elections, when the so-called Religious Question pitted bishops and freemasons against each other and shook church-state relations, the cartoon criticized Emperor Pedro II's planned trip to the United States (which would eventually be postponed to 1876).[31] In the accompanying crônica (on this genre of article, see Ludmila de Souza Maia's chapter), *O Mequetrefe* made its view clear:

> His Majesty is Going Traveling!
> And Brazil will stay here, divided into parties that hate each other, that attack each other, and that prepare themselves for a tremendous conflict. . . . The day of battle is drawing near and His Majesty is going traveling! He picked a good time to go; may God give him good weather and a nice trip[.] Here he leaves Her Imperial Highness to govern us, here he leaves his war chief ready to pull his sword on anyone who complains. . . . Thus, the emperor leaves! His people remain here.[32]

The illustration supports the writer's mocking tone. It shows the emperor, his back turned, dressed like a tourist, complete with a Panama hat, carrying his suitcase and a large bone on which is written the sum of 1,200:000$000 (US$660,000), a massive fortune equivalent to the value of 1,000 slaves. The bone is likely an allusion to the popular expression of "Don't let go of the bone [*não larga o osso*]," said to someone to advise not giving up something deeply desired or beneficial. Behind His Majesty, the political parties, portrayed as vicious curs, maul each other. In addition to the Liberals and the Conservatives, the cartoonist invented a third party, the "Ultramontane Party"—the only entirely black dog, a reference to clerical garb—which did not officially exist, but which was used to describe politicians who supported the church's cause. The dogs thus link the election and the Religious Question. The illustration suggests that the emperor preferred to turn his back on politics, letting the party dogs devour each other, while he escaped with a hefty sum from the Treasury.

Even more interesting than the canine imperial parties' backbiting is the sun that emerges from thick black clouds to illuminate the horizon. Framed by a republican Phrygian cap, the sun thumbs its nose at the fleeing emperor, as if predicting what would happen fourteen years later—the proclamation of a republic and Pedro's permanent exile. The artist is unknown; perhaps because of the daring nature of his critique, which certainly did not go unnoticed, he left the cartoon unsigned. In the end, Pedro delayed his journey by a few months and only arrived in New York on April 15, 1876.[33]

The Paraguayan War (1864–1870) provided material for a very large number of illustrations.[34] Rather than an example of one of the many cartoons about the war itself or about Brazil's enemies, the most common themes in wartime cartoons, figure 7.5 addresses another issue, the conflict's reception in Rio de Janeiro and its impact on the public spaces of debate in the capital. Ângelo Agostini's "Marechalitos da Rua do Ouvidor" (Ouvidor Street's little field marshals) shows a group of men, some of them sporting military headgear made out of folded newspapers and brandishing canes like swords, who discuss a map of the Chaco laid out on a table on which a puppet of Paraguayan president Francisco Solano López appears to dance. On the floor, two of the more vigorous participants in the discussion trade punches while a top hat rolls away. The cartoonist describes the scene as follows:

> To make good use of a few hours of leisure, Ouvidor Street's little field marshals open the way through the Chaco, crossing lakes and swamps with dry feet, lay siege to Angostura, attack and capture Villeta, imprison López and finally occupy [the country] ... with talk. Peace is reestablished! [And they do] this six hundred leagues away and while the devil rubs his eyes. And they say that we don't have manpower![35]

In this cartoon, Agostini innovates and even criticizes criticism—a sort of metacritique—of the war, pointing out that opposition to the conflict had turned into a sort of innocuous elite activity, a harmless pastime among the enlightened Rio de Janeiro elite, eager for news but unwilling to risk themselves on the Paraguayan battlefields. The cartoon was published as the allies were closing in on Asunción, which they would occupy after the Dezembrada, a

FIGURE 7.5 The Little Marshals of Ouvidor Street, 1868. *Vida Fluminense*, December 5, 1868.

series of battles later that month (Itororó, Avaí, Lomas Valentinas, and Angostura). The most interesting aspect of this illustration is the implication that the war had become a topic of enthusiastic discussion among the capital's elite. Of course, since the beginning of the conflict with Paraguay, the war had been a ubiquitous subject in the press; however, the lack of positive news and the length of a war that had been expected to be brief turned Brazilian public opinion against the conflict. Even as the war appeared to be nearing its end, armchair strategists continued to propose solutions. The use of military hats made from newspapers also suggests that the press had a central role in the establishment of this public space of debate. More than just a satire of debate about the war that, thanks to the cartoonist's exaggeration, leads to blows, what Agostini demonstrates here is that the press was an integral part of Brazilian political debates, so much so that he could satirize newspapers' role by turning them into headgear.

Although illustrated magazines had existed in Brazil since the late 1830s, illustrated satirical magazines only assumed their familiar form in the 1860s. This signaled a significant change in the meaning attributed to these magazines. Pedagogical and civilizing instruments in the variety magazines, images became tools of political and social criticism in illustrated satirical magazines. This trajectory, along with the multiple meanings of cartoons, are some of this genre's interesting features. As elements of interface among different cultural practices, these periodicals transformed the great space of debate that was the press and assumed a privileged cultural role, not just through their linkage of written and visual culture but also through their connection to other forms of public expression, such as theater and literature, frequently discussed in the illustrated press's pages and sometimes also serving as material for cartoons.

The illustrated press was at best a financially precarious venture as were all small businesses, and newspapers in general. Supported by only a handful of publishers, illustrated periodicals rarely achieved the success that their founders desired and they often folded after a few years or even months. The difficult relationship with printers led the most successful illustrated periodicals—notably *Semana Ilustrada* and, later, *Vida Fluminense* and Agostini's *Revista Ilustrada*—to establish their own printing presses, but most did not enjoy this level of success and quietly folded, begging subscribers to pay for the issues that they had already received.

Some writers and the predominantly immigrant caricaturists enjoyed considerable renown in Rio de Janeiro. Mill, for example, divided his time between drawing caricatures and teaching drawing to the children of the capital's cultured elite. Agostini and Fleiuss, about whom so much has been written, enjoyed lengthy careers and became important figures in political debate and in social circles. Others are but little known, although their work contributed to the cultural processes discussed in this chapter.

A quick glance at the world of the Brazilian illustrated press cannot do justice to the many analytical possibilities raised by this type of historical source. This chapter only provides glimpses into the dense web of themes and debates that can be analyzed through the illustrated press. These periodicals should not be used solely to illustrate historical arguments but also must be examined on their own terms to tease out the rich historical interpretations that they offer.[36] To paraphrase the Brazilian saying, "Tell me who are your friends and I'll tell you who you are," a scholar of the illustrated press might say, "Tell me what you laugh about and I'll tell you who you are."

Notes

1. See, for example, Alves, "Gênese"; Franco, *Gente*, 123; Pelegrini and Rocha, "Narrativas"; J. Araújo, "Imprensa."

2. Here it is important to acknowledge the sociology of taste as a key reference point, especially the work of Lizé and Roueff, "Fabrique"; and Bourdieu and Saint Martin, "Sens de la propriété."

3. Brazil, *Recenseamento*, 1872. For a fuller discussion of literacy rates, see the introduction.

4. *Museo Universal*, July 1, 1837. On *Museo Universal*'s primacy, see R. Cardoso, "Projeto," 20. *Museu Universal* was directly modeled after English periodicals like *Penny Magazine*, *Pinnock's Guide to Knowledge*, and *Instructor*, as well French counterparts like *Musée des Familles* and *Magazin Pittoresque*. Scholars who examine this type of publication include Heynemann et al., *Marcas*; J. Andrade, "Processos"; R. Santos, *Imagem*.

5. *Brasil Illustrado*, March 14, 1855.

6. On Manso's historical trajectory, see Hahner, "Feminism"; L. Lobo, "Juana Manso."

7. *O Jornal das Senhoras*, January 1, 1852.

8. In the first decades of the twentieth century, during the Old Republic, Nair de Teffé, wife of President Hermes da Fonseca (1910–1914), served as Brazil's first lady and continued to work as a cartoonist in respected illustrated magazines under the pseudonym of Rian (her first name spelled backwards); Lima, *História*, 3:1,266.

9. *Museo Universal*, July 7 and 14, 1838.

10. See, for example, *Brasil Illustrado*, September 15, 1855.

11. Sodré, *História*, 233. Those who accept Sodré's view include Martins, *História*, 66; Maringoni, *Angelo Agostini*, 29; H. Lima, *História*, 1:93. By contrast, Luciano Magno claims that *O Marimbondo* (1822) was the first Brazilian illustrated periodical; *História*, 24.

12. *Lanterna Magica* 1 (1844). This periodical did not include publication dates on its issues.

13. *Charivari Nacional*, August 25, 1859.

14. J. Andrade, "*Semana Ilustrada*"; Telles, *Desenhando*, 19–43; H. Lima, *História*, 1:95–97.

15. *Semana Illustrada*, November 2, 1860.

16. *Semana Illustrada*, November 2, 1860.

17. *Bazar Volante*, September 27, 1863.

18. *Bazar Volante*, September 27, 1863.

19. Scholars who examine the contrast between Agostini and Fleiuss include Balaban, *Poeta*; Telles, *Desenhando*; Lavarda, "Iconografia"; P. Soares, "Guerra."

20. Joaquim Nabuco, "Angelo Agostini," *O Paiz*, August 30, 1888.

21. R. Cardoso, "Projeto," 38.

22. Cagnin, "Bordalo x Agostini."

23. E. Lobo, "Evolução," 258.

24. Andrews, *Brazil*, 37.

25. Sant'anna, *Do* Brasil Ilustrado *(1855–1856)*, 791.

26. On the difficulty in precisely defining visual culture, see Mitchell, *Picture Theory*.

27. *Almanaque Laemmert* (1850): 216. On homeopathy in nineteenth-century Brazil, see Luz, *Arte*; Porto, "Artimanhas."

28. *Semana Illustrada*, February 25, 1866.

29. *Bazar Volante*, October 4, 1863.

30. On the development of political elites and the Brazilian party system, see J. Carvalho, *Construção / Teatro*; on the Liga Progressista, see A. M. J. F. Silva, "Crise partidária."

31. On the Religious Question, see Barros, "Questão."

32. *O Mequetrefe*, October 7, 1875. "Her Imperial Highness" is Princess Isabel, who would serve as regent during Pedro's absence. The "war chief" is a reference to Luiz Alves de Lima e Silva, the Duke of Caxias, army commander during the Paraguayan War and then prime minister.

33. On Pedro II's travels, see Schwarcz, *Barbas*, 373.

34. On the iconography of the Paraguayan War, see Toral, *Imagens*; Cuarterolo, *Soldados*; Salles, *Guerra do Paraguai*. On the war itself, see Izecksohn, *Slavery*; Kraay and Whigham, eds., *I Die with My Country*; Doratioto, *Maldita guerra*.

35. *Vida Fluminense*, December 5, 1868.

36. Balaban, *Poeta*; Maringoni, *Angelo Agostini*; Knauss et al., eds., *Revistas*; Martins, *Revistas*.

Hendrik Kraay

EIGHT TO "JUDGE THE STATE OF THIS PROVINCE" *Correspondence to Rio de Janeiro Newspapers from Bahia, 1868*

From the 1840s to the 1880s, Rio de Janeiro's major dailies published thousands of letters from provincial correspondents, who filled lengthy columns with miscellaneous news and political reporting from the Brazilian empire's far-flung provinces. Full of now obscure references to local affairs and their connections to imperial politics, these letters contributed to forging the imagined community of the Brazilian nation, to paraphrase the titles of two important books.[1] As historical sources, they provide invaluable information about provincial life and politics not available elsewhere, especially for provinces like Bahia from which very few nineteenth-century newspapers have survived—the 1912 federal bombardment of Salvador destroyed the state library and the 1913 fire in the Instituto Geográfico e Histórico da Bahia consumed some of its collection.[2] At the national level, provincial correspondence constituted a dense network, through which news and partisan political polemics flowed among the provinces, binding the newspaper-reading public together into a shared public sphere.

Despite its importance, no historian has, to my knowledge, written about provincial correspondence, and this chapter serves as a preliminary effort to assess the genre. I analyze the 128 letters from Bahia published in Rio de Janeiro's four dailies in 1868. This is, of course, but a small fraction of the provincial correspondence published that year, and much less of the total universe of these letters, but analyzing a connected set of letters together reveals the

---

Support for this research came from the Social Sciences and Humanities Research Council. I thank Renato Torres de Lira (Universidade Federal de Pernambuco), recipient of a 2016 Mitacs Globalink internship, for his skilled transcription of the 128 letters analyzed in this paper. Nina Olegovna Rojkovskaia provided additional research assistance in 2017. When the *JC* published more than one CP from Bahia in a single issue, they are numbered in order of appearance: CP 1, CP 2, etc.

sometimes-heated debates among their resolutely partisan writers, as well as the social and economic bases of news production and circulation. The letters reveal newspapers' partisan nature and financing, the expectations for correspondents who had to write about local events and interpret them for national readers, and the relationship between these writers and their readers. The publication of Bahian correspondence in Rio de Janeiro, normally less than a week after it was written, as well as its circulation back to Bahia as the capital's newspapers were distributed to the provinces, maps Brazil's public sphere, enabled by the steamship lines that carried passengers, cargo, and bundles of periodicals from one end of Brazil to the other.

Provincial and national politics suffused these letters. Their writers reported extensively on political questions and, more important, provincial correspondence was itself a venue for conducting politics. The choice of 1868 was somewhat arbitrary, but the year saw important political and military events. These included the turning point in the Paraguayan War (1864–1870), as the Brazilian navy forced its way past Humaitá in February and the last Paraguayan defenders surrendered the fortress in July, clearing the way for the allied advance toward Asunción, occupied on January 1, 1869.[3] The fall of Bahian lawyer Zacarias de Góes e Vasconcelos's Progressista cabinet (in office since August 3, 1866) and the Conservatives' return to power on July 16 under the Viscount of Itaboraí, Joaquim José Rodrigues Torres, constituted a major political realignment.[4] The Progressista Party (or League) had emerged in the early 1860s as an alliance of moderate Conservatives and moderate Liberals, encouraged by Emperor Pedro II, who saw it as a way of reducing partisanship, a policy that he had pursued since the Conciliação ministry of the mid-1850s. The Conservatives who rejected Progressismo were known as Vermelhos (Reds) or Emperrados (Stubborn Ones). The Liberals who rejected Progressismo were known as Historical Liberals.

Immediately after Pedro called the Conservatives back to power, Itaboraí's ministry lost a vote of confidence in the Chamber of Deputies, upon which the emperor dissolved Parliament and called elections for January 1869. As far as Progressistas and Historical Liberals were concerned, this amounted to a coup, all the more so because one of the main issues was the role of the Marquis of Caxias, commander of the allied forces in Paraguay. The Marquis, a former Conservative prime minister, attributed criticisms of his military strategy to cabinet members and threatened to quit if Progressistas remained in power.[5] For the remainder of the year, preparations for the elections dominated provincial and national politics. Former Progressistas and some former Historical Liberals created the Liberal Party; its senators founded the Centro Liberal and called for substantial reforms to the electoral and judicial systems. The Centro soon also recommended that Liberals boycott the January elections and concentrate their efforts on strengthening the party and developing its platform. While the differences between Historical Liberals and Progressistas could not be fully papered over, and some of the former would eventually sign the 1870 Republican Manifesto, these divisions had not yet become fully clear in 1868, so I will characterize the provincial correspondents as Conservative or Progressista before July 16 and as Conservative or Liberal after this date.

I begin with a brief history of provincial correspondence in the Rio de Janeiro press and provide an overview of the Bahian letters published there in 1868. The second section examines the writers and readers of these letters and their relationships with editors. Unfortunately, the anonymity surrounding these letters limits what we can know about their authors, but their content and the dialogue among correspondents reveal details about them and their intended audience. The third section examines the correspondents' reporting of the ministerial change's aftermath and the September 7 municipal elections. Rarely neutral in partisan politics, provincial correspondents represented a broad range of political positions and offered competing perspectives on politics.

A Year of Provincial Correspondence

Rio de Janeiro's major dailies regularly published provincial correspondence after the late 1840s. It consisted of periodic (and often quite lengthy) letters written by anonymous correspondents who described events in their province. Their format and style—regular letters by the same writer addressed to Rio de Janeiro readers—distinguished them from news reports reprinted from provincial newspapers, from letters to the editor, and from *apedidos* (paid articles published on request; Teresa Cribelli analyzes these in chapter 9), all of which might also treat provincial issues. Provincial correspondence was typically grouped under the headings of "Interior" and "Correspondência" and, in some issues, it filled entire pages. It constituted a distinct and, to nineteenth-century readers, familiar genre of article.

Newspapers had long published what the *Jornal do Commercio* called *cartas particulares* (private letters), a term that it continued to use during this period;

each of the 1868 letters were signed "carta particular" and published in the Interior section, grouped by province. Other newspapers referred to provincial letters as "correspondence" and published them in a section with that title.[6] Before the 1840s, these were typically brief commercial notices listing commodity prices and exchange rates—useful information for newspapers' business readership that some were willing to share publicly.[7] The earliest full-fledged Bahian carta particular that I have located dates from January 1842 and discusses several topics, including crime and policing, problems in recruitment and army and National Guard reorganization, personnel changes in the provincial government, rumors of corruption in the customs house, and high food prices. The writer concluded by apologizing for his letter's length and promised to recount the rest of Bahia's news in a future missive.[8]

By the 1850s, provincial correspondents' letters had become regular features of Rio de Janeiro's dailies. The *Jornal do Commercio*'s managing editor explained in 1850 to a prospective correspondent in Minas Gerais that he should write "with every mail shipment [*por todos os correios*]."[9] The *Correio Mercantil* soon had correspondents in Brazil's major ports and similarly insisted that they write with every steamer, much to the annoyance of its man in Belém, who grumbled in March 1855 that there was nothing interesting to report since the last steamer had sailed two weeks earlier, so he could only advise that, "happily," the province continued in peace.[10]

In 1868, Rio de Janeiro's four dailies collectively published at least 128 letters (figure 8.1) from what appear to have been seven different Bahian writers. Well over half of the letters (71 or 56.3 percent) appeared in the *Jornal do Commercio* (1827–2016). Described as "the *Times* of this capital,"[11] the *Jornal* was Rio de Janeiro's largest newspaper and, under its Franco-Brazilian absentee ownership, a profitable business. It maintained an impressively regular publication schedule and stopped its presses only on Easter Sunday, Christmas, and August 16 (for unspecified reasons), producing fully 363 issues in 1868 (a leap year). With a base of subscribers throughout Brazil, revenue streams from the publication of government notices, parliamentary debates, advertising, and apedidos, the *Jornal* maintained neutrality in party politics but hewed to a generally conservative position on most issues. While one foreigner lamented that the *Jornal*'s only program was to fill its coffers, partisan neutrality was the source of its success and longevity.[12] In the 1850 letter to a prospective correspondent, the managing editor explained that he wanted "the strictest impartiality" in the letters from Minas Gerais, even as he acknowledged that this would be difficult. If he touched on politics, "something that should be avoided," the correspondent should limit himself "to the role of mere chronicler."[13] Party activists, however, wasted no time in seeking to influence what appeared in the *Jornal*. In early 1851, Conservatives in Maranhão recommended that the president (governor) of neighboring Piauí have his "secretary or another reliable person write whatever [he] consider[ed] appropriate" to be added to the letters from Maranhão that one of that province's Conservative deputies was regularly writing.[14]

By the 1860s, all political parties had embraced provincial correspondence as a means to tell their version of provincial events and the *Jornal*'s principle of impartiality had turned into equal space for both parties. The seventy-one Bahian letters published in 1868 exemplify this in near-Solomonic fashion: The Conservative correspondent accounted for thirty-seven of them while his Progressista/Liberal rival contributed thirty-four and, on the twenty-two days that the *Jornal* published two or more letters, it led eleven times with the Conservative correspondence and eleven times with the Progressista/Liberal letter.

The second newspaper, the Conservative *Correio Mercantil* (1844–1868), known simply as *Mercantil* in its first years, published twenty-four letters by the same correspondent in 1868. Founded as a Liberal organ, this daily gradually moved to a more conservative position, until it was effectively a Conservative Party mouthpiece by 1867. In November 1868, in consultation with "their political allies," its owners resolved to close the *Correio* and, according to Matias Molina, merge with the *Diário do Rio de Janeiro*.[15]

The *Diário do Rio de Janeiro* (1821–1878) was then Rio de Janeiro's oldest newspaper and its twenty-one letters are more difficult to characterize. For most of the 1860s it was a Liberal organ under the direction of Joaquim Saldanha Marinho. This phase, during which the *Diário* enjoyed great political, cultural, and literary influence, came to an end in 1867 when its leading writers dispersed. In December, Luiz Antônio Navarro de Andrade was hired as chief editor to put the *Diário*'s financial affairs in order. His editorials in favor of Caxias aroused Zacarias's ire and the prime minister allegedly arranged his removal in April; the subsequent debate included accusations of bribery and excessive government interference in the press. Nevertheless, Zacarias failed to secure the *Diário*'s political support and it was bought by Conservative interests in May; the *Correio Mercantil*'s Bahian correspondent enthusiastically welcomed the newspaper to the party fold. At this point, Antônio Ferreira

Vianna took over as editor.[16] Unfortunately, the Hemeroteca Digital Brasileira's run of the 1868 *Diário* is missing issues 104 to 177 (April 16 to June 30) but the July 1 issue lists the new owner, Custódio Cardoso Fontes. As many as three Bahians wrote for the *Diário*. Five of the first six letters took a generally neutral position in partisan politics. The letter of January 24, apparently written by a different person, is much more critical of the Progressistas.[17] By June, the *Diário* had found a new Conservative correspondent and he produced fifteen letters from July to December.[18]

The *Diário do Povo* (1867–1869) only began publishing provincial correspondence when Lafaiete Rodrigues Pereira took over its editorship on July 12, 1868. After the Progressista cabinet's fall four days later, this small-format daily took an intransigently Liberal position (in 1870, Lafaiete would sign the Republican Manifesto, although he would later reconcile with the empire). Its Bahian correspondent described the *Diário do Povo* as the Liberal Party's "organ in the Court [capital]."[19] One cataloger of Rio de Janeiro newspapers identifies other leading Historical Liberals as contributors, including Aureliano Cândido Tavares Bastos, Pedro Luiz Pereira de Souza, and Francisco Otaviano de Almeida Rosa, most of whom had earlier written for *A Atualidade* and *Opinião Liberal*; they would go on to found *A Reforma* in 1869.[20] The twelve letters from Bahia published until the end of the year are stridently partisan and their author frequently transcribed the *Diário da Bahia*'s denunciations of Conservative government acts.

The 128 letters analyzed in this chapter are spread fairly evenly across the year (an average of 10 to 11 per month, with a minimum of 8 and a maximum of 13), although their distribution across the four newspapers fluctuated considerably (figure 8.1), an indication that none had achieved the regularity of reporting desired by the *Jornal do Commercio* and the *Correio Mercantil* in the 1850s. In January 1868, one of the *Diário do Rio de Janeiro*'s writers noted that he had agreed to send, "whenever possible, news from this province," an indication that he had not agreed to write on a schedule.[21] Earlier, he had apologized for not writing: summer heat had driven him and many others to the cooler suburbs where he sought to "enjoy fresh air in the shade of a mango tree."[22]

The letters varied considerably in length, ranging from 489 to 6,679 words. At 1,066 words, those in the *Correio Mercantil* were considerably shorter than those in the *Diário do Povo* (1,907 words), the *Jornal do Commercio* (2,350 words), and the *Diário do Rio de Janeiro* (2,390 words). Three-fifths of the letters (77 or 60.2 percent) are by Conservative correspondents. Progressistas

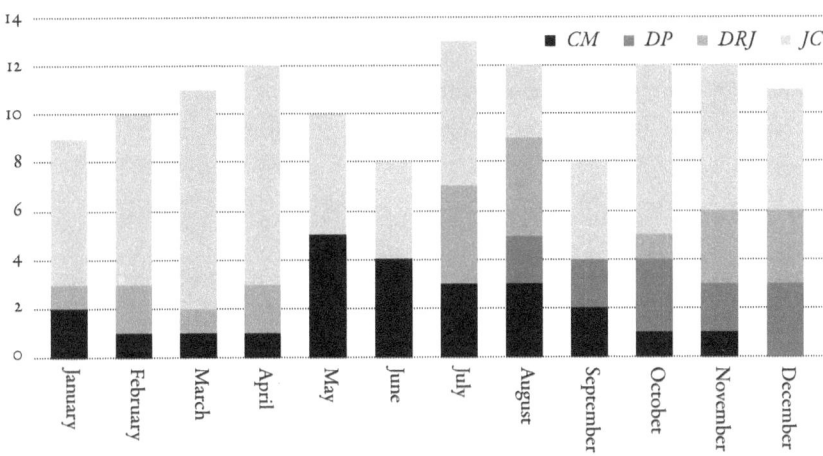

FIGURE 8.1 Number of Letters by Month and Newspaper, 1868. There were 128 letters from Bahia published in these 4 Rio de Janeiro newspapers in 1868.

accounted for nineteen letters and their Liberal successors produced twenty-seven. Five of the first six letters in the *Diário do Rio de Janeiro* express a largely neutral view on politics. The Conservative letters in the *Jornal do Commercio* were 14 percent longer on average than the Progressista/Liberal ones (2,501 versus 2,186 words).

This data suggests that provincial correspondents' reputation for prolixity was well deserved. Back in 1861, Bahia's correspondent for the *Diário de Pernambuco* made light of this "congenital flaw," which he shared with his fellow correspondents: "enraptured by the long columns" that they had written, they "savor a divine nectar" when reading them, while others, "horrified, turn away from these pages; those who brave them are soon overcome by deep drowsiness."[23] Despite noting that there was no "significant news" to report on August 31, 1868, the *Jornal do Commercio*'s Conservative correspondent managed to write 4,650 words![24] Noting that he had written three days earlier, the Progressista reported on April 19 that nothing had changed in Bahia's political situation, "and so there was nothing for a correspondent to say, unless he wanted to make something up, an effort for which the newspaper would certainly thank him." He would, however, never resort to this artifice, "preferring to be a sterile correspondent," for in this way he would best fulfill his obligations as he understood them.[25] He subjected his readers to only 865 words.

Collectively, Bahia's seven correspondents contributed well over 265,000 words to Rio de Janeiro's dailies in 1868. Every week, readers could count on two or three letters from Bahia, and many more from other provinces. They could have their political views confirmed or challenged and they could learn a great deal about what was happening in the province.

Writers in Bahia and Readers in Rio de Janeiro

These letters' authorship remains unknown. All of the 1868 letters (and indeed all of the others that I have seen) were published without bylines, and correspondents and editors publicly respected the principle of anonymity.[26] However, it is hard to believe that well-connected individuals did not know who was writing for the Rio de Janeiro newspapers from a relatively small center like Salvador, in which members of the lettered elite surely all knew each other. In fact, the *Jornal do Commercio*'s Conservative correspondent once indicated that he knew who his Progressista counterpart was, but he declined to reveal his rival's identity.[27]

Others apparently did not know who wrote these letters. The *Jornal do Commercio*'s Conservative correspondent claimed in February 1868 that Progressista Provincial President José Bonifácio Nascentes de Azambuja had called him "a cruel enemy"; fortunately, the president attributed his letters to someone else and would never discover his identity, thanks to "the obscurity in which I live, not involved in politics ... which gives me much freedom to judge with superior impartiality the course of our affairs."[28] Such protestations of isolation ring hollow in light of his admission that he had been in Santo Amaro at the same time that Azambuja had visited the town. There, he heard about a private conversation between the president and the local National Guard commander, the content of which he revealed in one of his letters.[29] He also learned about a private gathering during which the chief of police was overheard boasting to "a correspondent for the Corte" about his "great service," an indication that the chief both knew who the correspondent was and that he sought to influence his reporting.[30] Likewise, Azambuja's "friends" informed a *Diário do Rio de Janeiro* correspondent that a recent economy measure had been solely the president's idea.[31]

Publicly anonymous, politically well-informed, and well-connected, Bahia's correspondents were part of the province's small intellectual elite. The *Jornal do Commercio*'s Conservative correspondent claimed to have known Zacarias de Góes e Vasconcelos since his "university days," which indicates that he had studied at the Olinda law school, where Zacarias occasionally taught (he had a reputation as a brilliant teacher).[32] The frequent Latin interjections demonstrate these writers' education, as do the occasional classical references and their rich vocabulary.

Writing provincial correspondence required mastering the form. The first man to write for the *Diário do Rio de Janeiro* in 1868 promised to improve his style by studying his counterparts' recent letters, adding that this did not mean that he would follow their political line; he lamented that he would never match the inimitable prose of the *Correio Mercantil* correspondent's December 25, 1867, letter.[33] The new Conservative correspondent for the *Diário* apologized in one of his early letters in case that they did not meet expectations.[34] Evidently they did, for he went on to write thirteen more before year end.

There is no indication in the 1868 letters of how these writers were compensated for their work. Presumably, they were paid but this subject was never broached publicly, other than through accusations about "correspondents paid by the treasury" both before and after the July 16 ministerial change.[35] Nor are there any indications of what else they did for a living, but a *Diário do Rio de Janeiro* correspondent apologized for the "serious business" that prevented him from writing for a time.[36] At the end of the year, the *Jornal do Commercio*'s Conservative correspondent declared that he was not a candidate nor a "government employee"; this denial indicates that such people sometimes wrote provincial correspondence (as the 1851 evidence from Maranhão confirms).[37]

This correspondent insisted that he was an "impartial chronicler, who speaks the truth in all things," even as he admitted in late July that he was happy to see Azambuja leave the provincial presidency.[38] In another letter, he distinguished between his political reporting and his "task as a reporter" and, in December, he proclaimed that, "as a journalist I have been a true priest of the press . . . carrying my standard with the dedication and faith of a true believer."[39] He once even claimed that "passion" should never drive a correspondent's pen and that his only task was to recount "the events that take place in this province, so that readers in the Corte can accurately judge the state of this province."[40] The *Diário do Rio de Janeiro*'s new correspondent promised in late June that he would be "scrupulous in accompanying the events day by day," while one of his predecessors lamented that the transcriptions from the chief of police's report had forced him to "sacrifice the news part [of his letter]," which he preferred to write.[41] These comments indicate that the concept of journalistic neutrality existed, but Progressistas did not believe the Conservative correspondent's protestations of integrity and suggested in February that he also wrote for the opposition *Jornal da Bahia*.[42]

There are a few indications of how correspondents gathered their news. They assiduously read newspapers, to judge by the frequent transcription of articles from Bahian periodicals and their commentary on the press. Indeed, much of what they reported could have easily been gathered from a cursory reading of the local newspapers, but sometimes they wrote about things that they had seen. The *Jornal do Commercio*'s Conservative correspondent attended the funeral of Antônio Coelho de Sá e Albuquerque, the former minister of foreign affairs who had died on board a ship in the harbor, on February 29, 1868, but left before the end, for the Southampton packet had arrived and he felt obligated to tell his readers about "the latest events of this land."[43] Reliance on second-hand information led the *Diário do Rio de Janeiro*'s correspondent to make an "involuntary error" in his letter of August 2, in which he reported that the Baron of Cotegipe, João Maurício Wanderley, had been elected president of the newly founded Grêmio Conservador (Conservative Club); the Baron of São Lourenço, Francisco Gonçalves Martins, honorary president; and Dr. Joaquim José Fernandes da Cunha as a member of the board of directors. He had received this information from a friend who left the meeting early. While these three leading Bahian Conservatives—respectively the new minister of the navy, the newly appointed provincial president (who had not yet arrived to take office), and the acting chief of police—had been proposed for these positions, later in the meeting it was judged impolitic for the party to elect these men to such partisan roles while they also held office.[44]

Correspondents constantly commented on the steam packets that connected Bahia to Rio de Janeiro—and to European ports—and the mail service that they provided. The American, British, and French packets and the Brazilian coastal steamers were then Bahia's principal connection with the outside world (a telegraph line would not reach Salvador until 1874).[45] On Sunday, March 29, 1868, Salvador's port looked more impressive than it had for some time, for no less than six steamers lay at anchor, four large transatlantic ships and two Brazilian coastal vessels.[46] The Brazilian steamers linked the coastal provincial capitals and other major ports, while the foreign steamers carried passengers, mail, and newspapers among major Brazilian ports and usually stopped in Salvador and Recife en route to Rio de Janeiro and on their way back. Late arrivals prompted worries about the fate of ships and passengers at sea, while early arrivals forced correspondents to hastily complete their letters

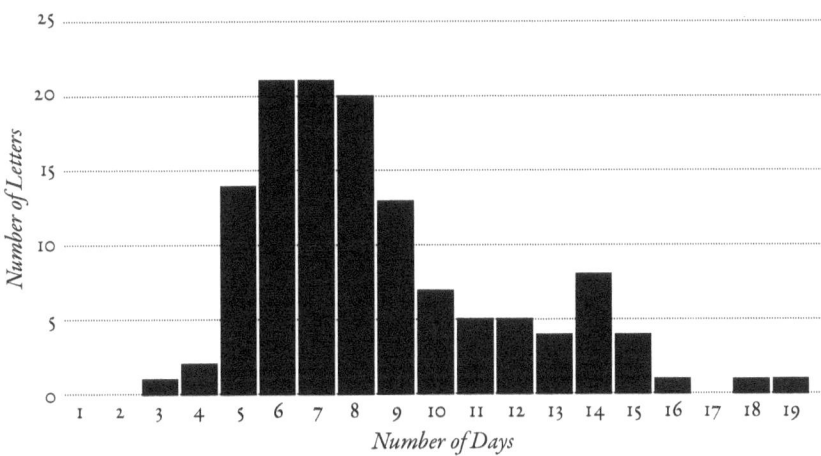

FIGURE 8.2 Number of Letters by Days from Writing to Publication, 1868. For sources, see figure 8.1.

before the mail bags closed. Early in the year, there was much complaint about packets that arrived and departed on Sundays or holidays, forcing all those engaged in business to go to work to prepare their correspondence. Another correspondent protested the British packet's lack of respect for "God's holy day." A week later, he missed sending a letter on the *Donati* (another British steamer), for he had thought that it would not sail on January 6—Epiphany, an important religious holiday. Worse yet, the Brazilian *Cruzeiro do Sul* arrived late at night on the Saturday before the major festival of Our Lord of Bonfim. It sailed at 1:00 p.m. the following day and the mail bags closed at 10:00 a.m. (apparently earlier than usual for there are indications that the mail deadline was normally one hour before ships' departures); despite rushing to complete their correspondence after they saw the vessel in port at dawn, many businessmen and journalists arrived at the post office too late to dispatch their correspondence.[47]

Once the letters arrived in Rio de Janeiro, they were usually published quite quickly. Three-fifths (76 or 59.4 percent) appeared between five and eight days of their dating at Bahia, but two made it in four days and one in three (I suspect a dating error in the latter case) (figure 8.2). Five days can thus be considered the normal time that it took news from Salvador to reach Rio de Janeiro, an indication of the speed of communication at this time, much faster than before the advent of coastal steamers in the late 1830s but much slower than the cryptic telegrams that carried the latest news to Bahia as of 1874. It was expected that newspapers publish the letters in chronological order and the *Diário do Rio de Janeiro* apologized for publishing a letter dated January 24 before the one dated January 9. The *Correio Mercantil* once also made this mistake and its correspondent worried that his earlier letter had been lost.[48]

Rio de Janeiro editors apparently did not edit what their correspondents wrote, although of course they selected writers who would conform to their political orientation (or, in the case of the *Jornal do Commercio*, represent both parties). No correspondent complained that a letter had been deliberately edited or censored. When something was cut, the newspaper carefully noted this, as on March 5, 1868, when the *Jornal do Commercio* cut the transcription of a report on a senator's funeral that had been copied from the *Diário da Bahia*; a footnote explained that this article had already been reprinted.[49] Its typographers once set both a correspondent's error and his correction, suggesting that the handwritten letter had gone straight from the mailroom to the composition table.[50]

The letters then returned to Bahia as part of the major newspapers' national distribution, completing their circular flow and underscoring how their authors were part of a national public sphere that tightly linked Brazil's major coastal cities. Whether the Bahian correspondents were enraptured by their long columns is not known, but they checked their letters carefully. The *Diário do Rio de Janeiro*'s correspondent immediately called attention to the errors that appeared in his letter of June 13; although he did not keep copies, he remembered "perfectly" what he had written.[51] Correspondents then sought to refute their rivals' letters. The *Jornal do Commercio*'s Progressista correspondent claimed that his Conservative counterpart naively believed everything that was said against Azambuja's administration, reproduced every rumor that appeared in "this city's petty periodicals," and even reported news "that seems to have only existed in the reporter's imagination."[52] As far as Azambuja's annoyance with his critic was concerned, how could the president be upset at someone whom he did not even know, much less at someone "whose arguments are so weak that reading them is enough to refute them?"[53] Not long after these jibes, the Conservative correspondent lamented, "When I describe the situation from my retreat, Progressistas think that I dislike them and they insult me.... If what I do is opposition, then may they imitate my unwavering rectitude and impartiality when they're out of power."[54]

Bahia's correspondents were writing for an audience outside of the province, so they had to present the news in a relatively factual manner, unlike cronistas who could assume that their local readers already knew what had happened.[55] In this respect, correspondents were closer to reporters than to cronistas, who increasingly delighted in literary flourishes, complex satires, and subtle wordplay, as Ludmila de Souza Maia shows in her overview of crônicas' evolution (chapter 5).[56] Few such crônica-like elements appeared in the letters. In one of his first missives, the *Diário do Rio de Janeiro*'s new Conservative correspondent mocked the Progressista deputy, [Francisco Maria] Sodré [Pereira], who had declared that, "thanks to the plethora of vitality with which it was born, the Progressista Party was destined to become the strongest of the empire's parties." While the deputy obviously meant "abundance" in his use of *plethora*, the correspondent recalled the word's medical meaning (an excess of humors) and explained: "The plethoric state, as doctors understand it, is always a sickly one." Thus, the deputy had inadvertently declared "that the period of Progressista rule had begun amid a fatal disease."[57] This was the only such instance of high-brow humor in the 1868 letters and its singularity highlights the differences between crônicas and provincial correspondence.

Little is known about the letters' readers, but many were no doubt Bahian expatriates who wanted to keep up with happenings in their home province. Obituaries of prominent individuals, notices about church and civic festivals, and comments about the theater season catered to such readers. So did stories like the accounts of the February 23 solar eclipse that some watched through smoky glass or paper with holes in it; others observed its reflection in still water.[58] Correspondents also noted a series of unusually severe thunderstorms and lightning strikes in Salvador and Santo Amaro.[59] But their audiences also included people with no ties to Bahia, so they sometimes had to explain Bahianisms. Thus, we learn from two correspondents that Bahians nicknamed the slaves freed to serve in the army or navy *andorinhas* (swallows).[60]

Those with business interests in Bahia could glean commercial intelligence from the letters. Every letter in the *Jornal do Commercio* (and most in the *Correio Mercantil* and the *Diário do Rio de Janeiro*) ended with a listing of customs and internal revenue, important indicators of trade conditions, and sometimes also exchange rates and commodity prices. Correspondents regularly noted unusual weather that might affect the harvest or trade. Early in 1868, excessive rains delayed the sugar harvest and drove up manioc prices.[61] In October, soon after the next sugar harvest began, drought threatened. The *Correio Mercantil*'s correspondent reported that "landowners are complaining about the lack of rain, but it should be noted that they're always grumbling about something."[62] By the end of the month, he no longer downplayed the urgent need for "copious rain," a concern shared by his counterparts.[63] The drought soon affected Salvador's beef supply. Scarcely any steers arrived at the slaughterhouse in December, lamented the *Diário do Povo*'s correspondent, and on some days as few as twenty-three sickly animals had to supply the entire population. Opposition correspondents blamed the poor quality beef for an outbreak of dysentery and added that recruitment efforts were scaring away farmers from bringing crops to market, thereby compounding the drought's effects.[64] Rains started in December and the Paraguaçu River swelled with silty runoff, which indicated heavy precipitation in its upper reaches and brought hope that the drought would soon end.[65]

While provincial correspondence was often a grab-bag of trivia, scribbled in haste by correspondents who leaped from topic to topic, these details are part of the letters' charm. They reveal much about daily life as it was experienced by regular readers and writers, even as their flow between Salvador and Rio de Janeiro maps the public sphere and reveals the technologies that underlay it. Provincial correspondence also contained sustained discussions of weightier subjects that reveal something of what writers, readers, and editors considered important political issues.

Provincial Politics through Correspondents' Eyes

The correspondents' declarations of political neutrality and journalistic integrity notwithstanding, these missives were integral parts of the political statements that were nineteenth-century Brazilian newspapers. The letters from Bahia can be read as a set of partisan narratives about provincial politics. Correspondents reported on the provincial assembly's work (March–June), described deputies' and senators' preparations for the general assembly's session (May–September), assiduously followed the national parliamentary debates, and reported the reception of rumors about an impending cabinet change. After the new cabinet dismissed Azambuja and appointed São Lourenço as provincial president, correspondents reported extensively on the personnel changes; the new government removed Progressistas from office throughout Bahia in preparation for the September 7 municipal elections and the January national vote.

Extreme partisanship characterized correspondents' reporting about politics. The purge of local officeholders that began under Antônio Ladislau Figueiredo Rocha (the vice president who administered the province for two weeks between Azambuja's dismissal and São Lourenço's arrival) was, for Conservative correspondents, an indispensable housecleaning: Most local officials had to be replaced, "for the most honest and worthy . . . had been sidelined by *Progressismo*."[66] The *Jornal do Commercio*'s Liberal correspondent complained that the vice president had given free rein to "the hatreds, vengeance, and rancor of his party's members."[67] In August, the *Diário do Povo*'s correspondent judged São Lourenço much worse than Figueiredo Rocha in this regard, for at least the latter had published most of his dismissals, while the former did everything in secrecy.[68]

In late July and early August, the "desperate" Progressista ex-deputies returned to Salvador, speaking about "resistance, agitation, etc.," but the *Correio Mercantil*'s correspondent assured his readers that the Conservative Party would "keep these pygmies in their place."[69] Manuel Pinto de Souza Dantas, Bahia's most prominent Progressista and the former minister of agriculture, returned on August 11 to what the *Diário do Povo*'s correspondent called "a brilliant reception on the part of his numerous friends."[70] He immediately set to work securing the Liberals' position in the press. The *Diário da Bahia*, the government's "official newspaper [*folha oficial*]" during the Progressista years, had just lost the lucrative contract to publish official notices and provincial assembly debates. The new government transferred this patronage to the former opposition *Jornal da Bahia*. An "association of Progressistas" bought the *Diário* in early August and the newspaper announced its "energetic and vigorous opposition" to the new administration, which an unsympathetic Conservative correspondent called "rabid opposition."[71] A Liberal correspondent reported that the new *Diário* quickly signed up "a large number of subscribers" throughout the province, while a Conservative claimed that Dantas had had little success in selling subscriptions, for no one wanted to support a newspaper "whose only mission has been to insult the government"; those who had subscribed were cancelling.[72]

For the new opposition, the press was "the only recourse that we can legitimately have"; for the rest of the year, the *Diário da Bahia* and the opposition correspondents never ceased denouncing what they saw as Conservative abuses of power.[73] There are no indications that the Conservative government sought to interfere directly with the *Diário* or with opposition correspondents, but Liberal newspapers in Recôncavo towns did not fare so well. At the end of the year, the correspondents who had earlier hailed these periodicals as evidence of the population's Liberal sympathies denounced the impressment of their typographers, which had forced them to cease publication.[74] Imperial Brazil's much-vaunted freedom of the press only went so far.

The September 7 municipal and justice of the peace elections were the first test for the new government and the new opposition. Azambuja had started preparing for this vote by, according to his critics, making personnel changes in the police, judiciary, and the National Guard to ensure that reliable Progressistas would oversee the balloting. The *Diário do Rio de Janeiro*'s correspondent sarcastically suggested that he save himself time by simply decreeing the "removal of all Conservatives who hold government posts," although it is unlikely that many Conservatives remained in key positions after several years of Progressista rule.[75] Figueiredo Rocha's dismissals were a first step in undoing Azambuja's work. In early August, the Grêmio Conservador prepared its slate of candidates for Salvador's city council as well as parish-level slates of candidates for justices of the peace.[76] Progressistas also sought to organize themselves but were hampered by a lack of leadership until Dantas arrived, less than a month before the vote.[77] All indications are that the government effectively controlled the electoral machinery in Salvador and Conservative correspondents hailed their triumph as evidence of their popularity, while Liberal correspondents denounced the coercion of government employees to vote for government lists, the numerous "ineligible voters [*fósforos*]" who cast ballots, and the thugs who kept Liberals from the polls. Conservative correspondents reported only one attempted fraud, in Brotas Parish, where a Liberal member of the electoral board had stuffed his jacket sleeve with ballots, which he tried to shake onto the counting table.[78] Conservatives had included one token Liberal on their slate, the respected Baron of Sauípe, but his continued partisanship prompted those in charge of the *apuração* (the certification of the votes) to discover an error that moved him from the last elected council member to the position of first alternate. All of the alternates, in fact, were Progressistas.[79] Correspondents wrote nothing about the new justices of the peace, an indication of how unimportant this position had become.

The municipal elections did not go so smoothly for the government in much of the interior. While the *Correio Mercantil*'s correspondent announced the Conservatives' "splendid and complete triumph" throughout the province, *duplicatas* from all over the province were reported to Salvador. Conservative correspondents dismissed these competing electoral results, which invariably showed an opposition victory, as the fruits of a Liberal plot to disrupt the electoral process. The provincial government eventually annulled these duplicatas and Conservative correspondents urged São Lourenço to punish those responsible for such electoral "farces," while Liberal correspondents continued to denounce these machinations.[80]

The political discussions in Bahia's provincial correspondence can easily be read to demonstrate, once more, the old aphorism that nothing more resembled a Conservative than a Liberal in power. Conservatives and Progressistas/ Liberals accused each other of the same misdeeds. The *Correio Mercantil*'s correspondent claimed that Progressistas only knew how to govern badly or to conspire against the government, while the *Jornal do Commercio*'s Liberal correspondent claimed that Vermelhos out of power spent all of their time creating "associations, resistance centers," and "promoting *meetings*" (he used the English word); when Liberals did the same in opposition, all that Conservatives could see was "anarchists and troublemakers."[81] The amount of space that the correspondents and the newspapers devoted to politics, however, indicates its importance to the newspaper-reading public.

Provincial correspondence was a distinctively imperial genre: in the 1880s, the frequency of letters from Bahia diminished and, by the 1890s, they completely disappeared from the capital's press. There was no room for such lengthy articles in the more popular newspapers like the *Gazeta de Notícias* and *O País*, whose shorter articles appealed to new reader preferences; the new popular press soon influenced the older newspapers.[82] To immerse oneself in provincial correspondence is to enter a world dominated by partisan politics, in which provincial life is tightly connected to the Corte and in which slaves or Africans scarcely appear; as far as correspondents were concerned, they were not part of political life. Life's rhythms follow the steam packets' comings and goings; readers eagerly await the bundles of newspapers carried in the ships' holds while writers hurry to make the mail deadline. To be sure, most Brazilians probably cared little about what appeared in the press (although yesterday's newspapers were no doubt useful for wrapping fish at the market). For a small, highly influential, educated elite—whose size grew significantly over the course of the empire, to judge by what we know about newspaper circulation—life revolved around the press. The provincial correspondence certainly contributed to their sense of belonging to the larger community of the Brazilian nation, refracted through the lenses of partisan politics. Much remains to be learned about provincial correspondence. I have focused on the reports from Bahia to the Corte, but correspondence also flowed in the other direction and both of Salvador's dailies published letters from Rio de Janeiro in 1868; there is no indication of how frequently they did so.[83] And there was correspondence among provincial capitals as well. Together they formed a dense network through which news and political polemics flowed around the Brazilian empire, a public sphere that undergirded the Brazilian nation in the nineteenth-century sense of a political community.

Notes

1. Barman, *Brazil*; Anderson, *Imagined Communities*.
2. Boccanera Junior, *Bahia*, 53, 87, 125. Many of the Bahian periodicals listed in late-nineteenth- and early-twentieth-century catalogs no longer exist, "Catalogo dos jornaes bahianos"; Torres and Carvalho, *Annaes*.
3. Doratioto, *Maldita guerra*.
4. The following paragraphs are based on Iglesias, "Vida," 85–112; Needell, *Party of Order*, 239–49; Barman, *Citizen Emperor*, 211–23; Nabuco, *Estadista*, 650–76. On the Progessista Party's origins, see S. Barbosa, "Política."
5. Caxias is scarcely mentioned in the correspondence, except in Conservative denunciations of Progressista provincial deputies' criticisms of the general, CP 1, March 17, *JC*, March 24, 1868; Corrs., May 3 and 18, *CM*, May 11 and 24, 1868.
6. Hence, I refer to the letters in the *JC* as CPs in these notes and those in the other newspapers as Corrs.
7. See, for example, CP, March 9, *JC*, March 21, 1841.
8. CP, January 25, *JC*, February 4, 1842.
9. Quoted in Mascarenhas, *Jornalista*, 208.
10. Corr., Belém, March 3, *CM*, March 23, 1855.
11. J. Clement Cobbold to Earl Granville, Rio, September 28, 1870, Great Britain, Public Record Office, Foreign Office 13, vol. 469, fol. 214.
12. Ribeyrolles, *Brasil*, 2:99–100; Sandroni, *180 anos*; Molina, *História*, 1:232–92.
13. Quoted in Mascarenhas, *Jornalista*, 208.
14. Francisco Xavier Paes Barreto to José Antônio Saraiva, São Luís, March 1, 1851 (postscript), Arquivo do Instituto Geográfico Brasileiro, lata 270, doc. 14.318. I thank Roderick J. Barman for sharing this source.
15. *CM*, November 15, 1868; Molina, *História*, 1:228; Mascarenhas, *Jornalista*, 318.
16. Corr., May 11, *CM*, May 28, 1868. On Andrade, see *Diccionario*, 342; Sacramento Blake, *Diccionario*, 5:353–54; L. Andrade, *Questão*. On Ferreira Vianna's editorship of the *DRJ* (1868–69), see Sacramento Blake, *Diccionario*, 1:166. My account of the *DRJ*'s trajectory differs slightly from Molina, *História* 1:226–28.

17. Corr., January 24, *DRJ*, February 1, 1868. This letter was not written by the same author as the one published the following day, but dated January 9 and 14, *DRJ*, February 2, 1868.

18. He wrote at least two letters that appeared before July 1, for he referred to "my earlier ones" in Corr., June 27, *DRJ*, July 3, 1868.

19. Corr., August 13, *DP*, August 19, 1868.

20. G. Fonseca, *Biografia*, 337; Mascarenhas, *Jornalista*, 342.

21. Corr., January 9, *DRJ*, February 2, 1868.

22. Corr., December 29, 1867, *DRJ*, January 4, 1868.

23. Corr., June 24, *Diario de Pernambuco* (Recife), July 2, 1861.

24. CP 1, August 31, *JC*, September 12, 1868.

25. CP 3, April 19, *JC*, April 27, 1868.

26. The only exception to this that I know of were the announcements in 1888 that described Alexandre José de Mello Moraes Filho as the correspondent for Salvador's *Jornal de Noticias*, "Imprensa Fluminense," *Diario de Noticias*, May 19, 1888; *Gazeta da Tarde*, May 19, 1888.

27. CP 1, December 31, *JC*, January 4, 1868.

28. CP 1, February 16, *JC*, February 29, 1868.

29. CP 2, February 17, *JC*, February 29, 1868.

30. CP, May 3, *JC*, May 14, 1868.

31. Corr., January 24, *DRJ*, February 1, 1868.

32. Vargas, *Conselheiro Zacarias*, 24; Sacramento Blake, *Diccionario*, 7:408.

33. Corr., January 9, *DRJ*, February 2, 1868.

34. Corr., July 4, *DRJ*, July 10, 1868.

35. CP 3, July 15, *JC*, July 21, 1868; CP 1, November 1, *JC*, November 17, 1868; CP 1, October 27, *JC*, November 4, 1868.

36. Corr., October 16, *DRJ*, October 22, 1868.

37. CP, December 15, *JC*, December 20, 1868.

38. CP 1, July 29, *JC*, August 5, 1868.

39. CP 1, May 29, *JC*, June 6, 1868; CP, December 15, *JC*, December 20, 1868.

40. CP 3, October 29, *JC*, November 4, 1868.

41. Corrs., June 27, *DRJ*, July 3, 1868; Corr., March 15, *DRJ*, March 26, 1868.

42. CP 3, February 16, *JC*, February 29, 1868.

43. CP 1, February 29, *JC*, March 5, 1868.

44. Corrs., August 2 and 12, *DRJ*, August 11 and 19, 1868. The *CM*'s correspondent also reported this incorrect news, but he did not publish a correction, Corr., August 2, *CM*, August 8, 1868.

45. Amaral, *Historia*, 282.

46. CP 1, April 1, *JC*, April 10, 1868.

47. CPs, December 31, 1867, January 8 and 19, 1868, *JC*, January 5, 19, and 28, 1868. On the mail closing one hour before a ship's departure, see CP, September 17,

JC, September 23, 1868. For a literary portrayal of the hustle and bustle in São Luís's port when steamers called, set in 1871, see A. Azevedo, *Mulatto*, 210, 224, 230–33, 234.

48. Footnote to Corr., January 9, *DRJ*, February 2, 1868; Corr., May 20, *CM*, June 4, 1868.

49. CP 1, February 29, *JC*, March 5, 1868.

50. CP, April 1, *JC*, April 10, 1868.

51. Corr., July 4, *DRJ*, July 10, 1868.

52. CP 1, March 6, *JC*, March 14, 1868; CP, March 29, *JC*, April 4, 1868; CP 2, May 16, *JC*, May 16, 1868.

53. CP 1, March 6, *JC*, March 14, 1868.

54. CP, May 14, *JC*, May 20, 1868.

55. R. Araujo, "Caminhos," 178.

56. On crônicas, see Chalhoub, Neves, and Pereira, eds., *História*.

57. Corr., June 27, *DRJ*, July 3, 1868.

58. CPs, February 29, *JC*, March 5, 1868.

59. Corr., February 29, *CM*, March 7, 1868; CPs, February 29 and March 17, *JC*, March 5 and 24, 1868.

60. CP, January 14, *JC*, January 23, 1868; Corr., January 17, *CM*, January 27, 1868.

61. CP, January 19, *JC*, January 28, 1868; Corr., January 24, *DRJ*, February 1, 1868; CP 1, January 30, *JC*, February 7, 1868; CP 1, February 13, *JC*, February 19, 1868.

62. Corr., October 16, *CM*, October 21, 1868.

63. Corr., October 31, *CM*, November 7, 1868; Corr., October 28, *DRJ*, November 6, 1868; CPs, November 1 and 2, *JC*, November 17, 1868.

64. Corr., December 15, *DP*, December 27, 1868; CP 1, December 15, *JC*, December 25, CP, December 15, *JC*, December 20, 1868.

65. CP 2, December 17, *JC*, December 25, 1868. This drought was much less severe than the major one of 1857–1861; G. Rodrigues, "Secas," 35–83, 84, 88.

66. Corr., July 29, *CM*, August 3, 1868.

67. CP, August 2, *JC*, August 7, 1868.

68. Corrs., August 16 and 23, *DP*, August 20 and September 10, 1868.

69. Corr., August 2, *CM*, August 8, 1868.

70. Corr., August 13, *DP*, August 19, 1868.

71. CP, August 2, *JC*, August 7, 1868; Corr., August 12 and 16, *DRJ*, August 19 and 24, 1868; Corr., August 13, *CM*, August 18, 1868. On the *Diario da Bahia*'s sale, see K. Silva, *Diario da Bahia*, 250–52.

72. CPs, September 6 and 29, October 12, *JC*, September 19, October 8 and 21, 1868.

73. CP, September 17, *JC*, September 23, 1868; CP 2, October 12, *JC*, October 21, 1868.

74. CP, September 6, *JC*, September 19, 1868; Corrs., November 26, December 4, *DP*, December 6 and 11, 1868; CP, December 4, *JC*, December 18, 1868.

75. CP 2, May 29, *JC*, June 7, 1868; CP, June 14, *JC*, June 23, 1868; Corr., July 13, *DRJ*, July 18, 1868; Corr., July 17, *DRJ*, July 22, 1868.

76. Corr., August 2, *CM*, August 8, 1868.

77. CP 1, July 29, *JC*, August 5, 1868.

78. Postscript of September 11 to CP, September 6, *JC*, September 19, 1868; CP 1, September 29, *JC*, October 8, 1868; Corr., September 14, *CM*, September 21, 1868.

79. Continuation of October 6 to CP 1, September 30, *JC*, October 10, 1868; Corr., October 28, *DRJ*, November 6, 1868. Whether any of these alternates actually took seats in the council is not known; the lists of councilors in Ruy's *História* appear to include only those elected. Allowing a token opposition member to win a seat was a common tactic to deprive the opposition of grounds for complaint and, in August 1868, Conservatives considered doing this for the upcoming elections; R. Graham, *Patronage*, 76.

80. Corr., October 16, *CM*, October 21, 1868; CP 2, October 15, *JC*, October 25, 1868; Corrs., October 16 and 28, *DRJ*, October 22, November 6, 1868; CPs 1 and 2, October 27, *JC*, November 4, 1868; CP 2, November 2, *JC*, November 17, 1868; CP, November 28, *JC*, December 9, 1868.

81. Corrs., September 14, October 16, *CM*, September 21, October 21, 1868; CP 2, August 31, *JC*, September 12, 1868.

82. This conclusion derives from my search for letters from Bahia in July of every year from the 1840s to the 1890s for Kraay, *Bahia's Independence*.

83. References to these letters appeared in Corr., March 15, *DRJ*, March 24, 1868; Corr., June 14, *CM*, June 24, 1868.

Teresa Cribelli

NINE   *APEDIDOS* AND PUBLIC DISCOURSE
Paid Letters and Articles in the Jornal do Commercio, *1870*

This chapter provides a preliminary examination of the Publicações a Pedido section (readers' letters or articles "published by request") of the *Jornal do Commercio*, one of the most widely circulated newspapers of imperial Brazil. Submitted by members of the public who paid to see their missives in print, *apedidos* can be considered a hybrid between *correspôndencias* (letters to the editor, printed for free at the publisher's discretion), a regular section that followed front-page news reporting, and *anúncios*, the paid want ads that filled the back pages of daily newspapers. Authors with "the cash" in hand, as one US visitor quipped, paid to print their views in the *Jornal do Commercio*.[1] Covering a diverse range of topics—from amateur poetry to polemics—apedidos offer a unique view into Brazilian public sentiment in the nineteenth century, shedding light on subjects that went beyond the usual political and economic fare of newspapers to capture local disputes, calls for action, and daily events.

This essay focuses on two lines of analysis. The first seeks to contextualize apedidos within a broader understanding of the genre of public letters in the eighteenth- and nineteenth-century transatlantic press. Similar in tone to published treatises and essays, the genre of readers' correspondence developed within the context of a new print culture rooted in the Enlightenment values of self-emancipation and civic engagement through print. Second, through the investigation of a sample of 923 apedidos printed in the *Jornal do Commercio* in January 1870, definitions of public opinion and topics important to the reading public come into view. Before the 1870s, cash-strapped Brazilian newspapers benefited from and may even have come to depend on the revenue produced by apedidos, a fact that likely contributed to editors' acceptance of a wide range of topics and viewpoints, perhaps more so than newspapers in the North Atlantic world. A similar variety of topics appeared in *remitidos*, the Spanish American counterpart to apedidos that were popular in the nineteenth-century Peruvian press. As Pablo Whipple notes, "any resident of Lima" could publish one with the proper payment, rendering each newspaper edition "a collaboration" between the public and the press.[2] The financial precariousness of newspaper publishing in general, and particularly in Latin America, likely contributed to the success of this distinctive genre as paid letters provided dependable revenue.

By January 1870 the Publicações a Pedido section had developed into a mature genre that appeared daily in the *Jornal do Commercio*. The column first appeared in the 1830s and evolved in tandem with the Brazilian press. While the apedidos of Brazilian luminaries such as the Afro-Brazilian engineer André Rebouças, abolitionist Joaquim Nabuco, and statesman Miguel Calmon du Pin e Almeida (the Marquis of Abrantes) regularly appeared in the section and have been studied by scholars, little attention has been focused on the everyday concerns of the reading public. The volume and tone of these letters and articles evidence a distinctly Brazilian space in which the actions, thoughts, and experiences of private individuals were transformed into an on-going public conversation. As printed expressions of daily life, apedidos—even when anonymous—expand our understanding of acceptable topics for public consumption beyond the traditional political commentary and economic reporting of the newspaper.

Apedidos demonstrate that in the nineteenth century, as now, the disgruntled and disaffected were highly motivated to take their complaints to print.[3] But apedidos also covered a diverse array of subjects that varied greatly in tone—from laudatory to caustic, from the cryptically personal to clear calls to end slavery or rally support for public works projects. Local businesses used the section to wage public relations campaigns, while individuals with sufficient cash pontificated on an astonishing spectrum of topics.[4] As a result, the "Publicações a Pedido" section contained a wide range of public sentiment, lending itself to a deeper understanding of the ways that the public and the press came together during the empire. Apedidos bring into focus vignettes of everyday life in nineteenth-century Brazil, ranging from support for girls' education, to praise for the funeral of US composer Louis Gottschalk who succumbed to yellow fever in Rio de Janeiro in 1869, to complaints about the circulation of fraudulent streetcar tickets.[5] As such, apedidos provide small windows into daily experiences that rarely appear in other sources.

Public Letters and the Enlightenment

"Letters," ideas circulated as printed text, acquired a newly emancipatory meaning during the Enlightenment. The printing press enabled the development of innovative textual genres (newspapers in the seventeenth century, for example, or Denis Diderot's multivolume *Encyclopédie* in the eighteenth) that gave voice to public inquiries intended to empower and emancipate the individual.[6] Examples of emancipatory texts ranged from ostensibly private letters exchanged between individuals but circulated to a broader audience (a genre that dated to antiquity) to pamphlets, broadsides, posters, essays, treatises, almanacs, encyclopedias, and, of special interest for this essay, newspapers. Michael Warner explains that in the pre-revolutionary United States printed texts were "[no] longer a technology of privacy underwritten by divine authority [the bible,] . . . [print became] a technology of publicity whose meaning [was] . . . civic and emancipatory."[7] In this sense, the genre of readers' letters that developed in the transatlantic periodical press emerged from the Enlightenment ideal of emancipation of the individual through the printed word. Expressing private thoughts through the "public prints" transformed the way that individuals understood themselves and their communities; what had once been private became increasingly acceptable for public discussion.

While reader correspondence or public letters—defined here as submissions to newspapers and journals by individuals outside of the usual cadre of journalists, editors, and printers—became popular sections of periodicals on both sides of the Atlantic by the eighteenth century, relatively little comprehensive research into their structure, thematic content, or role in shaping public debate has been undertaken by scholars. Recently, Elizabeth Andrews Bond forged new inroads into understanding this genre in her work on letters to the editor in the late eighteenth-century French provincial press. She argues that public letters offered French readers a forum to discuss issues of the day in print, giving voice to a "practical Enlightenment" that went beyond the Philosophes' insular debates to include members of the general public.[8] As one reader opined, letters captured the gist of readers' "rapid conversations, which touches on everything . . . where philosophical reflections intersect the neighborhood news."[9] Through her examination of more than 3,000 letters published in local and national newspapers in France in the decade before the revolution, Bond observes that published letters provided a venue for the reading public to practice the "habits of mind" exalted and promoted by Enlightenment thought. French letters to the editor expressed a range of sentiments from a fascination with new technologies (hot air balloons), precautionary information (the danger of poor ventilation in cellars), to the eminently practical (the use of potatoes as an ingredient in a healing ointment).[10] Popular letters were reprinted in provincial and national newspapers, demonstrating regional networks and flows of information between the provinces and Paris. Reader correspondence also generated conversations among individuals on the street—bringing the oral conversations that were often the genesis of printed letters full circle. By creating "buzz" about topics submitted by readers themselves, public letters also increased subscriptions, or so editors hoped.

Less comprehensive research has been completed about the development of public letters in the English-speaking press of Great Britain and the United States, although the genre appeared early on in both. In the latter, readers' letters comprised a vital and very visible section of pre-revolutionary newspapers, often taking up one page out of the usual four that comprised most editions. In this regard, public letters had greater visibility and were more important in terms of overall content than in present-day US newspapers.[11] The criteria for selecting reader correspondence in the British colony in the early decades of the 1700s depended on the "modesty and good manners" of submissions and focused on the staid topics of "education, marriage, medicine, and fashion."[12] By the 1740s, editors shifted toward more controversial topics, printing strongly opinionated reader submissions about politics, government, and social matters. The public sometimes charged that this tactic gave cover to editors to hide their personal views behind the voices of their readers. Colonial publishers were also accused of planting their own letters. While editors considered the publication of readers' letters a public service that provided a free and accessible forum for debating important topics, they not infrequently charged a fee for the privilege; even the famous printer Benjamin Franklin did so.[13] From its inception, the newspaper business was a financially precarious enterprise, and printers often looked for revenue streams beyond advertising and subscriptions.[14] Nineteenth-century French publishers, for instance, printed paid "editorial publicity" on the front pages of their papers in an effort to increase the bottom line.[15] A rare example of an editor's note on the fees charged to print a series of book reviews in an 1860s newspaper from New Jersey suggests that the practice was probably more common than can be quantified.[16] Charging to print submitted content, however, was controversial as it called into question a newspaper's credibility and journalistic independence; accordingly publishers had incentives to conceal paid submissions. As these publishing traditions in the United States and France indicate, nineteenth-century Latin American newspapers were not unique in printing readers' submissions for a fee, although the Publicações a Pedido section was fully transparent about the transactional nature of the arrangement.

In Great Britain, public letters were printed in a diverse swath of the seventeenth-, eighteenth-, and nineteenth-century press. In the eighteenth century, letters to the editor addressing political matters were considered a vital and effective forum for reaching the "common people," so much so that they diminished the popularity and distribution of pamphlets and printed essays.[17] By the nineteenth century, reader submissions evolved into a lively section in journals and newspapers, providing clues to present-day scholars about contributors' social class, gender, and political persuasion. In nineteenth-century Scotland, for example, the weekly *People's Journal* published poetry submitted by its working-class readers in the To Correspondents section. Immensely popular, the poems were subsequently critiqued and ranked by the editors, creating a space for a working-class "communal poetic identity" and a back-and-forth dialogue between the public and the journal.[18] The column was quickly imitated by two competing newspapers, underscoring the use of public submissions in generating content and attracting readers. In contrast to the niche genre exemplified in the *People's Journal*, British Victorian readers' correspondence more broadly took the form of amusing and instructive responses to a wide variety of topics.[19]

Readers' submissions also inspired more controversial debates as was the case with a collection of letters about the Victorian sex trade purportedly composed by several prostitutes and printed in the *Times* in London in 1858. One famous example, submitted under the pseudonym Another Unfortunate, was attributed to an affluent prostitute writing in defense of her livelihood. The letter drew a heated response from the public as well as follow-up editorials by the newspaper, not only broadening the manner in which prostitution was discussed in the public forum but eventually influencing government policy.[20] Whatever the original motive of the editors of the *Times* in printing the letters, they were almost certainly pleased by the amount of attention brought to their daily. Then, as now, controversy could be good for the bottom line.

As these examples show, public letters were very much a common and visible feature of the French- and English-language press on both sides of the Atlantic and served multiple roles: they provided a way to draw attention (and notoriety) to a particular newspaper; they created a forum for the reading public to see its thoughts in print as well as to exercise one's civic duty through public debate; and it was a free—and sometimes remunerative—method for generating newspaper content.

The Birth of the Press and Publicações a Pedido in Brazil

In contrast to a vibrant colonial press in British and Spanish America, printing presses were banned for most of the colonial period in Brazil; only with the arrival of the Portuguese court in 1808 (independence came fourteen years later) was the press legalized. During the final years of colonial rule, print emerged as a potent venue for political debates, ultimately playing a role in Brazil's break with Portugal. Scholars have noted that the Brazilian nation and the Brazilian press developed in tandem.[21]

The views expressed in the early Brazilian press reflected the emerging importance of the printed word in civic life, including its emancipatory potential so valued by the Enlightenment thinkers of the previous century. After independence, the press continued to play a central role in the creation of a public forum of print that paralleled the new public spaces—theaters, the botanical garden, and public parks and promenades—built after the arrival of the court. Marcel Morel and Mariana Monteiro de Barros define the community of private individuals who comprised the reading public during this formative period through the concept of *public opinion*, a term invoked in the masthead of period newspapers. Public opinion was not expressed through any one particular column or section of the newspaper, but represented the relationship between the newspaper's editors and readers who were assumed to be primarily white male subscribers.[22] Through purchase and subscription, readers supported the presumably rational, civic, and enlightened ideas expressed in newspapers, thereby influencing and reinforcing which topics were acceptable for print. The concept of public opinion later resonated in apedidos, and many authors explicitly invoked the term.

Because illiteracy was common in nineteenth-century Brazil, some additional observations on the definition of public (beyond the concept of public opinion) shed light on how literacy and illiteracy shaped the ways in which individuals experienced newspapers—and apedidos in particular—in the empire (see this volume's introduction for background on Brazilian literacy). Apedidos differed from other sections of the newspaper in that they were colloquial in tone and often prompted responses that were in essence a conversation in print. The public clearly felt a sense of ownership of the apedidos section and many expressed an obligation to challenge their compatriots in the pages of the *Jornal do Commercio* and other dailies.

For the purposes of this essay, *public* refers to the sense of "visibility of communication" or what is accessible and can be viewed (and what is acceptable for viewing) by a collective audience.[23] By and large, newspapers were published for white literate men from the middling and elite classes. While the economic and political reporting in the *Jornal do Commercio* was understood to be the province of male elites, access to newspapers extended beyond this group to include illiterate individuals, be they the enslaved, women, or those lower on the social ladder. Those who could not read were exposed to newspaper topics through conversation (both directly or through overhearing) as well as through public reading. This exposure happened in the very places where print was created; Rodrigo Camargo de Godoi demonstrates that enslaved people—both literate and illiterate—labored in printing offices as inkers and machine operators in addition to more specialized tasks that required reading and writing (see his chapter). Print workshops were also spaces where enslaved and free workers presumably listened to (or read) and almost certainly discussed the news topics of the day.[24] Outside of the printing office, scenarios of public reading and listening were equally likely; for example, one envisions a household of women, including enslaved people, listening in a drawing room or patio to the latest serialized novel in the *Jornal do Commercio*. After street sales appeared in the 1870s, passersby were subjected to the news shouted from the street corners by newsboys hawking the latest edition.[25] Andrew Hobbs observes that illiteracy was "no barrier to the consumption of print" in Victorian Britain; the same holds true for Brazil.[26]

In 1885, *O País*, one of the few Rio de Janeiro newspapers that did not print the genre, explained how apedidos were read publicly and inspired conversations:

> The Brazilian who picks up a copy of the *Jornal* [*do Commercio*] does not put it down for several hours. He zips through the news and soon settles on the great miscellany of—*apedidos*. By habit the reader soon searches for the little gems that he recognizes by title, signature, or context. One small *mofina* [anonymous insult] sometimes provides the topic of conversation for an entire day. The reader follows the

adventures of private disputes as one would follow the war in Paraguay, or the war between France and Prussia.[27]

As the above example poignantly demonstrates, apedidos were read aloud and discussed wherever newspaper readers gathered. Apedidos—many of them composed as letters that imparted a conversational and even intimate tone—differed substantially from sections of the newspaper that presented information alone. In his exploration of Mexican love letters exchanged at the turn of the twentieth century, William French argues that "letters are essentially conversation in written form, more a part of than separate from the world of everyday speech."[28] Although French examines manuscript letters that were never intended to circulate beyond an intimate group, the printed letters, opinions, declarations, arguments, and announcements of the Publicações a Pedido section resembled a conversation more than any other section of the periodical press. The many exchanges that unfolded in apedidos sometimes included weeks of back and forth that spilled over into rival newspapers.

The earliest appearance of a Publicações a Pedido section identified in this study dates to an 1834 edition of Recife's *Diário de Pernambuco* in which two signed apedidos on local politics appeared on the front page before the Correspondências (Letters to the Editor) section.[29] Apedidos appeared infrequently in the *Diário* in the 1830s but increased in number and prominence in subsequent decades. By the 1860s, apedidos became a regular feature and remained popular through the 1890s and into the twentieth century. Apedidos were also adopted by the Bahian press, first appearing in the *Correio Mercantil* in 1838.[30] The *Jornal do Commercio* ran the section in 1843, the first major Rio de Janeiro newspaper to do so, although the column did not appear on a daily basis until the 1850s. Other prominent Rio newspapers adopted the column by the late 1840s with the *Diário do Rio de Janeiro* doing so in 1847 and the *Correio Mercantil* in 1848.[31] By the end of the empire, newspapers across the nation published apedidos, underscoring their popularity—and profitability—as a national genre.[32]

Correspondências still appeared regularly in the 1850s, but by the 1860s the section became increasingly rare in the *Jornal do Commercio* where it was eventually eclipsed by the Publicações a Pedido section. On the surface, apedidos were similar to the letters published in the Correspondências section, especially in their commentary on political and current events, but the former included a much wider range of topics and writing styles. In the 1850s, apedidos averaged around 70 discrete articles or letters per month in the *Jornal do Commercio*; by the 1880s, the number increased to an average of 750 submissions per month.[33] The growing volume of apedidos suggests that they became an increasingly important—and perhaps even vital—source of income for newspapers. As Roderick Barman observes, until the 1870s when street sales became more reliable, it was difficult for newspapers to stay afloat on the basis of subscriptions and daily sales alone. The *Jornal do Commercio*, for example, supplemented its bottom line with contracts for government printing. The revenue generated by Publicações a Pedido was an important factor in its increasing presence in the periodical press as the century progressed.[34]

In the 1850s, Publicações a Pedido usually appeared on the second page of the *Jornal do Commercio* where it followed the national and international news, serialized fiction, and economic data printed on the front page. The section preceded Declarações (announcements about lectures and meetings), police reports, and local news about the arrival and departure of ships printed on the second page, while classified ads appeared on the third and fourth pages of most editions.[35] By the 1870s, apedidos were often featured on the front page of the *Jornal do Commercio* where they were prominently displayed, suggesting that their importance increased as editors realized their potential to attract readers and increase revenue. One anonymous observer charged that it was not the *Jornal do Commercio*'s "excellent foreign correspondents ... nor its reliable advertisements," but rather the apedidos section that held the "secret of its popularity."[36] This Latin American iteration of a daily pay-to-print genre appears to be a distinctive feature of the nineteenth-century press in Spanish and Portuguese America. Apedidos therefore pose several questions for understanding their role in producing both revenue and content.[37] US traveler and missionary James Fletcher claimed in 1852 that the volume of public letters in Rio de Janeiro newspapers surpassed that of newspapers in the United States and Europe, suggesting that reader participation in Brazil may have been more accessible to the public, printing fees notwithstanding. Nearly thirty years later, an entry in the Portuguese *Dicionário Popular* attested to the on-going popularity and variety of apedidos that "fill[ed] the greater part of Brazilian dailies."[38]

While comprehensive data on the exact fee structure for apedidos across nineteenth-century newspapers remains to be reconstructed, hints at the per line cost appear in a handful of Rio de Janeiro newspapers in the 1870s. Prices ranged from 80 réis (US$0.04) per line in the *Correio da Tarde* and *Diário de Notícias* to 120 réis (US$0.06) per line in the *Reporter*. In 1872 one line of print in an apedido cost double the newsstand price (40 réis—US$0.02) for the daily edition of *Diário de Notícias*. By comparison, anúncios (classifieds) were generally 80 réis per line.³⁹ Direct evidence for apedido fees for the *Jornal do Commercio* is more elusive. Rodrigo Cardoso Soares de Araujo provides the figure of 120 réis per line for the *Jornal do Commercio* in the 1870s, but a critique published in *A Pátria* in 1872 charged that the *JC* collected a prohibitive 240 réis (US$0.12) per line for the missives of "government ministers or their agents." Even more scandalous, *A Pátria* roundly complained, was that these fees were paid not out of the pockets of the ministers themselves but from the state treasury.⁴⁰ Even if the figure of 240 réis per line was exaggerated, at 120 réis per line apedidos would have made a tidy sum for newspaper printers. On January 2, 1870, the *Jornal do Commercio* printed 2,251 lines in the Publicações a Pedido section; at 120 réis per line this would have amounted to 270$120 or US$135.06 at that year's exchange rate of US$0.45 per mil-réis (1$000).⁴¹

The longest apedidos appeared at the front of the section, giving them prominence on the first or second page of daily editions. Medium-sized apedidos followed in descending order more or less by length, with the shortest—often only a few lines—printed at the end of the column. Apedidos probably appeared this way for aesthetic reasons but also because longer letters were more expensive to print and were therefore prominently placed. The most voluminous apedidos were usually signed by individuals or groups of high social standing with obvious financial means, as a series of letters regarding a slander lawsuit published by the powerful Carvalho clan from São Paulo attests. An apedido published by the family on January 2, 1870, ran for fully 239 lines (out of the 2,251 lines for the section on that day), which would have cost them 28$680 (US$12.91) at the estimated rate of 120 réis per line, or almost the price of an annual subscription to the *Jornal do Commercio* (30$000 or US$13.50). There is evidence that shorter apedidos were also accessible for those of more modest income, as a collective letter submitted by a group of self-described "poor residents" of Rio de Janeiro's Morro da Conceição neighborhood demonstrates.⁴² The apedido contained only 22 lines, but was printed on three consecutive days at the cost of 2$640 (US$1.19) per day or 7$920 (US$3.57) in total. The same residents printed a less expensive three-line version of their request for the following ten days to the tune of 360 réis per day or 3$600 (US$1.62) in total. The full cost of the residents' campaign to draw attention to the lack of piped water in the neighborhood came to the grand total of 11$520, or nearly the cost for one month's rent for a *cortiço* (tenement) room.[43]

These figures indicate that apedidos generated significant income for the *Jornal do Commercio*, though they were perhaps dominated by those with deeper pockets. The fees also suggest that apedidos were accessible but not necessarily easily affordable for those of more modest means, a fact that underscores the motivation of the individuals who printed them. The residents of the Morro da Conceição most likely pooled their resources or petitioned a patron to publish their collective request; the fact that they ran a shorter version of the apedido for a longer period of time suggests they were mindful of the cost. It is telling that they attempted to remedy their problem through the newspaper, underscoring their faith in a positive outcome. Bringing their grievance to the press was worth the price.

Sometimes authors referred directly to the expense of publishing apedidos, as did one anonymous submission in response to a criticism of the sale of lottery tickets: "So much hot air printed day after day, so much money squandered on the press. And to what end? Are lotteries not legal?"[44] As this example suggests, authors were very conscious of the paid format of apedidos, sometimes indicating a sense of ownership of the column. Even when cost was not explicitly mentioned, submissions often included declarations such as "Today I come to the press" or "If I receive no answer, I will return to the press," suggesting that readers thought of Publicações a Pedido as a public space in which they could express their views and enter and exit at will, albeit for a price.[45] In this vein, apedidos provided a forum through which private citizens could demand services from the state, develop (or defend) a reputation, and publicize an agenda.

Another elusive aspect of apedidos was the process of selection for publication. César Braga-Pinto cites an anonymous journalist in the *Revista Popular Brasileira* in 1861 who declared that it was more honest to call the section "Publications by Cash" because, he charged, selection criteria were so low that presumably anything, "bad poetry, flattery, and any type of personal attack or defamation," could be published for payment.[46] The level of vitriol expressed in many apedidos—an aspect of the Brazilian press that often took foreign observers aback—suggests that editors made little effort to enforce decorum and were willing to publish outrageous and offensive submissions as long as authors could pay.[47] While profanity was not published, insulting terms and tones frequently appeared. João José Fagundes de Rezende e Silva responded to an anonymous *apedido* that "made a wretched [insult] against my person" by demanding that the "leprous rat" who wrote it unmask himself.[48] Insults could also be erudite, arcane, and one imagines, entertaining for the newspaper public, as an *apedido* criticizing a priest in the provincial city of Barra Mansa illustrates. The anonymous author compared the priest and his town to the Boeotians, an ancient Greek community infamous for being dullards and invoked biblical figures in a scathing jibe: "What a devil Judas finds in the souls of priests!"[49] Other insults were more subtle. Apedidos were sometimes referred to in the diminutive as "*artiguinhos*" (little articles) and their authors, "*articulistas*" (article writers); the former term insinuated that the writer was amateurish or worse. By the 1870s a subgenre of anonymously printed apedidos, known as *mofinas* developed; a dictionary of that decade explained: "There are exchanged the most violent affronts, the most cruel insinuations, under the title *mofinas*."[50] Literally translated as "bad luck or misfortune," mofinas were usually brief, printed at the end of the column, and contained some of the most fiery and mean-spirited insults printed in the section.

The ad hominem attacks of anonymous authors could be irksome for the public and newspaper publishers alike; the latter were exposed to lawsuits when an anonymous apedido went too far. Referred to as *testas-de-ferro* (foreheads of iron, presumably for their aggressive tone as well as the fact that their identity was unknown), some anonymous authors made a living writing inflammatory apedidos intended to sway public opinion about a court case or other controversy. Even more nefarious were blackmailers who threatened to publish sensitive information about an individual or family unless they received a ransom. The pay-to-print format made the pages of the newspaper accessible to a wide swath of the public, but at the risk of printing harmful and untrue information that led to court cases and even social ostracism for those who participated in them.[51]

Along with the complaints and insults that filled the column, apedidos also displayed an irreverent sense of humor. A criticism of a performance of Mozart's *Requiem* by the Filharmônica Fluminense published on January 19, 1870 resulted in three strongly worded defenses of the musicians the very next day. One, written in the voice of the deceased Mozart observing the concert from his vantage point in the hereafter, quipped: "I am satisfied with the execution of my masterpiece.... Good sir, do you desire perfection? Then come to heaven."[52] As these examples illustrate, apedidos included a wide variety of voices, writing styles, creative insults, and humor; as such, they provide scholars with a range of idioms and language that shed light on the cultural registers of nineteenth-century Brazil.[53]

Aside from provocative language, the variety of subjects and detailed information contained in apedidos provides further evidence for relatively open publishing criteria. Topics from January 1870 included an accused deserter from the army; a judge with a gambling habit; a protest against brutal slave punishment; female and male sexual immorality; the abolition of slavery; a criticism of the *beija-mão* or hand-kissing ceremony that Brazilians were expected to perform before the emperor; a murder committed in defense of familial honor by the septuagenarian patriarch of a family in rural Rio de Janeiro; and all manner of governmental shortcomings, especially inadequate roads, trash pick-up, sewage, and yellow fever prevention.[54] The breadth of subjects suggests that, aside from outright vulgarity, editors did little to censor submissions. The intensity of criticisms of the government and government officials also speaks to a tolerance for opposing viewpoints and dissent; anonymity likely provided useful cover in this regard.

Political topics were also fair game. The *Jornal do Commercio*, for example, gained visibility and stature due to its ties to the Conservative Party, although it published apedidos from across the political spectrum and remained steadfastly nonpartisan in its reporting.[55] Opposing viewpoints by Liberal and Conservative politicians were printed side by side, which was perhaps an editorial tactic intended to provoke strong reactions and more paid submissions. The Conde d'Eu, Emperor Pedro II's son-in-law, accused the Brazilian press of disorienting readers with this practice:

> [Editors] accept and print everything on any subject . . . one often reads a missive glorifying Canavarro [*sic*] at the expense of the minister alongside a tirade against Canavarro justifying the minister. The public chooses between the two, or more often, I think they do not choose and remain ambivalent.[56]

As these examples indicate, while publishing letters in the Publicações a Pedido required access to literacy (either personally or through a scribe) and the necessary funds, nonetheless a diverse and even bewildering array of topics and viewpoints regularly appeared in print.

Anonymity and Its Discontents:
An Anatomy of a Month of Apedidos

In January 1870, the Publicações a Pedido section appeared in every daily print edition, usually a total of four pages, of the *Jornal do Commercio*, including four supplemental editions of eight pages each published under the title of Primeira Folha and Segunda Folha (First Section and Second Section).[57] Including supplements and special editions, a total of 36 discrete editions were published for the month, and they included 923 apedidos, an average of 26 per edition. The highest number of individual apedidos printed on a single day was 42 and the lowest was 4. A lower number of apedidos did not necessarily decrease the total space on the page dedicated to the section, suggesting that the newspaper devoted a finite amount of space to the section.

Three general categories characterize the submissions for January 1870: Complaints, Announcements, and Praise and Gratitude. Announcements, defined here as information printed for the public's benefit, included but were not limited to product advertisements, theater endorsements, eulogies, club and association information, descriptions of medical procedures and treatments, and exam results for local and regional schools. This category comprised the majority of apedidos at 46 percent of the total. Complaints came in second at 40 percent. This category included a wide catalog of misdeeds, criticism, and personal disputes; apedidos that referred to lawsuits (55), theatrical performances (43), and shortcomings in public works (32) comprised the most common topics for the month. The final category, Praise and Gratitude, included public declarations of thanks for firefighters, helpful strangers, the return of lost items, and successful medical treatments submitted (or so they claimed) by grateful patients. Apedidos of gratitude comprised 14 percent of the 923 published that month.

A slight majority of the 923 apedidos were printed anonymously (51.3 percent). This total included unsigned apedidos (13.4 percent) and those published under a pseudonym (37.9 percent), indicating that a hidden identity (or the creation of an alternate persona) was an important consideration for the majority of apedido authors. The notorious vitriol in the section, in mofinas in particular, was most likely attributable to the ability to speak freely (and perhaps untruthfully) without consequence from behind a pseudonym. More than one apedido author challenged an anonymous critic to unmask themselves.

TABLE 9.1   *Apedido* Signatories, January 1870. *JC*, January 1–31, 1870.

TYPE OF SIGNATURE	NUMBER	PERCENT
Pseudonym	350	37.9
Unsigned (anonymous)	124	13.4
Signature	240	26.0
Multiple Signatures	39	4.3
Initials	25	2.7
Unsigned (not anonymous)	145	15.7
TOTAL	923	100.0

Twenty-six percent of apedidos were signed with a personal name, 4 percent were signed by multiple individuals, and 2.7 percent were marked by initials—an action that did not fully reveal a person's identity, but did not hide it either. Nearly 16 percent of apedidos did not include a signature but were not anonymous as they were traceable to an individual, business, or institution; among these were product endorsements and announcements of association meetings and events. Out of 923 apedidos, 11 (1 percent) were signed by women; it is likely that anonymous apedidos were also submitted by women, though it is safe to assume the majority were authored by men (table 9.1).

Many apedidos were published in response to readers' letters in rival Rio de Janeiro newspapers and in newspapers from other provinces, demonstrating that the reading public engaged with a variety of publications. Five apedidos responded to readers' letters printed in the *Diário do Rio de Janeiro*, the *Diário Oficial* (the organ of the Brazilian state), the liberal *Quinze de Julho*, the *Diário de Pernambuco*, and *O Partido Liberal* (a newspaper from the capital of Alagoas). The section also contained articles reprinted from other periodicals, fourteen in total, from journals as diverse as the *Vida Fluminense* (published in Rio de Janeiro), the journal of the Abolitionist Society of Paris, a newspaper in Belgium, and newspapers from the southern and northern provinces of Rio Grande do Sul and Ceará respectively. Apedido authors hailed from at least nine provinces outside of Rio de Janeiro: Pará, Maranhão, Rio Grande do Sul, Alagoas, Ceará, Espirito Santo, Mato Grosso, Minas Gerais, and Rio Grande do Norte. Three French apedidos were also published in the month of January; foreign-language apedidos were not uncommon in a city with a large foreign-born population. French was also a language of public discourse in educated circles.

Public Opinion

An important concept invoked in many apedidos was public opinion. The notion of public opinion in the Brazilian press mirrored developments in the North Atlantic where the Enlightenment emphasis on reason as the pathway to personal and political emancipation appeared in newspaper discourse. Public opinion was seen as "the invocation of knowledge, the prudence of reasoned thinking," but it was contextualized in Brazil as an antidote to concentrated "political power, revolution, or abrupt changes in [the political] order."[58] At the same time in Brazil, as elsewhere, public opinion had multiple inflections; the first, influenced by the Enlightenment call to reason, was:

> intellectualized, private, critical, closer to the sphere of literature ... and founded on the supremacy of reason. The other, collective and normative, based on the will of the majority, [was] founded on the practice of the sociability of citizens assembling together to decide upon the common good.[59]

This latter meaning was explicitly invoked in apedidos from this sample set, demonstrating that authors very consciously crafted letters with a specific public in mind. Illuminating private matters in the public press was sometimes an attempt to influence fellow readers to the author's advantage, especially in the case of legal disputes or when personal and familial honor had been defamed.[60] In other cases, appealing to public opinion, apedido authors implicitly entreated, was intended to persuade those in power to enact a new policy or channel resources into a public works project. Regardless of whether the term *public opinion* was explicitly invoked, calling on the public's support was an important feature of many apedidos.

The letter of a wealthy widow from the southernmost province of Rio Grande do Sul illustrates this point in an apedido reprinted from her native Porto Alegre, the provincial capital. Infuriated by a lawsuit in which her legal claim to a gold mine inherited from her father and maintained by her husband before his death was denied, Henriqueta Figueiredo turned to the public for support in an apedido titled "Appeal to the Court of Justice by the Court of Public Opinion."[61] Figueiredo presented herself in the sympathetic figure of a widow facing a hostile court system in which her property rights had been usurped by a corrupt state. A matriarch such as herself, "burdened with many dependents," was the victim of biased magistrates who had openly and unabashedly favored the claims of her opponents. This example demonstrates that appealing to the public through the *Jornal do Commercio* was a potentially powerful way (or, in this case, probably a last resort) to pressure the courts, or at least publicly shame the judges, in a controversial case. Invoking and defending honor was a recurring theme in apedidos, a feature they shared with the public letters of the Spanish American press.[62] Figueiredo was a powerful figure with the social and economic resources to take her grievances to court and the means and standing to publish her complaint in the national press, despite the legal disadvantages faced by women in her time.

Not only the rich and powerful sought the support of public opinion in the apedidos section. Those lower in socioeconomic status also "came to the press," affirming the accessibility of the section to those of lesser economic means. The aforementioned collective letter from the residents of the Morro da Conceição neighborhood confidently addressed Emperor Pedro II directly, calling on his "unfailing good will and sense of justice" in remedying their lack of access to water.[63] Like the widow above, the authors cast themselves in a positive light as respectable workers at the military munitions factory (200 in total) and the Episcopalian Curia. Less demanding and inflammatory than the widow's missive (perhaps because they were a less politically powerful community), the letter respectfully called for the emperor, or any relevant government officials who might be reading, to treat the Morro da Conceição like other, more affluent neighborhoods.

Another exchange highlights the ways that apedido authors called upon public opinion by hurling clever insults and invoking virtue in their attempt to sway readers. In the apedido accusing Barra Mansa priest José Martins Pereira de Barros of corruption, favoritism, malice, and arrogance, an anonymous author signing as *Uma ovelha* (A sheep) requested that the church hierarchy in Rio de Janeiro intervene.[64] In response, another author using the not-so-subtle moniker, *O lobo* (The wolf), warned that the case demonstrated how public opinion could sometimes go too far and that *Uma ovelha* had abused the press to pillory an innocent man. *O lobo* argued that while the free expression of public opinion was a marker of a modern and progressive society, it also had its dangers: "The press's purpose is to instruct, provide counsel, defeat crime and vice; but many times it also attacks virtue." In his view, the expression of public opinion in the Publicações a Pedido section was "very useful, saintly even," but behind the "mask of anonymity and hypocrisy with which [the public] hides itself, one can see its shameless aspects."[65] In other words, anonymity encouraged incivility and the publication of lies, an abuse of the section that other authors echoed, although not always as pointedly as *O lobo*.

Announcements

Medical announcements comprised a different subcategory of apedidos that was less about persuading the public to take a stance on a local issue, and more about advertising medical services and building a doctor's reputation. These accounted for fifty-four apedidos (5 percent of the total for January). The majority described successful operations that ranged from what appears to have been the routine removal of cataracts to the more intimate repair of a woman's "recto-vaginal fistula (abscess)," a successful caesarian section (the apedido claimed that it was the first of its kind in Brazil), as well as a "half-castration" that resulted from "an alteration of the left testicle due to a hemorrhage."[66] Described in plain language that laid out the scientific facts of a procedure, medical apedidos underscored the precariousness of nineteenth-century health and the prominence it held in daily life. Medical apedidos were also one space within the newspaper where gender, race, and legal status (free or enslaved) were openly mentioned. One heart-breaking case described a dispute between two doctors about a difficult birth that resulted in a stillborn fetus. The article referred to the mother by her husband's name and listed very personal details of the ordeal, including the size of her uterus and the procedure by which the doctor attempted to extract the fetus.[67] The appearance of such graphic accounts demonstrates their worthiness for print and underscores that the public accepted—and perhaps had a prurient interest in—these vividly described ailments and calamities of the human body.

While the example above was a direct appeal to public opinion in defense of the doctor's reputation, the majority of medical apedidos functioned as advertising for doctors and medical institutes. The detailed measurements and descriptions showcased within the apedido format served to build one's reputation among the medical community as well as to invoke the authority of science in the advertisement of remedies and procedures. For the present-day scholar, these medical descriptions provide a micro-history of mostly anonymous individuals described vis-á-vis their ailments. The removal of cataracts from an enslaved woman, Constança, for example, restored her vision after six years of near-blindness. The apedido praised the young doctor's talent and was in part an advertisement aimed at slaveholders looking to heal their slaves' ailments and render them productive again, as was insinuated in the description of Constança's ordeal.⁶⁸ At the same time we have little insight into how Constança experienced her ailment and its cure. The frankness and frequency with which childbirth was described reveals an additional way in which women's experiences came to the surface in the press, albeit filtered through the men—doctors and husbands—who printed the majority of apedidos on the topic.⁶⁹ Descriptions of treatments and methods for preventing yellow fever bring to poignant life the fear and grief experienced by the public during the season of fevers. In a final example, an apedido describing an accident at the dock that crushed a young man's leg was accompanied by another apedido outlining the doctor's successful amputation of the leg on the same day. Illnesses and their cures, as described in the Publicações a Pedido section, provide useful insights into public discussion of the body as it related to gender, disease, and social relationships.⁷⁰

Gratitude

Another type of apedido that stands out for its sentiment (if also for its somewhat formulaic style) consisted of declarations of praise and gratitude for benevolent actions such as putting out fires or returning lost items. Kindness in the face of illness or bodily injury was a repeated theme. One dramatic example of this subgenre referred to a circus accident in which an acrobat fell from an elevated walkway during a performance and broke his arm.⁷¹ Antonio Pinto da Rocha, a friend of the performer, and his parents, Francisco and Leocadia Amoretti, published separate apedidos thanking the team of doctors, medical students, and members of the Rio de Janeiro community for "the part that they played in easing the suffering" of their son and friend during his recovery.⁷² In another example, a distraught father, João José Basilio Pereira, thanked the family of José Pinheiro de Souza Júnior from Valença for providing shelter to his family during a rainstorm, including his fifteen-month old daughter who had fallen ill. The child succumbed to her illness, the grieving father lamented, but not for lack of care by the Souza family for which he could only express his feelings with "tears of gratitude."⁷³ Another apedido, signed by seventeen workers of the Rio de Janeiro Street Railway Company, celebrated the generosity of the engineers Henrique Móra and "Master Emílio" for paying for "a decent burial for their coworker."⁷⁴

Aside from what appear to be genuine declarations of gratitude, what motived authors to print such heartfelt and intimate announcements in a public venue? These individuals composed and paid for an apedido that expressed their gratitude but also exposed their painful private travails (the death of a child!) in a deeply public way. In one sense, they demonstrate that public expressions of grief and gratitude were acceptable not only for print but also for public acknowledgement and discussion, inviting the community to participate as a spectator. Such acts affirmed values about proper displays of compassion, grief, and thanksgiving, perhaps assuring the public that all was well in the world despite everyday tragedies. In the case of the streetcar workers, such announcements reinforced paternalistic relationships of dependency and power; subordinates recognized the generosity of their benefactors but also affirmed their lower place within the social hierarchy. In another sense, these public expressions reinforced social values by representing and reinforcing proper behavior. Unlike complaints, which were by and large anonymous, declarations of gratitude referred to the benefactor by name and most were signed.

This short essay cannot do justice to the wealth of topics contained in even this one month of apedidos in one newspaper. Nonetheless, this research has attempted to bring to light the rich field of material that the Publicações a Pedido section offers to scholars. The prominent placement of apedidos in one of Brazil's most important nineteenth-century newspapers, the *Jornal de Commercio*, points to the central role that they played in the developing relationship between the public and the press during the empire. Although apedidos transformed private experiences into public topics, they did not necessarily diminish the importance of the private sphere, but rather transformed the contours of what was acceptable for public viewing. In the *Jornal do Commercio* the concept of public was amplified to the national level, making the local public also a national public. More inquiry into this interplay should prove fruitful. Additionally, further research into the thousands of apedidos published in local and regional newspapers will make for an interesting contrast to Rio de Janeiro, as well as for a more nuanced understanding of this newly national genre. Apedidos were part of a broader genre of readers' correspondence that developed in the periodical press in the eighteenth and nineteenth centuries across the Atlantic, but they evidence some distinctly Latin American features.

Although more information on the cost of publishing apedidos and how much they contributed to a particular newspapers' income needs to be unearthed, the increasing volume and prominent placement of the section on the first page by the 1870s suggests that apedidos became financially, and culturally, important to newspapers like the *Jornal do Commercio*. In this regard, apedidos were an innovative response to the revenue challenges that the periodical press faced in nineteenth-century Brazil. Editors capitalized on the public's willingness and desire to express its thoughts in print. Second, while the pay-to-print format contributed to the publication of contentious and perhaps untruthful letters, it also made the forum relatively democratic and accessible to the poor and women, perhaps more so than newspapers in other countries where there were presumably more editorial restrictions on public letters. Did the need to secure revenue streams inadvertently create a relatively accessible printed venue for the public, especially marginalized groups? Future research may clarify this point. Finally, the apedido section bypasses more traditional newspaper content about news and economics to show how very personal events reflected greater social norms and values. The graphic descriptions and personal information contained in medical apedidos may appear surprising to modern eyes, but they reveal deeper anxieties and curiosities about the body in Brazilian society. Nineteenth-century Brazilians complained vociferously about all manner of misdeeds, but they also took to the press to express gratitude and grace for their fellow humans, to announce their personal opinions and visions whether or not they successfully swayed public opinion, and many attempted to use the newspaper to negotiate for better conditions and services from the state. It is this wide-ranging content that makes the Publicações a Pedido section such a rich genre for study; hopefully this essay will inspire further research into the ways in which public voices appeared in apedidos and what they reveal about nineteenth-century Brazilian society.

Notes

1. Fletcher and Kidder, *Brazil*, 252.
2. Whipple, *Gente*, 77.
3. See also E. Silva, *Queixas*.
4. See, for example, the public relations campaign published in several Rio newspapers by Briton Thomas Rainey in defense of his ferry company in 1868; Saba, "American Mirror," 86–89.
5. "Collegio de Santa Rita de Cassia," *JC*, January 10, 1870; "As exequias de Gottschalk," *JC*, January 23, 1870; "Emmisão de Cartões," *JC*, January 27, 1870.

6. For a history of the development of the genre of newspapers in the Anglo-American world, see Slauter, "Rise."
7. Warner, *Letters*, 3.
8. Bond, "Circuits," 562.
9. *Journal de Paris*, February 27, 1778, cited in Bond, "Circuits," 535.
10. Bond, "Circuits," 542, 546–47.
11. Burns, *Infamous Scribblers*, 103.
12. Clark, *Public Prints*, 207.
13. Clark, *Public Prints*, 210.
14. John and Silberstein-Loeb, "Making News," 7.
15. Zeldin, *France*, 2:513.
16. Editor's manuscript notes on printing fees, *National Standard* (Salem, NJ), February 12, 1868, Serials Collection, American Antiquarian Society.
17. Adelman and Gardner, "News," 54.
18. Blair, "'Let the Nightingales Alone,'" 190.
19. Blair, "'Let the Nightingales Alone,'" 190.
20. Wendlin, "Prostitute's Voice," 53–56. My thanks to Karin Koehler for the citation.
21. Morel and Barros, *Palavra*, 7. See also Marcello Basile's chapter in this volume.
22. Although editors were largely white in this period, free people of color comprised about 30–35 percent of the population in Rio de Janeiro. Recent research has highlighted the importance of free persons of color, as well as enslaved people, in the printing world; Godoi, *Editor*, esp. chap. 9. See also Godoi's chapter in this volume.
23. "These two dimensions of the public-private distinction can well be applied to the analysis of the blending of public and private in texts. Visibility then refers to the communicative setting: the accessibility of a text. Collectivity applies to the content of the text," Landert and Jucker, "Private," 1,424.
24. Godoi, *Editor*, 148–50; see also R. Araujo, "Caminhos," 249–50.
25. R. Araujo, "Caminhos," 225.
26. Hobbs, "Provincial Periodicals," 227.
27. *O Paiz*, January 30, 1885, as cited in R. Araujo, "Caminhos," 253.
28. French, *Heart*, 93.
29. *Diario de Pernambuco* (Recife), September 11, 1834.
30. *Correio Mercantil* (Salvador), September 14, 1838.
31. *DRJ*, December 29, 1847; *CM*, January 11, 1848.
32. Data collected from keyword search for "Publicações a Pedido" in HDB.
33. Cribelli, *Industrial Forests*, 12–13.
34. Barman, "Periodical Press," 4–6.
35. Special or supplemental editions of the *JC* contained eight pages.

36. "Costumes valem mais que leis," *O Paiz*, January 30, 1885.
37. Whipple, *Gente*, chap. 3.
38. Chagas, *Diccionario*, 467.
39. *Correio da Tarde*, July 1, 1879; *Díario de Noticias*, September 9, 1872; *Reporter*, June 27, 1879.
40. R. Araujo, "Caminhos," 185; *A Patria*, June 12, 1872. An apedido in the *Diario do Rio de Janeiro* referred to the 240 réis per line fee in the *JC*, while a serialized short story in *A Comedia Social* cited 200 réis per line in 1871, "O ministerio e a propaganda abolicionista," *Diario do Rio de Janeiro*, June 18, 1871; "Uma vocação mallograda," *A Comedia Social*, July 20, 1871. The latter illustrated magazine also cited the figure of 120 réis per line in the *JC*, "Grande questão juridica," *A Comedia Social*, May 12, 1870.
41. Conversion rates are from Duncan, *Public and Private Operations*, 183.
42. "A S. M. o Imperador," *JC*, January 16–18, 1870; "A S. M. o Emperador e o Exm. Ministro das Obras Publicas," *JC*, January 19–28, 1870.
43. For cost-of-living and commodity figures see Arnaldo Lucas Pires Junior's chapter in this volume.
44. "Mofina Loterica," *JC*, January 4, 1870.
45. "Eterna gratidão," *JC*, January 11, 1870; "Barcas Fluminenses," *JC*, Segunda Folha, January 20, 1870.
46. Sebastianopolino, "A imprensa brasileira," *Revista Popular Ilustrada*, January–April 1861, p. 261, as cited in Braga-Pinto, "Journalists," 592. Thanks to Celso Castilho for this citation.
47. See also R. Araujo, "Caminhos," 187.
48. "O correspondente do Ouro Preto para o Diario do Rio de Janeiro e o barão [sic] de Cayapó," *JC*, January 2, 1870. Insults had a long history in the Brazilian press; Lustosa, *Insultos*.
49. "Urbanidade," *JC*, January 5, 1870; "Barra Mansa: o Vigario José Martins Pereira de Barros," *JC*, January 1, 1870.
50. Chagas, *Diccionario*, 467.
51. R. Araujo, "Caminhos," 185–88.
52. "Requiem," *JC*, January 20, 1870.
53. See also Nicolau, "Estudo," no pagination.
54. "Suum Ciuque," *JC*, January 6, 1870; "O Juiz que joga," *JC*, January 3, 1870; "Engenho Novo," *JC*, *Segunda Folha*, January 28, 1870; "Mofina," *JC*, January 20, 1870; "Homen de Industria," *JC*, January 21, 1870; "Vassouras: Crime Audacioso!!!," *JC*, January 10, 1870; "Muito Attenção," *JC*, *Segunda Folha*, January 12, 1870; "Chiquiero de Porcos," *JC*, January 29, 1870.
55. Sodré, *História*, 217–18.
56. Rangel, *Gastão de Orléans*, 126. Thanks to Roderick Barman for this citation. David Canabarro was a Brazilian general who fought in the Cisplatine War (1826–

1828) and the Farroupilha War (1835–1845). He remained an important political figure in Rio Grande do Sul until his death in 1867.

57. Supplemental editions sometimes covered special political or historical topics, but for the month of January these followed the same format as daily editions.

58. Morel and Barros, *Palavra*, 26.

59. Morel and Barros, *Palavra*, 31.

60. An accusation of nonvirginity was levied against a young bride by her new husband in 1878 in Salvador, Bahia. The controversy unfolded in the apedido section of the *Diario da Bahia*. The accuser and the bride's defenders published a series of heated apedidos that included a detailed description of a medical exam performed on the young woman; K. Silva, *Diário da Bahia*, 149–53.

61. "Rio Grande do Sul: Apello da Justiça dos Tribunaes Para a Justiça da Opinião Publica," *JC*, January 29, 1870.

62. Whipple, *Gente*, 83–84.

63. "A S. M. o Imperador," *JC*, January 17, 1870.

64. "Barra Mansa: o Vigario José Martins Pereira de Barros," *JC*, January 1, 1870.

65. "Barra Mansa: O Vigario José Martins Pereira de Barros," *JC*, January 15, 1870.

66. "Cantagallo," *JC*, January 25, 1870; "Casa de Saude do Senhor Bom-Jesus de Calvario," *JC*, January 16, 1870; "Casa da Saude da Nossa Senhora de Ajuda," *JC*, January 16, 1870; "Casa de Saude do Senhor Bom-Jesus do Calvario," *JC*, January 21, 1870.

67. "Dr. Emilio Guadagui," *JC, Segunda Folha*, January 7, 1870.

68. "Cantagallo," *JC*, January 25, 1870.

69. "Dr. Emilio Guadagui," *JC, Segunda Folha*, January 7, 1870; "Agradecimento," January 29, 1870; "Casa da Saude da Nossa Senhora de Ajuda," *JC*, January 16, 1870; "Quatis de Barra-Mansa," January 29, 1870.

70. "Barcas Fluminenses," *JC*, January 11, 1870; "Casa e saude allo-homeopathica de Nossa Senhora da Gloria," *JC*, January 11, 1870.

71. *Gazetilha*, *JC*, January 29, 1870.

72. "Agradecimento" and "Agradecimento," *JC*, January 30, 1870.

73. "[Title Illegible]," *JC*, January 21, 1870.

74. "Agradecimento," *JC*, January 21, 1870.

Roberto Saba

TEN THE SUN RISES IN THE NORTH
Brazilian Periodicals Published in the United States in the 1870s

In April 1864, Aureliano Cândido Tavares Bastos spoke in the Brazilian Parliament in favor of subsidizing a steamship line that would connect Rio de Janeiro to New York City. He imagined that, by being in touch with American society, Brazilian "young men will get used to indefatigable labor, to feverous activity, becoming fertilized by a solid education, practical, fundamental, professional, the only one capable of saving our youth."[1] A few months later, Antonio Francisco de Paula Souza told his peers in Parliament that, by having a direct means of transportation to the United States, young Brazilians would be able to attend agricultural schools "with excellent teachers, the first in the universe," and would have access to "ready-made [agricultural] models and machines." Moreover, in North America, Brazilian youths would find "a school of morality, of elevation and personal dignity."[2]

Whereas Tavares Bastos was a representative of the declining sugar-producing province of Alagoas, Paula Souza was the scion of prosperous coffee planters from São Paulo. Despite their different backgrounds, these two politicians shared an admiration for those who were crushing the proslavery rebellion in North America. Enthusiasts of Abraham Lincoln and the Republican Party, both men sought to establish closer relations with the northern section of the American Union. It would not be long before a new generation of reformers would take their project forward.

Scholars have long suggested that the outcome of the American Civil War created a sense of isolation in Brazil.[3] Recent research seems to support this claim. Ricardo Salles argues that, after the Emancipation Proclamation and key Confederate defeats, "it was evident to the attentive observer, like the [Brazilian] emperor and most statesmen of the empire, that slavery's days were numbered in the United States as well as in Brazil."[4] Jeffrey Needell adds that Pedro II moved against slavery after 1865 because he became worried about "the Empire's reputation among 'civilized' states. Now, Brazil alone among independent nations maintained slavery."[5] In other words, ashamed of their isolated position once slavery crumbled in North America, influential Brazilian statesmen embraced antislavery reform.

In addition to shaming powerful Brazilians into reform, scholars indicate that the American Civil War transformed the market for key commodities cultivated in Brazil. The growing predominance of Cuban sugar in the American market and the recovery of cotton production in the post-emancipation American South harmed the northern provinces of Brazil. Because the fast-industrializing postwar United States simultaneously expanded its consumption of Brazilian coffee, the coffee-growing southeastern provinces ended up concentrating the slave population. As Rafael de Bivar Marquese puts it, "By stimulating the growth of Brazilian coffee production while displacing Brazilian sugar and cotton in the world market, the economic performance of the United States in the last third of the nineteenth century contributed to widening the regional gap" in Brazil. A divided nation, Marquese concludes, could not hold on to slavery.[6]

As comprehensive as these arguments seem to be, they give the false impression that the American Civil War and its aftermath only brought fear and isolation to Brazil. In reality, many Brazilians saw the triumph of the free North over the slave South with optimism. Behind this positive attitude toward the downfall of American slavery were Brazilian men who lived in the United States during the 1870s. They edited monthly periodicals that arrived in Brazil via the steamship line that Tavares Bastos and Paula Souza had lobbied for. They discussed the achievements of the post-emancipation American economy while campaigning for agricultural modernization and slave emancipation in Brazil. Moreover, they directed northern technology and expertise to Brazilian society.

These publications were especially influential in the Oeste Paulista, the booming agricultural region northwest of São Paulo City, which had recently received thousands of slaves. Some of its editors were the coffee planters' sons who attended college in the United States. Their investment in slave labor notwithstanding, the planters did not shy away from these antislavery publications. On the contrary, Brazil's richest slaveholders used the Brazilian periodicals published in the postwar United States to plan for a future without slavery.

Until the 1970s, scholars of Brazilian slavery sought to demonstrate that the coffee planters of the Oeste Paulista had voluntarily transitioned from slave to free labor.[7] Reassessing this argument, Barbara Weinstein explains,

"From this structuralist perspective, to the extent that planters embraced the abolitionist cause, it was to advance a new set of class and material interests." The coffee planters were not benevolent masters who cherished their workers' freedom. According to Weinstein, "It was the amoral (if not immoral) forces of capitalist development, not moral compunctions about slave labor among elite Brazilians, that prepared the ground for the 'peaceful' abolition of slavery."[8]

Although the structuralist perspective has been under attack since the 1980s, it provides valuable clues for historians seeking to connect the process of Brazilian emancipation to the American Civil War and its aftermath. Avid readers of the Brazilian periodicals published in the postwar United States, the coffee planters of the Oeste Paulista did not feel afraid or isolated after the Confederacy fell. By examining the transformation of American capitalism after the Civil War, these publications helped Brazil's richest slaveholders to better understand "the amoral (if not immoral) forces of capitalist development." Like few other intellectual influences at the time, these periodicals contributed to the emergence of "a new set of class and material interests" in Brazil.

O Novo Mundo

José Carlos Rodrigues was born into a family of wealthy coffee planters in northeastern Rio de Janeiro.[9] A law student in São Paulo during the 1860s, he joined the youth insurgency of his time, which opposed the perpetuation of slavery and the centralizing tendencies of the monarchical regime.[10] In 1862, Rodrigues partnered with classmate Francisco Rangel Pestana to create a student newspaper titled *O Futuro*. In his articles, Rodrigues commented on the great event of the decade:

> The majestic edifice of democracy collapses. The adepts of slavery, the despots of all nations, sing Hosanna and continue their work of destruction. The United States, the land made sacred by the blood of the free, is the victim of a civil war, which sucks its life and threatens the cause of the republic.[11]

However upset, Rodrigues was confident that the cause of freedom would prevail in North America and set an example to the rest of the world. "Today," he proclaimed in September 1862, "the nations, submerged by the shadows of despotism, turn their eyes to the North, hoping that a star will shine on the horizon, which will guide them through the desert."[12]

After graduation, Rodrigues moved to Rio de Janeiro and started working at the Ministry of Finance. An accusation of embezzlement cut his public career short, however. Having few prospects in Brazil, he moved to the United States in 1867, first settling in Lowell, Massachusetts. His English teacher in Rio de Janeiro, American Presbyterian missionary George Whitehill Chamberlain, helped Rodrigues find work translating religious tracts, almanacs, and schoolbooks. James Cooley Fletcher, another Presbyterian missionary and coauthor of a widely read book about Brazil, who lived in Newburyport, Massachusetts, also became Rodrigues's close friend. The well-connected Fletcher introduced Rodrigues to prominent American intellectuals, politicians, and entrepreneurs.

Early in 1870, Rodrigues rented an office in the *New York Times* building. On October 24 of the same year, he published the first issue of *O Novo Mundo* (The New World). A monthly publication in Portuguese, *O Novo Mundo* was sent to Brazil by the New York–Rio de Janeiro line of steamers. Rodrigues modeled his illustrated review on American periodicals such as *Harper's Weekly* and *Frank Leslie's Illustrated Newspaper*.

The editor made his intentions clear in the first issue: "After the domestic war in the United States, Brazil and South America have sought to carefully study the things of this country." *O Novo Mundo* would contribute to this study "not only by providing news from the United States but also by exposing the principal manifestations of its progress and by discussing the causes and tendencies of this progress."[13] Rodrigues filled his publication with information about the economic prosperity and technological advancement of the postwar United States.

> A few years ago the farmer of the great West spent all his hot summer days cutting hay and grain with the reaper or the sickle: now he does the same work in a few hours by means of one of those American harvesters, drawn by the horse, and the farmer, gloves in hand and sitting down, finds great fun in what recently used to be a heavy task.
>
> In leather shoe manufacturing three men can now, with the aid of machinery, work as much as six did fifteen years ago.[14]

The heroes of *O Novo Mundo*, however, were not simple farmers or shoemakers. Rodrigues was an unapologetic admirer of corporate capitalists. For him, no one embodied American greatness better than Cornelius Vanderbilt, who had ascended from humble pilot of a small ferry to multimillionaire railroad and shipping magnate. "How it is possible in one life to accumulate such capital," Rodrigues sang Vanderbilt's praises, "is something impossible to explain to someone who does not know the value of indomitable energy allied to the good fortune of an American man."[15]

An enthusiast of major capitalists, Rodrigues was a sworn enemy of unions and socialists. He believed that freedom of contract was enough to guarantee a decent life for workers. Condemning a strike of Pennsylvania coal miners in December 1870, he denied that "the condition of the working classes is so awful that it justifies their general discontent or the concept of enmity which they have little by little formed against capital."[16]

Rodrigues's analysis of the American South during Reconstruction was consistent with his laissez-faire ideals. He saw corruption all around and singled out Radical Republicans as the root of all evil. "All these reforms," he lamented, "grew along with staggering corruption."[17] Rodrigues aligned himself with sections of the northern elite—the so-called Liberal Republicans—who disapproved of the military occupation of the southern states, high tariffs, monetary inflation, the income tax, labor organizations, and the enfranchisement of uneducated African Americans.[18] He concurred with the Liberal Republicans that Reconstruction should guarantee political stability in the South—which meant returning cotton planters to power—and secure ex-slaves' right to freely and individually negotiate labor contracts. Nothing more.[19]

Despite the many evils that he saw in Reconstruction, Rodrigues was convinced that slave emancipation had been a blessing to the American South, especially in economic terms: "The work of Reconstruction in the South is complete," he wrote in December 1873, "the Negro is not only a free man, he is a citizen; and the material wealth of the country is recovered under the wise and peaceful administration of those who forever crushed the terrible hydra of slavery."[20] Rodrigues was delighted to learn that cotton planters could now see the advantages of free labor in the form of the wage system or sharecropping. In October 1872, *O Novo Mundo* quoted one of them at length:

> Free labor costs much less than slave labor used to cost us. A Negro could not be rented for less than 300 to 350 dollars per year, and in addition, we had to pay taxes, and treat him in case of illness, etc., etc. The cost of owning a slave was more or less the same, if we calculate

the costs of taxes, medicine, interest, feeding, and maintaining him as a child and after old age. Currently, we can hire the same Negro for ten or fifteen dollars per month, in addition to home and food. It is true that Negroes now do not work as much as before, but, in any case, their proportional labor is much cheaper.

This cotton planter believed that wartime destruction—and not slave emancipation—caused difficulties for some of his neighbors. Nonetheless, he added, the planter who employed agricultural tools and fertilizers was making "more money planting cotton with free labor than he would with the slave's sweat."[21]

Rodrigues acknowledged that emancipation caused labor shortages, especially in cotton areas, because ex-slaves could now leave in search of better employment.[22] But he did not see this as a problem: "The difficulty caused by lack of hands has made agriculture more careful and scientific, and many Negroes, who have not emigrated from the South, now find more incentive in free labor than they found under the lash of the overseer." Progress, Rodrigues concluded, could be seen in the fact that by the late 1870s the cotton crop had reached "a number of bales superior to any year when the fiber was produced by slave hands."[23]

In addition to the recovery of cotton production, Rodrigues was thrilled that slave emancipation had brought economic diversification to the American South. Southerners had learned that "instead of sending cotton to Europe or the northern states to be woven, it is better to weave it at home and save in brokerage, freight, and other expenses."[24] In addition to textile mills, the South now had industries that processed "turpentine, yellow pine, grains, [and] precious minerals."[25]

Rodrigues never hid his objectives when describing the progress of the postwar United States in *O Novo Mundo*. "Let this eloquent example serve to calm the fears of those who worry about the future of agriculture in case of immediate slave emancipation," he wrote as early as January 1871, "and we shall soon have in the Empire [of Brazil] a great material prosperity such as the one we have here demonstrated to our readers!"[26] In 1872, after discussing the labor of ex-slaves in the American South, Rodrigues reiterated this point:

> This example shall serve to strengthen the courage of those Brazilians who, worried about the interests around them, fear a change that is now highly necessary, not only in regard to the great moral interests

of humanity, but also to their own material interests, and those of the country."[27]

Rodrigues had no doubt that slave emancipation would bring economic development to Brazil in the same way that it had done for the American South. He repeatedly returned to the idea that "the complete cessation of slavery is our greatest ambition. On the day no more slaves exist, our agricultural industry will begin its first era of true prosperity."[28]

When the Viscount of Rio Branco, prime minister from March 1871 to June 1875, set to work on the Free Womb Law, Rodrigues forcefully attacked the enemies of reform: "The system of slavery died a disgraceful and ridiculous death in the United States, thanks to its own madness; and it will die in the same way in Brazil if its supporters do not understand the spirit and the forces that work at the times they live in."[29] A few months after the law, which freed all children henceforth born to slave mothers, was ratified, however, Rodrigues started pressing for further measures to promote free labor in Brazil. He drew inspiration from the Homestead Act and the Pacific Railroad Acts, which Republican Congressmen passed in 1862.[30]

> Now that the country decreed the first step toward the complete abolition of slavery and seeks to attract to its shores the superabundant population of Europe, and that, as a consequence, agriculture and industry will receive the electrifying touch of free labor, the government needs to slice up its public lands, not only directly for the immigrants but also indirectly through concessions to railroads and other progressive institutions willing to help.[31]

By the mid-1870s, Rodrigues had joined those who criticized the Free Womb Law as imperfect and incomplete.[32]

As a complement to his antislavery stand, Rodrigues engaged in a campaign to modernize Brazilian agriculture. *O Novo Mundo* published several articles on coffee production, constantly advising the planters that "you must not only manage to produce large quantities of coffee, but also improve it, because if we now have access to all the markets of the world, we will only be able to secure them through the quality of our product, not its quantity."[33]

Rodrigues set to work on attracting American technology to Brazil, hoping that it would bring Brazilian agriculture up-to-date with the age of indus-

FIGURE 10.1 How Farming Is Done in the West of the United States, 1871. By 1871, Burr Oak Farm employed 250 wage earners who had the help of 350 mules, 100 oxen, and 50 horses to work 150 steel plows, 142 cultivators, 75 iron plows, and 45 seeders, among other implements. After three years of cultivation, Burr Oak produced an astonishing 540,000 bushels of corn. *ONM*, October 24, 1871.

try. Editors of American periodicals helped in this endeavor. In November 1870, *The Nation* informed its readers that *O Novo Mundo* "will be a valuable medium for spreading still further knowledge in Brazil of the products of American invention and skill, already so popular there."[34] The pages of *O Novo Mundo* soon were filled with ads for American locomotives, steam engines, steel tools, fertilizers, agricultural implements, and iron bridges, as well as laudatory portrayals of North American mechanized agriculture (figure 10.1).

An inexhaustible source of novelties, *O Novo Mundo* was a great success among Brazilian readers. "Go on, my friend," Tavares Bastos wrote to Rodrigues in 1872, "rendering services to our Brazil through your beautiful publication, which becomes every day more popular here."[35] By 1875, Brazilian newspapers reported that *O Novo Mundo* had reached 9,000 subscribers, a great success for the time.[36] In June 1878, John James Aubertin, the superintendent of the San Paulo Railway Company Limited, wrote to Rodrigues, "When I was in Rio, I often read your well-known and well-appreciated newspaper—*O Novo Mundo*. So much work, for sure, you must have had! The circulation, people say, is magnificent."[37]

After organizing a joint stock company called the Novo Mundo Association in New York City, Rodrigues took his project of channeling American products to Brazil one step further.[38] In July 1877, he created another monthly periodical titled *Revista Industrial* (Industrial Review). Rodrigues's new enterprise received the enthusiastic support of northern manufacturers, including the board of Baldwin Locomotive Works, whose members testified, "From our knowledge of the standing of these periodicals with the Brazilian public, and their circulation in that country, we believe them to be valuable means of advertising the business of American manufacturers and merchants in Brazil."[39]

The *Revista Industrial* preserved the tenets of *O Novo Mundo*, identifying slavery as the main cause of Brazilian backwardness. "Slave labor, and the consequent extensive cultivation of the soil, and also the extreme fertility and unlimited space," the first issue's editorial posited, "have contributed to maintaining us enslaved to antiquated and obsolete processes."[40] In his new periodical, Rodrigues forcefully expressed his contempt for the social order that slavery engendered in Brazil, condemning the permanence of "latifundia surrounded by miserable tenants, henchmen, parasites, and political firebrands, and worked by unfortunate and ignorant slaves."[41]

It is interesting that Rodrigues's most enthusiastic readers were located in one of the strongholds of slavery in Brazil, the coffee-producing Oeste Paulista, the new agricultural frontier northwest of São Paulo City. The *Correio Paulistano* used his writings as sources for discussing antislavery legislation, agricultural improvement, immigration policy, railroad construction, among other things. In 1874, it praised Rodrigues for his services to the country:

> Occupying himself assiduously about Brazil in brilliant articles, written within the intense glow coming from the place where he lives, our illustrious and solicitous countryman has become an independent thinker and journalist, impartial and profoundly judicious, and day to day offers invaluable services to our land through his wise observations.[42]

When the *Revista Industrial* came out, the *Correio Paulistano* commented, "No doubt, the new periodical will render an appreciable service to the progress of the country," recommending it "especially to our countrymen who dedicate themselves to agriculture, because they will find in the *Revista Industrial* a powerful tool always providing useful and beneficious information."[43] Writing to the *Gazeta de Campinas*, Manoel Ferraz de Campos Sales, a powerful coffee planter and republican leader in the Oeste Paulista (who would become president of the Brazilian republic in 1898), used Rodrigues's articles to criticize "the fatal belief, very common among our agriculturalists, that the free hand is absolutely impotent and incapable of cultivating coffee."[44] Far from being a political outsider connected to radical abolitionists, as historians have tried to portray him recently, Rodrigues had the esteem and attention of the richest coffee planters in Brazil.[45]

Rodrigues was aware that the Oeste Paulista was a net importer of slaves during the 1870s and that some of its coffee planters owned hundreds of slaves.[46] But he was no radical activist. Rather, Rodrigues wanted to work alongside the rich planters, hoping that his publications would inspire them to transition—even if slowly—to free labor. In São Paulo, he believed, "There is *self-help*; there is self-consciousness; there is individual initiative; there is trust in personal effort; there is unshakable certainty of the success of perseverance and labor."[47] Always favoring big capital at the expense of labor, Rodrigues made his antislavery publications into modernizing tools directed at advancing the interests of the great planters.

It is not surprising that many influential men in the Oeste Paulista embraced Rodrigues's campaign. In 1875, João Guilherme de Aguiar Whitaker, a major coffee planter in Rio Claro and provincial legislator, wrote to *O Novo Mundo* about the "multiplicity of enterprises and industrial associations through which [São Paulo] contributes to the common good." He mentioned the proliferation of railroads, plows, and steam-powered machines in the Oeste Paulista, which would help in the transition to free labor: "All around we see the agriculturalist trying to alleviate labor through the assistance of new instruments and understanding well that to invest in production is to sow capital which will produce advantageous fruits."[48] Many of these instruments were arriving in São Paulo from the United States thanks to Rodrigues's efforts.

In 1875, Rodrigues strengthened his bonds with the Oeste Paulista by sponsoring the establishment of a school in Itu, christened Instituto do Novo

Mundo. "The illustrious editor of *O Novo Mundo* had a very felicitous idea," *A Província de São Paulo* rejoiced; "his act is inspired by this noble sentiment which makes the North Americans be admired and esteemed by other peoples: to love one another." Rodrigues shipped more than 1,000 books from New York, along with desks, a printing press, and innovative didactic materials. The school would admit 200 students.[49]

Aurora Brasileira

Thanks to Rodrigues, coffee planters' sons would not only have access to the Instituto do Novo Mundo but also the opportunity to attend American universities. In this endeavor, he received the invaluable support of geologist Charles Frederick Hartt. Born in Nova Scotia, Hartt worked with Louis Agassiz at Harvard in the early 1860s. In 1865, he accompanied Agassiz to Brazil as a member of the Thayer Expedition; two years later, he returned to the country to continue his studies. In 1869, he became chair of geology at Cornell University and, the following year, published *Geology and Physical Geography of Brazil*.[50]

Rodrigues wrote an enthusiastic review of Hartt's work, emphasizing its importance for Brazil: "In an agricultural country, in which industry still needs to be developed, a work like the one we analyze here cannot be underestimated."[51] In January 1871, *O Novo Mundo* published Hartt's biography and portrait. During his third visit to Brazil, Hartt was struck by the reach of Rodrigues's publication, writing while exploring the Amazon that "I feel deeply indebted for what you have done for me in Brazil, I find I am known everywhere."[52]

Inspired by his friend, Rodrigues published a long article about Cornell in June 1871. He mentioned that Hartt was a faculty member, described the campus, and explained Cornell's origins in the 1862 Land Grant College Act. Rodrigues added that, like all other Land Grant colleges, Cornell's mission was to advance scientific agriculture and the mechanical arts. The students would learn through books and lectures while having hands-on experience at farms, workshops, construction sites, and laboratories.[53]

Although located in upstate New York, Cornell was well suited to Brazilian students willing to acquire knowledge applicable to their own country. Among its collections in natural history and agriculture, the university had the Hartt Brazilian Collection and the Prentiss Brazilian Collection in Botany.[54] An additional advantage, Rodrigues noted, was that "the costs here are not higher than in [the] São Paulo or Pernambuco [law schools]; and Brazilian parents will do well to send their sons to receive practical education in the United States."[55]

Rodrigues was pleased to report in June 1871 that "a few days ago a Brazilian youth, Mr. E. F. Pacheco Jordão, arrived from Itu, São Paulo."[56] Elias Fausto Pacheco Jordão was the son of a wealthy coffee planter from Rio Claro. He soon adapted to the American university. "Jordão is well and contented," Hartt informed Rodrigues, "he is a nice *filho* [son], I think he has come to the best place he could himself find."[57] More students from São Paulo soon followed him.

Rodrigues was the focal point of the network connecting São Paulo to Cornell. In 1874, he received a letter from journalist Joaquim Saldanha Marinho recommending two "young gentlemen of excellent demeanor, of distinguished families from Campinas ([province of] São Paulo).... They have the necessary means, and need only a friendly hand to guide them, and this friendly hand they will find in my friend and colleague J. C. Rodrigues."[58] Tomás de Aquino e Castro and his cousin arrived in New York City a few weeks after Saldanha Marinho's letter. They immediately "went searching for the office of 'O Novo Mundo' in order to visit the illustrious editor Mr. J. C. Rodrigues," who had already acquired a reputation as "the patron of the Brazilian students in the United States." Rodrigues accompanied the young men to Ithaca, introducing them to Hartt, who, "affable and kind," welcomed them "with deference and consideration." At the hotel, they had another nice surprise:

> We received the joyful visit of the students Elias [Fausto Pacheco] Jordão, [Luiz de] Souza Barros, [Carlos] Paes de Barros, [Antonio de] Queirós Teles Neto, Bento [de Almeida] Prado, and José Prado, who until then were the only Brazilians living there and who were enthusiastic about the growing community. We were eight then—and how odd!—all from the heroic province of São Paulo.[59]

Out of the thirty-four Brazilian students who enrolled at Cornell during the 1870s and 1880s, twenty-three came from the province of São Paulo. Like Pacheco Jordão, most were members of coffee planter families.[60]

Since the American Civil War, São Paulo had been the Brazilian province with closest ties to the United States. The most successful colony of ex-Confederates in Brazil was situated between Campinas and Limeira, where they used family labor to grow cotton and foodstuffs.[61] A New Jersey manufacturer called

William Van Vleck Lidgerwood had established his foundry in Campinas, where he became the most important producer of agricultural machinery in all of Brazil.[62] American missionaries had opened schools all over the province, including the famous Escola Americana in the city of São Paulo, whose owner was Rodrigues's former tutor George Whitehill Chamberlain.[63] Writing in 1875, Whitaker, the planter from Rio Claro, took great pride in one more element connecting his region to the United States.

> Around fifty men from São Paulo crossed the ocean to study in that country. Thankfully! Let us pray that they come back strengthened by example, by education, and capable of sowing the seeds which will fertilize our soil already so inclined to adopt North American uses and customs.[64]

To Whitaker's satisfaction, the Cornell students soon started transmitting what they were learning to Brazil. In October 1873, they published the first issue of a monthly review titled *Aurora Brasileira* (Brazilian Dawn).

The contributors to the *Aurora Brasileira* made clear that they drew inspiration from Rodrigues:

> The coming of so many Brazilians to this university happens thanks to that gentleman, who has shown the advantages of education in this country through the civilizing pages of *O Novo Mundo* and has welcomed all Brazilians in New York, advising that they come to this university, one of the best in the country.[65]

Like *O Novo Mundo*, the *Aurora Brasileira* portrayed the Oeste Paulista as the motor of Brazilian progress. In April 1874, it referred to the first experiments with immigrant labor, back in the 1840s and 1850s: "Long ago, through private initiative, the province of São Paulo first considered replacing the slave hand." Although these first experiments failed as immigrants often rebelled against poor treatment and left the plantations, the planters continued to search for ways to employ free workers. The *Aurora Brasileira* further claimed that São Paulo agriculture, "diverse and abundant as it is, has long rejected the old routine." Private initiative had brought plows, railroads, factories, and schools to "the Massachusetts of Brazil."[66]

The students planned to use the knowledge acquired at Cornell to carry out the transformation of São Paulo. As the *Aurora Brasileira* put it, "The movement begins: in all steamships young Brazilians depart for the United States, seeking to study the sciences—confident that they will render great services to their country."[67] The Cornell experience seemed to have instantaneous results. Upon arriving at the university, Aquino e Castro was pleased to see his compatriots' activities: Pacheco Jordão "worked with his own hands, spiking the soil of the Union with several miles of railway"; Souza Barros "breathed an atmosphere of acids in the chemistry laboratory"; Paes de Barros "surveyed university lands"; Vieira Bueno studied bridge building; and Almeida Prado "trained by moving agricultural instruments on the American soil." Aquino e Castro concluded that his colleagues' training represented much more than individual efforts: "It was Brazil which had come here to remake itself, undress the dull cloak of the royalty and take the garments of the humble worker of the century!"[68]

Rodrigues exulted at observing Brazilian students' experiences at Cornell. "They want to learn," he proclaimed; "they see on the walls of the near future the 'mene, mene, tekel, upharsin' [numbered, numbered, weighed, divided] of slavery." In the Old Testament (Daniel 5:25), these words appear on the wall during a feast and the prophet Daniel interprets them as God dooming Belshazzar's kingdom. Rodrigues also foresaw the demise of Brazilian slavery. "And through this sentence," he continued, "they see their country in need of all the energy from the men who will found the new order."[69] Rodrigues believed that American education, like American technology, would help extirpate the backward practices of Brazilian agriculture, not the least of which was slavery.

The coffee planters and their sons knew well what Rodrigues stood for. They were also fully aware of what kind of institution Cornell was. Before establishing the university, telegraph magnate Ezra Cornell had declared his detestation of slavery and concluded from his visits to Virginia that it bred ignorance and poverty. During the 1860s, he served as Republican state legislator in New York and supported the Union war effort. In 1871, the university librarian reported that abolitionist Samuel Joseph May had "generously presented to this Library his collection of books and pamphlets relating to the Slavery and Anti-Slavery contest in this country." Responding to the librarian's request, other abolitionists donated materials to the collection, making Cornell a center for the study of slavery and its pernicious effects.[70]

On September 7, 1873, eighteen Brazilian students at Cornell organized a parade to celebrate Brazil's Independence Day. Accompanied by a band, they marched to the university president's house. "If there is anything to stimulate us to new exertion," President Andrew Dickson White greeted them, "to arouse us to put forth new efforts to build up this new institution, it is the idea that its influence is to spread even beyond the borders of our own country."[71] The Brazilian youths were eager to receive Cornell's antislavery influence and forward it to Brazil through the *Aurora Brasileira*. Although the Oeste Paulista remained strongly attached to slavery during the 1870s, a new vision for the future of the coffee-producing region had already emerged in upstate New York.

Aurora Brazileira

In 1874, engineer William S. Auchincloss of Delaware traveled to Brazil. After visiting a plantation in Campinas, he enthused that "much progress has already been made in the introduction of labor-saving machinery and more scientific methods of tillage." Auchincloss was elated to find that the advancement of Brazilian society bore the mark of the United States: "Each year brings to our [American] shores new [Brazilian] students for our colleges and technical schools, who, on the completion of their education, immediately return to their native land."[72]

As the 1870s wore on, Brazilian students did not restrict themselves to Cornell. They found their way to Lehigh University and Lafayette College, in Pennsylvania; the University of Cincinnati, in Ohio; the Rensselaer Polytechnic Institute and Syracuse University, in New York; and the University of Massachusetts, among other northern institutions. Though their destinations varied, their objectives remained the same.

In 1875, José Custódio Alves de Lima, the son of a coffee planter from Tietê, province of São Paulo, transferred from Cornell to Syracuse and took with him the Brazilian students' publication. He renamed it *Aurora Brazileira*, with a z. Inspired by publications such as *Scientific American*, Alves de Lima sought to transform the periodical into a practical guide for Brazil's progress: "If there is a country in need of periodicals dealing with mechanics applied to industry and agriculture, this country certainly is Brazil."[73] He believed that "the American Union is a mirror in which the Brazilian will look if he wants to contribute his part to the material development of the country."[74]

Alves de Lima was first and foremost an agricultural reformer. "In a farm," he proposed in October 1877, "economy basically consists of performing labor with the least cost, the least waste, in the better way possible."[75] Emulating Rodrigues, Alves de Lima sought to solve the problems of Brazilian agriculture through American technology. He often announced, in English, that "parties who would like to have their goods known and introduced in Brazil, principally those manufacturers of engines, bridges, agricultural implements, locomotives, rolling stock, etc., will find at once that it pays to advertise in the *Aurora Brazileira*."[76]

Alves de Lima hoped that, by introducing American capital goods in Brazil, his periodical would help extirpate what he identified as the main cause of agricultural backwardness—slave labor. Work that could be performed by machines, he regretted, "is done in Brazil by slaves, who, we must admit, are always sluggish. Why should Brazil not imitate the United States at least in material improvements?"[77] Like other modernizers of his generation, Alves de Lima understood industrial technology as a force opposed to slavery.[78] He judged that the Free Womb Law would "only attain the beneficial results which our legislators envisioned if, from now on, we promote a complete revolution in our system of rural labor, replacing manual work with machines, creating a reasonable economy of time and money."[79] Technology, he suggested, would help Brazil replace the slave with the immigrant: "The German, Portuguese, Italian, or American colonists will work better if they have in hand a plow or an improved machine.... Thus, Brazilian agriculture needs to adopt machines, just like the United States did after slave emancipation."[80]

Alves de Lima chided Brazilian planters who "consider expensive a machine which does the work of ten slaves and still do not hesitate in paying ten times more for one slave!"[81] He looked down on the followers of Conservative Senator Bernardo Pereira de Vasconcelos, who had stated in the 1840s that "our civilization came from Africa." These were men fighting the spirit of the age: "The tortoise-statesman (as everyone knows) alluded to the benefit of importing more slaves to Brazil, the greatest error that our ancestors bequeathed to the present generation."[82]

But there were signs of progress among Brazilian planters. Like Rodrigues and the Cornell students, Alves de Lima praised the planters of his native region, the Oeste Paulista. "While in other regions of the Empire individual energy obtains nothing," he wrote in 1877, "in São Paulo, capital is raised in order to build railroads which take life and light everywhere." In addition to railroads, new schools emerged throughout the province. And now the planters' sons were flocking to the United States.

We are proud to say that here we find young men from Campinas, Piracicaba, Tietê, Capivari, Tatuí, Jundiaí, Santos, Itu, and other cities, who decided to come on their own or through advice from their parents. Some study engineering, others mechanics, agriculture, or medicine.... Our readers from other provinces will be surprised to learn that the students from São Paulo are the children of wealthy planters, who see in the education of their sons a great investment not only useful to themselves but also to society and their birthplace.[83]

The students had now taken the lead of the modernizing effort, helping the Oeste Paulista absorb technology from the United States. Alves de Lima rejoiced that "the Porter Manufacturing Company, which has always advertised in the *Aurora*, is presently building several steam-powered machines to be used in the townships of Tietê and Capivari in the province of São Paulo."[84] Luiz de Souza Barros, an engineering student at Columbia University and a contributor to the *Aurora Brazileira*, had sent "one hay-cutting machine, three different harvesters, one corn-planting machine, one grain-processing machine, one alfalfa-planting machine, several cultivators, and other instruments to the plantation of Mr. José de Souza Barros, a planter from Araraquara." Alves de Lima, who understood mechanization as the shortest—and safest—path to free labor, applauded "the progressive spirit of the Souza Barros family."[85]

The last issue of *Aurora Brazileira* came out in 1878. Its mission, however, lived on as Alves de Lima's fellow graduates would engage in modernizing their country upon returning from the American North. Cornell graduates assumed prominent roles in São Paulo during the late 1870s and 1880s. Pacheco Jordão served as assistant engineer of public works and later became superintendent of the Ituana Railroad. José Tibiriçá Piratininga first worked at the Mogiana Railroad, then became provincial engineer of traffic, and later served as general inspector of the Ituana Navigation Company. Domingos Correia de Morais worked as assistant engineer of São Paulo's municipal water works and, in 1888, became president of the São Paulo Streetcar Company.[86]

Graduates of other American universities also worked on developing transportation infrastructure in São Paulo. Alves de Lima served as assistant engineer of public works and later as inspector of the Mogiana and Sorocabana railroads. Eduardo de Andrade Vilares, another Syracuse graduate, worked as assistant engineer at the Mogiana Railroad and superintendent of the Ituana

Railroad.[87] Aquino e Castro, who had transferred to the University of Cincinnati, also served as assistant engineer of public works.[88] Eugenio de Lacerda Franco, a Rensselaer graduate, worked as assistant engineer at the Paulista Railroad. Luiz Gonzaga da Silva Lima, another Rensselaer graduate, became chief engineer of the Bragantina Railroad.[89]

Most graduates from American universities returned to their family plantations to modernize coffee production. According to a Dutch traveler who visited São Paulo in the 1880s, they made systematic use of the plow and built houses for the reception of immigrants.[90] Others engaged in commerce, extractive industries, and manufacturing. Fernando de Albuquerque, a Lafayette graduate, established an agency in Santos to import agricultural machinery from the United States.[91] Joaquim da Silveira Melo, a Cincinnati graduate, established a lumber company and a coffee-cleaning mill in Pirassununga.[92] Fernando Paes de Barros, a Syracuse graduate, established a steam-powered sawmill in Itu. Antonio de Queirós Teles Neto, also a Syracuse graduate, established a cotton mill in Jundiaí, while his fellow Syracuse alumni Francisco Fernando Paes de Barros Jr. and Otaviano Abdon Pereira Mendes established another near Itu.[93]

Proud of his protégés, Rodrigues left New York in 1879 feeling that he had accomplished his mission of bringing Brazil closer to the United States. He first went to the Colombian province of Panama to work as a correspondent for American newspapers, advocating for an American takeover of the projected canal route.[94] Subsequently, he moved to London, where he became a financial advisor for foreigners seeking to invest in Latin America. By the late 1880s, he returned to Brazil a rich man and bought the *Jornal do Commercio*.

In the wake of the American Civil War, Rodrigues and the Brazilian students worked together in directing northern expertise and technology to Brazil. Fulfilling Tavares Bastos's and Paula Souza's vision, they took advantage of pivotal changes in North America to push a modernizing project into their country. And they succeeded. Thanks to their efforts, Brazilian elites would not feel isolated or afraid of the changes to come. On the contrary, their publications made the aftermath of the American Civil War into a period of exciting opportunities and expanding networks for Brazilian society. Most important, these periodicals helped the slaveholding Oeste Paulista prepare for a future without slavery. *O Novo Mundo*, the *Revista Industrial*, and both versions of the *Aurora* reassured coffee planters that, like American capitalists, they had much to gain from rebuilding agriculture on the basis of wage labor.

The growing dominance of post-emancipation São Paulo in coffee production vindicated the antislavery vision of these publications.⁹⁵

Notes

1. Speech of Aureliano Cândido Tavares Bastos, April 22, 1864, *ACD* (1864), 4:246.
2. Speech of Antonio Francisco de Paula Souza, August 11, 1864, *ACD* (1864), 4:275.
3. Conrad, *Destruction*, 81; Toplin, *Abolition*, 41–43.
4. Salles, "Águas," 63.
5. Needell, *Party of Order*, 233.
6. Marquese, "U.S. Civil War," 237–38.
7. E. Costa, *Senzala*; Beigelman, *Formação*; Hall, "Origins"; Fernandes, *Revolução*.
8. Weinstein, "Decline," 83.
9. Gauld, "José Carlos Rodrigues"; Boehrer, "Jose Carlos Rodrigues."
10. On youth organizations, see Alonso, *Idéias*. For college students' political culture, see Kirkendall, *Class Mates*.
11. *O Futuro* (São Paulo), May 17, 1862.
12. "Os Patriotas," *O Futuro* (São Paulo), September 7, 1862.
13. *ONM*, October 24, 1870.
14. "O Valor das Machinas," *ONM*, May 23, 1875.
15. "Alguns Retratos," *ONM*, February 1877.
16. "As Classes Operarias nos Estados Unidos," *ONM*, December 23, 1870.
17. "Aspectos Politicos," *ONM*, April 23, 1872.
18. Foner, *Reconstruction*, 488–511.
19. Beckert, *Monied Metropolis*, 145–71.
20. "O Anno de 1870," *ONM*, December 23, 1870.
21. "O Trabalho dos Emancipados," *ONM*, October 23, 1872. On the restructuring of the plantation economy in the postwar South, see G. Wright, *Old South*, 51–197.
22. On ex-slaves' mobility in the post-emancipation South, see Hahn, *Nation Under Our Feet*.
23. "O Trabalho dos Libertos," *ONM*, February 1, 1879.
24. "Condição Economica do Sul dos Estados Unidos," *ONM*, October 24, 1871.
25. "O Trabalho dos Libertos," *ONM*, February 1, 1879.
26. "Prosperidade Industrial de 1870," *ONM*, January 23, 1871.
27. "O Trabalho dos Emancipados," *ONM*, October 23, 1872.
28. "O Trabalho dos Libertos," *ONM*, February 1, 1879.

29. "História da Escravidão nos Estados Unidos," *ONM*, August 24, 1871.
30. Richardson, *Greatest Nation*, 139–208; Hahn, *Nation Without Borders*, 237–43.
31. "Disposição das Terras Públicas," *ONM*, November 24, 1871.
32. Conrad, *Destruction*, 116–17.
33. "O Nosso Café," *ONM*, April 1877.
34. "Notes," *The Nation* (New York), November 3, 1870.
35. Tavares Bastos to Rodrigues, Rio, February 3, 1872, *ABN* 90 (1971): 162–63.
36. "O Novo Mundo," *Gazeta de Campinas*, July 29, 1875.
37. John James Aubertin to Rodrigues, Madrid, June 15, 1878, *ABN* 90 (1971): 233.
38. O Novo Mundo Association, *By-laws*.
39. "O Novo Mundo," *ONM*, November 1877.
40. "Aos Leitores," *Revista Industrial* (New York), July 1877.
41. "Irrigação—Fertilização pelo Limo," *Revista Industrial* (New York), July 1879.
42. "O Brasil visto dos Estados Unidos," *Correio Paulistano* (São Paulo), January 30, 1874.
43. "Revista Industrial Illustrada," *Correio Paulistano* (São Paulo), August 12, 1877.
44. "Questão do Dia," *Gazeta de Campinas*, November 5, 1871.
45. Marquese, "U.S. Civil War," 231.
46. On the domestic slave trade to São Paulo, see Motta, *Escravos*.
47. "Navegação Fluvial," *ONM*, June 24, 1876. *Self-help* appeared in English in the original.
48. "O Progresso de S. Paulo," *ONM*, February 22, 1875.
49. "O Instituto do Novo Mundo em Itu," *A Provícia de São Paulo*, January 4, 1875.
50. Freitas, *Charles Frederick Hartt*.
51. "Geologia do Brazil," *ONM*, October 24, 1870.
52. Charles Frederick Hartt to Rodrigues, Rio Tapajós, September 17, 1871, *ABN* 90 (1971): 138.
53. "A Universidade de Cornell," *ONM*, June 24, 1871. On the origins of the Land Grant colleges, see Richardson, *Greatest Nation*, 139–69.
54. Cornell, *Cornell*, 23.
55. "A Universidade de Cornell," *ONM*, June 24, 1871.
56. "A Universidade de Cornell," *ONM*, June 24, 1871.
57. Hartt to Rodrigues, Rio Tapajós, June 18, 1870, *ABN* 90 (1971): 138.
58. Joaquim Saldanha Marinho to Rodrigues, Rio, July 25, 1874, *ABN* 90 (1971): 224.
59. "Impressões de Viagem do Rio de Janeiro a Ithaca," *Aurora Brasileira* (Ithaca), May 20, 1874.

60. Freitas, *Contradições*.
61. C. Silva, "Capitalismo."
62. Camillo, "Modernização."
63. Vieira, *Protestantismo*.
64. "O Progresso de S. Paulo," *ONM*, February 22, 1875.
65. "O Novo Mundo," *Aurora Brasileira* (Ithaca), January 20, 1874.
66. "Propagadora da Instrução," *Aurora Brasileira* (Ithaca), April 20, 1874. On the free-labor experiments, see Beiguelman, *Formação*, 89–94.
67. "Aurora Brasileira," *Aurora Brasileira* (Ithaca), October 22, 1873.
68. "Impressões de Viagem do Rio de Janeiro a Ithaca," *Aurora Brasileira* (Ithaca), June 20, 1874.
69. "Educação no Exterior," *ONM*, January 23, 1874.
70. Willard Fiske to the Rev. Edmund Burke Wilson, Library of Cornell University, Ithaca, February 15, 1871, American Antiquarian Society, American Slavery Collection, no. 194249.
71. "The Brazilian Celebration," *Daily Journal* (Ithaca), September 8, 1873.
72. Auchincloss, *Ninety Days*, 76–77.
73. "Aurora Brazileira," *Aurora Brasileira* (Ithaca), March 1877.
74. "A Educação do Engenheiro Civil," *Aurora Brazileira* (Syracuse), January 1878.
75. "Verdadeira Economia," *Aurora Brazileira* (Syracuse), October 1877.
76. "Advertise in the Aurora Brazileira," *Aurora Brazileira* (Syracuse), May 1877–January 1878.
77. "Bombas para Uso Domestico," *Aurora Brazileira* (Syracuse), December 1875.
78. In her study of the Sociedade Auxiliadora da Indústria Nacional, Teresa Cribelli notes that its "central aim . . . was the dissemination of the latest in scientific and technological advances, especially . . . for agricultural improvement and as a way to transition from slave to free labor." *Industrial Forests*, 26.
79. "Aurora Brazileira," *Aurora Brazileira* (Syracuse), December 1875.
80. "O Segador de Bradley," *Aurora Brazileira* (Syracuse), January 1876.
81. "Nossa Resposta," *Aurora Brazileira* (Syracuse), May 1876.
82. "Influencia da Machina sobre o Trabalho," *Aurora Brazileira* (Syracuse), December 1875.
83. "Porque É que S. Paulo Progride," *Aurora Brazileira* (Syracuse), May 1877.
84. "Locomotivas e Machinas a Vapor Para o Brazil," *Aurora Brazileira* (Syracuse), December 1877.
85. "Em Geral," *Aurora Brazileira* (Syracuse), April 1876.
86. Cornell, *Ten-Year Book*, 125, 146, 189.
87. Syracuse University, *Alumni*, 637, 653.
88. University of Cincinnati, *Catalogue*, 59.

89. Rensselaer, *Annual Register*, 90, 94.
90. Laërne, *Brazil and Java*, 362.
91. Lafayette College, *Record*, 102.
92. University of Cincinnati, *Catalogue*, 61.
93. Syracuse University, *Alumni*, 643.
94. J. C. Rodrigues, *Panama Canal*.
95. Dean, *Rio Claro*; Holloway, *Immigrants*.

Celso Thomas Castilho

ELEVEN
A "GALLERY OF ILLUSTRIOUS MEN OF COLOR" Recife's O Homem, *the Black Press, and Transatlantic Literary Genres*

The launch of *O Homem* (The Man), a Black newspaper in the northeastern city of Recife in 1876, upended long-standing political and intellectual conventions. In confronting racial discrimination, the journal shattered the code of silence that muted public debate on racial discord.[1] In proposing that Recife's "men of color" coalesce around the abolitionist movement, *O Homem* also posited a racial, rather than the more customary partisan or class, political formation. And, through its running column titled "Galeria de homens de cor ilustres" (Gallery of illustrious men of color, hereafter "Gallery"), the paper refashioned the look and politics of a centuries-old literary tradition to critique the terms of national belonging. In so doing, *O Homem*'s "Gallery" subverted the aims of a genre that had historically drawn on portraiture and historical biography. In thus returning to this important, if also rather rare, example of a Black newspaper in nineteenth-century Brazil, this chapter probes *O Homem* for what it reveals about the relationship between the press and the practices of political claims-making in general, and for what it illuminates about the wider intellectual tradition of the "Gallery," in particular. In analyzing these processes together, I demonstrate why the study of Black newspapers is critical to reevaluations of trans-Atlantic intellectual currents.

An Afro descendant, law-school graduate, reputable schoolteacher, and prolific writer, Felipe Neri Collaço (1815–1894), edited *O Homem*.[2] The weekly ran for three months, totaling twelve issues. A mainstay in Conservative Party circles and a devout Catholic, Collaço descended from a prominent family. His paternal lineage dated to Pernambuco's storied colonial age. His great-grandfather, José Vaz Salgado, figured among the wealthiest merchants and imperial administrators of the eighteenth century, passing on sugar plantations and enslaved Africans to future generations, including Collaço's father. The father, however, bucked social norms and instead married a woman of mixed-African descent and of modest means. The decision estranged him and the couple's six children from the wealthy family's sphere. Yet, Collaço was still raised in a household maintained by enslaved domestic workers, and he received a primary and secondary education. His record in public life took off in his midtwenties when he served as the copyeditor for the city's most important daily, the *Diário de Pernambuco*, from 1846 to 1856; during this period, he also earned a law degree in 1853. Before publishing *O Homem*, Collaço edited literary, religious, political, scientific, and women's newspapers. With titles ranging from *O Recreio das Belas* (Recreation for the Fair [Sex], 1849–1850) and *O Jardim das Damas* (The Ladies' Garden, 1852), to the *Correio do Recife* (1865–1868) and *Caritas* (1874–1878), Collaço played a considerable role in shaping Recife's world of print. In 1866, he was acclaimed a "dignified representative of Gutenberg" at a national exposition.[3]

Meanwhile, Collaço's participation in jury trials and long career at the famed secondary school, the Ginásio Pernambucano, shored up his public reputation. At the Ginásio and in private classes, Collaço offered lessons in algebra, geometry, philosophy, French, English, and physics. In a recent study, historian Rafaella Valença de Andrade Galvão expanded upon Collaço's career in law and journalism. She commented on his work as a surveyor and an engineer with the municipality of Recife, and highlighted the reputation of his mathematics textbook, which went through at least sixteen editions.[4] Fittingly, Andrade Galvão characterizes him as much a man of numbers as one of letters. *O Homem*, then, needs to be understood as a serious publication by a man who had a long public career. His erudition both opened doors and fanned racism; from this richer view of Collaço's trajectory, we can begin to better appreciate how his rewriting of the "Gallery" drew on an extensive background in law, literature, and journalism.

To my knowledge, *O Homem* was the first Black newspaper in Recife. Given Collaço's self-presentation as a "man of color," as opposed to that of a "Black man," we can also use this chapter as an opportunity to reflect on the particularities and implications of using the category of the "Black press" when writing about newspapers in imperial Brazil. My use of *Black* accounts for the structural realities that Collaço in particular, and Afro descendants in general, navigated in the 1870s as a result of racial slavery. While it is true that Collaço was partially of African descent and that those whom he courted through *O Homem* were also more "men of color" than "Black," according to the social categories of the time, the racialized turn in his writing responded to processes of racism and exclusion that he and those in his privileged circle had recently endured. That is, he had not staked out as racialized a position in the press in the previous three decades of his public activity. It was thus a contingent move on his part in 1876. The paper's masthead, to be sure, used the phrase "men of color," which in terms of contemporary racial identities would have corresponded more to "*pardos*" than to "Blacks." Pardo, as we know, referred to the socially constructed identity of racially mixed people of African and European heritage. The differences between pardo and Black identity were well-understood distinctions among nineteenth-century Brazilians. Meanwhile, it was also the case that Collaço's conceptualization of "men of color" went beyond references to African heritage, and included men of Indigenous background. Therefore, equating his men of color with pardo identity does not fully capture the idea, either. Overall, I am not trying to reclassify Collaço's modes of self-representation or to suggest that he failed to see the converging realities faced by both pardos and Blacks. By referring to his work as invested in Black political rights, I am taking the position that his claims for political belonging were articulated through an expressly antiracist language that sought to recast the terms of Blackness. Recent work coming largely out of the Brazilian academy on the Black press, Black citizenship, and Black intellectuals has paved the way for this choice of terminology.[5]

The "Gallery" tradition in nineteenth-century Brazil engaged the wider Atlantic World developments in the genre, which increasingly became associated with visual articulations of the nation. To be sure, the history of the "Gallery" tradition extended back to the early-modern period, but it was only in the eighteenth century that the genre took a more recognizable form. In France alone there were at least fourteen collective biographies published prior to the revolution. According to David Bell, revolutionary-era iterations of the *Grands Hommes de la Patrie* (Great men of the fatherland) moved to nationalize, that is, Frenchify the heroes, and produce a "revolutionary vision in which the nation was embodied, potentially, in every citizen."[6] Similarly, the most important Brazilian adaptation, Sébastien Augusto Sisson's two-volume *Galeria dos brasileiros ilustres: os contemporâneos* (Gallery of illustrious Brazilians: The contemporaries), printed between 1859 and 1861, drew on the visual technologies and aesthetics of the time to render a specific idea about Brazil.[7] It appeared as titles of the same genre, such as *Portrait Gallery of Distinguished Americans* (1845), *National Portrait Gallery of Eminent Americans* (1862), and *The Black Man* (1863), were being published in the United States.[8] For our purposes, Sisson's work will serve as the primary basis from which to situate the innovations of Collaço's 1876 "Gallery of Illustrious Men of Color." Even absent the shiny lithographs that defined the "Galleries" being produced in France, the United States, and Rio de Janeiro, Collaço's own "Gallery" nonetheless offered a substantive reinterpretation of the genre, in terms of both its politics and form. The chapter thus begins with a deeper consideration of Sisson's 1850s *Galeria*, before turning more specifically to Collaço, *O Homem*, and the "Gallery of Illustrious Men of Color" in the second and third sections.

An Imperial Gallery

Sébastien Sisson's *Galeria dos brasileiros ilustres* channeled a specific vision and visual representation of national history. The book strove to consolidate specific values and experiences as exemplary, even normative. Yet, "there is more to it than the mere presentation of facts about these great men," he explains in the preface. "The nation, like a family, enjoys preserving an image," and this is best captured with "a visual [representation], of its most distinguished members."[9] More specifically, Sisson noted that the *Galeria* reflected Brazil's national era: the illustrious roster highlighted key figures from the 1820s to the 1850s. Certainly, this was a project about imperial nation making, that in its presentation included a glowing acknowledgement of the emperor's patronage; Sisson referred to him as a "man of science, letters, the arts, and industry."[10] Named the Imperial Lithographer in 1866, the French-born Sisson (1824–1898), shaped the history of the illustrated press in Brazil.[11]

Politically, the *Galeria* defended the status quo. In mid-1850s Brazil, this meant deepening the influence of Conservative rule, strengthening the mechanisms of centralization, and, at the same time, silencing discussions on slavery and racial discord.[12] Statesman and literary giant José de Alencar advanced the book's political project in several ways. According to Jesus Menezes, Alencar authored the first batch of biographies in the *Galeria*.[13] It is striking that in the entry on Eusébio de Queirós, who as prime minister in 1850 signed into law the prohibition of the African slave trade, Alencar never used the word *slavery* (or its derivatives). Instead, Queirós appears as a key reformer of Rio de Janeiro, who in his role as police chief in the 1830s, helped restore "order" and "integrity" to the rule of law.[14] We should not lose sight of the fact that it was Queirós who occupied this post as hundreds of thousands of Africans were being illegally imported into Rio de Janeiro, a process that several historians have shown to require the active complicity of the state.[15] Despite authoring antislavery plays at the same time that he wrote these entries, Alencar long maintained that slaveholders should preserve the final word over when and how to free the enslaved.[16] Nevertheless, he also contributed to the project's legacy in other ways. For example, he wove a reference to the *Galeria* into one of his novels. In *Senhora* (1875), two characters refer to it amid a discussion of the arts, celebrities, and national heroes.[17] Sisson's book also made a formidable impression on a still-maturing Joaquim Maria Machado de Assis. Machado recalled it decades later when writing a *crônica* about the "old Senate," writing that he referenced it to better understand this earlier generation's politicians.[18]

Indeed, Sisson's portrayal of Brazil's finest (men) created an aura around the imperial state. In fact, these men were the state. Forty-nine of those profiled worked, or previously had worked, for the state; twenty others were elected representatives, meaning that, altogether, sixty-nine of the eighty-nine chosen for the *Galeria* were the literal embodiments of the ruling class.[19] Their ties to the state, therefore, made them noteworthy and "created incentives for the sons of the nation" to also cultivate such ties.[20] Almost half—thirty-nine—possessed law degrees, most of which were obtained in Portugal at the University of Coimbra.[21] If a legal education comprised a core unifying element for Sisson, most also hailed from the largest provinces at the time: twenty-two from Rio, sixteen from Bahia, thirteen each from Minas Gerais and São Paulo, and five from Pernambuco.[22] The overrepresentation of these places does not surprise any scholar of nineteenth-century Brazil given these provinces' political and economic importance. They serve, however, to offer a loose geographic sense of the "us" that Sisson fostered, which when analyzed more closely, included a noticeable southeastern tilt. This tilt deliberately misrepresented the fact that both Salvador and Recife were considerably larger and arguably more intellectually vibrant cities than São Paulo city in the 1850s. Sisson's "nation," therefore, needs to be seen as comprising the regionally inflected idea of Brazil that it was, for recognizing this will put Collaço's own northeastern-dominated "Gallery" in better perspective.

To be sure, Sisson's imperial *Galeria* also included an elaborate presentation of the emperor, to whom the book was dedicated. The special attention that his entry commanded is immediately apparent from the portrait that Sisson used, which depicts the then thirty-three-year-old, sitting at a small table covered with books and writing ink. The emperor appears stately in this famous photograph that is today still used to illustrate his biography in *Encyclopedia Britannica*.[23] The accompanying text narrates the history of the nation as an extension of his personal trajectory. "The first stirrings towards independence began with the arrival of the Portuguese royal family," writes Sisson, in reference to the transatlantic move of the imperial court following the French invasion of the Iberian Peninsula.[24] From there, and in moving past—"for reasons that we right now do not need to revisit"—contentious events like the dissolving of the constitutional assembly in 1823, the entry expounds on his role as a "stabilizing force." Lauded for overcoming the gulfs that divided the "monarchy and the people," Pedro II is held as Brazil's shining light: "the first to be immersed in literary and industrial currents across the empire, a protector of the sciences and the arts, and a charitable man towards hospitals and the country's neediest."[25] These qualities, in short, conveyed a vision about political modernity, about an imperial modernity that was at once enlightened and, at the same time, restrained in its displays of power. Ending with an anecdote about him visiting those afflicted by the latest (cholera) epidemic, the entry underscores his connection with the people and reiterates the legitimacy of the imperial project.

Yet, if glossed over entirely by scholars of Sisson's *Galeria*, the imperial "us" construed in the portraits and the texts was also nothing short of a racial project, a white project that, of course, comes across as more incidental than deliberate. It appears that the "illustrious" men profiled were white because most of the accomplished male citizens were white; that is, the *Galeria* was at most a reflection of class and talent and not a racialized presentation of the nation. Sisson's book bypasses altogether some of the most prominent men of post-independence Brazil—like the Afro-Bahian jurist Antônio Rebouças— and includes just one Afro-descendant, the Viscount of Jequitinhonha (Francisco Gê Acaiaba de Montezuma). Curiously, Jequitinhonha's entry, which includes his heroic role during the independence wars and later career as a statesman, runs to nearly thirty pages. This is the most space devoted to any one figure, including the emperor. Still, the text silences Jequitinhonha's racial background and buries his interventions against the slave trade in the 1830s. The lithograph, nonetheless, brings out aspects of his African heritage. More generally, however, the point remains that the overwhelming majority of the men celebrated in the *Galeria* affirmed a connection between whiteness and power. It also bears repeating that the project's investment in maintaining the status quo entailed a notable erasure of slavery from the national narrative. It was this book, then, Sisson's *Galeria*, that most represented the wider Atlantic World tradition of the "illustrious men" genre in mid-nineteenth-century

Brazil, and it remains a text worthy of comparison when reengaging the decidedly Afro-descendant "Gallery" in Collaço's *O Homem*.

A Black Newspaper as Rights-Claiming

O Homem rattled the codes of racial discourse in a city where slavery and an entrenched seignorialism structured public life. A slaving port since the sixteenth century, Recife was the third-largest city in imperial Brazil with about 115,000 people in the early 1870s, three times the size of São Paulo city.[26] Approximately 10–15 percent of its population remained enslaved at this point, reflecting more or less the scale of urban slavery nationally. Also, like other cities, Recife's free people of color comprised about 40 percent of the urban population. An undeniably small, but still influential, number of these men attained success in law, education, business, and politics. And yet even with the decline in the urban and overall provincial ratios of enslavement over the nineteenth century, we should not necessarily assume that racial troubles diminished. Or that the continued abolitionist movement, which as of 1876 was about a decade old, had eased anti-Black sentiments. In fact, the opposite could probably be said: that, for however interracial the movement constituted and represented itself, the anti-abolitionist reaction emphasized and antagonized abolitionism's "Black" features. This defensive response stigmatized mass politics by racializing its participants, and anti-Black rhetoric gained space in the press. Furthermore, as *O Homem* launched in 1876, virtually every major newspaper in the country still published runaway-slave advertisements, illustrating the extent to which slaveholders' interests were taken as representative of broader social concerns.

The press in 1870s Recife played a major role in public life, filtering the importance of happenings from other pillars of local culture, including the law school, the theater arena, and the dozens of literary, political, and religious associations. Collaço's career prior to *O Homem* took him across most of these spaces, including the press where he began his career in the 1840s. Lacking an in-depth study of Pernambucan print culture, any summary of the press in the 1870s is still impressionistic. Between a half-dozen and a dozen dailies and scores of ephemeral titles energized urban life throughout the decade, which as was the case for other major cities, represented a notable increase from midcentury publications, and an even more substantial jump from the periodicals printed in the 1820s and 1830s. More than making a point about the number of newspapers, what matters is that we consider this a vibrant space of journalistic activity and political affirmation. It also matters that the largest dailies were nationally relevant and served as the main source of information on Pernambuco and the greater northern region (see Hendrik Kraay's chapter). Certainly, contemporaries recognized the press's importance, saw in it a space for participating politically, and disseminated its information through public collective readings. To brand newspapers an "elite" space is to profoundly misunderstand how involved Afro descendants were as printers, journalists, readers, and editors in these spaces (see Rodrigo Camargo de Godoi's chapter).

The publication of *O Homem* thus emerged in a context in which it was still more honorable to own people than to call that system into question. And the "Gallery" column became a way to connect antislavery sensibilities with the exclusions that free men of color experienced. Collaço explained in the introductory article that three separate incidents prompted the paper's existence. Recife's men of color were (1) being run out of public posts; (2) forced to disband a public meeting where they planned to sign and send a petition to Parliament; and (3) had endured the humiliation of having a prominent Afro-descendant candidate passed over for a law-school professorship. Emphatically, the paper cast these charges as not only illegal, a violation of their constitutional rights, but also as racially motivated. It stressed that such state acts went beyond personal circumstances and that these were, in fact, an attack on Recife's men of color. In putting these recent, and ostensibly unrelated events, in such terms, and in also trying to present these offenses as an offense to the wider "men of color population," the newspaper was audaciously breaking a long-held taboo against publicizing racial discrimination. Its existence and, by extension, its challenge to the rules of public discourse, elicited what would become a familiar reaction from white elites: *O Homem* was charged with trying to incite a race war. The most important Liberal paper in the city, *A Província*, called its entry into the print milieu "lazy and impolitic," and accused it of "sparking hate and disunity."[27] *A Província*, which was then an opposition newspaper, went down the well-trodden path of answering protests about racial problems with declarations that it was the protests themselves that were to blame for turning race into a problem; this became an increasingly important trope for proslavery sectors over the next fifteen years, including in the post-emancipation period when considerable numbers of Afro-descendants swelled the ranks of popular monarchical groups that challenged the sugar planter–based political machines.[28]

Collaço and contemporaries understood the importance of the press as a means of rights claiming. The practice of citizenship in nineteenth-century Brazil encompassed a broad range of rights and obligations as well as cultural processes of national belonging. The field of participation spanned from voting to forming part of associations to engaging the print sphere. *O Homem*, then, needs to be seen as both a statement and a strategy of national belonging. Building on Collaço's expertise in law, the newspaper made its case for Black political rights by quoting the constitution; it cited constitutional provisions directly on the masthead, pasting two clauses from the famed article 179. The first clause defended all [male] citizens' eligibility for civic, political, and military posts, and the second reiterated that those considerations must rest on "talent and merits alone, irrespective of other differences," which for Collaço clearly meant race.[29] It is interesting that this strategy of using constitutionalist language was also adopted in the Black press of the 1830s amid racialized disputes over access to employment. In Rio de Janeiro, a Black newspaper also quoted directly from article 179, and in Salvador (Bahia), public claims were made on behalf of the equal rights of men of color.[30]

Meanwhile, Collaço's legal arguments protested that "in the last year, six men of color have been pushed out from their jobs ... and that without faith or the rule of law ... a lasting peace cannot exist."[31] These developments worsened a political crisis for Recife's men of color, Collaço reminded readers, for they had been excluded from posts in the municipal council since the late 1840s.[32] Collaço also wrote about the violation of political rights that came with the violent dispersal of a public meeting where a group of men of color had gathered to sign a petition to Parliament. The incident encapsulated the disregard for their constitutional rights, he argued, for which they had to fight together to reclaim. The incident also revived anxieties over legislation from the preceding year that placed restrictions on where free and enslaved men of color could hang signs.[33] Because of these mounting affronts, Collaço felt it essential to respond with this paper to represent his "class of people, the most numerous and hardest working in Brazil."[34]

Doubtlessly, *O Homem* articulated a racial project. According to a series of guiding objectives presented on the front page of each edition, it aimed to "unite and instruct Pernambuco's men of color." This was no small goal in a city as large as Recife. The process of racial formation provided by *O Homem* required a smoothing over of class and gender distinctions to rewrite the political handbook for Pernambuco's men of color. The newspaper form allowed

Collaço a unique means to string together an unending series of "we's" and "our's" when referring to the men of color that when juxtaposed to the "they's" and "them's" gave the impression that oppositional, racial dialectics indeed shaped political dynamics. Also, the "we's" glossed salient class differences within the heterogeneous, free Afro-descendant male population. This "class of people," to use Collaço's words, encompassed carpenters and stonemasons, in addition to law-school graduates and influential businessmen.[35] Clearly, the men of color whom Collaço wrote about referred to those in the latter group. The gendered nature of the racial category is also explicit in the journal's title. The universalizing form of "man" feeds and reflects extant gendered discourses of power, and can be read as part of a nineteenth-century phenomenon of trying to preserve a "masculine" identification with the political arena.[36] For Collaço, who earlier in his career had edited "women's" and "family" newspapers, this contentious entry into public debate entailed reaffirming norms about the need to link masculinity and political practice.

The paper's abolitionist profile represented a crucial dimension of the racial project. Not someone who had previously registered a discernible antislavery record, Collaço championed the ending of slavery in 1876 as a way to confront racism. He connected the two matters explicitly in an editorial that appeared in the fourth issue: "We want the realization of constitutional equality for all Brazilians . . . we want our constitutional rights respected by the rule of law, not as an extension of personal favors . . . and we want the complete extinction of slavery in Brazil."[37] The racialized "we" here became defined by its call for abolition. In articles, and through the "Gallery," as we will turn to briefly, *O Homem* crafted a careful historical narrative about Black abolitionism. Collaço played a part in the local movement by reprinting articles from other antislavery periodicals, referring extensively to the recent experience in the United States as an inspiration. He praised "the equal citizenship that former slaves now enjoyed," and celebrated the United States' recognition of its Black veterans.[38] However optimistic his view of US racial politics, Collaço used these examples to expand Brazil's abolitionist horizons. He hailed the enthusiastic reception of *Uncle Tom's Cabin* in Europe, and in the last issue of *O Homem*, Collaço most imaginatively predicted that the United States would soon figure in Brazil's own process of abolition.[39] In an extended two-page article, he invited readers to imagine a scenario in which the emperor's upcoming trip to Philadelphia to participate in the US centennial celebrations would occasion further action in the legislature to end slavery (with a provision for indemnization, he added). *O Homem* argued that this was plausible given that the 1871 Free Womb Law had been passed while Pedro II was out of the country. The larger point, *O Homem* stressed, was that the press "worked to bring public opinion around to this perspective," and that in due time, the larger dailies across the country would also join in advocating abolition. "Could this all just be a dream, what we've just described," asked *O Homem* rhetorically?[40] This was how the paper's last issue closed. Other than knowing that the paper was bought by an association after its fourth issue—we do not know which one—it is still unclear why it ended when it did.[41] Overall, its twelve-issue run was not insignificant by the standards of the time, when so many periodicals remained ephemeral.

As part of the wider abolitionist movement of the 1870s, *O Homem* stoked the slavery debate in ways still not fully appreciated by historians. That is, because the most intense and popular-based forms of abolitionist mobilization peaked in the 1880s, this period where Collaço figured more prominently is taken as a prelude of sorts. In fact, in terms of the questions about racial equality put on the table, *O Homem*'s project actually had few precedents. It is plausible that a composite look at the press and juridical forms of abolitionism in the 1870s, which of course took shape in direct connection with slave resistance, would show it to eclipse previous levels of political protest. It is also more likely than not that new perspectives of the popular politics of the 1870s will bring out more connections between *O Homem* and budding labor activities, given Collaço's fury at seeing his peers excluded from different types of professions.

Rewriting the "Gallery" Genre and National Belonging

Much like Sisson's *Galeria* from two decades earlier, Collaço's column "Illustrious Men of Color" delivered a powerful statement about national belonging. It at once announced the paper's abolitionist stance, and more generally it made men and historical events from the northeast much more pertinent to the nation than had been the case in Sisson's book. Yet, beyond challenging the politics of Sisson's *Galeria*, Collaço's column also included poetry, bringing new forms to bear on this genre.

If particular in ways that we will explore briefly, it is necessary to acknowledge that Collaço's "Gallery" followed other local iterations of this genre. Antônio Joaquim de Melo (1794–1873) published a three-volume work,

Biografias de alguns poetas e homens ilustres da província de Pernambuco (Biographies of some poets and illustrious men from the province of Pernambuco, 1856–1859), which featured fourteen biographies. Most of these biographies were first printed in the *Diário de Pernambuco*.[42] Given that Collaço worked for the paper from 1846 to 1856 and remained at the center of Recife's print world thereafter, he must have known of this publication. Melo was an important public figure and a former president of Recife's municipal council. He wrote the *Biografias* to assert a provincial literary tradition, which, pointedly, did not include any men of color.

Collaço's "Gallery" appeared in the first issue of *O Homem*, beginning with a feature on the Afro-Bahian jurist Antônio Pereira Rebouças (1798–1880). The article heralded the statesman's long record in politics, highlighting what Collaço wanted to portray as an antislavery record. The text mentioned Rebouças's role in proposing an 1837 bill that had sought both to more definitively enforce the 1831 prohibition of the African slave trade and to restrict the buying and selling of enslaved people within Brazil. The bill signaled an attempt to curtail some aspects of the then-booming slave economy. Collaço also added that Rebouças later supported Britain's intervention in finally halting the Atlantic slave trade in 1850. Taken together, these points indicate that Collaço was presenting the jurist as more concerned with antislavery than what either Rebouças himself, or what most historians, have affirmed.[43] Collaço signaled Rebouças's national standing by pointing to a recent book published in Rio de Janeiro that contained the Bahian deputy's parliamentary speeches from 1830 to 1847.[44] Praising Rebouças "for his virtues and service to the *pátria* since its beginnings," Collaço used the first of the "illustrious men" columns to spell out some specific traits for Recife's men of color to emulate.[45] It was a story that created a Black antislavery lineage, while also opening a window into a recent past where talented Afro-Brazilians were integral to nation building. Incidentally, and as a nod to the visuals prominent in the wider "Gallery" tradition, the first issue of *O Homem* actually carried an insert of Rebouças. Lost to historians, it nonetheless suggested Collaço's intentions of working within the conventions of the genre, even if on a very modest scale. There are no references to other inserts appearing in future issues.

The theme of nation making, with a pronounced Pernambucan emphasis, ran through several other biographies. These sketches showcased Collaço's talents as an educator. They taught late nineteenth-century readers about pivotal figures from the independence era. He started with José da Natividade

Saldanha, the mulatto poet and cabinet member of the 1824 Confederation of the Equator. A constitutionalist and republican uprising against the central government in Rio de Janeiro, the Confederation remained an important reference in the local imaginary. At that point in the 1870s, a half-century after the events, recalling it stoked local pride in Pernambuco's history of political resistance, a history that had also been whitewashed. The whitewashing, it should be said, goes beyond which participants of 1824 get remembered, and extends to which chroniclers who later wrote about its memory also get acknowledged. Collaço, for example, felt it imperative to revive Saldanha's memory because he considered it forgotten, buried because the poet "was a republican and of color."[46] Incidentally, and symptomatically of the intersections between the politics of race and memory, Collaço's own reflections on the Confederation have also escaped the attention of scholars who write about the "cultural production of the Confederation."[47]

Collaço stressed the issue of talent when narrating Natividade Saldanha's life, having the poet's journey stand in for the possibilities and the hardships that his contemporaries, the men of color in Recife, had to endure in the 1870s because of rotten patronage (and racist) politics. Collaço made clear that Natividade Saldanha was a man who "lacked the traditional family and color" advantages associated with other important leaders of 1824.[48] Nevertheless, he had still won a trusted place in the Confederation's inner political circle, in part because of the reputation that he had recently earned by outranking many of his peers at the University of Coimbra. The Confederation's short-lived existence forced Saldanha into exile, where he moved between Philadelphia, Paris, Caracas, and Bogotá. In recounting Natividade Saldanha's inability to settle comfortably in any of those locations, Collaço did speculate as to whether racial prejudice may have hindered his prospects, his formidable record notwithstanding. Stylistically, the column included excerpts of Saldanha's poetry, affording his own thoughts a more prominent place in the retelling of his life; in so doing, it also added a distinct literary quality to the "Gallery" biographies.

The theme of national belonging hung over the last five of the "Gallery" columns, which turned their attention to the "heroes" from the era of the Dutch occupation (1630–1654). The historical events referred to the local alliances among Portuguese, Natives, and Africans that warded off the "occupying" Dutch West India Company. However, people from these same groups had also worked with the Dutch, so the making of this myth of resistance was, necessarily, a selective refashioning of the past. Still, for Collaço, as with an array of playwrights, novelists, and visual artists of the nineteenth century, these struggles against the Dutch inspired national myths about Brazil's interracial character.[49]

Collaço wrote about the military exploits of Henrique Dias, a man of African descent, and of Felipe Camarão, of Indigenous background, to establish the long history of service by men of color. These examples deepened the argument about Black triumph and belonging through Dias and, at the same time, suggested that Natives had also long flourished; were it not for racist exclusions, men of color would still be at the forefront of the nation's greatest accomplishments. In reprinting a text of Dias's military decorations, Collaço returned to a critique that he had made in earlier issues: that in the "province of Pernambuco, there were no pardo coronels or majors in the national guard."[50] Black and mulatto military exclusion had also been a major point of contention in the 1830s; displaced Black militia officers had been a key segment of the 1837 Sabinada revolt in Bahia, for example.[51] In this (one of the three) columns on Dias, Collaço emphatically asserted that "Black skin had not prevented him from receiving his due."[52] In turning to Camarão, whom he called "the Portuguese king's most loyal vassal in this America," Collaço again made the ideas of service and recognition central to the biography.[53] As had been the case with Dias's biography, Collaço pivoted from this historical discussion of Camarão to lament racial exclusions. And, for what it reveals about Collaço's geopolitical purview, he drew on Camarão's story to make connections to prominent Indigenous leaders from Chile, Mexico, and Peru "who figure in their political order."[54] He particularly noted Benito Juárez's recent triumph in Mexico as a "sign of the glorious republican possibilities in those countries."[55] In noticeable ways, Collaço's reflections about the Dutch resistance made the history of military service another of the cornerstones from which to press for a more meaningful mode of national belonging. These histories rendered the problems of contemporary exclusions as products of a corrupt political system, and not as intractable burdens of the past.

Beyond the stories about Saldanha Natividade, Dias, and Camarão, who share a common thread in that they defended a national project, Collaço's "Gallery" included contemporaries whose careers were derailed because of racism. One column featured the musical composer Elias Álvares Lobo (1834–1901), whom contemporaries regarded as highly as the famous Carlos Gomes.[56] The column on Lobo showcased another innovation of Collaço's in that it was reprinted from a newspaper in southern Brazil, the *Diário de Santos*. That article, along with others that he also borrowed, situates *O Homem* in national networks of print culture. Lobo's biography tells that he had written the musical score for the first "Brazilian" opera, *A noite de São João*. The imperial family, Collaço recalled, along with hundreds of others, attended the wildly successful premiere at Rio de Janeiro's Teatro Lírico (Lyric Theater) in 1857. The enthusiastic run of *A noite* should have propelled Lobo's career, yet jealous rivals isolated him. Disgusted, Lobo left Rio de Janeiro while seemingly at the height of his career and returned to his hometown of Itú, in the interior of São Paulo. The article then contrasts his inability to secure backing to study in Europe with Carlos Gomes's fate, who at the time was at best considered Lobo's equal, but would become Brazil's most celebrated composer by the 1870s, thanks to the specialized study in Italy financed by a government scholarship. Gomes, of course, gained international acclaim with the opera *Il Guarany* in 1870. From Lobo's story, then, and somewhat similar to the poet Saldanha's fate, the stories of these accomplished men of color risked being completely neglected were it not for such discussions in the "Gallery." For Collaço's purposes, Lobo's story represented yet another breach of the constitutional principle spelled out on the paper's masthead in that "virtue" and "talents" had not preceded all other considerations in determining people's life chances.

Broadly, then, when compared to earlier iterations of the "illustrious men" genre, Collaço's "Gallery" stands out for its antiracist discourse and hybrid form. It included poetry alongside biography, even while still generally lacking the all-important visual dimension. It was a text that interestingly worked at the individual and collective levels. Individually, the stories offered a deliberate counternarrative to real processes of exclusion, while collectively they provided a reformulation of the national imaginary. In this latter endeavor, the "Gallery" reached back into the colonial period to develop symbolic, foundational narratives, and in this respect, it was unlike Sisson's book that constructed national narratives only from men and episodes related to the years since from independence.

In ways big and small, Collaço's "Gallery" emerged from the political and cultural currents of the Atlantic World. In general, the paper drew on themes that were at the core of nineteenth century nation-building projects in Europe and the Americas, including, slavery, citizenship, and constitutionalism. To challenge prevailing trends in contemporary Recife, it had to break with both political and literary conventions. It had to break with the accustomed silence on race, a silencing that had proved instrumental to shoring up the slave-based political order. The "Gallery," then, not only redefined the recognized practices of rights claiming by interjecting an explicitly Black premise to its interventions, but it also illuminated previously overlooked dimensions of Franco-Brazilian intellectual exchange. It revealed the rather unknown Afro-descendant editor as an important player within this process of circulation.

It bears restating that the study of Black newspapers like *O Homem* remains promising, despite such titles' limited quantities, because of the insights it generates on the intellectual history of the African diaspora. In thus making the idea of the "Gallery" itself debatable, it allowed a space for Black assertion, on Black terms. This, and countless other Black intellectual counterpoints inscribed in the nineteenth-century press, compel us to keep thinking about newspapers as generative nodes of inquiry for better understanding Brazilian and Atlantic print culture. And, similarly, the breadth of Black intellectual production evidenced in Black-produced papers like *O Homem*, and also evidenced in the vast number of articles written by Afro-Brazilians in other newspapers, suggests that the press, writ large, signified a contentious and multiracial arena. The press was indeed a pillar of Brazilian public life, mediated, of course, by power dynamics of all sorts, but still constitutive of a long tradition of intellectual exchange.

Notes

1. Fischer, Grinberg, and Mattos, "Law."
2. The most recent and certainly the most incisive study of Collaço's career is R. Galvão, "Felippe Neri Collaço." The two other works that deal with *O Homem* proper are Hoffnagel, "'*O Homem*'"; A. F. M. Pinto, *Imprensa*, 53–102. The HDB's digital archive contains only two of the paper's issues (9 and 11), requiring researchers interested in the full run to work at the APEPe in Recife.
3. R. Galvão, "Felippe Neri Collaço," 52.
4. Collaço, *Aritmética*.
5. Pinto and Chalhoub, eds., *Pensadores*; A. F. M. Pinto, "Fortes laços"; Gomes and Domingues, eds., *Políticas*; Gomes and Domingues, *Da nitidez*; M. Machado, "Maria Firmina"; L. Ferreira, "Luiz Gama"; Neto and Gomes, "Escritos."
6. Bell, "Canon Wars," 712, 720, 738.
7. Sisson, *Galeria*; Menezes, "Sociedade"; Martins Júnior, "Galeria dos brasileiros," 1–10; Martins Jr., "Galeria de ilustres," 1–7.

8. Panzer, *Mathew Brady*, 55–60; Brown, *Black Man*.
9. Sisson, *Galeria*, 1:9.
10. Sisson, *Galeria*, 1:11.
11. Menezes, "Sociedade," 9–16.
12. Chalhoub, "Politics," 73–87; Needell, *Party of Order*, 167–222; Kraay, *Days of National Festivity*, 112–45; Cribelli, *Industrial Forests*, 37–75.
13. Menezes, "Sociedade," 85–86.
14. Sisson, *Galeria*, 1:19–22.
15. Chalhoub, *Força*, 45–70; Marquese, Parron, and Berbel, *Escravidão*, 220–56; Mamigonian, *Africanos*, 90–128.
16. Alencar, *Cartas*.
17. Menezes, "Sociedade," 88–89.
18. Menezes, "Sociedade," 90–91.
19. Menezes, "Sociedade," 73–74.
20. Martins Júnior, "Galeria dos brasileiros," 6.
21. J. Carvalho, *Construção / Teatro*, 55–74.
22. Menezes, "Sociedade," 73–74.
23. https://www.britannica.com/biography/Pedro-II (accessed September 15, 2017).
24. Sisson, *Galeria*, 1:123.
25. Sisson, *Galeria*, 1:127.
26. The best study on urban slavery in nineteenth-century Recife is M. Carvalho, *Liberdade*. On slavery, free people of color, and politics in late nineteenth-century Recife, see also Mac Cord, *Rosário* and *Artífices*; Cabral and Costa, eds., *História*; I. Cunha, *Capoeira*; F. Souza, *Eleitorado*; M. E. V. Santos, "Significados." On abolition, see Castilho, *Slave Emancipation*.
27. Quoted in *O Homem* (Recife), January 29, 1876.
28. Castilho, *Slave Emancipation*, 182–91.
29. *O Homem* (Recife), January 13, 1876.
30. A. F. M. Pinto, *Imprensa*, 61; I. Lima, *Cores*, 51–60; Kraay, *Race*, 150–51.
31. *O Homem* (Recife), January 13, 1876.
32. *O Homem* (Recife), February 24, 1876.
33. A. F. M. Pinto, *Imprensa*, 60.
34. *O Homem* (Recife), January 13, 1876.
35. Mac Cord's *Rosário* and *Artífices* convey well the class spectrum of Recife's free men of color.
36. If focused on the United States, an indispensable reference on public life is Barkley, "Negotiating," 107–46. On Brazil, see, Kittleson, "'Campaign'"; Martha Santos, "On the Importance."
37. *O Homem* (Recife), February 3, 1876.
38. *O Homem* (Recife), January 29, 1876.

39. *O Homem* (Recife), March 23, 1876.
40. *O Homem* (Recife), March 30, 1876.
41. *O Homem* (Recife), February 10, 1876.
42. A. Mello, *Biographias*, 1:3. The most detailed account of Mello's career was found on www.consciência.org, an open-access archive and space of philosophical debate maintained by Miguel Lobato Duclós (1978–2015) (accessed September 15, 2017).
43. Grinberg, "Em defesa," 111–46.
44. *O Homem* (Recife), January 13, 1876.
45. *O Homem* (Recife), January 13, 1876.
46. *O Homem* (Recife), January 20, 1876.
47. DeGoes, "1824 Confederation."
48. *O Homem* (Recife), January 20, 1876.
49. Collaço's columns about the "heroes" of the resistance appeared in *O Homem* (Recife), March 2, 9, 16, and 23, 1876. For more examples of nationalizing the memory of the Dutch resistance, see, Kraay, *Days of National Festivity*, 220–28. The classic study of Pernambucan memory and the Dutch resistance is E. Mello, *Rubro veio*.
50. *O Homem* (Recife), March 9, 1876.
51. Kraay, *Race*, 231–39.
52. *O Homem* (Recife), March 9, 1876.
53. *O Homem* (Recife), March 23, 1876.
54. *O Homem* (Recife), March 23, 1876.
55. *O Homem* (Recife), March 23, 1876.
56. *O Homem* (Recife), February 17, 1876.

BIBLIOGRAPHY

Abreu, Márcia. *Os caminhos dos livros*. São Paulo: Editora Mercado de Letras, 2003.

Abreu, Márcia, ed. *Trajetórias do romance: circulação, leitura e escrita nos séculos XVIII e XIX*. São Paulo: Editora Mercado de Letras, 2008.

Acree Jr., William. *Everyday Reading: Print Culture and Collective Memory in Río de la Plata, 1780–1910*. Nashville: Vanderbilt University Press, 2011.

Adelman, Joseph. *Revolutionary Networks: The Business and Politics of Printing the News, 1763–1789*. Baltimore: Johns Hopkins University Press, 2019.

Adelman, Joseph M., and Victoria E. M. Gardner. "News in the Age of Revolution." In *Making News: The Political Economy of Journalism in Britain and America from the Glorious Revolution to the Internet*. Edited by Richard R. John and Jonathan Silberstein-Loeb, 47–72. New York: Oxford University Press, 2015.

Aimard, Gustave. *Mon dernier voyage: le Brésil nouveau*. Paris: E. Dentu, 1886.

Alencar, José de. *Ao correr da pena*. Edited by João Roberto Faria. São Paulo: Martins Fontes, 2004.

———. *Cartas a favor da escravidão*. Edited by Tâmis Parron. São Paulo: Hedra, 2008.

Alencastro, Luiz Felipe de. "Prolétaires et esclaves: immigrés portugais et captifs africains à Rio de Janeiro, 1850–1872." *Cahiers du Centre de Recherches d'Études Ibériques et Ibero-Américaines de Rouen* 4 (1984): 119–56.

Almeida, Miguel Calmon du Pin e. *Memoria sobre o estabelecimento d'uma companhia de colonisação nesta provincia*. Bahia: Tip. do Diario de G. J. Bizerra e Companhia, 1835.

Alonso, Angela. *Flores, votos e balas: o movimento abolicionista brasileiro (1868–88)*. São Paulo: Companhia das Letras, 2015.

———. *Idéias em movimento: a geração 1870 na crise do Brasil-Império*. São Paulo: Paz e Terra, 2002.

Alves, Francisco N. "A gênese da imprensa caricata sul riograndense e a Guerra do Paraguai." *Historiae* 5 (2014): 9–46.

Amaral, Braz H. do. *Historia da Bahia do Imperio à Republica*. Salvador: Imprensa Official do Estado, 1923.

Anderson, Benedict. *Imagined Communities: Reflections on the Origins and Spread of Nationalism*. London: Verso, 1996.

Andrade, Débora El-Jaick. "A imprensa como tribuna dos intelectuais no século XIX: o *Guanabara* em defesa da arte e dos artistas nacionais." In *Os intelectuais e a imprensa*. Edited by Magali Gouveia Engel et al., 13–45. Rio de Janeiro: Mauad X and FAPERJ, 2015.

Andrade, Joaquim Marçal Ferreira de. *História da fotorreportagem no Brasil: a fotografia na imprensa no Rio de Janeiro de 1839 a 1900*. Rio de Janeiro: Elsevier, 2004.

———. "Processos de reprodução e impressão no Brasil, 1808–1930." In *Impressos no Brasil, 1808–1930: destaques da história gráfica no acervo da Biblioteca Nacional.* Edited by Rafael Cardoso, 50–75. Rio de Janeiro: Verso Brasil, 2009.

———. "A *Semana Ilustrada* e a Guerra contra o Paraguai." PhD diss., Universidade Federal do Rio de Janeiro, 2011.

Andrade, Luiz Antonio Navarro de. *Questão do Diario do Rio de Janeiro ou a retirada do seu redator em chefe.* Rio de Janeiro: Typ. Popular Azevedo Leite, 1868.

Andrade, Marcos Ferreira de. "Família e política nas Regências: possibilidades interpretativas das cartas pessoais de Evaristo da Veiga." In *Linguagens e práticas da cidadania no século XIX.* Edited by Gladys Sabina Ribeiro and Tânia Maria Tavares Bessone da Cruz Ferreira, 247–72. São Paulo: Alameda, 2010.

Andrews, Christopher C. *Brazil: Its Condition and Prospects.* New York: D. Appleton, 1887.

"Apelação criminal. A Justiça, autor. Theodoro, crioulo escravo de Junius Villeneuve e Cia, réu." AN, Corte de Apelação, n. 1184, caixa 160, Gal-C, 1863.

Araújo, Carlos Eduardo Moreira de. "Cárceres imperiais: a Casa de Correção do Rio de Janeiro. Seus detentos e o sistema prisional no Império, 1830–1861." PhD diss., UNICAMP, 2009.

Araújo, Dilton Oliveira de. "Política e imprensa da Bahia do período pós-Sabinada." In *200 anos de imprensa no Brasil.* Edited by Silvia Carla Pereira de Brito and Maria Letícia Corrêa, 121–44. Rio de Janeiro: ContraCapa, 2009.

Araujo, Iramir Alves. "A flecha, a pedra e a pena: um olhar sobre a primeira revista ilustrada do Maranhão—1879/1880." Master's thesis, Universidade Federal do Maranhão, 2013.

Araújo, Johny Santana de. *Bravos do Piauí! Orgulhai-vos. . . : a propaganda nos jornais piauienses e a mobilização para a Guerra do Paraguai (1865–1866).* Teresina: EdUFPI, 2011.

———. "A imprensa no Maranhão na segunda metade do século XIX: estado imperial, jornais e a divulgação da Guerra do Paraguai para um público leitor." *Dimensões* 33 (2014): 360–83.

Araujo, Rodrigo Cardoso Soares de. "Caminhos na produção da notícia: a imprensa diária no Rio de Janeiro (1875–1891)." PhD diss., Universidade do Estado do Rio de Janeiro, 2015.

———. "Pasquins e o submundo da imprensa na Corte imperial (1880–1883)." Master's thesis, Universidade Federal do Rio de Janeiro, 2009.

Armitage, John. *The History of Brazil from the Period of the Arrival of the Braganza Family in 1808, to the Abdication of Don Pedro the First in 1831.* London: Smith, Elder, 1836.

Assumpção, [Thomaz] Lino d'. *Narrativas do Brasil (1876–1880).* Rio de Janeiro: Livraria Contemporanea de Faro & Lino, 1881.

Auchincloss, William S. *Ninety Days in the Tropics or Letters from Brazil*. Wilmington, DE: n.p., 1874.
Azevedo, Aluísio. *Mulatto*. Edited by Daphne Patai. Translated by Murray Graeme MacNichol. Austin: University of Texas Press, 1993 [1881].
Azevedo, Elciene. *Orfeu de carapinha: a trajetória de Luiz Gama na Imperial cidade de São Paulo*. Campinas: Ed. UNICAMP and Cecult, 1999.
Azevedo, Manuel Duarte Moreira de. "Origem e desenvolvimento da imprensa no Rio de Janeiro." *Revista do Instituto Histórico e Geográfico Brasileiro* 28, no. 2 (1865): 169–224.
———. "Sociedades fundadas no Brazil desde os tempos coloniaes até o começo do actual reinado." *Revista do Instituto Histórico Geográfico Brasileiro* 48, no. 2 (1885): 265–322.
Badaró, F. C. Duarte. *Fantina (scenas da escravidão)*. Rio de Janeiro: B. L. Garnier, 1881.
Bagwell, Kyle. "Economic Analysis of Advertising." In *Handbook of Industrial Organization*, vol. 3. Edited by Mark Armstrong and Roy Porter, 1,701–1,844. Amsterdam: Elsevier, 2007.
Bagwell, Kyle, and Garey Ramey. "Advertising as Information: Matching Products to Buyers." *Journal of Economics and Management Strategy* 2 (1993): 199–243.
Baker, Keith Michael. *Inventing the French Revolution: Essays on French Political Culture in the Eighteenth Century*. Cambridge: Cambridge University Press, 1999.
———. "Politique et opinion publique sous l'Ancien Régime." *Annales: Économies, Sociétés, Civilisations* 42, no. 1 (January–February 1987): 41–71.
Balaban, Marcelo. *Poeta do lápis: sátira e política na trajetória de Angelo Agostini no Brasil imperial (1864–1888)*. Campinas: Ed. UNICAMP, 2009.
Baquaqua, Mahommah G. *Biography of Mahommah G. Baquaqua, a Native Zoogoo, in the Interior of Africa*. Edited by Samuel Moore. Detroit: George E. Pomeroy, 1854.
Barbosa, Marialva. *Os donos do Rio: imprensa, poder e público, 1880–1920*. Rio de Janeiro: Vício de Leitura, 2000.
———. *Escravos e o mundo da comunicação: oralidade, leitura e escrita no século XIX*. Rio de Janeiro: Mauad X, 2016.
———. *História cultural da imprensa: Brasil, 1800–1900*. Rio de Janeiro: Mauad, 2000.
Barbosa, Rosana. *Immigration and Xenophobia: Portuguese Immigrants in Early Nineteenth-Century Rio de Janeiro*. Lanham, MD: University Press of America, 2009.
———. "Portuguese Migration to Rio de Janeiro, 1822–1850." *The Americas* 57, no. 1 (2000): 37–61.
Barbosa, Silvana Mota. "A política progressista: parlamento, sistema representativo e partidos nos anos 1860." In *Repensando o Brasil do Oitocentos: cidadania, política e liberdade*. Edited by José Murilo de Carvalho and Lúcia Maria Bastos Pereira das Neves, 293–324. Rio de Janeiro: Civilização Brasileira, 2009.
Barkley, Elsa Brown. "Negotiating and Transforming the Public Sphere: African

American Political Life in the Transition from Slavery to Freedom." *Public Culture* 7, no. 1 (Fall 1994): 107–46.
Barman, Roderick J. *Brazil: The Forging of a Nation, 1798–1852*. Stanford, CA: Stanford University Press, 1988.
———. *Citizen Emperor: Pedro II and the Making of Brazil, 1825–91*. Stanford, CA: Stanford University Press, 1999.
———. "Justiniano José da Rocha e a época da Conciliação: como se escreveu 'Ação, Reação, Transação.'" *Revista do Instituto Histórico e Geográfico Brasileiro* 301 (October–December 1973): 3–32.
———. "The Periodical Press in Rio de Janeiro in the 1850s." Paper Presented at the American Historical Association and Conference on Latin America History Annual Meeting, Denver, CO, January 5–8, 2017.
Barros, Roque Spencer de. "A Questão Religiosa." In *História Geral da Civilização Brasileira*. Tomo 2, vol. 4. Edited by Sérgio Buarque de Holanda, 338–65. São Paulo: DIFEL, 1974.
Basile, Marcello Otávio Neri de Campos. "Anarquistas, rusguentos e demagogos: os liberais exaltados e a formação da esfera pública na Corte imperial (1829–1834)." Master's thesis, Universidade Federal do Rio de Janeiro, 2000.
———. *Ezequiel Corrêa dos Santos: um jacobino na Corte imperial*. Rio de Janeiro: Editora FGV, 2001.
———. "Governo, nação e soberania no Primeiro Reinado: a imprensa áulica do Rio de Janeiro." In *Linguagens e fronteiras do poder*. Edited by Miriam Halpern Pereira, José Murilo de Carvalho, Maria João Vaz, and Gladys Sabina Ribeiro, 172–85. Lisbon: Centro de Estudos de História Contemporânea, Instituto Universitário de Lisboa, 2012.
———. "O Império em construção: projetos de Brasil e ação política na Corte regencial." PhD diss., Universidade Federal do Rio de Janeiro, 2004.
———. "Inventário analítico da imprensa periódica do Rio de Janeiro na Regência: perfil dos jornais e dados estatísticos." In *Dimensões e fronteiras do Estado brasileiro no Oitocentos*. Edited by José Murilo de Carvalho and Lúcia Maria Bastos Pereira das Neves, 37–62. Rio de Janeiro: EdUERJ, 2014.
———. "O laboratório da nação: a era regencial (1831–1840)." In *O Brasil Imperial*, 3 vols. Edited by Keila Grinberg and Ricardo Salles, 2:53–119. Rio de Janeiro: Civilização Brasileira, 2009.
———. "*Luzes a quem está nas trevas*: a linguagem política radical nos primórdios do Império." *Topoi* 3 (September 2001): 91–130.
———. "O radicalismo *exaltado*: definições e controvérsias." In *Dimensões políticas do Império do Brasil*. Edited by Lúcia Maria Bastos Pereira das Neves and Tânia Bessone da C. Ferreira, 19–50. Rio de Janeiro: ContraCapa, 2012.
Basile, Marcello Otávio Neri de Campos, ed. "Regência e imprensa." *Dossiê* (Special Section) in Almanack 20 (September–December 2018): 1–193.

Beckert, Sven. *The Monied Metropolis: New York City and the Consolidation of the Bourgeoisie, 1850–1900*. New York: Cambridge University Press, 2001.
Bedoya H., María Elena. *Prensa y espacio público en Quito, 1792–1840*. Quito: FONSAL, 2010.
Beiguelman, Paula. *A formação do povo no complexo cafeeiro: aspectos políticos*. São Paulo: EdUSP, 2005 [1968].
Bell, David. "Canon Wars in Eighteenth-Century France: The Monarchy, the Revolution and the 'Grands Hommes de la Patrie.'" *MLN* 116, no. 4 (September 2001): 705–38.
Bellido, Remijio de. *Catalogo dos jornaes paraenses, 1822–1908*. Belém: Imprensa Official, 1908.
Bergamini, Atilio. "Escravos: escrita, leitura e liberdade." *Leitura, Teoria e Prática* 35, no. 71 (2017): 115–36.
Bessone, Tânia Maria Tavares, et al., eds. *Cultura escrita e circulação de impressas no Oitocentos*. São Paulo: Alameda, 2006.
Bessone, Tânia Maria Tavares, et al., eds. *Imprensa, livros e política no Oitocentos*. São Paulo: Alameda, 2018.
Bethell, Leslie. *A abolição do comércio brasileiro de escravos: a Grã-Bretanha, o Brasil e a questão do comércio de escravos, 1807–1869*. Translated by Luis A. P. Souto Maior. Brasília: Senado Federal, 2002.
Bettencourt, Angela Maria Monteiro, and Monica Rizzo Soares Pinto. "A Hemeroteca Digital Brasileira." Paper presented to the 25th Congresso Brasileiro de Biblioteconomia, Florianópolis, July 7–10, 2013. https://portal.febab.org.br/anais/article/view/1321/1322.
Binzer, Ina von [Ulla von Eck]. *Alegrias e tristezas de uma educadora no Brasil*. São Paulo: Anhembi, 1965.
Bissigo, Diego Nones. "O censo de 1872 e a simplificação da liberdade." Paper presented at the 7º Encontro da Escravidão e Liberdade no Brasil Meridional, Curitiba, May 13–16, 2015. http://www.escravidaoeliberdade.com.br.
Bitis, Alexander, and Janet Hartley. "The Russian Military Colonies in 1826." *Slavonic and East European Review* 78, no. 2 (April 2000): 321–30.
Blackburn, Robin. *The American Crucible: Slavery, Emancipation and Human Rights*. London: Verso, 2009.
———. *The Overthrow of Colonial Slavery, 1776–1848*. London: Verso, 1988.
Blair, Kristie. "'Let the Nightingales Alone': Correspondence Columns, the Scottish Press, and the Making of the Working-Class Poet." *Victorian Periodicals Review* 47, no. 2 (Summer 2014): 188–207.
Bly, Antonio T. "'Pretends he can read': Runaways and Literacy in Colonial America, 1730–1776." *Early American Studies* 6, no. 2 (Fall 2008): 261–94.
Boccanera Junior, Silio. *Bahia historica: reminiscência do passado, registo do presente*. Salvador: Typ. Bahiana, 1921.

Boehrer, George C. A. "Jose Carlos Rodrigues and *O Novo Mundo*, 1870–1879." *Journal of Inter-American Studies* 9, no. 1 (January 1967): 127–44.

Bond, Elizabeth Andrews. "Circuits of Practical Knowledge: The Network of Letters to the Editor in the French Provincial Press, 1770–1788." *French Historical Studies* 39, no. 3 (August 2016): 535–65.

Bösche, Eduardo Theodoro. "Quadros alternados de viagens terrestres e maritimas, aventuras, acontecimentos politicos, descripção de usos e costumes de povos durante uma viagem ao Brasil." Translated by Vicente de Sousa Queirós. *Revista do Instituto Histórico e Geográfico Brasileiro* 83, no. 137 (1918): 133–241.

Bourdieu, Pierre. *O poder simbólico*. Translated by Fernando Tomaz. Lisbon: Difel; Rio de Janeiro: Bertrand Brasil, 1989.

Bourdieu, Pierre, and Monique Saint Martin. "Le sens de la propriété (la genèse sociale des systèmes de préférences)." *Actes de la Recherche en Sciences Sociales* 81–82 (March 1990): 52–64.

Braga-Pinto, César. "Journalists, Capoerias, and the Duel in Nineteenth-Century Rio de Janeiro." *Hispanic American Historical Review* 94, no. 4 (November 2014): 581–614.

Brazil. Directoria Geral de Estatistica. *Recenseamento da população do Brazil a que se procedeu no dia 1 de agosto de 1872*. 21 vols. Rio de Janeiro: Leuzinger & Filhos, 1873–76.

Brazil. Fundação Biblioteca Nacional. *Catálogo dos periódicos brasileiros microfilmados*. Rio de Janeiro: Fundação Biblioteca Nacional, 1994.

Briggs, Asa, and Peter Burke. *A Social History of the Media: From Gutenberg to the Internet*. Cambridge: Polity, 2009.

Brown, William Wells. *The Black Man, His Antecedents, His Genius, and His Achievements*. 2nd ed. New York: Thomas Hamilton, 1863.

Browne, George P. "Government Immigration Policy in Imperial Brazil, 1822–1870." PhD diss., Catholic University of America, 1972.

Buffington, Robert M. *A Sentimental Education for the Working Man: The Mexico City Penny Press, 1900–1910*. Durham, NC: Duke University Press, 2015.

Buitoni, Dulcília Schroeder. *Imprensa feminina*. 2nd ed. São Paulo: Ática, 1990.

Burlamaqui, Frederico Leopoldo Cesar. *Memoria analytica acerca do commercio d'escravos e acerca dos malles da escravidão domestica*. Rio de Janeiro: Tip. Commercial Fluminense, 1837.

Burns, Eric. *Infamous Scribblers: The Founding Fathers and the Rowdy Beginnings of American Journalism*. New York: Public Affairs, 2006.

Cabral, Alfredo do Valle. "Anais da imprensa nacional, 1823–1831." *Anais da Biblioteca Nacional* 73 (1953): 39–115.

Cabral, Flávio José Gomes. *Conversas reservadas: "vozes públicas", conflitos políticos e rebeliões em Pernambuco no tempo da Independência do Brasil*. Rio de Janeiro: Arquivo Nacional, 2013.

Cabral, Flávio José Gomes, and Robson Costa, eds. *História da escravidão em Pernambuco*. Recife: Editora da UFPE, 2012.
Cadena, Nelson Varón. "O Dois de Julho: a imprensa como protagonista." *Revista do Instituto Geográfico e Histórico da Bahia* 108 (2013): 201–17.
Cagnin, Antonio. "Bordalo x Agostini—'nestas mal tratadas . . . intrigas.'" In *Rafael Bordalo Pinheiro—o português tal e qual: da caricatura à cerâmica, o caricaturista*. Edited by Emanuel Araújo, 57–75. São Paulo: Pinacoteca do Estado, 1996.
Caimari, Lila. "News from around the World: The Newspapers of Buenos Aires in the Age of the Submarine Cable, 1866–1900." *Hispanic American Historical Review* 96, no. 4 (November 2016): 607–40.
Caldeira, Jorge, ed. *Diogo Antônio Feijó*. São Paulo: Editora 34, 1999.
Calhoun, Craig, ed. *Habermas and the Public Sphere*. Cambridge, MA: Massachusetts Institute of Technology Press, 1996.
Camillo, Ema Elisabete Rodrigues. "Modernização agrícola e máquinas de beneficiamento: um estudo da Lidgerwood Mfg. Co. Ltd., década de 1850 a de 1890." Master's thesis, Universidade Estadual de Campinas, 2003.
Campos, Adriana Pereira, Karulliny Silverol Siqueira, and Kátia Saussen da Motta, eds. "Imprensa, partidos e eleições no Oitocentos." Special Issue of *Ágora* 31, no. 1 (2020).
Cândido, Antonio. "A vida ao rés-do-chão." In *A crônica: o gênero, sua fixação e suas transformações no Brasil*. Edited by Antonio Cândido, 13–20. Campinas: Ed. UNICAMP, 1992.
Cândido, Antonio, ed. *A crônica: o gênero, sua fixação e suas transformações no Brasil*. Campinas: Ed. UNICAMP, 1992.
Cano, Jefferson. "Justiniano José da Rocha, cronista do desengano." In *História em cousas miúdas: capítulos de história social da crônica no Brasil*. Edited by Sidney Chalhoub, Margarida de Souza Neves, and Leonardo Affonso de Miranda Pereira, 23–66. Campinas: Ed. UNICAMP, 2005.
Canstatt, Oskar. *Brasil: a terra e a gente, 1871*. Translated by Eduardo de Lima Castro. Rio de Janeiro: Conquista, 1975.
Cardoso, Rafael. "Projeto gráfico e meio editorial nas revistas ilustradas do Segundo Reinado." In *Revistas ilustradas: modos de ler e ver o Segundo Reinado*. Edited by Paulo Knauss et al., 17–41. Rio de Janeiro: Mauad X and FAPERJ, 2011.
Cardoso, Tereza Maria Rolo Fachada Levy. "A *Gazeta do Rio de Janeiro*: subsídios para a história da cidade (1808–1821)." Master's thesis, Universidade Federal do Rio de Janeiro, 1988.
Carneiro, Maria Luiza Tucci, ed. *Minorias silenciadas: história da censura no Brasil*. São Paulo: FAPESP, Imprensa Oficial, EdUSP, 2002.
Carvalho, Alfredo de, and João N. Torres. *Anais da imprensa da Bahia: 1.º centenário, 1811–1911*. 2nd ed. Salvador: Empresa Gráfica da Bahia, 2007 [1911].
Carvalho, José Murilo de. "A modernização frustrada: a política de terras no Império." *Revista Brasileira de História* 1, no. 1 (1981): 39–57.

———. *"Clamar e agitar sempre": os radicais da década de 1860*. Rio de Janeiro: Topbooks, 2018.

———. *A construção da ordem: a elite política imperial / Teatro de sombras: a política imperial*. Rev. ed. Rio de Janeiro: EdUFRJ and Relume Dumará, 1996.

———. *D. Pedro II: ser ou não ser*. São Paulo: Companhia das Letras, 2007.

———. "Escravidão e razão nacional." In *Pontos e bordados: escritos de história e política*, 35–64. Belo Horizonte: EdUFMG, 2005.

———. "História intelectual no Brasil: a retórica como chave de leitura." *Topoi* 1 (September 2000): 123–52.

Carvalho, José Murilo de, Lúcia Bastos, and Marcello Basile. "Introdução." In *Às armas, cidadãos! panfletos manuscritos da Independência do Brasil (1820–1823)*. Edited by José Murilo de Carvalho, Lúcia Bastos, and Marcello Basile, 7–32. São Paulo: Companhia das Letras; Belo Horizonte: Editora UFMG, 2012.

Carvalho, José Murilo de, Lúcia Bastos, and Marcello Basile, eds. *Às armas cidadãos! panfletos manuscritos da Independência do Brasil (1820–1823)*. São Paulo: Companhia das Letras; Belo Horizonte: Editora UFMG, 2012.

———. *Guerra literária: panfletos da Independência (1820–1823)*. 4 vols. Belo Horizonte: Editora UFMG, 2014.

Carvalho, Marcus Joaquim Maciel de. *Liberdade: rotinas e rupturas do escravismo, Recife, 1822–1850*. Recife: Editora da UFPE, 1998.

———. "O 'tráfico de escravatura branca' para Pernambuco no ocaso do tráfico de escravos." *Revista do Instituto Histórico e Geográfico Brasileiro* 149, no. 58 (1988): 22–51.

Castilho, Celso Thomas. "The Press and Brazilian Narratives of *Uncle Tom's Cabin*: Slavery and the Public Sphere in Rio de Janeiro, ca. 1855." *The Americas* 76, no. 1 (January 2019): 77–106.

———. *Slave Emancipation and Transformations in Brazilian Political Citizenship*. Pittsburgh: University of Pittsburgh Press, 2016.

Castro-Klarén, Sara, and John Chasteen, eds. *Beyond Imagined Communities: Reading and Writing the Nation in Nineteenth-Century Latin America*. Baltimore: Johns Hopkins University Press, 2003.

"Catalogo de jornais e revistas do Rio de Janeiro (1808–1889) existentes na Biblioteca Nacional." *Anais da Biblioteca Nacional* 85 (1965): 7–208.

"Catalogo dos jornaes bahianos publicados de 1811–1899." *Revista do Instituto Geográfico e Histórico da Bahia* 21 (1899): 409–20, 22 (1899): 549–79.

Catálogo dos periódicos da Coleção Plínio Doyle. 2nd ed. Rio de Janeiro: Edições Casa de Rui Barbosa, 2000.

Cavallini, Marco Cícero. "Monumento e política: os comentários da semana de Machado de Assis." In *História em cousas miúdas: capítulos de história social da crônica no Brasil*. Edited by Sidney Chalhoub, Margarida de Souza Neves, and Leonardo Affonso de Miranda Pereira, 299–340. Campinas: Ed. UNICAMP, 2005.

Chagas, Manoel Pinheiro. *Diccionario popular: historico, geographico, mythologico, biographico, e litterario.* Lisbon: Tip. do Diario Illustrado, 1880.
Chalhoub, Sidney. "A crônica machadiana: problemas de interpretação, temas de pesquisa." *Remate de Malês* 29, no. 2 (2009): 231–46.
———. *A força da escravidão: ilegalidade e costume no Brasil oitocentista.* São Paulo: Companhia das Letras, 2012.
———. "John Gledson, leitor de Machado de Assis." *ArtCultura* 8 (2006): 110–15.
———. "The Politics of Silence: Race and Citizenship in Nineteenth-Century Brazil." *Slavery and Abolition* 27, no. 1 (April 2006): 73–87.
———. "População e Sociedade." In *A construção nacional: 1830–1889.* Edited by José Murilo de Carvalho, 37–81. Rio de Janeiro: Fundação Mapfre, 2012.
———. "Precariedade estrutural: o problema da liberdade no Brasil oitocentista (século XIX)." *História Social* (Campinas) 19, no. 2 (2010): 33–62.
Chalhoub, Sidney, and Fernando Teixeira da Silva. "Sujeitos no imaginário acadêmico: escravos e trabalhadores na historiografia brasileira desde os anos 1980." *Cadernos AEL* 14, no. 26 (2009): 15–45.
Chalhoub, Sidney, and Leonardo Affonso de Miranda Pereira, eds. *A história contada: capítulos de história social da literatura no Brasil.* Rio de Janeiro: Editora Nova Fronteira, 1998.
Chalhoub, Sidney, Margarida de Souza Neves, and Leonardo Affonso de Miranda Pereira. "Apresentação." In *História em cousas miúdas: capítulos de história social da crônica no Brasil.* Edited by Sidney Chalhoub, Margarida de Souza Neves, and Leonardo Affonso de Miranda Pereira, 9–22. Campinas: Ed. UNICAMP, 2005.
Chalhoub, Sidney, Margarida de Souza Neves, and Leonardo Affonso de Miranda Pereira, eds. *História em cousas miúdas: capítulos de história social da crônica no Brasil.* Campinas: Ed. UNICAMP, 2005.
Chartier, Roger. "L'Ancien Régime typographique: réflexions sur quelques travaux récents." *Annales: Économies, Sociétés, Civilisations* 36, no. 2 (1981): 191–209.
Chartier, Roger. *Leituras e leitores na França do Antigo Regime.* Translated by Álvaro Lorencini. São Paulo: Editora da UNESP, 2004.
Chávez Lomelí, Elba. *Lo público y lo privado en los impresos decimonónicos: libertad de imprenta, 1810–1882.* Mexico City: UNAM/Miguel Ángel Porrúa, 2009.
Chrysostomo, Maria Isabel de Jesus, and Laurent Vidal. "De depósito à hospedaria de imigrantes: gênese de um 'território da espera' no caminho da emigração para o Brasil." *História, Ciências, Saúde-Manguinhos* 21, no. 1 (February 2014): 195–217.
Clarence-Smith, William Gervase, and Steven Topik, eds. *The Global Coffee Economy in Africa, Asia, and Latin America, 1500–1989.* New York: Cambridge University Press, 2003.
Clark, Charles E. *The Public Prints: The Newspaper in Anglo-American Culture, 1665–1740.* New York: Oxford University Press, 1994.

Coelho, Geraldo Mártires. *Anarquistas, demagogos e dissidentes: a imprensa liberal no Pará de 1822*. Belém: CEJUP, 1993.

Collaço, D'Felipe [sic] Nery. *Aritmética prática para uso das escolas primarias de ambos os sexos*. 16th ed. Recife: Livraria Franceza, 1888.

Collecção de documentos relativos ao tratado de commercio concluido entre o Brazil e Portugal, aos 19 de maio de 1836. Rio de Janeiro: Typ. Imp. e Const. de J. Villeneuve, 1836.

Conrad, Robert Edgar. *The Destruction of Brazilian Slavery, 1850–1888*. Berkeley: University of California Press, 1972.

———. *Tumbeiros: o tráfico escravista para o Brasil*. Translated by Elvira Serapicos. São Paulo: Brasiliense, 1985.

Contier, Arnaldo de. *Imprensa e ideologia em São Paulo, 1822–1842 (matizes do vocabulário politico e social)*. Petrópolis: Vozes; Campinas: Universidade Estadual de Campinas, 1979.

Cooper-Richet, Diana. "Paris, capital editorial do mundo lusófono na primeira metade do século XIX?" *Varia História* 25, no. 42 (2009): 539–55.

Coratini, Odaci Luiz. "Grandes famílias e elite 'profissional' na medicina no Brasil." *História, Ciências, Saúde—Manguinhos* 3, no. 3 (November 1996–February 1997): 425–66.

Cornelius, Janet Duitsman. *"When I can read my title clear": Literacy, Slavery and Religion in the Antebellum South*. Columbia: University of South Carolina Press, 1991.

Cornell University. *Cornell University: What It is and What It is Not*. Ithaca, NY: University Press, 1872.

———. *The Ten-Year Book of Cornell University*. Vol. 2, *1868–1888*. Ithaca, NY: Andrus & Church, 1888.

"Correspondência passiva de José Carlos Rodrigues." *Anais da Biblioteca Nacional* 90 (1971): 8–339.

Costa, Carlos. *A revista no Brasil do século XIX: a história da formação das publicações, do leitor e da identidade do brasileiro*. São Paulo: Alameda, 2012.

Costa, Emília Viotti da. *Da Senzala à Colônia*. São Paulo: Editora Unesp, 1998 [1966].

———. *The Brazilian Empire: Myths and Histories*. Chicago: University of Chicago Press, 1985.

Cribelli, Teresa. *Industrial Forests and Mechanical Marvels: Modernization in Nineteenth-Century Brazil*. New York: Cambridge University Press, 2016.

Cuarterolo, Miguel Angel. *Soldados de la memoria: hombres e imágenes de la Guerra del Paraguay*. Buenos Aires: Editorial Planeta, 2000.

Cunha, Israel Ozanam de Souza. *Capoeira e capoeiras entre a guarda negra e a educação física no Recife*. Recife: Editora da UFPE, 2013.

Cunha, Maria Clementina Pereira da. *"Não tá sopa": sambas e sambistas no Rio de Janeiro*. Campinas: Ed. UNICAMP, 2015.

Cury, Cláudia Engler, et al., eds. *O Império do Brasil: educação, impressos e confrontos sociopolíticos*. São Luís: Café & Lápis; Editora UEMA, 2015.

Dantas, Monica Duarte. "Da Luisiana para o Brasil: Edward Livingston e o primeiro movimento codificador no Império (o Código Criminal de 1830 e o Código de Processo Criminal de 1832)." *Jahrbuch für Geschichte Lateinamerikas* 52 (2015): 173–205.

Darnton, Robert. *O grande massacre de gatos e outros episódios da história cultural francesa*. Translated by Sonia Coutinho. São Paulo: Paz e Terra, 1984.

———. *Poesia e polícia: redes de comunicação na Paris do século XVIII*. Translated by Rubens Figueiredo. São Paulo: Companhia das Letras, 2014.

Davis, Natalie Zemon. *Culturas do povo: sociedade e cultura no início da França Moderna*. Translated by Mariza Corrêa. Rio de Janeiro: Paz e Terra, 1990.

Dean, Warren. *Rio Claro: A Brazilian Plantation System, 1820–1920*. Stanford, CA: Stanford University Press, 1976.

DeGoes, Plinio Tadeu. "The 1824 Confederation of the Equator and Cultural Production in Brazil." PhD diss., Harvard University, 2015.

Delumeau, Jean. *História do medo no ocidente: 1300–1800, uma cidade sitiada*. Translated by Maria Lucia Machado and Heloisa Jahn. São Paulo: Companhia das Letras, 1989.

Dénis, Ferdinand. *Brésil*. Paris: Firmin Didot Frères, 1837.

Diccionario bibliographico portuguez: estudos de Innocencio Francisco da Silva aplicaveis a Portugal e ao Brazil, continuados e ampliados por Brito Aranha. Lisbon: Imprensa Nacional, 1885.

Diouf, Sylviane A. *Servants of Allah: African Muslims Enslaved in the Americas*. New York: New York University Press, 1998.

Dobranravin, Nikolai. "Não só mandingas: Qasidat Al-Burda, poesia ascética (Zuhdiyyat) e as Maqāmāt de Al-Hariri nos escritos dos negros muçulmanos no Brasil oitocentista." *Afro-Ásia* 53 (2016): 185–226.

Domingues, Petrônio. "Imprensa negra." In *Dicionário da escravidão e liberdade*. Edited by Lilia M. Schwarcz and Flávio Gomes, 253–59. São Paulo: Companhia das Letras, 2018.

Doratioto, Francisco. *Maldita guerra: nova história da Guerra do Paraguai*. São Paulo: Companhia das Letras, 2002.

Drescher, Seymour. *The Mighty Experiment: Free Labor versus Slavery in British Emancipation*. New York: Oxford University Press, 2002.

Duarte, Constância Lima. *Imprensa feminina e feminista no Brasil: século XIX, dicionário ilustrado*. Belo Horizonte: Autêntica, 2016.

Duncan, Julian Smith. *Public and Private Operations of Railways in Brazil*. New York: Columbia University Press, 1932.

Dunham, George F. "Journal of George Dunham, 1853." Woodson Research Center, Rice University, Americas Collection, ms. 518. Manuscript.

Durkheim, Emile. *The Division of Labor in Society*. Translated by W. D. Halls. New York: Free Press, 1997 [1893].

Dutra, Eliana de Freitas, and Jean-Yves Mollier, eds. *Política, nação e edição: o lugar dos impressos na construção da vida política no Brasil, Europa e Américas nos séculos XVIII e XIX*. São Paulo: Annablume, 2016.

Earle, Rebecca. "The Role of Print in the Spanish-American Wars of Independence." In *The Political Power of the Word: Press and Oratory in Nineteenth-Century Latin America*. Edited by Ivan Jaksić, 9–33. London: Institute of Latin American Studies, 2002.

Eisenberg, Peter. *The Sugar Industry in Pernambuco, 1840–1910: Modernization without Change*. Berkeley: University of California Press, 1974.

El Far, Alessandra. "Bilhetes de namoro abertos ao público: mensagens e encontros às escondidas anunciados no *Jornal do Commercio* (década de 1870)." *Revista Brasileira de História* 37, no. 74 (2017): 1–20.

Ellis Jr., Alfredo. *Feijó e a primeira metade do século XIX*. São Paulo: Companhia Editora Nacional, 1980.

Engel, Maria Gouveia, et al., eds. *Os intelectuais e a imprensa*. Rio de Janeiro: Mauad X and FAPERJ, 2015.

Estatutos da Sociedade Promotora de Colonisação. Rio de Janeiro: Tip. Americana de I. P. da Costa, 1836.

Ewbank, Thomas. *Life in Brazil: Or, A Journal of a Visit to the Land of the Cocoa and the Palm*. New York: Harper & Brothers, 1856.

Façanha, Dayana. *Política e escravidão em José de Alencar:* O tronco do ipê, Sênio *e os debates em torno da emancipação (1870–1871)*. São Paulo: Alameda, 2017.

Farge, Arlette. *Dire et mal dire: l'opinion publique au XVIIIe siècle*. Paris: Seuil, 1992.

Fernandes, Ana Carla Sabino. *A imprensa em pauta: jornais* Pedro II, Cearense *e* Constituição. Fortaleza: Museu do Ceará, Secretaria da Cultura do Estado do Ceará, 2006.

Fernandes, Florestan. *A revolução burguesa no Brasil: ensaio de interpretação sociológica*. Rio de Janeiro: Zahar Editores, 1974.

Ferraria, Maria José, and Fernando de Sousa. "A emigração portuguesa para o Brasil e as origens da Agência Abreu (1840)." In *Nas duas margens: os portugueses no Brasil*. Edited by Ismênia Martins, Izilda Matos, and Fernando de Sousa, 13–32. Porto: Edições Afrontamento and CEPESE, 2009.

Ferreira, Ligia Fonseca. "Luiz Gama autor, leitor: revisitando as *Primeiras Trovas Burlescas* de 1859 e 1861." *Estudos Avançados* 96, no. 33 (2019): 109–34.

Ferreira, Ligia Fonseca, ed. *Com a palavra, Luiz Gama: poemas, artigos, cartas, máximas*. São Paulo: Imprensa Oficial do Estado de São Paulo, 2011.

Ferreira, Roquinaldo. "Biografia, mobilidade e cultura atlântica: a micro-escala do tráfico de escravos de Benguela, séculos XVIII–XIX." *Tempo* 10, no. 20 (January 2006): 23–49.

Fischer, Brodwyn, Keila Grinberg, and Hebe Mattos. "Law, Silence, and Racialized Inequalities in the History of Afro-Brazil." In *Afro-Latin American Studies: An Introduction*. Edited by Alejandro de la Fuente and George Reid Andrews, 130–78. Cambridge: Cambridge University Press, 2018.

Fletcher, James C., and Daniel P. Kidder. *Brazil and the Brazilians Portrayed in Historical and Descriptive Sketches*. 9th ed. Boston: Little Brown, 1879.
Flinter, George D. *An Account of the Present State of the Island of Puerto Rico*. London: Longman, Rees, Orme, Brown, Green & Longman, 1834.
Florentino, Manolo. *Em costas negras: uma história do tráfico de escravos entre a África e o Rio de Janeiro, séculos XVIII e XIX*. São Paulo: Companhia das Letras, 1997.
Florentino, Manolo, and José Roberto Góes. *A paz das senzalas: famílias escravas e tráfico atlântico, Rio de Janeiro (c. 1790–c. 1850)*. Rio de Janeiro: Civilização Brasileira, 1997.
Flory, Thomas. "Race and Social Control in Independent Brazil." *Journal of Latin American Studies* 9, no. 2 (November 1977): 199–224.
Foner, Eric. *Reconstruction: America's Unfinished Revolution, 1863–1877*. New York: Harper & Row, 1988.
Fonseca, Gondim da. *Biografia do jornalismo carioca (1808–1908)*. Rio de Janeiro: Quaresma Editora, 1941.
Fonseca, Marcus Vinicius. *A educação dos negros: uma nova face do processo de abolição da escravidão no Brasil*. Bragança Paulista: EdUSF, 2002.
Fonseca, Silvia Carla Pereira de Brito. *A ideia de República no Império do Brasil: Rio de Janeiro e Pernambuco (1824–1834)*. Jundiaí: Paco, 2016.
Fonseca, Silvia Carla Pereira de Brito, and Maria Leticia Corrêa. "Apresentação: a imprensa e os historiadores." In *200 anos de imprensa no Brasil*. Edited by Silvia Carla Pereira de Brito Fonseca and Maria Leticia Corrêa, 8–20. Rio de Janeiro: ContraCapa, 2009.
Fonseca, Silvia Carla Pereira de Brito, and Maria Leticia Corrêa, eds. *200 anos de imprensa no Brasil*. Rio de Janeiro: ContraCapa, 2009.
França Júnior, J[oaquim] J[osé] de. *Política e costumes: folhetins esquecidos (1867–1868)*. Rio de Janeiro: Civilização Brasileira, 1957.
Franco, Sérgio da Costa. *Gente e espaços de Porto Alegre*. Porto Alegre, EdUFRGS, 2000.
Frank, Zephyr L. *Dutra's World: Wealth and Family in Nineteenth-Century Rio de Janeiro*. Albuquerque: University of New Mexico Press, 2004.
———. *Reading Rio de Janeiro: Literature and Society in the Nineteenth Century*. Stanford, CA: Stanford University Press, 2016.
———. "Urban Property in Nineteenth-Century Rio de Janeiro." In *The Routledge Companion to Spatial History*. Edited by Ian Gregory, Don DeBats, and Don Lafrenière, 544–66. New York: Routlege, 2018.
Frank, Zephyr L., and Whitney Berry, "The Slave Market in Rio de Janeiro circa 1869: Movement, Context, and Social Experience." *Journal of Latin American Geography* 9, no. 2 (2010): 85–110.
Freitas, Marcus Vinícius de. *Charles Frederick Hartt: um naturalista no Império de Pedro II*. Belo Horizonte: Editora UFMG, 2002.

———. *Contradições da modernidade: o jornal* Aurora Brasileira *(1873–1875)*. Campinas: Ed. UNICAMP, 2011.
French, William E. *The Heart in the Glass Jar: Love Letters, Bodies, and the Law in Mexico*. Lincoln: University of Nebraska Press, 2015.
Freyre, Gilberto. *O escravo nos anúncios de jornais brasileiros do século XIX*. São Paulo: Editora Nacional; Recife: Instituo Joaquim Nabuco de Pesquisas Sociais, 1979.
Gallagher, Catherine. "The Rise of Fictionality." In *The Novel*. Edited by Franco Moretti, 336–63. Princeton, NJ: Princeton University Press, 2007.
Galvão, B. F. Ramiz. *Catálogo da Exposição de História do Brasil*. 3 vols. Facsimile ed. Brasília: Editora da Universidade de Brasília, 1981.
Galvão, Rafaella Valença de Andrade. "Felippe Neri Collaço: um homem de cor, de letras e de números, Recife, 1815–1894." Master's thesis, Universidade Federal de Pernambuco, 2016.
Galves, Marcelo Cheche. *"Ao público sincero e imparcial": imprensa e Independência na província do Maranhão (1821–1826)*. São Luís: Café & Lápis and Editora UEMA, 2015.
Gantús, Fausta, ed. "La libertad de imprenta en el siglo XIX: vaivenes de su regulación." *Historia Mexicana* 69, no. 1 (July–September 2019): 93–310.
Gauld, Charles A. "José Carlos Rodrigues, o patriarca da imprensa carioca." *Revista de História* 7, no. 16 (1953): 427–38.
Girardet, Raoul. *Mitos e mitologias políticas*. Translated by Maria Lucia Machado. São Paulo: Companhia das Letras, 1987.
Giron, Luis Antonio. *Minoridade crítica: a ópera e o teatro nos folhetins da Corte*. São Paulo: EdUSP, 2004.
Gledson, John. "Introdução." In *Bons Dias! Machado de Assis*. 2nd ed. Edited by John Gledson, 13–62. Campinas: Ed. UNICAMP, 2008.
———. "Introdução." In *A Semana, Crônicas (1892–1893)*. Edited by John Gledson, 14–15. São Paulo: Hucitec, 1996.
———. *Machado de Assis: ficção e história*. 2nd ed. Rio de Janeiro: Paz e Terra, 2003 [1986].
Godoi, Rodrigo Camargo de. "As cartas dos livreiros: manuais escolares e mercado editorial entre Rio e Paris, 1870–1874." *Anais da Sociedade Brasileira de Estudos do Oitocentos*, 2017. http://www.seo.org.br/images/Anais/Anais_II_Encontro/Rodrigo_Godoi_completo.pdf.
———. *Um editor no Império: Francisco de Paula Brito (1809–1861)*. São Paulo: EdUSP, 2016.
———. "Trabalho escravo e produção de impressos no Rio de Janeiro oitocentista." Escola São Paulo de Estudos Avançados sobre Globalização da Cultura no Século XIX, Campinas, 2012. http://www.espea.iel.unicamp.br/index.php.
Godwin, William. *Of Population: An Enquiry Concerning the Power of Increase in the Numbers of Mankind*. London: Longman, Hurst, Rees, Orme, & Brown, 1821.

Gomes, Angela Maria de Castro, Kaori Kodama, and Maria Rachel Fróes da Fonseca, eds. "Imprensa e mediadores culturais: ciência, história e literatura." *Dossiê* (Special Section) in *Varia História* 34, no. 66 (September–December 2018): 593–762.

Gomes, Flavio [dos Santos], and Maria Helena P. T. Machado. "Da abolição ao pós-emancipação: ensaiando alguns caminhos para outros percursos." In *Tornando-se livre: agentes históricos e lutas sociais no processo de abolição*. Edited by Maria Helena P. T. Machado and Celso Thomas Castilho, 19–42. São Paulo: EdUSP, 2015.

Gomes, Flávio dos Santos, and Petrônio Domingues. *Da nitidez à invisibilidade: legados do pós-emancipação*. Belo Horizonte: Fino Traço, 2013.

Gomes, Flávio dos Santos, and Petrônio Domingues, eds. *Políticas da raça: experiências e legados da abolição e da pós-emancipação no Brasil*. São Paulo: Editora Selo Negro, 2014.

Gonçalves, Paulo Cesar. "Procuram-se braços para a lavoura: imigrantes e retirantes na economia cafeeira paulista no final do Oitocentos." *Revista Brasileira de História* 34, no. 67 (2014): 283–308.

González, Anibal. *Journalism and the Development of Spanish American Narrative*. Cambridge: Cambridge University Press, 1993.

Gouvêa, Myriam Paula Barbosa Pires. *Impressão, sociabilidades e poder: o Diário do Rio de Janeiro e fundação da sua tipografia (1821–1831)*. Jundiaí: Paco Editorial, 2016.

Graham, Richard. *Patronage and Politics in Nineteenth-Century Brazil*. Stanford, CA: Stanford University Press, 1990.

Graham, Sandra Lauderdale. "Writing from the Margins: Brazilian Slaves and Written Culture." *Comparative Studies of Society and History* 49, no. 3 (2007): 611–36.

Granja, Lúcia. "Crônica, Chronique, Crónica." *Revista da ANPOLL* 38 (2015): 86–100.

———. "Das páginas dos jornais aos gabinetes de leitura: rumos dos estudos sobre a crônica de Machado de Assis." *Teresa: Revista de Literatura Brasileira* 6, no. 7 (2009): 385–99.

———. *Machado de Assis, escritor em formação: à roda dos jornais*. Campinas: Mercado de Letras, 2000.

Gravier, Marina Garone, and Ana Utsch, eds. *Red Latinoamericana de Cultura Gráfica: Bibliografía Latinoamericana de Cultura Gráfica—2018*. Belo Horizonte: Faculdade de Letras, UFMG, 2018.

Grinberg, Keila. "Em defesa da propriedade: Antônio Pereira Rebouças e a escravidão." *Afro-Ásia* 21–22 (1998–1999): 111–46.

Guerra, François-Xavier. "Forms of Communication, Political Spaces, and Cultural Identities in the Creation of Spanish American Nations." In *Beyond Imagined Communities: Reading and Writing the Nation in Nineteenth-Century Latin America*. Edited by John Charles Chasteen and Sara Castro-Klarén, 3–32. Baltimore: Johns Hopkins University Press, 2003.

———. *Modernidad e independencias: ensayos sobre las revoluciones hispánicas*. México: Fondo de Cultura Económica, 1993.

Guerra, François-Xavier, and Annick Lempérière, eds. *Los espacios públicos en Iberoamérica: ambigüedades y problemas, siglos XVIII–XIX*. Mexico City: Fondo de Cultura Económica, 1998.

Habermas, Jürgen. *Mudança estrutural da esfera pública: investigações quanto a uma categoria da sociedade burguesa*. Translated by Flávio R. Kothe. Rio de Janeiro: Tempo Brasileiro, 1984.

Habermas, Jürgen. *The Structural Transformation of the Public Sphere: An Inquiry into a Category of Bourgeois Society*. Translated by Thomas Burger with the assistance of Frederick Lawrence. Cambridge, MA: MIT Press, 1991.

Hahn, Steven. *A Nation Under Our Feet: Black Political Struggles in the Rural South from Slavery to the Great Migration*. Cambridge, MA: Harvard University Press, 2005.

———. *A Nation Without Borders: The United States and Its World in an Age of Civil Wars, 1830–1910*. New York: Viking, 2016.

Hahner, June. "Feminism, Women's Rights and the Suffrage Movement in Brazil, 1850–1932." *Latin American Research Review* 15, no. 1 (1980): 65–111.

Hall, Michael. "Origins of Mass Immigration in Brazil, 1871–1914." PhD diss., Columbia University, 1969.

Hall, Michael, and Verena Stolcke. "The Introduction of Free Labor on São Paulo Coffee Plantations." *Journal of Peasant Studies* 10, no. 2–3 (January 1983): 170–200.

Hallewell, Laurence. *O livro no Brasil: uma história*. 3rd ed. São Paulo: EdUSP, 2012 [1985].

Heynemann, Cláudia B., Maria do Carmo Teixeira Rainho, and Rafael Cardoso Denis. *Marcas do progresso: consumo e design no Brasil do século XIX*. Rio de Janeiro: Arquivo Nacional, 2009.

Hilliard, Henry W. *Politics and Pen Pictures at Home and Abroad*. New York: G. P. Putnam's Sons, 1892.

Hobbs, Andrew. "Provincial Periodicals." In *The Routledge Handbook to Nineteenth-Century British Periodicals and Newspapers*. Edited by Andrew King, Alexis Easley, and John Morton, 221–33. New York: Routledge, 2016.

Hoffnagel, Marc Jay. "'O Homem': raça e preconceito no Recife." *Clio* (Recife) 1 (1977): 52–62.

Holanda, Sérgio Buarque de. "Do Império à República." In *História geral da civilização brasileira*. Tomo 2. *O Brasil monárquico*. 5 vols. Edited by Sérgio Buarque de Holanda, 5:7–435. São Paulo: Difel, 1966–1971.

Holloway, Thomas H. "The Defiant Life and Forgotten Death of Apulco de Castro: Race, Power, and Historical Memory." *Estudios Interdisciplinares de América Latina* 191 (January–June 2008): 637–76.

———. *Immigrants on the Land: Coffee and Society in São Paulo, 1886–1934*. Chapel Hill: University of North Carolina Press, 1980.

Hudson, Frederic. *Journalism in the United States, from 1690–1872.* New York: Harper & Brothers, 1873.
Huerne de Pommeuse, Michel L. F. *Les colonies agricoles et leurs avantages.* Paris: Imprimerie de Madame Huzard, 1832.
Iglesias, Francisco. "Vida política, 1848–1866." In *História geral da civilização brasileira.* Tomo 2. *O Brasil monárquico,* 5 vols. Edited by Sérgio Buarque de Holanda, 3:9–112. São Paulo: Difel, 1966–1971.
Ignotus [Joaquim Serra]. *A imprensa no Maranhão: sessenta anos de jornalismo, 1820–1880.* Rio de Janeiro: Faro & Lino, 1883.
Ingersoll, Thomas N. "Releese Us Out of This Cruell Bondegg": An Appeal from Virginia in 1723." *William and Mary Quarterly* 51, no. 4 (October 1994): 777–82.
Izecksohn, Vitor. *Slavery and War in the Americas: Race, Citizenship, and State Building in the United States and Brazil, 1861–1870.* Charlottesville: University of Virginia Press, 2014.
Jacobsen, Nils. "Public Opinions and Public Spheres in Late Nineteenth-Century Peru." In *Political Cultures in the Andes.* Edited by Nils Jacobsen and Cristóbal Aljovín, 278–300. Durham, NC: Duke University Press, 2005.
Jinzenji, Mônica Yumi. *Cultura impressa e educação da mulher no século XIX.* Belo Horizonte: Editora UFMG, 2010.
John, Richard R., and Jonathan Silberstein-Loeb. "Making News." In *Making News: The Political Economy of Journalism in Britain and America from the Glorious Revolution to the Internet.* Edited by Richard R. John and Jonathan Silberstein-Loeb, 1–18. New York: Oxford University Press, 2015.
Karasch, Mary. *Slave Life in Rio de Janeiro, 1808–1850.* Princeton, NJ: Princeton University Press, 1987.
Kirkendall, Andrew J. *Class Mates: Male Student Culture and the Making of a Political Class in Nineteenth-Century Brazil.* Lincoln: University of Nebraska Press, 2002.
Kirschner, Tereza Cristina. *José da Silva Lisboa, visconde de Cairu: itinerários de um ilustrado luso-brasileiro.* São Paulo: Alameda; Belo Horizonte: PUC-Minas, 2009.
Kittleson, Roger. "'Campaign All of Peace and Charity': Gender and the Politics of Abolitionism in Porto Alegre, Brazil, 1879–1888." *Slavery and Abolition* (December 2001): 83–108.
Klein, Herbert S. *The Atlantic Slave Trade.* 2nd ed. Cambridge: Cambridge University Press, 2010.
Knauss, Paulo, et al., eds. *Revistas ilustradas: modos de ler e ver o Segundo Reinado.* Rio de Janeiro: Mauad X and FAPERJ, 2011.
Koselleck, Reinhart. *Crítica e crise: uma contribuição à patogênese do mundo burguês.* Translated by Luciana Villas-Boas Castelo-Branco. Rio de Janeiro: EdUERJ and Contraponto, 1999.
Kraay, Hendrik. *Bahia's Independence: Popular Politics and Patriotic Festival in Salvador, Brazil, 1824–1900.* Montreal: McGill-Queen's University Press, 2019.

———. *Days of National Festivity in Rio de Janeiro, Brazil, 1823–1889*. Stanford, CA: Stanford University Press, 2013.

———. *Race, State, and Armed Forces in Independence-Era Brazil: Bahia, 1790s–1840s*. Stanford, CA: Stanford University Press, 2001.

Kraay, Hendrik, and Thomas L. Whigham, eds. *I Die with My Country: Perspectives on the Paraguayan War, 1864–1870*. Lincoln: University of Nebraska Press, 2004.

Kury, Lorelai Brilhante, ed. *Iluminismo e império no Brasil: O Patriota (1813–1814)*. Rio de Janeiro: Editora FIOCRUZ, Ministério da Cultura, Fundação Biblioteca Nacional, 2007.

Laërne, C. F. Van Delden. *Brazil and Java: Report on Coffee-Culture in America, Asia and Africa, to H. E. the Minister of the Colonies*. London: W. H. Allen, 1885.

Laet, Carlos de. *Crônicas*. 2nd ed. Edited by Homero Sena. Rio de Janeiro: Academia Brasileira de Letras, 2000.

Lafayette College. *Record of the Men of Lafayette: Brief Biographical Sketches of the Alumni of Lafayette College from Its Organization to the Present Time*. Easton, PA: Skinner and Finch, 1879.

Landert, Daniela, and Andreas H. Jucker. "Private and Public in Mass Media Communication: From Letters to the Editor to Online Commentaries." *Journal of Pragmatics* 43 (2011): 1,422–34.

Lara, Silvia H. "Biografia de Mahommah G. Baquaqua." *Revista Brasileira de História* 8, no. 16 (1988): 269–84.

Lavarda, Marcus Túlio. "A iconografia da Guerra do Paraguai e o periódico *Semana Ilustrada*." Master's thesis, Universidade Federal da Grande Dourados, 2009.

Lebrun, Isidore. *Tableau statistique et politique des deux Canadas*. Paris: Treuttel et Würtz, 1833.

Lefebvre, Georges. *O Grande Medo de 1789: os camponeses e a Revolução Francesa*. Translated by Carlos Eduardo de Castro Real. Rio de Janeiro: Campus, 1979.

Lepler, Jessica. *The Many Panics of 1837: People, Politics, and the Creation of a Transatlantic Financial Crisis*. New York: Cambridge University Press, 2013.

Lessa, Monica Leite, and Silvia Carla Pereira de Brito Fonseca, eds. *Entre a Monarquia e a República: imprensa, pensamento político e historiografia (1822–1889)*. Rio de Janeiro: EdUERJ, 2008.

Lima, Herman. *História da caricatura no Brasil*. 4 vols. Rio de Janeiro: José Olympio Editora, 1963.

Lima, Ivana Stolze. *Cores, marcas e falas: sentidos da mestiçagem no Império do Brasil*. Rio de Janeiro: Arquivo Nacional, 2003.

Lizé, Wenceslas, and Olivier Roueff. "La fabrique des goûts." *Actes de la Recherche en Sciences Sociales* 181–82 (2010–11): 4–11.

Lobo, Eulalia M. Lahmeyer. "Evolução dos preços e do padrão de vida no Rio de Janeiro, 1820–1930." *Revista Brasileira de Economia* 25, no. 4 (October–December 1971): 235–65.

Lobo, Luiza. "Juana Manso: uma exilada em três pátrias." *Revista Genero* (Niterói) 9, no. 2 (2009): 47–74.
Lopes, Antonio. *História da imprensa no Maranhão (1821–1925)*. Rio de Janeiro: Imprensa Nacional, 1959.
Lopes, Aristeu Elisandro Machado. *Traços da política: a imprensa ilustrada em Pelotas no século XIX*. Porto Alegre: Editora Fi, 2017.
Lopez, Telê Porto Ancona. "A crônica de Mário de Andrade: impressões que historiam." In *A crônica: o gênero, sua fixação e suas transformações no Brasil*. Edited by Antonio Cândido, 165–88. Campinas: Ed. UNICAMP, 1992.
Lovejoy, Paul. "Identidade e a miragem da etnicidade: a jornada de Mahommah Gardo Baquaqua para as Américas." *Afro-Ásia* 27 (2002): 9–39.
Loveman, Mara. "The Race to Progress: Census Taking and Nation Making in Brazil, 1870–1920." *Hispanic American Historical Review* 89, no. 3 (August 2009): 435–70.
Lustosa, Isabel. *Insultos impressos: a guerra dos jornalistas na Independência, 1821–1823*. São Paulo: Companhia das Letras, 2000.
———. *O nascimento da imprensa brasileira*. Rio de Janeiro: Jorge Zahar, 2003.
Luz, Estevão de Melo Marcondes. *Incendiárias folhas: ação política, imprensa e instrução pública na trajetória do padre Antonio José Bhering (1829–1849)*. Curitiba: Prismas, 2017.
Luz, Madel Therezinha. *A arte de curar versus a ciência das doenças: história social da homeopatia no Brasil*. Porto Alegre: Editora Rede UNIDA, 2014.
Lyall, Robert. *Notice sur l'organisation, l'administration, et l'état présent des colonies militaires de la Russie*. Translated by C. J. Ferry. Paris: Anselin et Pichard, 1825 [1824].
Mac Cord, Marcelo. *Artífices da cidadania: mutualismo, educação e trabalho no Recife oitocentista*. Campinas: Editora da UNICAMP, 2012.
———. *O Rosário de D. Antônio: irmandades negras, alianças e conflitos na história social do Recife, 1848–1872*. Recife: Editora da UFPE, 2005.
Mac Cord, Marcelo, Carlos Eduardo Moreira de Araújo, and Flávio dos Santos Gomes, eds. *Rascunhos cativos: educação, escolas e ensino no Brasil escravista*. Rio de Janeiro: Editora 7 Letras, 2017.
Macedo, Joaquim Manuel de. *Anno Biographico Brazileiro*. 2 vols. Rio de Janeiro: Tip. e Lithographia do Imperial Instituto Artístico, 1876.
———. *Memórias do sobrinho do meu tio*. Edited by Flora Sussekind. São Paulo: Companhia das Letras, 1995 [1867–1868].
———. "O primo da Califórnia." In *Teatro Completo*. 3 vols., 1:97–148. Rio de Janeiro: Serviço Nacional de Teatro, 1979–1982.
Machado, Humberto Fernandes. "Imprensa abolicionista e censura no Império do Brasil." In *Entre a monarquia e a República: imprensa, pensamento político e historiografia (1822–1889)*. Edited by Monica Leite Lessa and Silvia Carla Pereira de Brito Fonseca, 243–59. Rio de Janeiro: EdUERJ, 2008.

———. *Palavras e brados: José do Patrocínio e a imprensa abolicionista do Rio de Janeiro*. Niterói: Editora da UFF, 2014.

Machado, Maria Helena Pereira Toledo. "Maria Firmina dos Reis: escrita íntima na construção do si mesmo." *Estudos Avançados* 96, no. 33 (2019): 93–108.

Machado, Maria Helena Pereira Toledo, ed. "Tinta negra, papel branco: escritas afrodescendentes e emancipação." *Dossiê* (Special Section) in *Estudos Avançados* 33, no. 96 (May–August 2019): 93–224.

Machado de Assis, Joaquim Maria de. *Bons Dias! Machado de Assis*. 2nd ed. Edited by John Gledson. Campinas: Ed. UNICAMP, 2008.

———. *História de quinze dias*. Edited by Leonardo Affonso de Miranda Pereira. Campinas: Ed. UNICAMP, 2009.

———. *A Semana, crônicas (1892–1893)*. Edited by John Gledson. São Paulo: Hucitec, 1996.

Mackintosh, Phillip Gordon. *Newspaper City: Toronto's Street Surfaces and the Liberal Press, 1860–1935*. Toronto: University of Toronto Press, 2017.

Magno, Luciano. *História da caricatura brasileira: os precursores e a consolidação da caricatura no Brasil*. Rio de Janeiro: Gala Edições de Arte, 2012.

Mamigonian, Beatriz Gallotti. *Africanos livres: a abolição do tráfico de escravos no Brasil*. São Paulo: Companhia das Letras, 2017.

———. "Bilhete do africano Cyro." In *História social da língua nacional*. Vol. 2, *Diáspora africana*. Edited by Ivana Stolze Lima and Laura do Carmo, 379–88. Rio de Janeiro: Nau, 2014.

———. "Do que 'o preto mina' é capaz: etnia e resistência entre africanos livres." *Afro-Ásia* 24 (2000): 71–95.

Mangueira, Xangô. *O rei do partido-alto* (LP). Rio de Janeiro: Copacabana, 1972.

Margingoni, Gilberto. *Angelo Agostini: a imprensa ilustrada da Corte à Capital Federal, 1864–1910*. São Paulo: Devir Editora, 2011.

Marques, [Francisco] Xavier [Ferreira]. *Uma família bahiana*. 2nd ed. Salvador: Imprensa Popular, 1888.

Marques, João Pedro. *Os sons do silêncio: o Portugal de oitocentos e a abolição do tráfico de escravos*. Lisbon: Imprensa de Ciências Sociais, 1999.

Marques Júnior, Nelson Ferreira. "'Os Verdadeiros Constitucionais, Amigos do Rei e da Nação': áulicos, ideias e soberania na Corte fluminense (1824–1826)." Master's thesis, Universidade do Estado do Rio de Janeiro, 2013.

Marquese, Rafael de Bivar. "The U.S. Civil War and the Crisis of Slavery in Brazil." In *American Civil Wars: The United States, Latin America, Europe, and the Crisis of the 1860s*. Edited by Don H. Doyle, 222–45. Chapel Hill: University of North Carolina Press, 2017.

Marquese, Rafael, and Dale Tomich. "O Vale do Paraíba escravista e a formação do mercado mundial do café no século XIX." In *O Brasil Imperial*. 3 vols. Edited by

Keila Grinberg and Ricardo Salles, 2:41–83. Rio de Janeiro: Civilização Brasileira, 2009.
Marquese, Rafael, Tâmis Parron, and Márcia Berbel. *Escravidão e política: Brasil e Cuba, 1790–1850.* São Paulo: Hucitec, 2010.
Martins Júnior, Leandro Augusto. "Galeria de ilustres: escrita biográfica e formação da nação, 1840–60." Paper presented at the 25th Meeting of ANPUH, Fortaleza, Ceará, 2009.
———. "Galeria dos brasileiros ilustres: escrita biográfica e imaginário nacional na consolidação do Império do Brasil, 1840–1860." Paper presented at the 13th Meeting of ANPUH-RJ, 2008.
Martins, Ana Luiza. *História da imprensa no Brasil.* São Paulo: Contexto, 2013.
———. *Revistas em revista: imprensa e práticas culturais em tempos de República.* São Paulo: EdUSP, 2008.
Martins, Ana Luiza, and Tânia R. de Luca, eds. *História da imprensa no Brasil.* São Paulo: Editora Contexto, 2008.
———. *Imprensa e cidade.* São Paulo: EdUNESP, 2006.
Mascarenhas, Nelson Lage. *Um jornalista do Império (Firmino Rodrigues Silva).* São Paulo: Companhia Editora Nacional, 1961.
Mattos, Ilmar R. de. *O tempo saquarema: a formação do Estado Imperial.* São Paulo: Hucitec, 2009 [1986].
Mattos, Raimundo José da Cunha. "Memoria historica sobre a população, emigração e colonisação, que convem ao Império do Brasil." *O Auxiliador da Industria Nacional* 5, no. 11 (1837): 344–64.
McIntyre, Jerilyn. "The Avvisi of Venice: Toward an Archaeology of Media Forms." *Journalism History* 14, no. 2–3 (1987): 68–87.
Meirelles, Juliana Gesuelli. *Imprensa e poder na Corte joanina: a* Gazeta do Rio de Janeiro *(1808–1821).* Rio de Janeiro: Arquivo Nacional, 2008.
Mello, Antonio Joaquim de. *Biographias de alguns poetas e homens illustres da provincia de Pernambuco.* 3 vols. Recife: Tip. Universal, 1856–1859.
Mello, Evaldo Cabral de. *Rubro veio: o imaginário da restauração pernambucana.* Rio de Janeiro: Editora Nova Fronteira, 1986.
Menezes, Paulo Roberto de Jesus. "Sociedade, imagem e biografia na litografia de Sebastião Sisson." Master's thesis, Universidade Federal do Rio de Janeiro, 2008.
Meyer, Marlyse. *Folhetim: uma história.* São Paulo: Companhia das Letras, 1996.
———. "Voláteis e versáteis: de variedades e folhetins se fez a chronica." In *A crônica: o gênero, sua fixação e suas transformações no Brasil.* Edited by Antonio Cândido, 93–151. Campinas: Ed. UNICAMP, 1992.
Milligan, Ian. "Illusionary Order, Online Databases, Optical Character Recognition, and Canadian History, 1997–2010." *Canadian Historical Review* 94, no. 4 (2013): 540–69.

Mitchell, W. J. T. *Picture Theory: Essays on Verbal and Visual Representation*. Chicago: University of Chicago Press, 1994.
Mizuta, Celina Midori Murasse, et al., eds. *Império em debate: imprensa e educação no Brasil oitocentista*. Maringá: EdUEM, 2010.
Molina, Matías M. *História dos jornais no Brasil*. Vol. 1, *Da era colonial à Regência (1500–1840)*. São Paulo: Companhia das Letras, 2015.
Moniz Barretto, Rozendo. *Cantos d'aurora*. Rio de Janeiro: E. & H. Laemmert, 1868.
Morais, Christianni Cardoso. "Ler e escrever: habilidades de escravos e forros? Comarca do Rio das Mortes, Minas Gerais, 1731–1850." *Revista Brasileira de História da Educação* 12, no. 36 (September–December 2007): 493–505.
Morel, Marco. *Cipriano Barata na Sentinela da Liberdade*. Salvador: Academia de Letras da Bahia; Assembleia Legislativa do Estado da Bahia, 2001.
———. "Da gazeta tradicional aos jornais de opinião: metamorfoses da imprensa periódica no Brasil." In *Livros e impressos: retratos do setecentos e do Oitocentos*. Edited by Lúcia Maria Bastos P. das Neves, 153–81. Rio de Janeiro: EdUERJ, 2009.
———. "Escravidão e imprensa no Brasil do século XIX." In *Imprensa, história e literatura*. Edited by Isabel Lustosa, 75–82. Rio de Janeiro: Casa de Rui Barbosa, 2008.
———. *As transformações dos espaços públicos: imprensa, atores políticos e sociabilidades na cidade imperial (1820–1840)*. São Paulo: Hucitec, 2005.
Morel, Marco, and Mariana Monteiro de Barros. *Palavra, imagem e poder: o surgimento da imprensa no Brasil do século XIX*. Rio de Janeiro: DP&A, 2003.
Mota, Isadora Moura. "O vulcão negro da Chapada: rebelião escrava nos sertões diamantinos." Master's thesis, UNICAMP, 2005.
———. "On the Imminence of Emancipation: Black Geopolitical Literacy and Anglo-American Abolitionism in Nineteenth-Century Brazil." PhD diss., Brown University, 2017.
Motta, José Flávio. *Escravos daqui, dali e de mais além: o tráfico interno de cativos na expansão cafeeira paulista*. São Paulo: Alameda, 2012.
Motte, Dean de la, and Jeannene M. Przyblyski. "Introduction." In *Making the News: Modernity and the Mass Press in Nineteenth-Century France*. Edited by Dean de la Motte and Jeannene M. Przyblyski, 1–12. Amherst: University of Massachusetts Press, 1999.
Mulhall, M[ichael] G[eorge]. *Handbook of Brazil*. Buenos Aires, 1877.
Muniz Barreto, Domingos Alves Branco. *Memória sobre a abolição do commercio da escravatura*. Rio de Janeiro: Typ. Imparcial de F. de Paula Brito, 1837.
Mussell, James. "Digitization." In *The Routledge Handbook to Nineteenth-Century British Periodicals and Newspapers*. Edited by Andrew King, Alexis Easley, and John Morton, 17–28. New York: Routledge, 2016.
Muzart, Zahidé Lupinacci. "Uma espiada na imprensa das mulheres no século XIX." *Revista Estudos Feministas* (Florianópois) 11 (January–June 2003): 225–33.

Nabuco, Joaquim. *Um estadista do Império*. 4th ed. Rio de Janeiro: Nova Aguilar, 1975 [1897–1899].
Naeher, Julius. *Excursões na província da Bahia: a terra e a gente da província brasileira da Bahia*. Translated by Osvaldo Augusto Teixeira. Salvador: CIAN, 2011.
Nascimento, Luiz do. *História da imprensa de Pernambuco (1821–1954)*. 14 vols. Recife: Arquivo Público and Imprensa Oficial, 1962–1994.
Needell, Jeffrey D. "Party Formation and State-Making: The Conservative Party and the Reconstruction of the Brazilian State, 1831–1840." *Hispanic American Historical Review* 81, no. 2 (May 2001): 259–308.
———. *The Party of Order: The Conservatives, the State, and Slavery in the Brazilian Monarchy, 1831–1871*. Stanford, CA: Stanford University Press, 2006.
———. *A Tropical Belle Époque: Elite Culture and Society in Turn-of-the-Century Rio de Janeiro*. Cambridge: Cambridge University Press, 1987.
Neto, Alexandre Ribeiro, and Flávio Gomes. "Escritos insubordinados entre escravizados e libertos no Brasil." *Estudos Avançados* 96, no. 33 (2019): 155–77.
Neves, Lúcia Maria Bastos Pereira das. *Corcundas e constitucionais: a cultura política da Independência (1820–1822)*. Rio de Janeiro: FAPERJ and Revan, 2003.
———. "Opinião pública." In *Léxico da história dos conceitos políticos do Brasil*. Edited by João Feres Júnior, 181–202. Belo Horizonte: Editora UFMG, 2009.
Neves, Lúcia Maria Bastos Pereira das, ed. *Livros e impressos: retratos do setecentos e do Oitocentos*. Rio de Janeiro: EdUERJ, 2009.
Neves, Lúcia Maria Bastos Pereira das, and Lúcia Maria Paschoal Guimarães, eds. *Minerva Brasiliense: leituras*. Rio de Janeiro: ContraCapa, 2016.
Neves, Lúcia Maria Bastos Pereira. das, Marco Morel, and Tania Maria Bessone da C. Ferreira, eds. *História e imprensa: representações culturais e práticas de poder*. Rio de Janeiro: DP&A and FAPERJ, 2006.
Neves, Margarida de Souza. "Uma escrita do tempo: memória, ordem e progresso nas crônicas cariocas." In *A crônica: o gênero, sua fixação e suas transformações no Brasil*. Edited by Antonio Cândido, 75–92. Campinas: Ed. UNICAMP, 1992.
Nicolau, Rosane. "Estudo dos apedidos presentes em jornais paraibanos do século XIX sob a ótica da teoria da enunciação." *Temática: Revista Electrónica* 4, no. 4 (2010).
Nord, David Paul. "The Victorian City and the Urban Newspaper." In *Making News: The Political Economy of Journalism in Britain and America from the Glorious Revolution to the Internet*. Edited by Richard R. John and Jonathan Silberstein-Loeb, 73–106. Oxford: Oxford University Press, 2015.
Nunes, Tassia Toffoli. "Liberdade de imprensa no Império brasileiro: os debates parlamentares (1820–1840)." Master's thesis, Universidade de São Paulo, 2010.
O Novo Mundo Association. *By-laws of 'O Novo Mundo Association' of the City of New York (Incorporated 1875)*. New York, 1875.

Oliveira, Carlos Eduardo França de. *Poder local e palavra impressa: São Paulo, 1824–1834*. São Paulo: Annablume and FAPESP, 2011.

Oliveira, Cecília Helena L. de Salles. *A astúcia liberal: relações de mercado e projetos políticos no Rio de Janeiro (1820–1824)*. Bragança Paulista: EdUSF and Ícone, 1999.

Oliveira, Klebson. "E agora, com a escrita, os escravos!" In *Do português arcaico ao português brasileiro*. Edited by Sônia Bastos Borba Costa and Américo Venâncio Lopes Machado Filho, 139–62. Salvador: EdUFBA, 2004.

———. "Textos de escravos no Brasil oitocentista: os tempos de uma edição filológica e de uma antologia comentada de alguns fatos linguísticos." *Revista de Filologia e Linguística Portuguesa* 10–11 (2009): 189–220.

Paiva, Eduardo França. "Leituras (im)possíveis: negros e mestiços leitores na América portuguesa." In *Política, nação e edição: o lugar dos impressos na construção da vida política no Brasil, Europa e Américas nos séculos XVIII e XIX*. Edited by Eliana de Freitas Dutra and Jean-Yves Mollier, 481–93. São Paulo: Annablume, 2006.

Paixão, Alexandre Henrique. "Elementos constitutivos para a formação do público literário no Rio de Janeiro e em São Paulo no Segundo Reinado." PhD diss., Universidade de São Paulo, 2012.

Panzer, Mary. *Mathew Brady and the Image of History*. Washington, DC: Smithsonian Institution Press, 1997.

Paranhos, José Maria da Silva. *Cartas ao amigo ausente*. Edited by José Honório Rodrigues. Rio de Janeiro: Ministério das Relações Exteriores, Instituto Rio Branco, 1953.

Parron, Tâmis. "A política da escravidão na era da liberdade: Estados Unidos, Brasil e Cuba, 1787–1846." PhD diss., Universidade de São Paulo, 2015.

———. *A política da escravidão no Império do Brasil, 1826–1865*. Rio de Janeiro: Civilização Brasileira, 2011.

Passos, Alexandre. *Um século de imprensa universitária (1831–1931)*. Rio de Janeiro: Pongetti, 1971.

Patroni M. M. P., F. A. [Filippe Alberto Patroni Martins Maciel Parente]. *A Bíblia do Justo Meio da Politica Moderada ou Prolegomenos do Direito Constitucional da Natureza Explicado pelas Leis Fysicas do Mundo*. Rio de Janeiro: Imprensa Americana, 1835.

Pelegrini, Sandra de Cássia Araújo, and Danilo Aparecido Chapman Rocha. "As narrativas visuais sobre a Guerra do Paraguai no *Diabo Coxo*." *Navigator* (Rio de Janeiro) 14, no. 27 (2018): 87–98.

Pereira, Leonardo Affonso de Miranda. *O carnaval das letras: literatura e folia no Rio de Janeiro do século XIX*. 2nd ed. Campinas: Ed. UNICAMP, 2004.

———. "Introdução." In *História de quinze dias*. Edited by Leonardo Affonso de Miranda Pereira, 9–58. Campinas: Ed. UNICAMP, 2009.

Perelman, Chaïm, and Lucie Olbrechts-Tyteca. *Tratado da argumentação: a nova retórica*. São Paulo: Martins Fontes, 1996.

Piccato, Pablo. "Notes for a History of the Press in Mexico." In *Journalism, Satire, and Censorship in Mexico*. Edited by Paul Gillingham, Michael Lettieri, and Benjamin T. Smith, 33–60. Albuquerque: University of New Mexico Press, 2019.

———. "Public Sphere in Latin America: A Map of the Historiography." *Social History* 35, no. 2 (2010): 165–92.

———. *The Tyranny of Opinion: Honor in the Construction of the Mexican Public Sphere*. Durham, NC: Duke University Press, 2010.

Pinho, [José] Wanderley [de Araújo]. *Cotegipe e seu tempo: primeira phase, 1815–1867*. São Paulo: Companhia Editora Nacional, 1937.

Pinto, Ana Flávia Magalhães. "Fortes laços em linhas rotas: literatos negros, racismo e cidadania na segunda metade do século XIX." PhD diss., UNICAMP, 2014.

———. *Imprensa negra no Brasil do século XIX*. São Paulo: Editora Selo Negro, 2010.

Pinto, Ana Flávia Magalhães, and Sidney Chalhoub, eds. *Pensadores negros—pensadoras negras, Brasil, século XIX e XX*. Belo Horizonte: Editora Fino Traço, 2016.

Pinto, Antonio Pereira. *Apontamentos para o direito internacional*. 4 vols. Rio de Janeiro: F. L. Pinto e Cia, 1864–1869.

Pinto, Luis Maria da Silva. *Diccionario da lingua brasileira*. Ouro Preto: Tip. de Silva, 1832.

Pires Junior, Arnaldo Lucas. *A imprensa em guerra: caricaturas e Guerra do Paraguai*. Rio de Janeiro: Multifoco, 2018.

Pirola, Ricardo Figueiredo. *Senzala insurgente: malungos, parentes e rebeldes nas senzalas de Campinas (1832)*. Campinas: Editora da UNICAMP, 2011.

Ploux, François. *De bouche à oreille: naissance et propagation des rumeurs dans la France du XIXe siècle*. Paris: Aubier, 2003.

Polanyi, Karl. *The Great Transformation: The Political and Economic Origins of Our Time*. Boston: Beacon, 1944.

Porto, Ângela de Araújo. "As artimanhas de esculápio: crença ou ciência no saber médico." Master's thesis, Universidade Federal Fluminense, 1985.

Posada-Carbó, Eduardo. "Newspapers, Politics, and Elections in Colombia, 1830–1930." *Historical Journal* 53, no. 4 (December 2010): 939–62.

Putnam, Lara. "The Transnational and the Text-Searchable: Digitized Sources and the Shadows They Cast." *American Historical Review* 121, no. 2 (April 2016): 377–402.

Quadros, Jussara Menezes. "Print Technologies, World News and Narrative Form in Machado de Assis." In *Books and Periodicals in Brazil, 1768–1930: A Transatlantic Perspective*. Edited by Ana Cláudia Suriani da Silva and Sandra Guardini Vasconcelos, 199–214. London: Legenda, 2014.

Quinn, Sarah. "The Transformation of Morals in Markets: Death, Benefits, and the Exchange of Life Insurance Policies." *American Journal of Sociology* 144, no. 3 (November 2008): 738–80.

Radiguet, Max. *Souvenirs de l'Amérique espagnole: Chili-Pérou-Brésil*. New ed. Paris: Calmann Lévy, 1890.

Ramos, Ana Flávia Cernic. "'Balas de Estalo' de Machado de Assis: humor e política no Segundo Reinado." *Revista de Letras da UNESP* 48 (2008): 151–70.

———. *As máscaras de Lélio: política e humor nas crônicas de Machado de Assis (1883– 1886)*. Campinas: Ed. UNICAMP, 2016.

———. "Política e humor nos últimos anos da Monarquia: a série 'Balas de Estalo.'" In *História em cousas miúdas: capítulos de história social da crônica no Brasil*. Edited by Sidney Chalhoub, Margarida de Souza Neves, and Leonardo Affonso de Miranda Pereira, 87–122. Campinas: Ed. UNICAMP, 2005.

Rangel, Alberto. *Gastão de Orléans (o último Conde d'Eu)*. São Paulo: Companhia Editora Nacional, 1935.

Rasmussen, Birgit Brander. "'Attended with Great Inconveniences': Slave Literacy and the 1740 South Carolina Negro Act." *PMLA* 25, no. 1 (January 2010): 201–3.

Read, Ian, and Kari Zimmerman. "Freedom for too Few: Slave Runaways in the Brazilian Empire." *Journal of Social History* 48, no. 2 (December 2014): 404–26.

Refutação á Exposição, que á Nação Brasileira offererão 32 Cidadãos em o dia 25 de Julho de 1831, e relatorio dos accontecimentos da noite de 14, e dia 15 do mesmo Julho, e anno corrente. Rio de Janeiro: Typ. Imperial d'E. Seignot-Plancher, 1831.

Rego, Ana Regina Barros Leal. *Imprensa piauiense: atuação política no século XIX*. Teresina: Fundação Cultural Monsenhor Chaves, 2001.

Reis, João José. *Rebelião escrava no Brasil: a história do levante dos Malês em 1835*. Rev. and ex. ed. São Paulo: Companhia das Letras, 2003.

Reis, João José, Flávio dos Santos Gomes, and Marcus J. M. de Carvalho. *O Alufá Rufino: tráfico, escravidão e liberdade no Atlântico negro (c. 1822–1853)*. São Paulo: Companhia das Letras, 2010.

Renault, Delso. *O Rio antigo nos anúncios de jornais, 1808–1850*. Rio de Janeiro: J. Olympio, 1969.

———. *Rio de Janeiro, a vida da cidade refletida nos jornais (1850–1870)*. Rio de Janeiro: Civilização Brasileira, 1978.

Rensselaer Polytechnic Institute. *Annual Register, April 1897*. Troy, NY: Wm. H. Young, 1897.

Ribeiro, Gladys Sabina. *A liberdade em construção: identidade nacional e conflitos antilusitanos no Primeiro Reinado*. Rio de Janeiro: Relume Dumará, 2002.

Ribeyrolles, Charles. *Brasil pitoresco: história-descrições-viagens-colonização-instituições*. Translated by Gastão Penalva. 3 vols. in 2. São Paulo: Martins, 1941 [1859–1861].

Ricci, Maria Lúcia de Souza Rangel. *A atuação de um publicista: Antônio Borges da Fonseca*. Campinas: Pontifícia Universidade Católica de Campinas, 1995.

Richardson, Heather Cox. *The Greatest Nation of the Earth: Republican Economic Policies During the Civil War*. Cambridge, MA: Harvard University Press, 1997.

Rizzini, Carlos. *O livro, o jornal e a tipografia no Brasil, 1500–1822: com um breve estudo geral sobre a informação—meios de comunicação, correio, catequese, ensino, sociedades literárias, Maçonaria, etc*. Rio de Janeiro: Kosmos, 1945.

Rodrigues, Graciela Gonçalves. "As secas na Bahia do século XIX (sociedade e política)." Master's thesis, Universidade Federal da Bahia, 2000.

Rodrigues, Jaime. "Ferro, trabalho e conflito: os africanos livres na Fábrica de Ferro de Ipanema." *História Social* 4–5 (1997–1998): 29–42.

Rodrigues, José Carlos. *The Panama Canal: Its History, Its Political Aspects, and Financial Difficulties*. New York: C. Scribner's Sons, 1885.

Rosas, Suzana Cavani. "Da 'Constituinte Soberana' à 'Conciliação política sobre as bases das reformas': o Partido Liberal em Pernambuco e o Gabinete Paraná de 1853." *Revista de História* (São Paulo) 170 (January–June 2014): 291–316.

Ruy, Affonso. *História da Câmara Municipal da Cidade do Salvador*. 2nd ed. Salvador: Câmara Municipal de Salvador, 1996.

Saba, Roberto. "American Mirror: The United States and the Empire of Brazil in the Age of Emancipation." PhD diss., University of Pennsylvania, 2017.

Sabato, Hilda. *Republics of the New World: The Revolutionary Political Experiment in Nineteenth-Century Latin America*. Princeton, NJ: Princeton University Press, 2018.

Sabato, Hilda, ed. *Ciudadanía política y formación de las naciones*. Mexico City: Fondo de Cultura Económica, 1999.

Sacramento Blake, Augusto Victorino Alves. *Diccionario bibliographico brazileiro*. 7 vols. Rio de Janeiro: Tip. Nacional, 1883–1902.

Salles, Ricardo. "As águas do Niagara: crise da escravidão e o ocaso saquarema." In *O Brasil Imperial*. 3 vols. Edited by Keila Grinberg and Ricardo Salles, 3:39–82. Rio de Janeiro: Civilização Brasileira, 2009.

———. *Guerra do Paraguai: memórias e imagens*. Rio de Janeiro: Biblioteca Nacional, 2003.

Sanders, James. *The Vanguard of the Atlantic World: Creating Modernity, Nation, and Democracy in Nineteenth-Century Latin America*. Durham, NC: Duke University Press, 2014.

Sandroni, Cícero. *180 anos do Jornal do Commercio—1827–2007: de D. Pedro I a Luiz Inácio Lula da Silva*. Rio de Janeiro: Quorum, 2007.

Sant'anna, Benedita de Cássia. *Do* Brasil Ilustrado *(1855–1856) à* Revista Ilustrada *(1876–1898): trajetória da imprensa periódica literária ilustrada fluminense*. Rio de Janeiro: Paço Editorial, 2011.

Santos, Maria Emília Vasconcelos dos. "Os significados dos 13 de maio: a abolição e o imediato pós-abolição para os trabalhadores dos engenhos da Zona da Mata Sul de Pernambuco, 1884–1893." PhD diss., UNICAMP, 2014.

Santos, Mário Márcio de A. *Um homem contra o Império: vida e lutas de Antônio Borges da Fonseca*. Recife: Fundação do Patrimônio Histórico e Artístico de Pernambuco, 1995.

Santos, Martha. "On the Importance of Being Honorable: Masculinity, Survival, and Conflict in the Backlands of Northeast Brazil, Ceará, 1840s–1890." *The Americas* 64, no. 1 (July 2007): 35–57.

Santos, Renata. *A imagem gravada: a gravura no Rio de Janeiro entre 1808–1853*. Rio de Janeiro: Casa da Palavra, 2008.

Schudson, Michael. *Discovering the News: A Social History of American Newspapers*. New York: Basic Books, 1978.

———. "Was There Ever a Public Sphere? If so, When? Reflections on the American Case." In *Habermas and the Public Sphere*. Edited by Craig Calhoun, 143–63. Cambridge, MA: MIT Press, 1992.

Schwarcz, Lilia Moritz. *As barbas do imperador: D. Pedro II, um monarca nos trópicos*. São Paulo: Companhia das Letras, 2003.

———. *Retrato em branco e negro: jornais, escravos e cidadãos em São Paulo no final do século XIX*. São Paulo: Companhia das Letras, 1987.

Schwartz, Stuart B. "Resistance and Accommodation in Eighteenth-Century Brazil: The Slaves' View of Slavery." *Hispanic American Historical Review* 57, no. 1 (February 1977): 69–81.

Schwarz, Roberto. "Autobiografia de Luiz Gama." *Novos Estudos Cebrap* 25 (1989): 136–41.

Secreto, María Verónica, and Giselle Martins Venancio. "Apresentação." In *Cartografias da cidade in(visível): setores populares, cultura escrita, educação e leitura no Rio de Janeiro imperial*. Edited by Giselle Martins Venancio, María Verónica Secreto, and Gladys Sabino Ribeiro, 9–16. Rio de Janeiro: Mauad X and FAPERJ, 2017.

Sena, Consuelo Pondé de. *A imprensa reacionária na Independência:* Sentinella Bahiense. Salvador: Centro de Estudos Baianos, 1983.

Seyferth, Giralda. "The Slave Plantation and Foreign Colonization in Imperial Brazil." *Review, a Journal of the Fernand Braudel Center* 34, no. 4 (2011): 339–87.

Shenkman, Rick. "Here's What Historians Said in Private about Trump's Election." History News Network. January 20, 2017. www.historynewsnetwork.org.

Sigaud, J.-F.-X. *Du climat et des maladies du Brésil: ou, statistique médicale de cet empire*. Paris: Chez Fortin, Masson et Cie., 1844.

Silva, Alberto da Costa e. "Buying and Selling Korans in Nineteenth-Century Rio de Janeiro." In *Rethinking the African Diaspora: The Making of a Black World in the Bight of Benin and Brazil*. Edited by Kristin Mann and Edna G. Bay, 83–90. New York: Frank Cass, 2001.

Silva, Adriana Maria Paulo da. "A escola de Pretextado dos Passos Silva: questões a respeito das práticas de escolarização no mundo escravista." *Revista Brasileira de História da Educação* 4 (July–December 2002): 145–66.

Silva, Ana Cláudia Suriani da, and Sandra Guardini T. Vasconcelos, eds. *Books and Periodicals in Brazil, 1768–1930: A Transatlantic Perspective*. London: Legenda, 2014.

Silva, Antonio de Moraes. *Diccionario da lingua portugueza: recopilado dos vocabularios impressos até agora, e nesta segunda edição novamente emendado, e muito *accrescentado*. Facsimile ed. 2 vols. Rio de Janeiro: Oficinas da S. A. Litho-Tip. Fluminense, 1922 [1813].

Silva, Antonio M. Jackson F. da. "Crise partidária e labirinto político no Brasil império." *Histórica* (São Paulo) 30 (2008). http://www.arquivoestado.sp.gov.br/site/publicacoes/revista_historica.

Silva, Célio Antônio Alcântara. "Capitalismo e escravidão: a imigração confederada para o Brasil." PhD diss., Universidade Estadual de Campinas, 2011.

Silva, Eduardo. *Prince of the People: The Life and Times of a Free Man of Colour*. Translated by Moyra Ashford. London: Verso, 1993.

———. *As queixas do povo*. Rio de Janeiro: Paz e Terra, 1988.

Silva, Ignacio Accioli Cerqueira e. *Memorias historicas e politicas da provincia da Bahia*. 6 vols. Edited by Braz do Amaral. Salvador: Imprensa Official do Estado, 1919–1940 [1835–1836].

[Silva, José Carneiro da]. *Memoria sobre o comercio dos escravos, em que se pretende mostrar que este tráfico é, para eles, antes um bem do que um mal*. Escrita por ***, natural dos Campos dos Goitacazes. Rio de Janeiro: Tip. Imperial e Constitucional de J. Villeneuve, 1838.

Silva, Juremir Machado da. *Raizes do conservadorismo brasileiro: a abolição na imprensa e no imaginário social*. Rio de Janeiro: Civilização Brasileira, 2017.

Silva, Kátia Maria de Carvalho. *O Diario da Bahia e o século XIX*. Rio de Janeiro: Tempo Brasileiro, 1979.

Silva, Lígia Osório. *Terras devolutas e latifúndio: efeitos da lei de 1850*. Campinas: Ed. UNICAMP, 1996.

Silva, Maria Beatriz Nizza da. *Diário Constitucional: um periódico baiano defensor de D. Pedro—1822*. Salvador: EdUFBa, 2011.

———. *A Gazeta do Rio de Janeiro (1808–1822): cultura e sociedade*. Rio de Janeiro: EdUERJ, 2007.

———. *Movimento constitucional e separatismo no Brasil (1821–1823)*. Lisbon: Horizonte, 1988.

———. *A primeira gazeta da Bahia:* Idade d'Ouro do Brazil. Salvador: EdUFBA, 2005.

———. *Semanário Cívico: Bahia, 1821–1823*. Salvador: EdUFBa, 2008.

Silva, Marilene Rosa Nogueira da. *Negro na rua: a nova face da escravidão*. São Paulo: HUCITEC, 1988.

Silva, Rodrigo Fialho. "O universo das letras: debates impressos e mediações culturais—São João d'El-Rey (1827–1829)." In *História urbana: memória, cultura e sociedade*. Edited by Giselle Sanglard, Carlos Eduardo Moreira de Araújo, and José Jorge Siqueira, 49–72. Rio de Janeiro: Editora FGV, 2013.

Silva, Roger Anibal Lambert da. "Em nome da ordem: o *Jornal do Commercio* e as batalhas da abolição." PhD diss., Universidade Federal Fluminense, 2016.

Silva, Susana Serpa. "Emigração legal e clandestina nos Açores de oitocentos (da década de 30 a meados da centúria)." In *Nas duas margens: os portugueses no Brasil*. Edited by Ismênia Martins, Izilda Matos, and Fernando de Sousa, 381–400. Porto: Edições Afrontamento and CEPESE, 2009.

Silva, Wlamir. "'Amáveis patrícias': o *Mentor das Brasileiras* e a construção da identidade da mulher liberal na província de Minas Gerais (1829–1832)." *Revista Brasileira de História* 28, no. 55 (2008): 107–30.

Silveira, Daniela Magalhães da. "O trabalho feminino no espaço doméstico: gênero e classe no *Jornal das Famílias*." *Topoi* 16, no. 31 (July–December 2015): 689–706.

Silveira, Mauro Cesar. *A batalha de papel: a Guerra do Paraguai através da caricatura*. Porto Alegre: L&PM, 1996.

Sirinelli, Jean-François. "As elites culturais." In *Para uma história cultural*. Edited by Jean-Pierre Rioux and Jean-François Sirinelli. Translated by Ana Moura, 259–80. Lisbon: Estampa, 1998.

Sisson, Sebastião Augusto. *Galeria dos brasileiros ilustres: os contemporâneos*. 2nd ed. 2 vols. São Paulo: Livraria Martins Editora, 1948.

Slauter, Will. "The Rise of the Newspaper." In *Making News: The Political Economy of Journalism in Britain and America from the Glorious Revolution to the Internet*. Edited by Richard R. John and Jonathan Silberstein-Loeb, 19–46. New York: Oxford University Press, 2015.

Slenes, Robert. "'Malungu, ngoma vem!': África coberta e descoberta do Brasil." *Revista USP* 12 (1992): 48–67.

Soares, Carlos Eugênio, and Flávio Gomes. "Sedições, haitianismo e conexões no Brasil escravista: outras margens do Atlântico negro." *Novos Estudos Cebrap* 63 (July 2002): 131–44.

Soares, Luiz Carlos. *O "povo de Cam" na capital do Brasil: a escravidão urbana no Rio de Janeiro do século XIX*. Rio de Janeiro: FAPERJ and 7Letras, 2007.

Soares, Marcus Vinícius Nogueira. *A crônica brasileira do século XIX: uma breve história*. São Paulo: Realizações Editora, 2014.

Soares, Pedro Paulo. "A guerra da imagem: iconografia da Guerra do Paraguai na imprensa ilustrada fluminense." Master's thesis, Universidade Federal do Rio de Janeiro, 2009.

Sodré, Nelson Werneck. *História da imprensa no Brasil*. 2nd ed. Rio de Janeiro: Graal, 1977.

Sousa, Octavio Tarquínio de. *História dos fundadores do Império do Brasil*. Vol. 6, *Evaristo da Veiga*. 2nd ed. Rio de Janeiro: José Olympio, 1957.

———. "Tentativa de golpe de Estado de 30 de julho de 1832 (A revolução dos três padres)." In *Três golpes de estado*, 82–106. Belo Horizonte: Itatiaia; São Paulo: EdUSP, 1988.

Souza, Christiane Laidler de. "Mentalidade escravista e abolicionismo entre os letrados da Corte (1808–1850)." Master's thesis, Universidade Federal Fluminense, 1994.

Souza, Felipe Azevedo e. *O eleitorado imperial em reforma*. Recife: FUNDAJ, 2014.
Souza, Flavia Fernandes de, and Rosane dos Santos Torres. "Liberdade e instrução: projetos e iniciativas abolicionistas para a educação popular (Rio de Janeiro, década de 1880)." In *Os intelectuais e a nação: educação, saúde e a construção de um Brasil moderno*. Edited by Karoline Carula, Magali Gouveia Engel, and Maria Letícia Corrêa, 49–83. Rio de Janeiro: ContraCapa, 2013.
Souza, Iara Lis Carvalho. *Pátria coroada: o Brasil como corpo político autônomo, 1780–1831*. São Paulo: EdUNESP, 1998.
Souza, Roberto Acízelo de. *O império da eloquência: retórica e poética no Brasil oitocentista*. Rio de Janeiro: EdUERJ and EdUFF, 1999.
Strzoda, Michelle, ed. *O Rio de Joaquim Manoel de Macedo: jornalismo e literatura no século XIX*. Rio de Janeiro: Casa da Palavra, 2010.
Studart, Guilherme, Baron of. *Catalogo dos jornaes de grande e pequeno formato publicados no Ceará*. Fortaleza: Typ. Minerva de Assis Bezerra, 1904.
Syracuse University. *Alumni Record and General Catalogue of Syracuse University, 1872–1910*. Syracuse, 1911.
Taunay, Carlos Augusto. *Manual do agricultor brasileiro*. Edited by Rafael Bivar de Marquese. São Paulo: Companhia das Letras, 2001 [1839].
Telles, Angela da Motta. *Desenhando a nação: revistas ilustradas do Rio de Janeiro e Buenos Aires nas décadas de 1860–1870*. Rio de Janeiro: FUNAG, 2010.
Thérenty, Marie-Ève. "La crónica en el periódico francés del siglo XIX: caso irónico, rúbrica mediática o taller literario." *Boletín* 9, no. 1–2 (2006): 131–60.
———. *La littérature au quotidien: poétiques journalistiques au XIXe siècle*. Paris: Seuil, 2007.
———. "Pour une histoire littéraire de la presse au XIXe siècle." *Revue d'histoire littéraire de la France* 103, no. 3 (2003): 625–35.
———. "Vies drôles et 'scalps de puce': des microformes dans les quotidiens à la Belle Époque." *Études Françaises* 44, no. 3 (2008): 57–67.
Tinhorão, José Ramos. *A imprensa carnavalesca no Brasil: um panorama da linguagem cômica*. São Paulo: Hedra, 2000.
Tinoco, Antonio Luiz Ferreira. *Codigo Criminal do Imperio do Brazil annotado*. Facsimile ed. Brasília: Senado Federal, 2003 [1886].
Toplin, Robert Brent. *The Abolition of Slavery in Brazil*. New York: Atheneum, 1972.
Toral, André Amaral. *Imagens em desordem: a iconografia da Guerra do Paraguai (1864–1870)*. São Paulo: Humanitas, 2001.
Torre, Laura Beatriz de la, ed. *Empresa y cultura en tinta y papel: 1800–1860*. Mexico City: Instituto de Investigaciones Dr. José María Luis Mora, 2001.
Torres, João N., and Alfredo de Carvalho. *Annaes da imprensa da Bahia*. Salvador: Typ. Bahianna de Cincinnato Melchiades, 1911.
Trumper, Camilo. *Ephemeral Histories: Public Art, Politics and the Struggle for the Street in Chile*. Berkeley: University of California Press, 2016.

University of Cincinnati. *Catalogue of the Academic Department, 1890–1891*. Cincinnati: Office of the University, 1891.
Unzueta, Fernando. "Periódicos y formación nacional: Bolivia en sus primeros años." *Latin American Research Review* 35, no. 2 (2000): 35–72.
Uribe-Uran, Victor. "The Birth of a Public Sphere in Latin America during the Age of Revolution." *Comparative Studies in Society and History* 42, no. 2 (April 2000): 425–57.
Vaillant, Alain. "A crônica no século XIX: as metamorfoses midiáticas de um gênero literário." *Revista da ANPOLL*, 38 (2015): 186–94.
Vargas, Tulio. *O conselheiro Zacarias (1815–1877)*. 2nd rev. ed. Curitiba: Juruá, 2007.
Vasconcelos, Bernardo Pereira. *Relatório da Repartição dos Negócios do Império*. Rio de Janeiro: Tip. Nacional, 1838.
Venancio, Giselle Martins, María Verónica Secreto, and Gladys Sabino Ribeiro, eds. *Cartografias da cidade in(visível): setores populares, cultura escrita, educação e leitura no Rio de Janeiro imperial*. Rio de Janeiro: Mauad X and FAPERJ, 2017.
Vianna, Hélio. *Contribuição à história da imprensa brasileira (1812–1869)*. Rio de Janeiro: Imprensa Nacional, 1945.
———. *D. Pedro I jornalista*. São Paulo: Melhoramentos, 1967.
Vicuña Mackenna, Benjamin. *Paginas de mi diario durante tres años de viaje, 1853–1854–1855*. 2 vols. Santiago: Universidad de Chile [1936].
Vieira, David Gueiros. *O protestantismo, a maçonaria e a questão religiosa no Brasil*. Brasília: Editora Universidade de Brasília, 1980.
Vitorino, Artur José Renda. "Os sonhos dos tipógrafos na corte imperial brasileira." In *Culturas de classe: identidade e diversidade na formação do operariado*. Edited by Claudio Henrique de Moraes Batalha, Fernando Teixeira da Silva, and Alexandre Fortes, 187–203. Campinas: Editora da UNICAMP, 2004.
Walker, Charles. "'La orgia periodística': prensa y cultura politica en el Cuzco durante la joven república." *Revista de Indias* 61, no. 221 (March 2001): 7–26.
Warner, Michael. *The Letters of the Republic: Publication and the Public Sphere in Eighteenth-Century America*. Cambridge, MA: Harvard University Press, 1990.
Weber, Johannes. "Strassburg, 1605: The Origins of the Newspaper in Europe." *German History* 24, no. 3 (2006): 387–412.
Weinstein, Barbara. "The Decline of the Progressive Planter and the Rise of the Subaltern Agent: Shifting Narratives of Slave Emancipation in Brazil." In *Reclaiming the Political in Latin American History*. Edited by Gilbert M. Joseph, 81–101. Durham, NC: Duke University Press, 2001.
Wendlin, Greta. "The Prostitute's Voice in the Public Eye: Police Tactics of Security and Discipline Within Victorian Journalism." *Communication and Critical/Cultural Studies* 7, no. 1 (March 2010): 53–69.
Wetherell, James. *Brazil: Stray Notes from Bahia*. Edited by William Hadfield. Liverpool: Webb & Hunt, 1860.

Whipple, Pablo. *La gente decente de Lima y su resistencia al orden republicana: jerarquías sociales, prensa y sistema judicial durante el siglo XIX*. Lima: Instituto de Estudios Peruanos and Centro de Investigaciones Diego Barras Arano, 2013.
Wildberger, Arnold. *Os presidentes da Provincia da Bahia*. Salvador: Tip. Beneditina, 1942.
Wissenbach, Maria Cristina Cortez. "Cartas, procurações, escapulários e patuás: os múltiplos significados da escrita entre os escravos e forros na sociedade oitocentista brasileira." *Revista Brasileira de História da Educação* 4 (2002): 103–22.
———. "Letramento e escolas." In *Dicionário da escravidão e liberdade*. Edited by Lilia M. Schwarcz and Flávio Gomes, 292–97. São Paulo: Companhia das Letras, 2018.
Wisser, William M. "Rhetoric and Riot in Rio de Janeiro, 1827–1831." PhD diss., University of North Carolina at Chapel Hill, 2006.
Wood, Marcus. *Black Milk: Imagining Slavery in the Visual Cultures of Brazil and America*. Oxford: Oxford University Press, 2013.
Wright, Frances. *Views of Society and Manners in America*. New York: E. Bliss & E. White, 1821.
Wright, Gavin. *Old South, New South: Revolutions in the Southern Economy Since the Civil War*. Baton Rouge: Louisiana State University Press, 1986.
Youssef, Alain El. *Imprensa e escravidão: política e tráfico negreiro no Império do Brasil (Rio de Janeiro, 1822–1850)*. São Paulo: Intermeios and FAPESP, 2016.
Zeldin, Theodore. *France, 1848–1945*. Vol. 2, *Intellect, Taste, and Anxiety*. Oxford: University of Oxford Press, 1977.
Zeltsman, Corinna. "Defining Responsibility: Printers, Politics, and the Law in Early Republican Mexico City." *Hispanic American Historical Review* 98, no. 2 (May 2018): 189–222.

CONTRIBUTORS

MARCELLO BASILE holds a doctorate in social history from the Universidade Federal do Rio de Janeiro and is an associate professor of Brazilian history at the Universidade Federal Rural do Rio de Janeiro. He is the author of more than fifty publications, including *Ezequiel Corrêa dos Santos: um jacobino na Corte imperial* (FGV Editora, 2001) and, with José Murilo de Carvalho and Lúcia Bastos, *Às armas, cidadãos! Panfletos manuscritos da Independência do Brasil (1820–1823)* (Companhia das Letras, 2012) and *Guerra literária: panfletos da Independência (1820–1823)* (Editora da Universidade Federal de Minas Gerais, 2014).

CELSO THOMAS CASTILHO is an associate professor of history at Vanderbilt University. His research focuses on the political, cultural, and literary histories of slavery and abolition in Brazil and comparatively. His current book is about the circulation of *Uncle Tom's Cabin* in Latin America. In 2016, he published *Slave Emancipation and Transformations of Brazilian Political Citizenship* (Pittsburgh, 2016), and more recently coedited a special issue of *Historia Mexicana* (October 2019) titled "Los ecos atlánticos de las aboliciones hispanoamericanas."

TERESA CRIBELLI is an associate professor of history at the University of Alabama. She is the author of *Industrial Forests and Mechanical Marvels: Modernization in Nineteenth-Century Brazil* (Cambridge University Press, 2016). Her present research follows two lines of inquiry: readers' letters and the newspaper press, and a comparison of narratives of progress in nineteenth-century Brazil and the United States. She is a member of the Rede Proprietas, organized by Márcia Motta at the Universidade Federal Fluminense. She offers courses on Latin America, comparative frontiers in the Americas, and environmental history.

ZEPHYR FRANK is professor of history at Stanford University and the founding director of the Stanford Center for Spatial and Textual Analysis (CESTA). His research interests focus on Brazilian social and cultural history, the study of wealth and inequality, and the digital humanities. He is the author of *Dutra's World: Wealth and Family in Nineteenth-Century Rio de Janeiro* (University of New Mexico Press, 2004) and *Reading Rio de Janeiro: Literature and Society in the Nineteenth Century* (Stanford University Press, 2016).

RODRIGO CAMARGO DE GODOI is a professor of history at UNICAMP. His research focuses on Brazilian press culture in the nineteenth century. He is the author of *Francisco de Paula Brito: A Black Publisher in Imperial Brazil* (Vanderbilt University Press, 2020), a translation of his *Um editor no Império: Francisco de Paulo Brito, 1809–1861* (EdUSP, 2016). He has also edited *O Futuro* (Editora da UNICAMP, 2014), a collection of chronicles by Machado de Assis.

HENDRIK KRAAY is a professor of history at the University of Calgary. He is the author of *Race, State, and Armed Forces in Independence-Era Brazil: Bahia, 1790s–1840s* (Stanford University Press, 2001), *Days of National Festivity in Rio de Janeiro, Brazil, 1823–1889* (Stanford University Press, 2013), and *Bahia's Independence: Popular Politics and Patriotic Festival in Salvador, Brazil, 1824–1900* (McGill-Queen's University Press, 2019). His research has been funded by the Social Sciences and Humanities Research Council (Canada).

LUDMILA DE SOUZA MAIA received her dual PhD in history from Rice University and from the Universidade Estadual de Campinas (UNICAMP). She has been a postdoctoral fellow at the Rice University history department. Her research focuses on female writers in the nineteenth-century Atlantic World, analyzing the relation between gender, literature, and press. Her articles have appeared in the *Revista Brasileira de História*, *Cadernos Pagu*, *Revista de História da USP*, and *Varia História*. She currently teaches global history at the American School of Campinas.

MATTHEW NESTLER is a PhD candidate in history at Stanford University. He is currently writing his dissertation, provisionally titled "Inflation and Inequality in Urban Brazil, 1944–1994." He received a BA in Spanish Language and Literature from Wesleyan University, an MA in the Social Sciences (MAPSS) from the University of Chicago, and an MA in Political Science from Stanford University.

JOSÉ JUAN PÉREZ MELÉNDEZ is a historian of Latin America and the Caribbean who specializes on nineteenth-century Brazil. He has held a Max Weber Fellowship at the European University Institute and serves as an assistant professor at the University of California, Davis. His research examines governmental capacity-building in postindependent Latin America, and has received support from the Fulbright-Hays Program and the American Council of Learned Societies. His current book manuscript focuses on the role played by migrations and subsidized colonization schemes in the development of the early Brazilian Empire.

ARNALDO LUCAS PIRES JUNIOR received his PhD from the Universidade Federal do Rio de Janeiro in 2019. He holds an MA in comparative history from that university and a BA in history and social science education from the Universidade Federal Fluminense. His research interests are in the comparative history of Brazil and the Americas, with special attention to state formation, military recruitment, and the role of the press in shaping public opinion in these processes. He is the author of *A imprensa em guerra: caricaturas e a Guerra do Paraguai* (Multifoco, 2018).

ROBERTO SABA received his BA (2007) and MA (2010) in history from the Universidade de São Paulo. In 2017, he received his PhD from the University of Pennsylvania. He subsequently held the Hench Postdoctoral Fellowship at the American Antiquarian Society and the Henry G. Fairbanks Visiting Humanities Scholar-in-Residence position at Saint Michael's College. He is currently an assistant professor of American Studies at Wesleyan University. He has published articles in the United States and Brazil, including a study of Confederate migration to Brazil after the American Civil War for *Traversea: Journal of Transatlantic History*.

ALAIN EL YOUSSEF holds a PhD (2019) from the University of São Paulo. He specializes in the study of slavery, the slave trade, and abolition in nineteenth-century Brazil. He is a member of the Laboratório de Estudos Sobre o Brasil e o Sistema Mundial (Lab-Mundi/USP), and coordinates the research group, Capital, State, and Labor: The Crisis of Black Slavery in the Long Nineteenth Century. He is the author of *Imprensa e escravidão: política e tráfico negreiro no Império do Brasil, Rio de Janeiro (1822–1850)* (Intermeios/FAPESP, 2016) and is currently writing a book on Brazilian abolition in global context.

INDEX

Page numbers in *italic* text indicate illustrations.

abolitionist movement, 59–60, 80, 81, 161, 242, 248, 252
Additional Act (1834), 61–62, 66
advertisements. *See* classified advertisements
Africans, liberated, 78–79, 86
Agostini, Ângelo, 13, 22, 161, 162, 170–71, *171*, 172
Alencar, José de, 115, 119, 121–22, 245–46
Almeida, Cipriano José Barata de, 6, 7
Almeida, Miguel Calmon du Pin e (Marquis of Abrantes), 68, 95–96, 101, 104–5, 106, 197
Anglo-Brazilian anti-slave trade treaty (1826-1827), 57, 65
Anglo-Brazilian Times, The, 107
apedidos: ad hominem attacks, 206–7; Announcements, 209, 213–14; anonymity in, 206–7, 208, 209–10, *210*, 212–13; Complaints, 209; humor in, 207–8; illiteracy, and print consumption, 201–2; letters to the editor (*Correspondências*), distinguished from, 196, 203–4; medical announcements, 213–14, 216; *mofinas*, 202, 207, 209; and oral culture, 202–3; pay-to-print, practice of, 196, 199–200, 204–5, 207, 216; Praise and Gratitude, 209, 214–15; prices for printing, 204–6; Publicações a Pedido section, 196, 197, 200, 203–4, 206, 215–16; public letters, 198–201; public opinion, concept of, 201–2,
211–13; *remitidos*, 196–97; selection criteria, for publication, 206–7, 208; signatories, 209–10, *210*; subject matter, 197, 207–10, 213–15. *See also Jornal do Commercio*
Astreia, 7, 8, 93
Aurora Brasileira, 232–33
Aurora Brasileira, 234–35, 236
Aurora Fluminense, 6, 44, 45, 56, 67, 101
Azambuja, José Bonifácio Nascentes de, 182, 186, 188, 190

Bahian samba (partido-alto) music, 85
Baquaqua, Mahommah Gardo, 79
Barros, Domingos Borges de (Viscount of Pedra Branca), 105
Bazar Volante, 160–61, 162, 166–69, *168*
Biblioteca Nacional, 11, 35–36
Biografias de alguns poetas e homens ilustres da província de Pernambuco (Biographies of some poets and illustrious men from the province of Pernambuco, 1856-1859), 252–53
Bivar, Diogo Soares da Silva, 97, 100, 102, 103
Black press: Black abolitionism in, 251–52; Black newspapers, 6, 257; Castro, Apulco de, 8, 22; citizenship and rights claiming, 23, 250; Santana, Aristides Ricardo de, 8, 22. *See also* Brito, Francisco de Paula; Collaço, Felipe Neri; *Homem, O*
Bocaiuva, Quintino, 84, 107
Brito, Francisco de Paula, 11, 40, 78–79

Camarão, Felipe, 255
Caramuru, O, 45–46, 56
Caramurus, 39, 43, 44, 56, 61–62
cartoonists and caricaturists, 161, 162, 172
cartoons. *See* magazines, illustrated satirical
Carvalho, José da Costa, 94
Casa de Correção, 78–79
Castro, Apulco de, 8, 22
censorship, 5–6, 158
census data, 14, 15–18, *16*, *17*, 47, 81–82, 155
Charivari Nacional, 157, 158
classified advertisements: addresses appearing in, analysis of, 148–49; brokers, property, 145–47; efficacy of, 134–35, 143–45; for enslaved persons, 77, 135–37, 138, 143, 248; landlords placing, 147–48; language of, 150–51; literacy rates, estimating from, 82–83, *83*; and markets, relationship between, 132–36; for rent and sale in newspapers, analysis, 137–42, *139*, *140*, *141*. See also *Diário do Rio de Janeiro*; *Jornal do Commercio*; markets for property rentals and sales; newspapers
coffee production, Brazilian, 62–63, *63*, 221, 237. See also *Novo Mundo, O*
Collaço, Felipe Neri: Black abolitionism, promoting, 251–52; early life and career, 242–44; "Galeria de homens de cor ilustres" (Gallery of illustrious men of color), 242, 244–45, 249, 252–57; *Homem, O*, founding of, 248–49; "man of color," self-presentation as, 243–44; racial discrimination, confronting, 242, 249–51. *See also* Black press; *Homem, O*
colonization: Associação Central de Colonização, 106; Azoreans, 90, 97, 100, 101; *colonos* (immigrant settlers), 90, 91, 92, 97, 100–102, 105, 106; Companhia do Mucury, 106; epidemic crisis (*colonos canarinos* affair), 98–99; newspapers, coverage of, 90–92, 95, 96, 97–98, 103–7; organizing companies, 90–91, 92, 95–99, 104, 106; political response, 91, 93–94, 96–97; press coverage of foreign examples, 93–95, 96; projects, criticisms of, 92, 97–99; and slave trade, 99–100; statute, *prestação de serviços* (September 13, 1830), 101. *See also* Almeida, Miguel Calmon du Pin e (Marquis of Abrantes); Bivar, Diogo Soares da Silva; Sociedade Promotora de Colonização
Conciliador, O, 6, 48
Conde d'Eu, 208
Conservative Party, 12, 39, 55, 176, 179, 190–91
Constituent Assembly (1823), 6, 37, 43, 104
Correio da Tarde, 12, 204
Correio do Recife, 243
Correio Mercantil (Rio de Janeiro), 121, 178, 179, 180, 186, 187–88, 203
Correio Mercantil (Salvador), 105, 203
Correio Oficial, 68, 94, 96
correspondence, provincial: 1868 letters, characteristics of, 178–82, *181*; in *Correio Mercantil* (Rio de Janeiro), 179; correspondents, 175–76, 182–85, 186–87; in *Diário do Povo*, 180; in *Diário do Rio de Janeiro*, 179–80; editing, 186; historical significance of, 175–76, 191–92; in *Jornal do Commercio*, 178–79; politics, reporting on, 176, 178–79, 183–84, 188–91; private letters (*cartas particulares*), overview, 177–78; readers, 187–88; steamship packets and mail service, 184–86, *185*

See also Conservative Party; Liberal Party; Paraguayan War

Correspondências (letters to the editor), 196, 203–4

crônicas: "Aquarelas," 124; "Balas de Estalo," 125–26; Belona, 122–23; "Crônica dos Salões," 122–23; "Crônicas do Dr. Semana," 123–24; dialogical writing style, 122; Dr. Semana (multiple authors), 123–24, 157–58; *feuilleton*, 22, 113, 114–15, 119–20; fictional elements in, 113, 122, 124–25, 126, 128–29; Folhazinha (section title, in *O Cronista*), 120; *folhazinha* (section, like *feuilleton*), 120; *folhetim* (*folhetins*, plural), 19, 20, 22, 115, 120, 121, 122; Folhetim (section title, in *Jornal do Commercio*), 115; "Gazeta de Holanda," 111, 112, 126–29; genre, emergence as, 111–13, 119–22; genre origins, French, 113–15; Malvolio, 111–12, 126–29; modernization, effects on, 125–26; newspapers, mutual dependency between, 112, 118–19, 124–25, 126, 128, 129; periodicals, non-mainstream, appearances in, 122; pseudonyms, importance of, 118–19, 123–24; scholarship on, 22, 115–19; series, characteristics, 118, 126; Variedades, 114–15. *See also* Alencar, José de; Machado de Assis, Joaquim Maria

Cronista, O, 68, 98–99, 103–4, 119–20

cronistas, 112, 115, 118, 122, 129, 187

Dantas, Manuel Pinto de Sousa, 84, *84*, 189, 190

Diário da Bahia, 104, 180, 186, 189

Diário de Notícias, 10, 204–5

Diário de Pernambuco, 10–11, 18, 181, 203, 210, 243, 253

Diário do Povo, 100–101, 180

Diário do Rio de Janeiro: circulation, 46; classified advertisements, estimating literacy rates from, 82–83, *83*; classified advertisements, for property, 137; colonization, content related to, 12, 90, 97, 99–100, 102, 105, 107; content, types of, 8–9, 41, 120; correspondents' letters, 179–81, *181*, 183, 184, 186, 187, 190; printing press (Tipografia do *Diário*), 38, 40, 158; Publicações a Pedido section, 203

Diário do Vintém, 82, 97

Dias, Henrique, 255

Dutch occupation, 254–55

editors, 6, 34, 40, 42–43

education, for enslaved persons, 80–81

Emperrados. *See* Conservative Party

enslaved persons: African Muslims, 72; autobiographies, 79–80; in classified advertisements, 77, 135–37, 138, 143, 248; education, opportunities and restrictions, 80–81; literacy, 74, 82–83, *83*; literacy, as challenge to slave system, 72, *73*, 80, 83–86, *84*; press, appearances in, 73, *73*, 77; print materials, consumption of, 74, 85–86, 202; print shops, working in, 74, 77–78, 202; Theodoro (print shop worker), 74–77; uprisings, 66, 72, 73, 84–85. *See also* Africans, liberated; Black press; oral culture

Espada da Justiça, 2, 11

Exaltados, 38, 39, 40, 42, 44, 56, 60–62

Faria, Cândido Aragonês, 162

Farol Paulistano, O, 93–94

Feijó, Diogo Antonio, 58, 60–62, 63–65, 66, 67–68

Fleiuss, Henrique, 22, 159, 160, 161, 166–67, 172
Floresta, Nísia, 42
Fluminense, O, 65, 67
Fonseca, Antônio Borges da, 6, 8
France: collective biographies published in, 244; literary influence on Brazil, 113–15, 119–20, 150; public letters, 198–99
free Blacks, 80–81
free population of color, 15, 17, 82
Free Womb Law (1871), 81, 226, 235

"Galeria de homens de cor ilustres" (Gallery of illustrious men of color), 242, 244–45, 249, 252–57
Galeria dos brasileiros ilustres: os contemporâneos (Gallery of illustrious Brazilians: The contemporaries), 244–48
Gama, Luiz, 79–80
"Gazeta de Holanda," 111, 112, 126–29
Gazeta de Notícias, 10, 12, 21, 111, 125, 126, 191
Gazeta do Brasil, 46, 47
Gazeta do Rio de Janeiro, 1, 5, 33
Gomes, Carlos, 255–56
Great Britain: abolition, and anti-British press coverage, 67, 69; antislavery press subsidies, 12; colonies, Upper and Lower Canada, 94; public letters, 199, 200; slave-trade policing, 55, 57, 62, 64, 65

Hartt, Charles Frederick, 230, 231
Heaton, George, 78, 79
Hemeroteca Digital Brasileira (HDB), 23–24, 115, 138–39, 148, 151
Historical Liberals, 176–77, 180
Homem, O: Black abolitionism in, 251–52; Black press, 243–44;
"Galeria de homens de cor ilustres" (Gallery of illustrious men of color), 242, 244–45, 249, 252–57; publication, racially-repressive context for, 248–49; racial discrimination, confronting, 242, 249–51. *See also* Black press; Collaço, Felipe Neri
Homem e a América, O, 46–47

Idade de Ouro do Brazil, 5, 97
Imperial Library, 14, 19, 77
Imprensa Ituana, 84, *84*

Jornal da Bahia, 12, 14, 184, 189
Jornal das Senhoras, 9, 122–23, 156–57
Jornal do Commercio: advertisements, 137–42, *139*, *140*, *141*, 144, 146, 149; circulation, 13, 21, 41, 46, 178; content, types of, 8–9, 115, 120, 178; correspondents' letters, 178–79; cost, 18; economics of publishing, 13, 178, 204, 205, 215–16; founding, 3, 98; politics, partisan neutrality on, 178–79, 208; private letters (*cartas particulares*), 177–78; Publicações a Pedido section, 196, 197, 203, 204, 205; slave labor, 76, 77–78; slave trade, discussion in, 66, 67. *See also* apedidos; classified advertisements; correspondence, provincial; markets for property rentals and sales
journalism, 6, 10, 12–13, 34, 164. *See also* crônicas; magazines, illustrated satirical; newspapers; press, Brazilian
journalists, 3, 10, 23, 34, 42, 45, 49

Lanterna Mágica, 157–58
Leão, Honório Hermeto Carneiro, 61, 62, 65
letters to the editor (*Correspondências*), 196, 203–4

Liberal Party, 39, 44, 177, 180
Lima, José Custódio Alves de, 234–36
Lima, Pedro de Araújo (Marquis of Olinda), 62, 68, 91, 97, 104, 105, 106
Lima e Silva, Luiz Alves de (Marquis, later Duke of Caxias), 176, 179
Lisboa, José da Silva (Baron, later Viscount of Cairu), 43
literacy: as challenge to slave system, 72, 73, 80, 83–86, *84*; estimating rates from classified advertisements, 82–83, *83*; rates, in Brazil, 14–18, *16*, *17*, 47–48, 72, 81–82, 155; and schools, 80–81. *See also* oral culture
lithograph shops, 78
Lobo, Elias Álvares, 255–56

Macedo, Joaquim Manuel de, 2, 150
Machado de Assis, Joaquim Maria, 21, 111, 115–17, 119, 124, 126–28, 246
magazines, illustrated satirical: "A Homeopathic Coachman," *166*, 166–67; cartoons (caricatures), satirical, emergence of, 154, 155, 172; circulation, *163*; cost, 18–19, 163–64; economics of publishing, 11, 158–59, 161, 163, 172; fictional characters (*personagens-símbolo*), 157–58; "His Majesty Is Traveling," *168*, 169–70; humor, use of, 159–60, 165–70, *166*, *168*; layout, 162–63; magazines, illustrated variety, as origin for, 154, 155, 156–57, 172; Paraguayan War, in cartoons, 170–71, *171*; provincial, 11, 155, 161–62; "Retrospective Mirrors," 167–69, *168*; "The Little Marshals of Ouvidor Street," 170–71, *171*; and visual culture, 10, 154–55, 164–65. *See also* Agostini, Ângelo; Fleiuss, Henrique; Mill, Joseph; *Semana Ilustrada*

Malê Rebellion, 72
Malvolio, 111–12, 126–29
manuscript texts, 3, 4, 5–6, 47, 48
Marinho, Joaquim Saldanha, 107, 179, 231
markets for property rentals and sales: addresses in classified advertisements, analysis of, 148–49; brokers, property, 145–47; and classified advertisements, relationship between, 132–36; classified advertisements for rent and sale, analysis of, 137–42, *139*, *140*, *141*; estate inventories, 136, 142; frames of reference for, 132–34; landlords, 147–48; language of classified advertisements, 150–51. *See also* classified advertisements
Martins, Francisco Gonçalves (Baron of São Lourenço), 184, 189, 191
Martins Pena, Luiz Carlos, 121
Melo, Antônio Joaquim de, 252–53
Memórias do sobrinho do meu tio (Memoirs of my uncle's nephew, 1867–1868), 2
Memória sobre o estabelecimento d'uma Companhia de colonisação (1835, Memoir on the establishment of a colonization company), 95
Mequetrefe, O, 162, *168*, 169–70
migrant trade. *See* colonization
Mill, Joseph, 160, 162, 167, *168*, 169, 172
Moderados, 38, 39, 56, 58–62, 63, 65–66. *See also* Feijó, Diogo Antonio; Veiga, Evaristo Ferreira da
Montezuma, Francisco Gê de Acaiaba de (Viscount of Jequitinhonha), 105, 247
"Moro na Roça," 85–86
Mosquito, O, 82
Mougenot, R.A., 76
Mulher do Simplício, A, 46

Museu Universal: Jornal das Famílias Brasileiras, 41, 156, 157

newsboys, 10, 18, 19, 164, 202
newspapers: charging to print content, practice of, 199–200; circulation, 13–14; *commercial*, 41; content included in, 8–9, 41, 50, 112; cost, 18–19, 35; growth in, 33, 35–40, *36*, *37*, *39*, 55–56, *56*; illiteracy, and print consumption, 201–2; in manuscript form, 3, 5–6, 48; national communities, creation of, 4–5, 14; "new journalism," 10, 12–13; political dictionaries, 50; politics, engagement with, 33, 34–35, 37, 38, 39, 40; profitability, 12–13, 196–97, 199–200; provincial, 10–11, 13, 33, *36*, 37; public opinion, concept of, 45, 74, 201–2, 211–13; scholarship on, overview, 21–24; subscribers, characteristics of, 45–47, *46*; subventions and subsidies, 11–12; technology, effects of, 21, 125, 184–85. *See also* apedidos; classified advertisements; correspondence, provincial; crônicas; markets for property rentals and sales
Noronha, Juana Paula Manso de, 9, 156
Nova Luz Brasileira, 44, 50, 56
Novo Mundo, O, 223–28

Oeste Paulista region, 221–22, 228–30, 235–36, 237–38
oral culture: and the press, 18, 19, 47, 48, 49–50, 74, 199; reading aloud, 6, 19, 20, 47–48, 83–86, *84*, 202–3
Ottoni, Teófilo, 106

País, O, 13, 18, 21, 84, *84*, 191, 202–3
pamphlets (*papelinhos*), 4, 5, 33, 40, 48, 198

Paraguayan War, 170–71, *171*, 176
pardos (mixed-race persons), 80–81, 244, 255
pasquins (small-format newspapers), 9, 35
Pedro I (Emperor), 5, 6, 36–38, *37*, 43, 55, 93
Pedro II (Emperor), 7, 38–39, *168*, 169–70, 176, 220, 246–47
Pereira, Lafaiete Rodrigues, 180
periodicals. *See* magazines, illustrated satirical; manuscript texts; newspapers; pamphlets (*papelinhos*)
periodicals, Brazilian, published in the United States. *See Aurora Brasileira*; *Aurora Braziliera*; Lima, José Custódio Alves de; *Novo Mundo, O*; Oeste Paulista region; Rodrigues, José Carlos; United States of America
Picot, François Antoine, 76–77
Pinheiro, Rafael Bordalo, 162
Plancher, Pedro (Pierre), 38, 76
political associations, 40, 55–56, *56*
Pontes, Felisberto Caldeira Brant (Marquis of Barbacena), 57, 65, 105
press, Brazilian: audience for, 21, 48, 50, 201; growth of, 8–11, 35–40, *36*, *37*, *39*; publishing, nature of, 34–35; rhetoric, political, 48–50. *See also* crônicas; literacy; magazines, illustrated satirical; newspapers; oral culture; press freedom; printing presses; print shops
press freedom, 5–8, 42, 120
press law of September 20, 1830, 6–7, 42
printing presses: equipment and supplies, 78; establishment in Brazil, 33, 36–37, 38, 40, 77, 201; types, physical, 20, 34
print shops: 1844 tax decree, 79; enslaved persons, employed in, 77–78,

86, 202; liberated Africans, employed in, 78–79; and print culture, 74, 83–86; Theodoro (enslaved print shop worker), 74–77; workers, 20, 77, 78
private letters (*cartas particulares*), 177–78
proclamations, public (*bandos*), 48
Progressista Party, 39, 176–77
property rentals and sales. *See* markets for property rentals and sales
Provincia, A, 249
public letters, 198–201
public opinion, 45, 74, 201–2, 211–13
public sphere: concept of, 4, 18; and the press, 6, 50–51, 82, 154–55, 175–76, 186, 188
publishers, 34

Queirós, Eusébio de, 245

Radical Liberals. *See* Exaltados
railroads, 14, 21, 125, 235
reader correspondence. *See* public letters
reading aloud, 6, 19, 20, 47–48, 83–86, *84*, 202–3
Rebouças, Antônio Pereira, 247, 253
Recife, 243, 246, 248
Regresso, 39, 50–51, 65–66, 67–69
Rensburg, Eduardo, 78, 160
reporters, 12
Republican Manifesto (1870), 177, 180
Restauradores. *See* Caramurus
Revista Ilustrada, 13, 18–19, 83–84, *84*, 161, 162, 172
Revista Industrial, 228–29
Revista Popular Brasileira, 206
Rio de Janeiro: literacy rate, *16*; newspapers, characteristics of, 35–36; newspapers, *commercial*, 41; periodical press, growth of, 35–36, *37*, 37–38, *39*, 39–40; printing presses, 33, 38; publishing trade, role in, 33–34; schools, 80–81; Sociedade Defensora da Liberdade e Independência Nacional, 44, 46, 56; Sociedade Federal Fluminense, 44, 56. *See also Diário do Rio de Janeiro*; *Gazeta do Rio de Janeiro*; *Jornal do Commercio*; newspapers
Rocha, Antônio Ladislau Figueiredo, 189, 190
Rocha, Justiniano José da, 12, 68, 98, 103–4, 107, 119–20
Rodrigues, José Carlos: agriculture, modernization, 226–27, *227*, 229; *Aurora Brasileira*, 232–33; capitalists, corporate, views on, 223–24; career, after leaving the United States, 237; Cornell University for Brazilian students, promotion of, 230–34; Emancipation, views on, 224–26; free labor, campaign for, 224–25, 226, 229; Instituto do Novo Mundo, 229–30; *Novo Mundo, O*, 223–28; Novo Mundo Association, 228; *Revista Industrial*, 228–29; youth and early career, 222–23

Saldanha, José da Natividade, 253–54
Santana, Aristides Ricardo de, 8, 22
Santana plantation uprising, 73–74
Santos, Ezequiel Corrêa dos, 6, 43, 44–45
Semana Ilustrada: "Crônicas do Dr. Semana," 123–24, 157–58; finances, 159; printing press, establishment of, 172; as the standard for illustrated satirical magazines, 159–61; "Um bom criado malcriado," 72, *73*
Sete d'Abril, O, 61, 66–67, 68, 96

Sigaud, Joseph François Xavier, 76, 98
Silva, Ernesto Augusto de Souza e, 160
Silva, Pretextato dos Passos, 81
Sisson, Sébastien, 244–48
slaves. *See* enslaved persons
slave trade: Anglo-Brazilian treaty against (1826-1827), 57, 65; coffee production, effects on, 62–63; "Do tráfico dos pretos Africanos" (On the African slave trade), 63–65; press debates, 54–55, 58–59, 67–70; prohibition of (law of November 7, 1831), 57–58, 59, 63, 64, 66, 99; volume of, 57, *57*, 58, 60, 69. *See also* Caramurus; Exaltados; Great Britain; Moderados; Regresso
Sociedade Promotora de Colonização, 91, 92, 94, 96–99, 100, 102–6. *See also* colonization
Souza, Antonio Francisco de Paula, 220
steamship lines, 14, 21, 176, 184–86, 220

Tavares Bastos, Aureliano Cândido, 180, 220, 227
telegraph networks, 21, 125, 184
Torres, Joaquim José Rodrigues (Viscount of Itaboraí), 62, 65, 68, 176

United States of America: Brazilian students, pursuing higher education in, 230–34; Civil War, effects on Brazil, 220–22; coffee tariffs, 62; collective biographies published in, 244; enslaved persons, literacy, prohibition on, 81; as model for Brazil, 93; press, 5, 12, 21, 78, 198, 199–200
Universal, O, 93, 105, 106

Variedades, 90, 92, 114–15
Vasconcelos, Bernardo Pereira de, 61, 62, 66–67, 68, 69, 91, 235
Vasconcelos, Zacarias de Góes e, 176, 179, 182–83
Veiga, Evaristo Ferreira da, 6, 34, 43–44, 59–60, 62, 66
Vermelhos. *See* Conservative Party
Vida Fluminense, 161, 163, *171*, 172, 210
Villeneuve, Junius, 76–77

women: literacy rates, 81–82; periodicals for, 9–10, 41–42, 243; property owners, 148; publishing, roles in, 9–10, 41–42, 156–57
Wright, Frances, 96

www.ingramcontent.com/pod-product-compliance
Lightning Source LLC
Chambersburg PA
CBHW030523230426
43665CB00010B/735